Rebirth

*Mexican Los Angeles
from the Great Migration
to the Great Depression*

D0176626

Douglas Monroy

UNIVERSITY OF CALIFORNIA PRESS
Berkeley · *Los Angeles* · *London*

University of California Press
Berkeley and Los Angeles, California

University of California Press, Ltd.
London, England

© 1999 by
The Regents of the University of California

Grateful acknowledgment is made for the use of material from
Jimmy Santiago Baca, *Immigrants in Our Own Land.* Copyright
© 1982 by Jimmy Santiago Baca. Reprinted by permission of
New Directions Publishing Corp. Thanks also to Simon Ortiz for
permission to include excerpts of his poems, which originally appeared in *Woven Stone,* published by the University of Arizona
Press, 1992.

Library of Congress Cataloging-in-Publication Data

Monroy, Douglas.
    Rebirth: Mexican Los Angeles from the great migration to
the Great Depression / Douglas Monroy.
       p. cm.
    Includes bibliographical references (p.   ) and index.
    ISBN 0-520-21332-7 (alk. paper). — ISBN 0-520-21333-5
(alk. paper)
      1. Mexican Americans—California—Los Angeles—
History—20th century. 2. Mexican Americans—California—
Los Angeles—Ethnic identity. 3. Immigrants—California—
Los Angeles—History—20th century. 4. Los Angeles
(Calif.)—Ethnic relations. 5. Mexico—Emigration and
immigration—History—20th century. 6. Los Angeles
(Calif.)—Emigration and immigration—History—20th
century.
    I. Title.
    F869.L89M455 1999
    979.4'940046872073—dc21   98-50013
                                     CIP

Printed in the United States of America
9 8 7 6 5 4 3 2 1

The paper used in this publication meets the minimum
requirements of American National Standards for Information
Sciences—Permanence of Paper for Printed Library Materials,
ANSI Z39.48-1984.

For my children,
Mara and Luis

Contents

Illustrations

Introduction

This is an old story about people who leave their homeland for some new place. A story ages as it survives over time. This signifies that the story lives. If it is alive, then it is always growing and changing, like all living things, in response to the urgencies of the moment. Which is why this old story can be retold here, and will be told again later, in different ways, for different purposes.

Here, the purposes turn on muted intentions, earnest re-creations, and unintended consequences for people who moved from Mexico to a place where they tried to re-create the familiar. Mexican people came *al norte,* to the north, to continue in life as they had known it, or imagined that it had been or could be.

This story, and indeed other histories of the Mexican people of the United States, has been increasingly well told in recent years. The book in hand could not have happened without the efforts of my predecessors. This book is not an argument with any of them, only a building on the foundations that they have laid. The social scientific study, the oppression-resistance dichotomy, and how Mexicans responded to their second-class status in America have each provided points of departure for such works. More recent writers have concentrated on issues of identity and culture, or—with the knowledge of the usual outcome of the immigrant experience—on the creation of something new, in this case, the Mexican Americans. I mention first the fine books by my two friends and colleagues Ricardo Romo and George Sánchez, which treat much the same period as this volume does.[1] And I cannot omit Richard Griswold del Castillo, Antonio Ríos-Bustamante, Pedro Castillo, Vicki Ruiz, Juan Gómez-Quiñones, Rodolfo Acuña, Abraham Hoffman, Francisco Balderrama, and Carey McWilliams, whose more general or more specific works have made important contributions to our understanding of Mexican Los Angeles in the first half of the twentieth century.[2] Special acknowledgment must go to Lisbeth Haas and Gilbert González: not only have their books on Mexican Southern California informed this narrative, but their effective critiques of this manuscript model the collegiality for which our profession is not often properly credited.[3] How this book differs from those that made it possible shall unfold in this introduction. Let me say here only that I shall try to view the history not from the outcome, but from the intentions of those who made it. The exertions to, and conflicts over, this attempt to re-create Mexico—in the constraining context of the political economies of California and Mexico, and the weight of history and culture—form the essence of this narrative.

My own purposes are similarly various. Readers should know that the stories in this book parallel the story of my father's family. I can only imagine how my grandfather, a participant both in the turbulence of the Mexican Revolution described in chapter 2 and in the contention in La Placita described in chapter 5, would have related this history. He was a passionate political partisan who would have told this story with much more verve and detail, but probably more narrowly. Some of my father's telling (more partisanship) weaves its way into chapter 5. And at least one of my uncles would tell about the boxing. I have the historian's perspective: it is not so much one of detachment (I am a partisan too) as one in which a myriad of sources—social work studies, newspapers (in Spanish and English), government reports, popular magazines, contemporary scholarly journals, interviews with participants—and knowing in part how the story would come out all inform the narrative.

In another way, I am radically, often distressingly, detached. I have not resided in Los Angeles—the place of my birth and the only place where my soul feels at home—for twenty years. I have learned, though, to be thankful for other grand blessings. The Colorado College, especially its Hulbert Center for Southwest Studies, is a marvelous home away from home. Its generous institutional support for this project, especially its Benezet grants, and cooperative and personalized atmosphere are what have made this book possible.

My method here may at times be perplexing. A huge amount of research has gone into this project, but I have not "written up the re-search." Rather, I have tried to use my investigations into that array of sources to create a narrative that is about the interaction of the forces of history and economics with the endeavors and passions of human beings. This complex effort to re-create the familiar has remained frag-mentary because the urgencies of such grand notions as the family, lib-eralism and conservatism, urbanization and modernity, the economic marketplace, the spiritual world and fate, and more, all came to bear on Mexican Los Angeles. Thus, these issues, as I understand them, are all woven into the telling. These grand notions and other, more ancil-lary ones, such as the world market and the Mexican Revolution, Ameri-can tastes in fruits and vegetables and movie stars, classic Latin Ameri-can conservatism, the New Deal, and notions of progress, to name only a few, all intertwined with Mexicans' efforts to continue upon a new landscape. This is why my narrative appears to stray from the subject at hand. Readers will encounter digressions—strands, I would call them— that weave together the explanations for why and how people did what they did. Different readers will, I hope, find that they can grasp different threads that will help draw them into the overall narrative. All of these concerns must be part of the story because it is how people make his-tory—under, of course, circumstances, restraints, and habits that formed their historical legacy.

This, then, is the point of view and method of this book: the most meaningful, indicative, and pivotal aspects of Mexican Los Angeles in the first four decades of the twentieth century—history, political econ-omy, popular culture, and fate—are taken apart and analyzed. So too are *la gente*'s intentions, passions, and disappointments. It is the inter-weaving of this human saga and the material world that makes under-standable the rebirth of Mexican Los Angeles.

This story is one historian's creation. Of course, it could not have hap-pened without the pathbreaking works and the accumulation of sources cited above. Nonetheless, only I can take responsibility and credit for the interpretations of events, juxtapositions of historical forces and human passions, and choices about which sources to include and, most impor-tant, which to believe. Thus I make no claim to scientific method or de-tachment, just to genuine efforts at openness and theoretical sophistica-tion and to an attempt to amass as much knowledge and compassion as I am capable of. That is the methodology of this book.

Chapter 1 describes how Mexican people and their institutions ap-peared on the landscape, how they came into view: that is, how the An-glo Americans superficially viewed them and how they themselves, in the process of re-creating the familiar, came into view by building homes and institutions and by conducting themselves in particular ways in such important matters as the spirit world and pastimes. On this old Spanish/ Mexican homeland, immigrants lived mostly hidden from view, except when they were called a labor or health "problem." They built only for themselves on a landscape called not just Los Angeles but also, in a popular phrase of the time, *México de afuera*, "Mexico outside" or "outer Mexico."

This is a transnational history, or perhaps better, this is a transborder history. Chapter 2 analyzes the causes of what I have called "the First Great Migration" (I would say that we are in the process of the "Second" right now), as well as the historical legacies of California, especially regarding matters of work and race, awaiting them in that new place. I hope that readers will think of this not as a long digression but rather as an explanation: an understanding of the hearts and minds of the people of Mexican Los Angeles, their received wisdom and their aspirations, requires an understanding of the history and culture of both Los Angeles and the place from which Mexicans were coming.

Mexicans in the United States have often been portrayed as marginal to both the economy and the society of Southern California. Octavio Paz asserted that "This Mexicanism—delight in decorations, carelessness and pomp, negligence, passion and reserve—floats in the air" in Los Angeles, and old-style urban histories mention Mexicans only in passing.[4] Chapter 3 shows how perceived marginality is the opposite of reality. Indeed, Mexicans have been central to the functioning of the agricultural economy of this most productive farming state in the union. Then, too, they have been constructed as a problem when "Mexican" is associated with "dirty," and as fantasy figures when "Mexican" has been reconstructed as "Spanish."

Chapter 4 tells the extraordinary story of the three-way encounter between American popular culture, the children of México de afuera, and their parents and cultural leaders, who sought to counter the subversive influences of that repulsive and attractive notion we call "modernity." So many things mixed together: a profusion of necessities and opportunities associated with children and with new ways of conducting oneself; everyday tasks and joys usually having to do with the daily labors of subsistence and family; and ancestral commands and human inconsistency. In this, my favorite chapter, about movies, fashion, courtship, and schools, we see how people with both diverse intentions and various degrees of intentionality break free from old subjections; how they become subjects of new institutions, ways of thinking, and spirits;

how, in other words, Mexican culture changed in an American city; how Mexicans continued in the new place, in some ways the same, in some ways different.

Chapter 5 should, if nothing else, divest readers of any prejudices about a single Mexican point of view about politics north or south of the border, or about life in the north. While this chapter often treats the conflicts between Mexicans and Americans, it emphasizes the different positions that *mexicanos de afuera* took regarding the Mexican Revolution, labor organization, and how to deal with American politics and institutions.

This transborder perspective makes the issue of language difficult. Spanish and English are both beautiful, captivating, and expressive languages, which, while they have much in common, do not always translate easily. In some cases, I have tried to communicate the meaning of Spanish words by giving a translation. Where Spanish words have appropriately been left in the Spanish, I hope that either the context will make them clear or they are close enough to English for those without Spanish to understand them. (I did most of the translating myself, but with my classic third-generation Mexican-American Spanish sometimes not up to the challenge of the flowery and archaic language of the early twentieth century, I received help from my esteemed friend and colleague Clara Lomas.) Words and phrases like *México de afuera, el norte* (the north), and *sociedades* (the Mexicans' fraternal and cultural institutions) have been left in Spanish because no English word or phrase can evoke the meaning of these original Spanish terms. I often use *americanos,* and, I judge, quite effectively. Of course the term "Americans" is at best confusing since they have been a polyglot people. But Mexicans themselves called all those we can grossly group in the category of fairskinned, English-speaking people *americanos.* Our learned perspective informs us that there was much diversity among those people, but the Mexicans saw their foremen, teachers, social workers, movie stars, policemen, and so on simply as *americanos.* We certainly know that Americans of German, Slavic, and Irish descent cannot be accurately called Anglo Americans, just as Puerto Ricans, Colombians, and Mexicans cannot be reliably lumped together as "Hispanics." Thus I use *americanos* often, especially when I want to give my readers the sense of how Mexicans were perceiving white English speakers. (Mexicans did not include, for example, African Americans in this appellation, but simply called them *los negros.*) I have appended a glossary that gives simple translations, and deeper meanings, of all the Spanish words used here.

One more caveat: it is worthwhile to reflect on what it means to become a subject of historical analysis. *Subject* derives from the Latin *subjicere,* which means "to place or put under." It seems to me that historians often act to put people under the superior perspective, information, and detachment that our positioning later in time permits. One outcome is that our voice and tone are frequently ironic, bemused, and patronizing. From our panorama in the present, we see much more clearly and wholly than our subjects did the events, issues, and ideas that confronted them. A good example is the treatment of the migrations of Mexican families presented in the second chapter.

One of the qualities of a good book, in my view, is that it makes us think about things in new ways, that it transforms our sense of reality rather than simply confirming our suppositions, cleverness, and preeminence. We must proceed then with some humility and empathy: people will indeed be our subjects here, but if this is to be a good book, then, reader, you and I both must subject ourselves to ("place under," in other words) these historical subjects. If we do, we will wonder, criticize, hope, and despair, and be perplexed, saddened, reconciled, and optimistic, all a little more.

The Making of México de Afuera

It has to do with stories, legends
full of heroes and traveling.
It has to do with rebirth and growing
and being strong and seeing.

Simon Ortiz, in Woven Stone

INTRODUCTION: WAYS OF SEEING

In Los Angeles, the first days of May 1903 exuded much excitement over the elaborate and splendid preparations for the gala of the Fiesta Days. One of the daily newspapers anticipated that its "beloved 'Angel City'" would soon be "turreted and pillared with the pomp of a Moslem mosk, [and] gay in the riotous coloring of southern Spain." The city was not like this usually: mostly it wore "too commercial an aspect during eleven months and three weeks of the year." The businessmen who sponsored the fiesta typically concerned themselves primarily with work and production, and they judged the quality of their labors by the quantity of money and possessions they got. "However, this cannot be said during Fiesta Week. . . . It needs now but a slight imagination to garb all Broadway's pedestrians as peasants of Andalusia." Another paper noted, "One of the characteristic features . . . was a band of forty caballeros, led by Oscar Chavez. Many of the riders being of Spanish-American birth . . . [were] dressed in charro suits and 'Mexican sombreros.'" The fancy festival featured "an electric flower parade," a dreamy nighttime procession of floats and blossoms illuminated by electric light: "Nature's great floral symphony played by man's orchestra of light," extolled one daily. The celebration's provocative and alluring imagery "awoke the slumberous memory of a Spanish past, and brought with it the buoyant West of an American present." And it transformed the rich and complicated history of that warm and beautiful place, the city named for the Virgin Mother of our Lord, the Queen of the Angels, the place now called simply Los Angeles.[1]

A month before, those who were laying the rails for the electric railway cars that would transport the spectators and carry the floats, men who spoke Spanish and answered to the same sorts of names as those of the "Spanish past," had gone on strike (see figure 1). On April 24 the track workers, organized into the Union Federal Mexicano, demanded 17 1/2 to 20 cents per hour for daytime work and more for evenings and Sundays. The alteration of history, which the festival reflected and engendered, rendered this event indecipherable in any authentic way. With remarkable presumption, the Los Angeles Times spoke for the Mexican workers, who allegedly "thought Huntington's $1.50 a day a good sized chunk of heaven." Those in the "cholo union . . . are like dumb beasts being driven," mere dupes of local labor leaders. At first the Pacific Electric Railway conceded, but then Henry E. Huntington, the owner of the company and many of the rest of California's railroads, countermanded the pay increase. At that point all of the approximately 700 Mexican workers put down their tools and walked off the job. Huntington offered 22 cents an hour to anyone who would replace the strikers, and, by April 27, Japanese, African-American, and new Mexican workers filled the crews that now continued laying the tracks.[2]

Peasant women, many of them descendants of Andalusians who had intermixed with Mexican Indians, arrived as the new crews appeared, but not as decoration for the upcoming fiesta. "The women [who] had come from various parts of Sonoratown . . . ," reported the newspaper, "approached the workers and began seizing the shovels, picks and tamping irons which they were using." Numbering "more than thirty," the women tossed the tools away, but "the workmen simply walk[ed] over and pick[ed] them up again, laughing all the time." The police threatened the women with arrest, and they went away. A few days later, the mystic woman called Santa Teresa led a procession to the job site, but got only 50 to join the strike. The 764 car men, most of whom were Anglo, were supposed to support the effort, but on April 29 only 12 of them walked out. "We have plenty of laborers on whom we can depend," stated Superintendent McClure of the Pacific Electric. The strike was over.[3]

But as the festival days approached, few outside the Mexican community worried much about those matters. The entrepreneurs' big man would be the honored guest for the festivities. Though he could not see very well, Theodore Roosevelt was a man best described as a bully fel-

Figure 1. Mexican workers building the Los Angeles Railroad, 1903. (Reproduced by permission of The Huntington Library, San Marino, California.)

low: truly all of the dictionary definitions of "bully" fit him nicely. Fleeing the life of patrician Victorian New York with its tinges of domesticity, he had made himself a great game hunter and a western cowboy, like the ones in the dime novels. With saber in hand he had captured Puerto Rico from the Spanish, adding it to the United States as his predecessors had done with California just over fifty years before. He had been vice president of the country until a foreigner—a blacksmith and an anarchist—shot down the previous president in 1901. As president he would try and make America an even greater country, with enlightened and progressive corporations and the swift application of a big stick against those who would not cooperate. Some of his essays and speeches had been collected in a book, *The Strenuous Life*, in which he urged Americans to "boldly face the life of strife, resolute to do our duty well and manfully." The Los Angeles Public Library circulated more copies of it than any other book: "Requests pile up for it," reported Miss Darrow, a librarian there. The library contained few books about Mexicans, and no one was much interested anyway, except in the "gorgeous allegorical tableaux" of genteel Spanish California.[4]

The attention Anglo Angelenos paid the Mexicans in the ensuing decades varied widely, but the Anglos almost always problematized the Mexicans. Truly, the imaginary, pastoralist image of old California, which they made Spanish, served Anglo Californians' requirements for the "Hispanic" history of the place where most of them actually had arrived only recently. Such a telling, with its festal reliving in Fiesta Days, was one reason for the puzzlement about the errant track workers. Was it puzzlement, or obliviousness, or self-serving objectification, or indifference? The newspaper most associated with the business class's point of view called the workers "credulous and ignorant peons," and the tool-grabbing women "Amazons." They had been brought to Los Angeles "by clever evasion of contract labor laws" and "are in a condition not far different from slavery." The Socialist paper saw the fiesta strikers simply as "the dusky workmen." Just before the strike rumblings, the *Los Angeles Times* recognized, "The condition of the large numbers of peons now here is one of the questions to which the greatest attention will be paid."[5]

The confused ways in which these observers identified Mexicans confirm the need to pay attention to this issue. In contradictory fashion Mexicans were simultaneously manifest and concealed upon the landscape. The Mexicans' strike did more than threaten the progress of the fiesta preparations: now those people who picked and hoed in the fields, and dug and hauled on the streets and railroads, and then went away to Sonoratown, or across the river, or back to Mexico, or somewhere, now began to presence themselves in American history. The fanciful reminiscences of halcyon days gone by in California had erased the true story of their past. Mexicans, in their enclaves, shops, churches, and celebrations—most of which their predecessors had founded—could assume a place on the landscape, but one unacknowledged in any substantial way by those who defined and named the cityscape at the turn of the century. Now Mexicans began to make scratches upon the historical slate. They would become part of the history as they began to build and dwell upon the land of Southern California.

It seemed like such an ingenuous affair, those Fiesta Days of 1903. But two cultures with their two histories, as intensely connected as they were divergent, converged there on the streets of downtown Los Angeles. The big man, President Roosevelt, forcefully affirmed his people's ways and their stature upon the landscape. The celebration of "Spanish" California served to obscure further the Mexicans who had sought some affirmation when they struck the street railway. Except when their strikes, revolutions, or "contamination" threatened, Mexicans remained concealed in the *colonias*, across the tracks or rivers, or in the migrant stream. It was "particularly unfortunate," noted an editorial in the *Imperial Valley Press* that ran when the Mexican pickers struck the fields in 1928, that the walkout came "at a time when a determined effort is being made to put Mexican immigrants on a quota basis." Mexicans who had fled the troubles of the old country and come to work in the United States had little authentic presence in the Southwestern panorama, at least as far as the newly arrived but imposing Anglo-American culture beheld it. This was because their ancestors had become fantasy figures for the new Californians, or at best survived in isolated locales like Sonoratown or rural places like San Juan Capistrano. Mexican liminality and impermanence on this landscape, which their ancestors had conquered, settled, and named a mere century before, meant that they did not yet again build much; thus they dwelled only superficially upon the land. Negligible building, transitory dwellings, little knowledge of, or imagining of, or continuing on a place: marginal being.[6]

How, then, to proceed in a narrative about such people? Because their own voices from the turn of the century remain mostly silent in the source materials, we may have to proceed with the descriptions that strangers to their ways and predicaments offered. Likely no better indicator exists for the situation of Mexicans in Los Angeles at the turn of the century than the fact that many of them lived in "Boxcarville." There "the Southern Pacific workers are living in box-cars, on a siding east of the river," reported the *Times* as Fiesta Days approached. The railroad, its steel roads emblematic of the lifeblood of capitalism, the bleeding of the subsistence village, and provider of mobility variously yearned for, disturbing, and unintended, now gave its cast-off cars to Mexicans for temporary quartering. "In an open place shorn of all beauty, we found an encampment of peons, Mexicans just brought over the border to work on the Southern Pacific Railroad," noted a social worker in 1903. "They will soon be transferred to the barracks provided by the railway management—a line of disused freight cars," she explained. Concealed across the river, or the tracks, or something, such an image of Boxcarville contrasts meaningfully with the ebullience of the Fiesta Days exhibition. Around this relative deprivation we could build our story of Mexican Los Angeles.[7]

Then, too, maybe the most appropriate description comes from research published in 1912 about Los Angeles's Mexican community: "On one of the streets now being paved, fifty-three men work, fifty of them are laborers, two are assistant foremen and one man who is an American, is head foreman."[8] That Mexicans worked for wages substantially lower than those of other groups, almost exclusively in gangs under "American" foremen, and without much opportunity for advancement, suggests that their work experience must be central to an analysis of their lives in Los Angeles. Perhaps their confinement in the secondary labor market, essentially defined in the previous sentence, and their concealment upon the landscape, evoked in the first paragraph, are actually expressions for much the same thing.

This chapter could have begun with something else the social worker said: "They have come far, the women will tell you, from the City of Mexico."[9] That they more likely came from Jalisco or Michoacán tells us something about the problem of relying on impressionistic sources. But the point here is that this account could now proceed to emphasize not housing or work, but instead the efforts of women to reconstitute family life in the new place. And how American schools and popular culture competed with the Mexican parents for the allegiance of the children; how the wage economy, in which women and youth earned money, challenged the patriarchal ways that had evolved through centuries of kin-based, subsistence production in the old villages.

What of "the Mexicans who will render their tribute of love to the brown Virgin," as *La Opinión,* the Mexican daily, reported in December 1944, a date by which we would have expected more religious deculturation? Peoples' relationships to the spirit world fundamentally define and orient them, some would say more meaningfully than these transitory material concerns. Could a candle flickering before a small statue of the Virgin of Guadalupe in the corner of a boxcar have meant more to uprooted Mexican migrants than the facts of their liminality or their position in the secondary labor market? People gathered before other icons too: Mexican movie stars and troubadours performed regularly on the stages and screens of the theaters on Main Street.[10]

Many of those of the immigrant middle class, and indeed some émigré elites, would themselves take issue with the focus on the masses of Mexicans, *la chicanada,* as they called the unsophisticated peasants who made up most of the Mexicans in the United States. The middle class and elites, who affirmed order and deference to institutions (especially the Church) and to what they considered the natural social hierarchy, would have emphasized the cultural elegance and political refinement of *la gente bién,* "the better sort," those who allegedly made Mexican society and culture respectable in the eyes of the Americans and the world.

And what of la gente's conversations about all of these matters? The several Mexican newspapers; patriotic, fraternal, and insurance societies; and labor unions all expounded on both the nature of the Mexican presence in the United States and what was the best way to live one's life in the new land, all the while, though, emphasizing the events and passions of Mexico. Perhaps the nature of Mexican America, or la gente's consciousness of it, best emerges from their own discussions about it.

It can safely be said that different readers will find that certain of these relationships speak to them more meaningfully than others. Much depends on whether we think of humans as productive, consuming, gendered, desirous, spiritual, hierarchically ordered, or thoughtful beings. It is my view that each of these characteristics, and even some others, is powerfully significant; any ranking would depend on the time, the place, and persons. Thus this narrative will proceed to observe and ponder all of these notions with the aspiration of achieving a worthwhile understanding of the emergence of Mexican America in Southern California in the first decades of the twentieth century.

PART A: HIDDEN ON THE
MEXICAN LANDSCAPE OF LOS ANGELES

Several meanings of "Boxcarville" are probably apparent. Obviously the term indicates that people lived poorly. Unlike the adobes of old California or the villages of Mexico, boxcars sheltered woefully in heat and cold. They had no windows, they did not furnish well, and they were not amenable to children's play. And they symbolized the mobility and transiency that characterized their inhabitants' lives. Less readily apparent than the squalor and hardship, but no less important: these habitations deprived people of any sense of place. The relocated elders did not know the stories and myths about Los Angeles, or about the Mexican ancestors of the area, to tell the young; in these localities "shorn of all beauty" children could not easily run about and imbue the place with their elaborate and wondrous fantasies; and adults could not think that they were building and continuing anything of much importance in or around the boxcars. A comprehensive meaning of the statement that the sojourning people had little belonging to the new place needs this fuller consideration.[11]

The word *colonia*, as the Mexican press, consulate, and literati all used it, refers to a group of Mexicans living in a cluster of boxcars or any other assemblage of tents, shanties, "house courts," old adobes, apartments, or even houses. (Sometimes, though, the press used *colonia* to refer to all of the Mexicans residing in Los Angeles.) The word carries with it the connotation of newborn settlement, even of impermanence. A colonia differs in essence from a *barrio,* or neighborhood, in which the affinities of kin ties, godparentage, church attendance, and schools connect people in more organic ways. Colonias expressed a new ideal for a cityscape: the division of the people by spatial area according to their history, culture, appearance, and wealth (which some would argue has been the principal determining factor). Los Angeles was once a Mexican pueblo of considerable caste divisions wherein everyone participated, unequally but often gathered together, in such experiences as drought and earthquakes, the remarkable fiestas and the brutalizing fights with the Indians, and vice and faith. The colonias (like Indian reservations, harbingers of the ghetto) marked the advent of the modern era in which disparate people, now more spatially separated, experienced and imagined the events of the city in sharply different ways—the advent of segregation, in other words.[12]

The dwelling places of Sonoratown near the Plaza (see figure 2), the physical and spiritual center of Spanish and Mexican Los Angeles, had a rich history of graceful and place-appropriate architecture, warm and inviting spaces for children, and people who imagined a future for themselves and their successors upon the landscape. Most of the Mexicans of the nineteenth and very early twentieth centuries lived there, with Italians and Chinese, but isolated from everyone else. An outsider's description of the Macy Street district, adjacent to the Plaza, evokes this impression of simultaneous rootedness and isolation: "The streets form a veritable maze," noted a sociology student in 1924. "There are 27 of them, 7 only leading out to the district boundaries and but four crossing into adjacent territory."[13] Here la gente lived something of the actual history of the archaic pueblo of Los Angeles among those 27 streets, but with routes in and out quite limited (see map).

Some few people actually derived from the Spanish and Mexican days, some came in the decades after the conquest of 1846–48, and some others had arrived only very recently. The buildings seemed to gather around the old plaza, allegedly the site at which Governor Felipe de Neve and the mission padres had ceremonially founded and blessed the little pueblo in 1781. The people abided literally and figuratively under the shadow of the old Roman Catholic church prominently situated at one end of the Plaza. Their adobe homes, which actually did date from the Spanish and Mexican days, came directly from the earth, and they proved extraordinarily efficient at maintaining warmth in winter and

Figure 2. The old adobe houses from Mexican Los Angeles became the new homes of Mexican immigrants. (Reproduced by permission of The Huntington Library, San Marino, California.)

coolness in summer. The old Californios, at least the few that maintained some property and social integrity during the last half of the nineteenth century, customarily used the front of the house for living quarters and entertaining and had plenty of room in back for gardening and their large families. In the half century after the conquest, though, most of Californio society had either moved back to Mexico, intermarried with Anglos or more recently arrived Mexicans, or moved out of Sonoratown, which was rapidly filling with poor Mexican migrants.

In the last decades of the century, candles, made of tallow from the few cows remaining from the old pastoralist economy, no longer illuminated within the adobes the shabby gentility of remnant Californios. Instead, the dim light flickered on the faces of several poor families living in what was actually one long room that included cooking, sleeping, and socializing areas. The courtyards in back now filled with shacks thrown together with whatever materials could be scrounged from the industrializing environment. In 1900 from 3,000 to 5,000 Mexicans lived in Sonoratown and other less substantial colonias scattered around

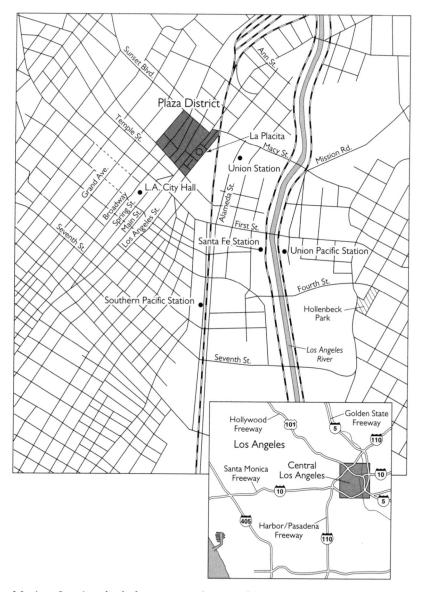

Mexican Los Angeles before 1940 with inset of Greater Los Angeles in 1990s.

the city. The historical record lacks the same degree of precision about the proportion of families, extended families, and single men in the colonia at the turn of the century as it does about what happened when the Mexican street railway workers struck the Fiesta Days: that each category comprised about one-third of the people in Sonoratown makes a sensible and informed guess. Sometimes a family might have a whole two-room, makeshift building to itself, but usually at least two families, broadly understood, crowded into a shack. Common washing areas and toilets (for use by up to a dozen families) provided a fruitful arena for socializing and the accumulation of filth and contagion.[14] In the same way that the Fiesta Days parade vividly illustrated much about how certain men's creations fulfilled the prospects of increasing material wealth associated with linear notions of history, the crumbling adobes candidly depicted the historical process by which other people and their things return to the earth from which they came.

Such suggestions of an organic succession, or eternal return, were not to be. For one thing, people's unruly passions almost inevitably mean that there is no such thing as a natural cycle where humans are involved. And for another, the engine of capitalist development complicates the picture. These roomy old houses and sprouting house courts proved inefficient when it came to the dollar return on the land use. "The rent exacted for the wretched homes of the courts is of course exorbitant," noted a contemporary observer, but more could be gotten for what was becoming prime real estate. As the region's population and economy grew, market pressure and astute businessmen connived to haul down many of the functional, and even by Fiesta Days standards, picturesque old adobes (see figure 3). Small industries—especially those associated with the railroad shops—warehouses, and "modern" brick tenements all irrevocably pushed land values and rents up and Mexicans out. Indicative of the modernization of Los Angeles, "the roomy old houses are fast being pulled down to make way for more profitable brick tenements," reported our social work informant, "and modern filth and squalor are invading Sonoratown." Businesses wanted to be near the railroads for supply and distribution, and their acquisition of land drove Mexicans out and prices even higher in Sonoratown. The trains that early on brought Mexicans later pushed them out: the construction of Union Passenger Terminal, the splendid mission-style depot begun in 1933 and completed in 1939, displaced more of the few Mexicans, but especially the Chinese, who remained there at that time.[15] This would not be the first time that Mexicans would be pushed to live

Figure 3. Several old adobes remained in Los Angeles through the 1920s. All of la gente would know about the performances at the teatros. (Reproduced by permission of The Huntington Library, San Marino, California.)

"across" something, a river or the tracks usually. Such positioning on the geographic fringes marked them in the eyes of American society, as would their distinct occupations, language, culture, and appearance. Still, Mexicans continued in this isolated center for a good while, and the Plaza area remained the cultural center of Mexican Los Angeles for many decades.

Sonoratown had once included in the area north of the Plaza the infamous "Nigger Alley," a place of destitution, vice, violence, and mayhem. By the 1890s this area had become, and today remains, Chinatown. Nigger Alley or no, there was much economic hardship in this still small Mexican community and, as a concomitance, much suffering and social chaos. There was sharing with, and compassion for, those out of work, the homeless, and the infirm. Then, too, there was much sickness (often a direct result of such charity), squalor, and discouragement.

In the first place one could never count on consistent employment. Until 1915 no numerical data exist to specify unemployment exactly, but the few who published their observations at the turn of the century agreed that work was not steady. When railroad tracks were completed, or when the local harvest ended, one could only hope that some new job would open up. Mexicans unable to speak English could get work only as part of a gang of Mexican laborers. No wage work for the men meant dependence on the compassion of one's (poor) neighbors. Saloons, pool halls, brothels, and bawdy entertainments, concentrated on North Main Street just above the Plaza, provided dubious solace to the men—what proportion of them we will never know—and untold dread, disgust, and anger for so many of the women.

Studies done when migration more fully commenced, and to which we shall eventually return, tell us that about one-fourth of the women earned money, largely by doing laundry or by taking in single men as borders. Otherwise the labor market for Mexicans, which wanted physically strong men at this time, and their own culture's norms about women's place, mostly confined women's labors to the domestic sphere. These were the women who went downtown to seize the strikebreakers' tools. By taking the jobs of the striking men, these recreants had strained the attachments of the precariously bonded Mexican community. Casting down those picks and shovels affirmed the women's preference for community unity regarding who should not be working on the track at that particular moment. The words we have used here surely would not (even if they were Spanish) be the ones that the women would have used in their discussions around the communal washtubs among the shacks. They spoke through their actions. Almost needless to say, the dread of having no money with which to buy food for their families moved them to toss aside the strikebreakers' tools. The menfolk's limited opportunities in the job market made everyone fearful about survival when any crisis happened.

A direct relationship existed between job structure and the formation of these colonias. "To the vicinity of Watts many of the Mexicans have been brought by the Pacific Electric Company to be employed on their tracks," explained a district nurse there. Those who came to build the railroads "first lived in box cars with their families, later in tents, and finally in rows of four-room houses, each house occupied by two families with a common shelter outside for wash days for the women." This pattern should not be confused with permanence: "They were employed for a time and then discharged and others have taken their places. No inspection is ever made of the Pacific Electric camps as they employ their own nurses and all others must be kept out." We notice immediately that what the Mexicans called a colonia, the Anglos simply called a "camp," a term quite evocative of the meagerness and impermanency of the domicile. We note as well how the Pacific Electric "brought" them in, then "kept" them sequestered away from everyone else, and then replaced them. These houses in the railroad camps "are built either in barrack-like rows, with only a thin board wall to separate one family from another," noted a researcher of the Plaza district in 1914, "or in small two- and three-room houses with narrow passageways between them." The "partition walls have large cracks between the boards," another pointed out, "and in order to make them [the rough boards] look more habitable they are whitewashed on the inside and painted red on the outside. This makes them resemble so many stalls for cattle instead of homes for human beings." The transiency, combined with the railway companies' lack of concern for the Mexicans and the Mexicans' acceptance of the lousy lodgings their employers provided, meant that improvements were few and deterioration was fast.[16]

Working Mexicans more often arranged their own lodging. For example, in Watts "the Mexicans discharged or not living in the camps have settled in homes that they can afford at their low wages." Such "homes" varied, but only within the parameters of segregation and what they could afford. "The worst congestion that existed in the city," reported a 1907 book about Los Angeles whose subtitle referred to it as a modern city, "was found on Utah Street, just east of the river, where those Mexicans live who were brought in from Mexico to work on the trolley lines." The evocative description continues: "The land in that locality was divided into tiny lots which were rented for one or two dollars a month. On each of these lots was built a shack of hammered-out cans, old boxes, or burlap, with no yard space nor sanitary appliances of any sort. The toilets were of earth, and were used in common." Needy or recently arrived kinfolk crowded in; children ran about, some gleefully and others furtively; now and then people celebrated a family event; and sometimes they huddled in misery. Several beds, and children sleeping on the floor, cramped a room.[17]

Many lived in agricultural camps, indeed simply in tents, which sometimes meant a canvas stretched between trees or poles. Again these dwellings corresponded to the structure of work. As we shall see when we turn to a fuller portrayal of Mexican labor in Los Angeles, the county's agricultural production ranked among the highest in the nation. Farms ranged throughout the county and produced a wide variety of crops: from celery and onions on the west side, to citrus and vegetables in the San Fernando Valley, to berries and lettuce on the east side. Small encampments came and went with the growing season in those places. Some were semipermanent if there was continuous labor, as in the old days of hired hands. The more efficiently organized and sharply diversified agriculture became, the more fluid the labor supply needed to be. People came and went a lot as they worked in fields that could give only short-term employment. Moreover, this sort of labor provided the simplest entry into the job market in el norte, particularly for a single man.[18]

Often the irrigation ditches provided the water that was used for drinking, laundry, and bathing. Sanitation was none too good; people toileted themselves as best they could with the most meager of facilities. In camps people lived essentially outside, exposed to the air (see figure 4). When it was warm and dry, this could be acceptable, and the weather was usually nice in Los Angeles. But during the two weeks' worth of dense rain, people in the open lived in muck and misery. When it was wet, lungs could not recover from infections. People abided not only in destitution but also in sickness because of the gastrointestinal disorders they got from the foul water and because viruses and bacteria infected their respiratory systems. They lived in a fair amount of confusion and ignorance about the causes of these afflictions. Nearly everyone in the camps got diarrhea and hacked at some point, but mostly it was the little children who frantically, too often fatally, coughed or purged. If they could, people searched out new habitations in a more settled environment.

When Mexicans sought to settle outside of these transient and rootless camps, they typically located themselves in a variety of "house courts." The deteriorated adobes in the Plaza district dating from the Spanish and Mexican days portended these haphazard, at times chaotic, lodgings. Some were old adobes, but as the Mexican population grew, the house courts were increasingly shacks of scavenged materials, or boards held together with battens, or strips of wood hammered over the ends of the boards where they connected, rather than fitted and grooved. Landlords of these barracks-style flats sometimes provided a double wall with felt insulation to partition each unit, but the residents could still hear a lot from the next room. In places without this consideration, many sounds came wafting and bursting through the habitations. Housing inspectors insisted that cracks be battened for privacy, and now and then they were. Sometimes these house courts consisted of two- to four-room bungalows crowded onto a vacant tract.

The physical space within these courts usually consisted of a kitchen and a compartment that served as the *sala,* a living room and sleeping

Figure 4. A Southern California agricultural workers' camp. (Courtesy Seaver Center for Western History Research, Natural History Museum of Los Angeles County.)

quarters. Some inhabitants papered the walls with inexpensive wallpaper, some with newspapers, to which postcards might be added, and some not at all. The kitchen had a small cookstove; a table, for which a scrounged box often served; and perhaps another box nailed to the wall, which served as a pantry. People sat on chairs, more boxes, the family's prize trunk if there was one, or the floor. In the sala there might be one bed, and the children slept on blankets on the floor. Unemployed or recently arrived kin or *paisanos* often crowded in.

House courts came in barracks-style rows—a single row, a double row, or perhaps two rows of ten flanking a shorter row of four—arranged around a courtyard. There in the enclosure were the faucets and hoppers for washing clothes, dishes, and children, and the toilets. Residents shared these privies, with one on average for every nine or ten people. Garbage containers, junk heaps (that is, stuff with possibility for use), and woodpiles took up leftover space. Here, too, the children played. In the rain, the courtyards turned detestable and foul.

As integral to the economy as these low-wage and itinerant workers were, the local housing and health officials saw Mexican households as a nuisance. In support of campaigns for their elimination, local authorities gathered statistics about the house courts, which will now help us complete our picture of how these Mexicans lived. Unfortunately, the statistics regarding the number of courts vary widely, and not all of the residents were Mexicans. The Los Angeles Housing Commission reported: "On June 30th, 1912, 294 active house courts were on record, which were only 12 more than the preceding year. This small increase was due to the fact that 94 house courts have been demolished. . . . Within the last nine months 409 new house courts have been added, so that by March, 1913, there are 621 active house courts, comprising 3,671 habitations, containing 9,877 inhabitants." An academic study published in 1916 recorded, "Upon 1,200 house-courts there are 5,934 habitations." The discrepancy here likely derives from differences in the definition of a house court as well as from genuine fluctuations in their numbers. "The average number of habitations per house-court is 4.94. . . . The smallest number of habitations per house-court is three and the largest number runs up to 35, 40, or even 50," calculated the latter study. Two- to four-room house courts predominated overwhelmingly. This study also computed a population of 6,490 men, 4,920 women, 2,640 boys, and 2,460 girls.[19]

This largely impressionistic and statistically vague description hopefully provides a likeness of life in the house courts. But to paint a deeper and more significant portrait of such a place, we would need to go beyond such simple issues as the definition of batten construction and wonder more about what could be heard through the boards. The modern obsession with privacy notwithstanding, babies crying in the night; people's awareness of intimate activities such as feuds, sexual relations, drinking habits, and comings and goings; and practices regarding the spirit world fueled what were no doubt interesting complications in house court society.

That neighbors and spouses come in all qualities has always incited conversation in neighborhoods and villages everywhere. Observers typically noted about the house courts: "Many of the houses are ill-kept, although a few are neat and clean."[20] Some disposed of waste as appropriately as they could under the circumstances, but others tossed their kitchen slops in the courtyard, and were careless in the toilets. Ideally, women were to stay secluded in the home, while men had access to the public world of wage labor and public entertainments, many of them dubious. Men often socialized at the pool halls and bars, with unfortunate domestic consequences.

Likely, the most telling conversations in the house courts about all of these matters would have been those of the women at the communal washtubs. They had secrets about others and themselves to reveal or to withhold. They knew who had messed the toilets and whose husband or boarder had not bothered to use them at all after a night at the saloon. And what happened when certain men came home from drinking. The joy and anxiety, and too often the ultimate sorrow, that their children brought them provided common ground for the women. Whose children were obedient and whose were not underpinned invidious judgments between them, as did whose house was "ill-kept" and whose was "neat and clean." Although husbands and wives appear not to have conversed much (we will turn to such issues later), some evidence and conventional wisdom tells us that women did. The words exchanged around the washtubs will remain obscure, though.

But how, and here is one of those places where we must proceed delicately with our subjects, did their language allow them to specify the meaning of these sorts of experiences? For such folks, I refer to any peasantry here, "the primary use of language," according to Mary Douglas, "is to affirm and embellish the social structure which rests upon unchallengeable metaphysical assumptions." Thus, exploration and elaboration in words, whether spoken to oneself or to others, of their thoughts and feelings about life's trials and ordeals are not something we would expect to find. Mexicans of the lower classes came with a worldview that customarily provided answers based on immutable received wisdom. Their language facilitated fixed guidance based on established patterns and roles, not complex edification of the self's inner turmoil.[21] People lay awake at night crowded together on an old mattress or lying with several family members, even a vaguely familiar single male relative, on a blanket on the board floor. We have only informed speculation to help us imagine how these people formulated for themselves, in their time before sleep, their responses to this fearful, exciting, curious new place and what, if anything, they said to one another about their thoughts the next day.

The words likely came in the form of stories, and the winds carried one in particular to the north: La Llorona could be heard through the cracks wailing for her children, whom she had drowned after her adulterous husband had betrayed her. Her story has been told with scores of variations throughout Mexico, and we can interpret her figure in at least two ways. On the one hand, she has acted against the most serious prescriptions for a Mexican woman and committed the most heinous of crimes: she has not suffered dutifully her husband's transgression, and she has manifestly forsaken her true role as mother. Appropriately she has been condemned to wander in search of her children. And as she wanders she punishes. In variants of the tale not only does she get bad children who are out when they are not supposed to be, but she kills men too. Thus, we can also see La Llorona as vengeful; her phantasm punishes men for their treacheries and violations of women. Through the agency of such stories, then, the women could make familiar new happenings in the house courts and colonias by plugging them into such prosaic mediums.[22]

The single men, the *sólos*, remain the most concealed. The greater number of men in the house courts seems to indicate that some men lived with relatives or acquaintances from the old village or boarded with families they had recently met. Groups of men who traveled together no doubt set up housekeeping as best they could. Single men could stay in one of the lodging houses in the Plaza district. One of the larger rooms would contain up to thirty beds, which rented for from 10 to 20 cents per night. These floating proletarians, maximally ideal from the employers' point of view, moved around a lot, from colonia to lodging house to the abodes of generous relatives and paisanos, and back to Mexico.

Since men rarely worked steadily, they had time on their hands to look for work or for social activities, which could and did refer to a wide array of things. Long-time Mexican residents of Los Angeles remember La Placita as "a gathering place for people who used to hang around" and as "a public forum where almost any subject could be spoken about" and "a helluvalot of complaining" was done about work and life north and south of the border (see figures 5 and 6). In the Plaza

Figure 5. Hanging out in La Placita. (Courtesy Seaver Center for Western History Research, Natural History Museum of Los Angeles County.)

Figure 6. A broad view of La Placita. When people moved they went to La Placita and hired one of these trucks. (Courtesy Seaver Center for Western History Research, Natural History Museum of Los Angeles County.)

one could find jobs offered at employment agencies, shop in familiar stores, listen to speakers extolling or condemning faith or one side or another of the Revolution, or simply lounge. When one got a good job or there was something else to be celebrated, like the arrival of a paisano, the ever-handy bar (in these days before Prohibition) provided a convivial place for merrymaking. Stereotypical male pursuits could be reestablished in el norte: in February 1928, for example, authorities arrested Valentín Ortega and Jesus Salas of Belvedere, who "had devoted themselves for a good while to exploiting such vices as cock fights, making wine, and selling marijuana."[23]

The sólos encountered a new, unnamable feeling. In the Spanish language there is the word *soledad,* which means "solitude," but none that means "loneliness." That no such word exists most likely stems from the various organic bonds that Latin American peoples ideally have to family and kin, village and place, and faith and the spirit world: no one is "alone," in other words. Travel to the new place severed those connections, with the result that many, especially single men, were actually alone. When this new, confusing sensation or the discouragement of unemployment, or both, set in, the saloon provided the single man's special solace. Regardless of the occasion, sometimes such men wound up broke and sick, and occasionally they hurt one another with their fists and knives; sometimes the men made new *compañeros,* or the drink loosened their tongues and they articulated the remarkable things about their lives that could only be revealed to strangers.

Whether one was single or with family, it was difficult for working-class Mexicans to dwell in much comfort. Observers agreed that "the rent exacted for the wretched homes of the courts is of course exorbitant." "In general," as the California Commission of Immigration and Housing reported, "houses in the Mexican quarter of the city rented for more than similar houses in other sections of Los Angeles," and these high rents derived from a number of factors.[24] As noted previously, the demand for downtown real estate increased steadily, and as industry replaced more and more residences, the supply of available housing diminished. Mexicans, though, faced segregation.

Discriminatory housing practices meant that the best deals on residences were quite apparently and matter-of-factly closed to Mexicans. As Mexican immigration increased in the years during and after World War I, more and more suburban communities sought to enhance their desirability to Anglo migrants by excluding Mexicans and blacks and then touting their absence: El Segundo bragged in 1927 that it "had no negroes or Mexicans," and in 1930 the emerging industrial suburb of Lynwood affirmed how it could "furnish ample labor of the better class" by "being restricted to the white race."[25]

Such segregation obviously affronts the humanity of those against whom it is directed, but its financial costs remain less acknowledged. With the available housing supply thus limited, demand for what was left and the declining space in the Mexican quarter drove up rents. Thus Mexicans in the 1920s, and any group similarly discriminated against, had to pay more for housing. While such factors remained largely out of the control of Mexican renters, Mexican preferences for housing did drive up demand in other ways. La gente did not simply shop the housing market for a new abode. They relied on kin ties and the bonds they maintained with people from the old village to locate a new home. Primarily, they lived life in accordance with these sorts of obligations. Living in the city center meant that they could walk to work in the railroad shops or other industries and be near kin. Mexican politicians and merchants may have wondered why Mexicans paid high rents in the industrial center or why the emotional and financial disadvantages of doing so did not spur them to political action. But, for reasons that we will survey in the next chapter, most Mexicans (and indeed humanity's vast majority, which had not embraced ideas of the market) approached such life decisions in the context of their customary conduct, which included the notions that walking to work and organic human bonds were good.

Thus, in the years before World War I, rents for a one-room house court averaged about $3.50 or $4.00 per month; for a two-room, about $6.00; and for a three-room, about $12.00. A state study from the same time period put the average rental in the Plaza district at $9.30 per month and indicated that income averaged $36.85 per month. A study done in 1916 of 172 Mexican families in the Ann Street district, a few blocks to the north of the Plaza, calculated the average rent Mexicans paid as $6.36 and wages as $41.40. It is difficult for us, nearly a century later, to gauge the meaning of such statistics. There is a gap between what people paid for rent and what they earned, though we must recall that a wage earner spent from one-third to one-quarter of the year unemployed, and that what people got for their money was truly dismal. The student of the Ann Street district concluded that virtually all were "living on a wage too small to secure the necessities of life."[26]

In those days before stringent building regulations, Mexicans could rent or even buy a lot, and then several families would build upon it.

The Los Angeles Housing Commission reported in 1913: "in the heart of the city, on Hollenbeck Street near East 7th Street, a Mexican settlement, built on rented ground, existed, consisting of a group of shacks laboriously built up board by board of second-hand lumber and new lumber. These 'Homes' had minute gardens, seeds having been supplied through the Commission by a benevolent lady." "Together the heads of several families buy a lot upon which they each build a house," noted a researcher in the 1920s. "There are community toilets, but usually the water, gas and electricity are connected in each house . . . The families who enter into this sort of agreement are usually related by blood or marriage. Small 'clans' they are." One immediately surmises here an effort to re-create an older village community on an urban landscape. People started their homes with such materials as "flattened oil cans, cardboard cartons, lumber discarded in repairing box-cars, or other refuse of American economic life."[27]

While the sounds of talk and the smells of food surely identified them as Mexican, colonia dwellers fundamentally lived like poor people everywhere. In the Macy Street district, a few blocks north and east of the Plaza, Mexicans shared terrain with packinghouses that abutted the train tracks. A 1924 study of the area noted, "In recent years . . . the surrounding packing houses have so polluted the air with poisonous gasses as to stunt all vegetation and to make the process of breathing at times disagreeable because of disgusting odors." An environment not so different (excepting the winter weather) from the jungle that Jurgis Rudkus encountered in Chicago: "There is always a heavy cloud of smoke hanging low over the district from the ever passing trains, making the air full of soot and all things grimy to the touch."[28]

All of the inhabitants of these downtown districts—the Chinese, the remaining Italians, and Mexicans—lived crowded with their compatriots. We have seen how they lived cramped within their abodes, but it is important to note that the condition of urban sprawl did not apply to the downtown areas. Urban congestion prevailed there. The California Commission of Immigration and Housing noted in 1916, "the 500 cubic feet of air rule is constantly violated." Another student of these downtown districts indicated, "At least 54.5 per cent of the Mexicans live in conditions which are overcrowded." While the criteria for these standards of living change over time, and while the apparent exactness of these numbers often masks their actual imprecision, there can be no doubt about the congestion that prevailed in these colonias.[29]

People moved around a lot. The demands of work or unemployment took them to new places, they sought better lodgings, or rising prices or demolition crews cleared them out. Early in the century the city passed regulations against the contaminating disorder of the house courts, but "rather than submit to the expense of renovating the houses and repairing the courts, [the landlords] have evicted their tenants," according to our authority on the modern city, who continues the imagery that the term "Boxcarville" first evoked: "This is especially true on Utah Street, where nearly all the courts were cleared out."[30]

Recall, too, the homes on Hollenbeck Street with their "minute gardens": "Suddenly just as vegetables and flowers were growing beautifully, the 'March of Progress' loomed up, to be built on that spot. Sixty days were given to find new ground." The housing commission assisted them in finding new "land that could be rented or bought on the installment plan[;] fifty of the 85 families took up their little houses bodily, set them on wagons and moved to a new location, leaving the cherished gardens behind." For the remaining 35 families, the commission found another three-acre plot: "the ground was subdivided and the houses on wheels were placed on 25 x 100 foot lots." The 1916 Ann Street study showed that 8.7 percent (15) had been in their homes over five years; 28 percent from one to five years; 11 percent from six to nine months; 33 percent for one to five months; and 5 percent less than a month (14 percent were "not obtained"). In other words, nearly half (49 percent) had lived in their home for less than a year.[31]

Much goes into a process of urbanization such as the one in Los Angeles and its growing Mexican population. Cities cannot exist, however, unless food is conveyed in and sewage is taken out. American perception of Mexican food (a cuisine of great regional variation) has altered over the course of the twentieth century. Once viewed as food of the underprivileged and lacking in nutrition, it has more recently become fashionable and appreciated for its protein content and the salubrious effect of chilies on the digestive system. The issue for Mexicans in the colonias, however, has usually revolved around not its trendiness, but how to get enough of it. Diet in the colonias varied primarily in accordance with the steadiness of work and the amount of pay received relative to the number of mouths to feed. During hard times there were only beans, tortillas, and coffee. Inexpensive meat and rice could be added. Stable employment could bring to the table an "almost steady diet . . . of flour tortillas (the corn ones are too expensive), beans, chili, tomatoes, onions, and cheap cuts of meat."[32] The women combined these staples in various ways to make assorted dishes, and they made tamales for special occasions. Even the youngsters drank black coffee when there was money for it. The exceptional healthfulness of the pinto bean notwithstanding, the lack of green vegetables and milk for the children constituted the glaring shortcoming of this diet, even in its steady form.

Again, though, what must be emphasized is how the family menu depended on employment and on such contingencies as the presence of a passel of unemployed relatives. Ultimately, too, we are discussing the foodways of impoverished people—the poor have never eaten well. In the Ann Street district breakfast consisted usually of "bread and coffee, the remains of the previous evening meal, and perhaps some fruit. Lunch was often conspicuous by its absence. Where there was any at all, it was similar to breakfast."[33] The shortage of food, and milk for children, could not replenish the life force expended in merciless labor and childhood ailments, and such shortages left Mexican bodies ill-fortified for the afflictions of urban life.

A young woman with tuberculosis from the Mexican community of Watts explained to a sociology student of the early 1930s why she left the sanitarium:

> While my father was ill [he soon died], I felt I should earn money. After school hours, I would go to fish canning places which were often all night according to the way the fish came in. When there was a big catch, we would sometimes work till one or two in the morning. The work was always in a damp room with a wet floor because we were constantly washing the fish.

In such conditions the small nodules (tubercles) in her lungs, infested with the bacterium, could not heal; her sputum and coughing easily spread infection in close quarters, especially if lungs breathed contaminated air and bodies received poor sustenance. This misery repeated itself in Mexican households well out of proportion to their numbers in Los Angeles. The 1916 Ann Street study reported that while 17.4 percent of all deaths in the city arose from TB, it caused 39.2 percent of Mexican deaths in the Ann Street district. In 1930 Mexicans comprised about 12.5 percent of the city's population, and 13.5 percent of the county's, but they accounted for 27 percent of the clientele of the tuberculosis clinics operated by the city in 1928 and 21.25 percent of the deaths recorded in the county from the disease in 1929.[34]

Disease's grim harvest reaped its greatest toll on the babies and little children. The 1916 Ann Street study recorded that of 227 deaths, 60 (25 percent) were "infantile diseases of the digestive tract." Presumably some of the TB casualties were children. A study of Pasadena published in 1923 noted that children under nine years of age accounted for most of the deaths in the Mexican community there. Fifteen percent were from "stomach trouble," and 36 percent were from contagious diseases; but 30 percent of the deaths were from "weak constitutions" and occurred "before the first eight months of life." A religious reformer cited statistics in 1925 showing that "of the children born in the whole city last year, 7.9 per cent were Mexicans; of the children of the city who died, 12.2 per cent were Mexicans." For the weak bodies, only limited treatment was available. "Diarrhoea and enteritis" took the most grievous toll on the little ones in the Mexican communities and colonias.[35] There was plenty of infection and not much knowledge about the causes of or cures (usually simple rehydration, we now know) for the children's running bowels.

These were tragic deaths, intensified by their occurrence in an alien place where interment with the ancestors could not happen. But for the Euro-Americans in Southern California these sicknesses were one of the ways in which working-class Mexicans presenced themselves on the landscape. Obviously, they did so in this case in a negative way, as a diseased people. The construal of poor Mexicans as a problem, in spite of their centrality to the functioning of the labor market, is a pattern we see continuing in this narrative.

There were some Mexicans who did not appear so problematical. Again, not only did those with nothing but their labor power to sell arrive, but so too did Mexicans from the middle and elite classes, as well as disaffected or exiled intellectuals. The Mexican petite bourgeoisie, teachers, lawyers, entertainers, doctors, shopkeepers, and so on, who came because they had lost their customers or because of the chaos of revolution, often tried to limit their association with poorer immigrants. The glamorous ones, the great movie stars who will be a subject of chapter 4, even lived on the west side of town, and the few old elites who could escape the Revolution with cash lived there too. These Mexicans, like the Anglos, tended to see their working-class compatriots as a problem, but one of a different sort.

Because middle-class Mexicans were still Mexicans, and thus associated with poor Mexicans in the eyes of the Anglo majority, they experienced limited access to the city's housing. In addition, they had to be near their clients. So while they often lived in the barrios, this middle class took on upper-class sensibilities and values. They presumed the inability of the lower classes to ever amount to much socially or politically. They referred to *los modos rancheros*, or worse, when speaking of people they considered peasants. The excesses of Villa's and Zapata's armies proved the dangers of unbridled rustics. Middle-class Mexicans aspired to refinement and culture. They valued individualist family enterprise. Presumably, their well-bred sensibilities would provide leadership and models for *la chicanada,* as they would have called the less fortunate masses of Mexicans. Their *sociedades* and *comisiones,* to which we shall return shortly, established their prominence within the barrios and provided much of the cultural activities for all Mexicans.

In other words, other social forms besides the rough peasant communalism of the working classes in Mexican Los Angeles appeared on the landscape. In the years between 1914 and 1916, before and after some insurrectionary undertakings, two brothers, Ricardo and Enrique Flores Magón, rented five acres just north of downtown Los Angeles, on which they lived and farmed communally with several others. They were called *Liberales.* There, women and men lived together without formal marriage. The Liberales could be seen carting their fruit downtown to sell. They published a provocative newspaper and organized support committees for a great movement that would free the workers from the bonds of capitalism and the Church. It was hard to decide what to make of them, but we will hear much more about them later on.

The colonias and barrios began to teem with life as immigration surged. I am drawn here to a metaphor from Greek mythology: a chthonian eruption, that is, something emanating from the underworld of the dead and its gods and spirits. The vibrancy of the barrios surely seemed mysterious at the time for anyone who bothered to observe this furtive reemergence of Mexicans in the old pueblo of Spain and Mexico, now the metropolis of Los Angeles. It was life coming, life with all its diversity (the stuff of evolution), chaos, contingency, drama, charm, and above all its growth and increase.

PART B: PRESENCING ON THE LANDSCAPE OF LOS ANGELES URBANIZATION

There is much to be said for the quality of a life in the country, but certainly not, however, for the vast majority of itinerant field laborers. The conditions under which agricultural workers lived, worked, schooled their children, and attempted to progress socially and economically argued compellingly for the fortunes of city life. Think for a moment of the typical attractive marketing image for Southern California in the

early decades of the century: pictorial reproductions of sun-kissed orange groves under a blue sky backgrounded by a snow-capped mountain appeared everywhere from citrus crate labels, to railroad advertisements, to Chamber of Commerce booster brochures. Suburban houses
have replaced the groves of Orange County and the San Gabriel and
San Fernando Valleys by now, and the smog would obscure the view
anyway, but it often used to look like that; it would be a nice place to
live. Absent from the pretty pictures, though, were the pickers. They
stood on ladders for hours on end with a sack that could weigh up to
50 pounds. In the beginning of the season the cold blew down from the
mountains, and harvesters had to handle chilly fruit while their clothing
and shoes grew frigidly wet from the damp on the trees and the ground
cover. Rarely was there ever drinking water or toilet facilities. Toward
the end of the season the temperature in the groves could reach 100
degrees. Closer to the ocean, in the *limoneras* of a place like Ventura,
there was fog and dampness year-round, especially in the morning. It
would settle in the lungs, and the coughing would start.[36]

There was a time around the turn of the twentieth century when
Americans genuinely wondered at the preciousness of the fruits and vegetables reaped from California's intensive agriculture. But the delicate-
ness of the berries, grapes, asparagus, and tomatoes and the vibrancy
of the oranges, lettuce, and melons have obscured the grueling and consuming toil it takes to produce them. Notwithstanding employers' foolishness about the innate predisposition of Mexicans for stoop labor
(made so by the short-handled hoes, *cortitos*, which employers provided)
or the apparent stoicism of the immutable brown figures bent over in
the lush fields, the work is consistently miserable; people have done it
because their resourcelessness leaves them few other choices. This agriculture succeeded so excellently because irrigation enabled farmers to
take advantage of the rich soil and long growing seasons of what were
actually deserts. People worked in tremendous heat, or early morning
frosts, often without suitable water. Death or impairment from heat
prostration and tuberculosis were familiar events, especially for the old
and the young. When one of these jobs was done, a man or a family
just moved on to the next one.

The seasons continued to orient the agricultural worker in space and
time, but not in the way they did for agricultural peons or small hold-
ers. Now workers did not act in the old rhythm of the seasons—sowing,
maintaining, and harvesting crops and then fixing and mending things
in the off-season—in their own place. Instead, they moved from place

to place depending on which crop was in season and with the important difference that now the labor market ultimately drew people to some new place. It was still a cyclical way of being in time, but now the wheel of time moved about the landscape as it spun around. Stories of a place could never take root and grow: instead, the elders told of those who had died of heat prostration or coughing. For agricultural people, time has revolved around repeatable events of the growing cycle, around the motions and actions undertaken for, and associated with, survival. Especially for those sometimes called the peasantry, occurrences will ideally be the same year to year, and thus the family will survive year to year. The sense of time orients around repeatable events, not toward a future where things will be different. For migratory workers, though, there is no place. They are always arriving someplace, but because they are always leaving that place, they are never really arriving anywhere. These have been people "neither here nor there."[37]

Some continued in the migratory stream with the goal of returning to their place in Mexico. Others transformed their colonias into more permanent domiciles. Others moved to the city. Not culturally predisposed to nomadism, many of those borne by the migratory streams began to settle. Shallow roots began to steady people upon the new place, land that actually once belonged to the old mother country. We would not want to generalize too much about the process—sometimes people found dwellings their Mexican predecessors had built, or they constructed shacks upon some ground rented or even purchased, or they transformed makeshift colonias into little neighborhoods.

In the Imperial Valley, in many ways the paradigm for field labor transiency, many Mexicans began to make houses. In the larger towns of Brawley, Calipatria, and El Centro, a Mexican family would buy a lot, on the other side of the tracks, and proceed to assemble what some would deem a shack, but what was certainly the building of a home. More materials were acquired and more shaky structures arose on the same lot. As these were rented to other paisanos or given over to married children and other relatives, village communities issued from the otherwise barren soil. Truly homes of the laboring poor, these abodes appeared chaotic and unkempt, but before World War I such home ownership was virtually unknown. By the late 1920s more than one-half of the Mexican schoolchildren in the Imperial Valley had been born in the United States. In other words, some of the people carried along in the immigrant stream were becoming a more stable agricultural proletariat. It was still field work, though, with the heat and the contractors and the inconsistent employment. Fluctuations in distant markets made work disappear, and nature could not be completely controlled: in late 1934 the waters to irrigate the valley did not come because little snow had fallen in Colorado (a problem the completion of Boulder Dam in 1936 would regulate), and two years later frost killed most of the pea crop.[38] These roots in agricultural colonias could prove shallow; people pulled up and moved to the metropolis.

People wound up in the city via diverse processes. Winter gardens notwithstanding, the fields of California required about one-third of the workers in December that they did in June. Unemployed Mexican agricultural workers from all over the state wintered in Los Angeles, in a movement that was typical of such midwestern cities as Chicago and Detroit as well. The depression of 1907–8 first drew attention to this phenomenon in Los Angeles. Paul Taylor, the era's remarkable scholar of Mexican labor in the United States, claimed, "In February, probably 80 percent or more of the Mexican population of the state is found there."[39] Winter sojourners in the city crowded in with their relatives or compatriots. If they could find some consistent employment away from the damp, the heat, and the labor contractors, but especially if doing so was amenable to their family life, they often stayed.

In places like Pacoima and El Monte colonias became barrios, suburban neighborhoods of the working poor. In Pacoima (which its denizens called "Pacas"), at the far end of the San Fernando Valley, shacks sprang up near the fields. Improvements were made and the makeshift edifices became houses, homes for families. Because of such factors as the ability to succeed in the job market, the ability of lodgers and children to contribute to the family economy, and personal preference and diligence, the houses began to distinguish themselves from one another. A former resident of the Pacoima barrio recalled the houses "ranging from a one-room shack where people slept in the 'front room,' to the more elegant." They "had some similarities: a window on each side and a door smack in the middle. Others appeared lopsided because of the many additions tacked on as the family grew." The yards varied from bare to full of flowers, fruits, and vegetables. But "they had one thing in common: each had a junk pile somewhere in the backyard."[40]

Reformers and other observers echoed such residents' descriptions. In El Monte most Mexicans lived in Hick's Camp, which presented "deplorable housing conditions." But some, reported a Protestant reformer in the late 1920s, "live in comfortable homes . . . where the houses and yards are well kept." These homes were "humble dwellings of four and five rooms, but so infinitely better than the rest" because they had "clean yards, neat homes and flowers everywhere." For the sake of public safety, sanitation, and utility companies' financial solvency, gas, electricity, and running water arrived. Now and then the streets were paved: "Some time ago the city fathers ordered the paving of the street (where the nicer homes were), with the hope that the Mexicans would move out" (because of the resulting tax assessment). "They were, however, happy to have this improvement and have met all payments cheerfully."[41]

No single factor can be identified to explain this process of settling. Out of habit or family considerations or both some remained in the city central. Others responded to the escalating costs of such housing by moving to a barrio in one of several ways. Real estate companies subdivided tracts and sold lots and houses to Mexicans for about $600 in the World War I era. (This practice continued, but prices increased.) In these Mexican tracts, "Many of the homes [were] garden spots, a wealth of flowers and vegetables providing an inspiring contrast to the hideous, jammed, foul-smelling courts of New High, Alameda, Olivera [sic], North Broadway, and other streets near the heart of the city." A sociology student who later became a housing administrator noted that some in the Mexican tracts lived "on the hill-top, shaded by large pepper trees, where the cool fresh breeze can always be felt. At the bottom of the hill and down in the valley are numerous newly-built bungalows, and here and there can be seen garages and autos standing in the yards."[42]

Or maybe the heads of families would buy a lot and begin building; an old resident of Hollenbeck recalled of Maravilla Park: "It has always been almost 100 percent Mexican. The first houses were the worst kind of shacks, like hobo jungles, built of old oil cans, old tin, boxes, scrap lumber, etc., that could be found. Since the school was built out there the houses have improved much." Just before World War I, the Los Angeles Housing Commission reported how the mother of a family who lived on Macy Street near the gas works

> heard that it was possible to secure a house and lot on the out skirts of the city . . . by paying $25.00 down and $10.00 a month. She made up her mind to secure a home of her own. The family had driven to Los Angeles from Bakersfield some time ago. One of their team of mules had died, but the $25.00 they expected to receive for the surviving animal, Mrs. M. resolved to use as the first payment on a home. She interested her husband. Together they bought a place in the Mexican tract. That was about a year ago. The

garden produces many vegetables and flowers, as well as giving healthy interest and occupation to all the family. . . .
    Another room has been added to the original three room house and a
shed built in the yard.

The days of turning a mule into a down payment on a house are long
gone, and such episodes have been much the exception rather than the
rule.[43] But in these humble settlements, children could run about and
start to imbue the place with their stories, and family heads would start
to think that their future could be different from their past.

MÉXICO DE AFUERA

It was on a landscape nominally the domain of the United States that
Mexicans were situating themselves, but there are few things more important to remember than the fact that they understood themselves
to be reestablishing Mexican communities in the new land. Their new
places, whether colonias, barrios, or the old pueblo of Los Angeles
around the Plaza, were very much México de afuera. These were largely
economic but sometimes political emigrants who sought to sustain their
families and find safety from violence and chaos; blending into the American cultural, social, or political landscape was never the intent of the
vast majority of them. Notions of white Protestant superiority kept it
largely closed to them anyway. The objective was either to return to the
homeland when conditions became more satisfactory or to reinstitute
the familiar in the new place. The conservative Mexican newspaper in
Los Angeles, *El Heraldo de México,* noted in 1920 that those who migrated did so because of "the misery occasioned by the lack of work and
the neediness of the laborers." But they "continue, in spite of that ab-
sorbing [American] civilization, feeling as Mexicans, with all of their
defects and all of their virtues." The more liberal *La Opinión* similarly
acknowledged in 1928 that even though la gente came north for better
conditions than those "created by the revolution, we must always respond to the requirement of continuing to feel fully Mexican, in love, in
intent, in deeds, [and] we have the clear right to express our opinions
about our problems."[44]
    Significantly, "our problems" (*nuestros problemas*) refers to Mexico's
problems. Perhaps the newspapers overstated the nationalism of Mexicans residing in the United States, and probably they responded to a
perceived waning of la gente's loyalty to the mother country. But na-

tionalism works in very curious ways, to say the least. Life in a new land often transforms people with a fealty to a mere locality in the old land into people with a national identity. In the same way that Sicilians and Neapolitans became Italians in New York, Jalisqueños and Sonorüenses became Mexicans in Los Angeles. Ernesto Galaraza tells how in Sacramento:

> Crowded as it was, the colonia found a place for these *chicanos*, the name by which we called an unskilled worker born in Mexico and just arrived in the United States. The *chicanos* were fond of identifying themselves by saying they had just arrived from *el macizo*, by which they meant the solid Mexican homeland, the good native earth. Although they spoke of *el macizo* like homesick persons, they didn't go back. They remained, as they said of themselves, *pura raza*.

They settled into a new Mexico, one without so many of the troubles of the old. And living in the new place seems to have enhanced their opinion of the old one.[45]

Typical of many immigrants to the United States, newcomers expected to return to the familiar homeland; but in the meantime they would re-create the ways of the old village in the new country. Recall that Mexicans did not emigrate to become Americans; they aspired not to become un-Mexican but to get away from what was making their lives intolerable. "You see," stated a night school student in the 1920s, "our people love their country very much, and everyone hopes to go back to his own place some time." Another who did become a citizen explained, "Most of the Mexican people do not want to be American citizens, though. I can see why they don't. They all think that they will go back to Mexico. You don't see many of them going, do you?" "Señor S.G." told how community opinion pressured people away from naturalization: "I have a store in the Mexican district. If I become a citizen of the United States the Mexicans wouldn't trade with me, because they wouldn't think that I was fair to them or loyal to my country. I read the papers and would like to vote, but I must not become a citizen. I have to have the Mexican trade to make a living." While the presumption of return played the largest role, other considerations maintained the formal allegiance of the residents of México de afuera to *la madre patria*. (Mexicans in legal trouble, for example, were relatively helpless in an American court if they were citizens, but they could rely on the aid of the Mexican consul if they were not.) "Never will I become an American citizen. Never!" emphatically declared the most renowned resident of México de afuera, glamorous movie star Dolores del Río.[46]

Indeed, few Mexicans became citizens of the United States. Although about one-half of foreign-born whites in California were naturalized citizens in 1920, only about one in twenty Mexicans were. This situation owed in part to the relative newness of most immigrants, but one 1919 study that considered Mexican districts in Los Angeles where many had lived in the United States for more than ten years found that only 8 to 25 percent applied for naturalization, whereas 40 to 60 percent of Italians did so. As more and more immigrants came to Los Angeles in the 1920s, the proportion of those choosing naturalization decreased. Of the total admitted to citizenship in the United States, 6.5 percent were Mexicans in 1920, but only 0.1 percent in 1928. By this latter date, of an average of 726 naturalizations in Los Angeles County, only 3 were Mexicans. The americanos did and did not appreciate this situation: the presence of apparently unassimilating immigrants made them nervous and offended the notion that everyone should want to become an American, but so too did the specter of too many Mexicans joining their country. Then, too, virtually none of the 75,000 Americans living in Mexico in 1910 and none of those who ventured back there after the Revolution became citizens of Mexico.[47]

All immigrants to the United States, whether through their religious institutions, social and family networks, bars, or workplace relationships, continued on with the familiar ways to various degrees; and many of them—with the exception of Jews from the shtetls of Eastern Europe, where pogroms ever threatened—expected to return. In this regard Mexicans were unique only in that their proximity to the mother country, and continuous migration broken only by the Depression, meant that new immigrants perpetually fortified the culture of México de afuera. The ethnic enclaves in the Mexican districts of Los Angeles, and in the rest of the country where migration has been uninterrupted, have received more ongoing and extensive cultural sustenance than those where immigration has declined.

THE FAMILIAR CITYSCAPE

Not only with the family, where one heard the familiar language, smelled the familiar foods, and worshipped the familiar gods, but also on certain of the streets of Los Angeles did one know that one lived in México de afuera. There was much to see as one walked south from the Plaza down Main Street. A solo worker, a family whose patriarch or grand-

Figure 7. Teatro Hidalgo at 373 North Main Street. Note that *solos* could rent "clean beds" upstairs next door for 15 cents. (Courtesy Seaver Center for Western History Research, Natural History Museum of Los Angeles County.)

mother watched carefully over the brood whose heads swayed back in forth in furtive anticipation, or a small cluster of youths just escaped from the literal and figurative confines of the family encountered signs in Spanish (some of the men and a few of the women could read them) and pictures indicating entertainments that they would find congenial. The railroad connections between the United States and Mexico enabled a variety of Mexican touring companies to come to the lands outside, especially after the turn of the century. The years of revolution proved plainly inhospitable for theater in Mexico. Many artists and companies traveled north, especially to Los Angeles and San Antonio, to wait out the chaos; as we would expect, some stayed. And there, on Main Street at the most prominent and enduring of the Mexican auditoriums in Los Angeles, Teatro Hidalgo (1911–34, see figure 7), Mexican companies found responsive audiences. Just over on Spring Street were Teatro Zendejas (later Novel, 1919–1924) and the first Teatro México. Farther down

Figure 8. La gente bién at a gala movie opening. (Courtesy Seaver Center for Western History Research, Natural History Museum of Los Angeles County.)

Main Street were Teatro Principal (1921–29), the second Teatro México (1927–33), and Teatro California (1927–34). These, and several others, provided a steady supply of Mexican performances, as did more than a dozen others on a more irregular basis.[48]

These theaters represented different things to different people. The first Teatro México aspired to provide la gente bién with comforts, such as richly upholstered seats, and theater appropriate to their social status (see figure 8). Owners had charged up to $1.50 for box seats and 60 cents for general admission for special events. But la gente bién inconsistently supported the plays, operettas, and urbane touring companies, so that genteel presentations had only sporadic runs; the first Teatro México apparently (the sources are confusing) came and went several times. (When it was not Teatro México it was the Walker Theater, also used by Mexicans and for a variety of purposes, and originally it had been the Lyceum.)

The demand for Mexican entertainments represented an opportunity to make some money. If, because of their small numbers, la gente bién could not support an entire house with high-priced seats, *la gente tra-*

bajadora could compensate with their purchasing of higher numbers of seats. Most of la gente could be counted upon to frequent the less pretentious presentations, which included *revistas* (variety reviews), *zarzuelas* (a format, originated in Spain, of musical plays or comedies), dramas of various themes and tempers, dance troupes, circus-type shows, comedy acts, burlesques, and, eventually, Spanish-language movies. In spite of their largely non-Mexican ownership, the theaters provided a wonderful variety of Mexican shows at assorted prices.[49]

A walker along Spring and Main Streets (the former angled into the latter at Ninth Street) typically saw the signs for such acts as the circus acrobats Trio Rivas; such dramas as *La Dama de las Camelias* by Alexander Dumas, *La Mujer Adultera,* "the emotional historical drama, Maximiliano I. Emperador de México," *La Guerra de México*, and the "extravaganza of Don Juan Tenorio"; or such dance presentations as "Amparito Guillot—la bailarina de los pies desnudos" ("the ballerina with the naked feet"); or maybe simply an "Orquesta Típica." On special occasions one could see promoted on the marquee "Virginia Fábregas, El Orgullo [Pride] de la Raza," the famed Mexican actress whose company performed the latest European, and sometimes Mexican, plays; and typically in the late 1920s and early 1930s one saw advertised Los Pirríns, whose revistas starred the picaresque comic Don Catarino.[50]

Several theaters, especially the Hidalgo, showed the new motion pictures. At first, unlike immigrants in eastern cities, only Mexican men went to unrefined venues to see rough productions, often about the Mexican Revolution. By 1920 both the movies of Mexico's thriving film industry and American ones with Spanish captions (both very much the fare in Mexico City or Guadalajara) flickered on the screens of the Mexican theaters, which catered to all of la gente. In February 1920 one could see at the Hidalgo Charlie Chaplin's *El Nuevo Portero* for 10 cents or the Mexican *Revelación* with "La celebrada artista Madame Nazinova." Several months later the marquee advertised, with faulty chronology, the ten-part *Ramona*, "an exquisite and vivid historical narrative of the times when California belonged to Mexico."[51] The management showed consideration for, and reinforced, Mexican proprieties when it tendered such films as *¿Está Segura Su Hija?* (*Is Your Daughter Safe?*), which presented "¡La Verdad Ante Sus Ojos!" ("The Truth Before Your Eyes!"): Teatro California showed it for several weeks in 1927 for men only and then later "solamente para mujeres" (only for women), at 50, 40, and 25 cents per ticket.

One entered not only into the salacious world of some Hollywood movies and their Mexican imitators, or into escapist comedy, or into some simplified world of a happy or oppressed or naive folk society. Mexican theatergoers could chose portrayals of life in all of its complexities. Nicolás Kanellos's careful reconstruction of the Mexican theater scene in Los Angeles reveals its remarkable richness and depth. The popular revistas, offered at various prices and aimed at assorted appreciations of humor and parody, typically satirized such issues as the culture shock immigrants experienced upon arrival in the americano metropolis, the resulting vitiation of Mexican culture, and, quite commonly, the Mexican Revolution. Los Pirríns' revistas, largely the creations of the ingenious Don Catarino, lampooned everything from Hollywood to Hell to the Depression to el niño Fidencio (a crackpot spirit boy in Mexico) to repatriation to "Whiskey, morfina, y marihuana." Other writers, often under contract to one of the theaters, created revistas with similar themes and aimed at both working- and middle-class audiences.

Fleeing the turmoil of Mexico, several playwrights made Los Angeles their semipermanent home. Eduardo Carrillo, Adalberto Elías González, and Gabriel Navarro turned Los Angeles into a centerpiece of Mexican dramaturgy. These expatriates were fundamentally Mexican writers, but their themes often dealt with the predicaments of Mexicans in the north. (González's most successful play, an adaptation of *Ramona,* broke Los Angeles box office records in 1927, toured throughout the Southwest, and sometimes starred Virginia Fábregas.)[52] Mexican people of different classes and aspirations produced, staffed, and attended these Mexican theaters physically located in Los Angeles, but most certainly situated in México de afuera.

It was a remarkable walk down Main Street in Los Angeles. There numerous peoples emerged from their concealment into a diverse public space, where sometimes they mixed and sometimes they segregated. English and Yiddish and Spanish intermingled in the sounds and sights of downtown. Many considerations steered an individual or family into one door or another or into none at all. How much money was available for such diversions, one's social standing or aspirations, and one's moral sense—or the conflict between that moral sense and one's ardent yearnings—all meant that immigrants went into some shows and not others; or maybe they did go into some of those "others," but anxiously. (The doors to the americano theaters opened to Mexicans as well, but Mexicans entered with consequences to which we shall soon turn.) The marquees of Spring and Main Streets held something to strike the fancy or the longings of almost everyone. I would have liked to have attended the longings of *Ramona* not only to see a dramatization of the fictional character to whom I am so drawn—its illusory re-creation of history notwithstanding—but also to observe the people's responses to the poignant story about their predecessors upon the landscape of Southern California.[53] Quite definitely, though, when travelers from across the international border traversed from the culturally diverse streets of downtown Los Angeles into one of the Mexican theaters, they straightforwardly reentered the familiar milieu of Mexico.

Yet other doorways afforded passage in and out of México de afuera. Emerging from one of the theaters, a walker on Main Street reentered the public and culturally assorted American city. On the way back to the Plaza, however, the doors of La Ciudad de México beckoned shoppers. According to its newspaper advertisements, this department store on North Main Street offered "la colonia mexicana residente en Los Angeles" everything from clothing to chilies to milk to lunch boxes. A few doors away the Farmacia Hidalgo (with another store on Los Angeles Street) asserted that "we have the largest stock of medicines and Mexican herbal remedies." Many of the colonias around the county had such *farmacias*, which also functioned as typical drugstores tendering Mexican sodas, ice creams, and candies. A block farther on North Main was the Repertorio Musical Mexicana, which featured for 75 cents "Discos Victor" of the latest Mexican popular tunes. A loudspeaker proclaimed the availability of the familiar music to be played on the new machines and usually attracted an assembly of male listeners.[54] This was not the old Mexican village, because people came from all over, but it was fundamentally Mexico that Mexican people sought to build upon the cityscape of Los Angeles.

THE PASSIONS OF MÉXICO DE AFUERA

We might say that there were cultural transplants that blossomed differently in the new soil, such as revistas with Chicano themes. And worship of the beautiful Virgin of Guadalupe truly bloomed again. We might also say that other activities, such as baseball, express a universal male parthenogenesis, a *mestizaje* of sports. Or we might say that Mexican men consciously and intuitively sought validation in the new place through organized competitions, or that, for various reasons, they simply enjoyed recreations, especially the big favorite, boxing, and that money could be made by marketing these activities.

At any rate baseball was reimported to México de afuera. This all-American sport has gained a top spot in the aspirations of young men in Mexico, Cuba, Puerto Rico, the Dominican Republic, Venezuela, and Nicaragua—almost all places where American economic and military presence has been very intense. Baseball arrived in Mexico in the 1870s and 1880s via American sailors in Guaymas and mine employees in Cananea, and via Cuban players on tour. Although Mexican miners first took up the sport, during the regime of Porfirio Díaz, the middle class and elites looked upon baseball as a way of emulating the cricket-playing English gentry. Quickly, though, the ball diamonds attracted working-class Mexicans, and the sport waxed more clamorous and competitive. Increasingly baseball in Mexico became more an opportunity for the middle class to manage and promote working-class athletic youth and less a club sport for socially aspiring Mexicans. North of the border Mexicans were playing baseball in Arizona and New Mexico in the 1880s, and baseball, along with the Church and the mutual-aid societies, provided weekend entertainment and social cohesion.

Mexicans in Los Angeles rounded the bases too. In 1916 *El Heraldo de México* reported, "Several youthful companions, amateur enthusiasts of 'baseball,' have begun practicing this lovely sport in the lawn tennis patio of the club." This was the Club Anahuac, "where the principal families of our reputable society always meet." Club Anahuac likely combined recently arrived Mexican elites with the remnants of Californio society. (At a club dance, the names included Señorita Couts, no doubt an offspring of the marital alliance between the Californio Bandini family and the mildly Hispanicized Yankee entrepreneur Cave Couts.)[55] The appeal of the great game, though, could never be confined to such aristocratic pretensions.

By the late 1920s "sides" sponsored usually by local Mexican businesses regularly competed with one another, with other ethnically identified teams, with local Anglo clubs, and with touring professionals from the United States and Mexico. The most renowned local Mexican teams in the era seem to have been those of the El Paso Shoe Store, the El Porvenir Grocery, and the Ortiz New Fords. El Porvenir Grocery, on First Street in Belvedere, had a ballpark next to it, El Gran Parque Mexicano, but the El Paso Shoe Store had the best team. Itinerant workers could not have participated consistently of course, but, because of the high level of competition and the number of teams, a cross section of Mexican social classes undoubtedly took to the field together. In 1929 Doctor A. C. Tellez, former catcher and captain of the University of California team, caught for the El Paso Shoe Store.

Sports have greater meaning than simple competition, and Mexican baseball in Los Angeles of the 1920s and 1930s was no exception. It was one way the various people from south of the border forged an identity as Mexicans, a way for Mexicans to garner respect in the eyes of the americanos, and a public reinforcement of the traditional manly family values of forceful, dynamic activities. El Porvenir Grocery sponsored various baseball games and charged admission for "an afternoon of enthusiasm, healthy fun, and genuine emotions," "an afternoon simply Mexican." The crowds cheered for "their team," and their teams were often organized by ethnic group: when El Paso Shoe Store played the Nippons, we can be sure that Mexicans rooted for their "estrellas mexicanas" and that Japanese fans rooted for their "Nips" (which was emblazoned on their uniforms). Mexicans in Los Angeles, at least the men, could feel a bit more upstanding when in the spring of 1929 El Paso Shoe Store defeated the Paramount Studios Sheiks, the Commercial Club Millionaires, and especially the Pacific Electric Trainmen in "an emotional game" on Cinco de Mayo. Similarly when the championship team from Mexico, San Luis, played the Philadelphia Negro Giants in November 1929 (they split a two-game series), we can be quite certain about who was cheering for whom. I am sure that the scene in the stands at such games was a remarkable one, as people from all over the world played and watched baseball together in Los Angeles. I hasten to add that the sources do not mention altercations between the different peoples.[56]

Of course the appeal of the baseball games centered around the competition. Much was reflected in these contests: "El evento beisbolístico más importante," exclaimed *La Opinión*: "The most important baseball event that has registered in the bosom of the Mexican colony in the past years, will take place tomorrow afternoon in White Sox Stadium when the Mexicans of the mighty El Paso Shoe Store Club battle the orientals of the Los Angeles Nippons for the 'foreign championship of baseball' of the United States." I do not know how the Japanese press portrayed the series of games, and the americano press remained predictably silent about the matter, but the Mexican press proclaimed that the "Mexican stars" won "the championship" by a score of ten to five on May 12, 1929. Sports writers have always embellished their articles with such rhetoric about "world championships," but we can be sure that they expressed some truth when, after the Mexicans won the first game in April, *La Opinión* reported that the El Paso Shoe Store team "established themselves as the idols of the hundreds of aficionados [overwhelmingly male, I'm sure] of our raza who attended [the game] yesterday."[57]

We are discussing not only the outcome of the games but also complicated issues of allegiance as well, ones that have much to do with
maleness and national identity. They also concern appearances, how *la
raza*, "the Mexican people," appeared to themselves and to others, how
they presenced themselves in this curious new land of movie studio sheiks
and Nippons. After one victory over the latter in April 1929, *La Opinión* explained, "The task these boys are undertaking on the sports field,
which is the most appreciated among the American people, to elevate the
good name of our raza, should not be overlooked." The El Paso Shoe
Store team had demonstrated its suitability "to participate in the major leagues of Los Angeles," that is, the triple A minor leagues that the
Hollywood Stars and the Los Angeles Angels represented. (Perhaps some
non-Mexican local promoters had suggested this possibility too.)[58] Baseball simultaneously created cohesion and identity in "the Mexican colony," provided recreation, and displayed Mexicans' (at least the men's) desire for the validation of the broader Los Angeles populace, for, in other
words, the acknowledgment of various mexicanos as dwellers, Mexican
ones, of the place.

There is much to see when one looks at a baseball game. Aficionados
emphasize the constant strategizing, the shaving of odds through positioning infielders for the *doble play* or countering with the hit-and-run,
while others celebrate the excitement of the *jonrun*, especially if the
round-tripper comes at a dramatic moment. That it is a game of such
calculation and aggressive, forceful actions marks it as a masculine activity, the game's recent appeal to women notwithstanding. Perhaps we
should not make too much of the shapes of the central accouterments
of the game—bats and balls—but that baseball has always been a male
undertaking is beyond doubt. The newspapers did not say much about
who sat in the stands for any of the games mentioned above. A local
mexicana beauty queen appeared at one, but, given the practice of sequestering women and the paucity of Mexican females at other public
events, there is no reason to surmise that many women attended. The
baseball diamond overall represented a masculine space on the landscape. Not only did men's participation in baseball prove to Mexican
contemporaries, especially women, that men were just like boys—playing games and getting dirty and bragging about their exploits—but baseball also provides a useful medium for understanding some aspects of
the male character in general.

Another Sunday activity offers a window into the Mexican immigrant female character in the decades of mass migration. While men (in

frocks) lorded over the ceremonies and males did attend, the Church embodied a feminine presence upon the landscape. Catholicism arrived in Mexico in the 1520s and 1530s via the priests who accompanied the Spanish soldiers. Together, but with intense rivalry, the priests and the soldiers sought to turn Indians into loyal subjects of His Catholic Majesty and bring them everlasting salvation. The great moment in the Christianizing effort came in 1531 when the Virgin Mary appeared to the Indian boy Juan Diego on the hill that had been home to the popular Tonantzin, the vanquished Aztec mother goddess of the earth, fertility, and corn. Indianlike in Her features, this beautiful Virgin of Guadalupe came not only to attract many Indians to the True Faith, but to epitomize the mestizaje of old and new world religions: She endures as a central figure of Mexican Catholicism and as the symbol of Mexican nationalism.

On another level She protects and forgives, brings health and happiness, and offers solace and comfort in times of fear and tragedy. (Her hands on Her holy shroud on which appears Her True Image in the Basilica of the Virgin of Guadalupe in Mexico City are placed in the Indian position of offering rather than the Christian one of supplication.) She is, nonetheless, a universal goddess, not a local one whose being animated only a particular place. As mother of the omnipresent Savior, Her spirit could be conveyed to new places. Indeed, the new immigrants transported Her to Los Angeles, a place named not for the angels but rather for *la reina de los angeles*, the Queen of the Angels, the great mother Guadalupe/Tonantzin. Bringing Her to Los Angeles was another way that Mexican people presenced themselves in México de afuera.

It is a remarkable religion, this Roman Catholicism. It celebrates, according to the Catechism, its "God the Father Almighty . . . " and "Jesus Christ, His only Son, our Lord; who was conceived by the Holy Ghost, born of the Virgin Mary . . . [and who] was crucified. . . . He arose again from the dead; He ascended into heaven, sitteth at the right hand of God; . . . from thence He shall come to judge the living and the dead." It has erected majestic places of worship with spires pointing heavenward, in which celibate men have ruled with divine authority. And then, through Her esoteric rituals and imagery, the Church has opened a window for so many people into the spirit world. No figure has been so meaningful for Mexican people in this regard as the Virgin of Guadalupe. In Her honor, the priests founded the first Church of the True Faith on this landscape, the one on the Plaza about which we have already heard a little bit.

The Church, though, had changed profoundly since those first masses said in the small pueblo of Los Angeles in the waning decades of the eighteenth century, when the place was still part of the increasingly decadent Spanish empire. The Church that those who followed their nineteenth-century forebears al norte encountered was the American one, of course. Its northern European austerity was clearly out of step with the spiritual richness of what might be called the "folk Catholicism" of the Mexican immigrants. The leaders of the American Church have adhered more stringently to Trinitarianism than has the Mexican Church, where local spirits and beliefs have found more tolerance. On an institutional level, though, the American Church in the Southwest, manned mostly by clergy of German and Irish descent (over 80 percent at the turn of the twentieth century), did not pay much attention to its Mexican believers until after World War II. Coupled with the historical antipathy of many Mexicans toward the Church and its tremendous economic and political power, which always has been exercised on the side of the wealthy classes, the lack of attention paid the flock in Los Angeles meant that many strayed either into the Protestant fold or mostly into simple apathy. Most of the sources note that no less than 90 percent of the Mexicans who came in the great migrations were nominally Catholic but "mostly poorly instructed in the faith." Street paver Bonifacio Ortega professed in Los Angeles in 1926 a common attitude, though: "I am Catholic, but the truth is I hardly follow out my beliefs. I never go to the church nor do I pray. I have with me an amulet which my mother gave to me before dying. This amulet has the Virgin of Guadalupe on it and it is she who always protects me." A resident of the Pacoima barrio recalled, "To the practicing Catholics of our town, the month of May was el mes de María, dedicated to the Blessed Virgin Mary." It included "the nightly offering of flowers to Our Lady. This Mexican custom, brought by our parents to this country, was something I enjoyed." And how the place was reanimated with the spirit of the Virgen Morena. Later I will comment briefly on the institutional presence of the Church in Los Angeles; for now we will follow up on the rich symbolism of Mexican religious practice.[59]

Not an easy task. Many find oppression in religious belief. It gives behavioral directives that violate human rationality and biological impulses and then scares people into obeisance. Its messages to women have typically been the most harsh. For Karl Marx, it "is at the same time an *expression* of real suffering and a *protest* against real suffering. Religion is the sigh of the oppressed creature, the sentiment of a heartless world, and the soul of soulless conditions."[60] But those who take these views of religion (myself included) have a difficult time appreciating how belief provides the faithful with a window into the spirit world, an entry into the supernatural and mystical, a deep knowledge of the sacred. We must acknowledge, too, the notion that such instruments as the Bible are divinely revealed truths. The view we take positions us in richly assorted ways to embark upon an analysis of religious meaning. Perhaps we should recall that most of the faithful of all religions accept their creed "as it is given"—"the chief truths we believe or profess to believe," as the Catechism says—but take it to heart and soul in distinct ways, on different levels, and with disparate consequences.

Thus how people practice their religion usually unveils more about belief than does the degree to which they adhere to its dogmas or discourses about its doctrines. An uncomprehending priest stated about the Mexicans of the Imperial Valley town of Wasco that they "are like children of nature, and do not take their religion very seriously. . . . Many of the Mexicans have devotions in their own homes—they have little altars. They like the trimmings better than the essentials; it is better that way than if they had nothing." Of course such altars have been common in Mexican homes on both sides of the border. They have continued as the focus of private religious expression for so many of the faithful: these devotions are the location of profound belief.[61] Public professions of faith, ones that bore upon the streets and parks of Los Angeles, came largely in the form of processions in honor of the Virgin of Guadalupe or Her Son, or both.

If religion and politics tend to cause disputes, then we can be sure that when the two are mixed, as they so often have been in Mexico, strife will abound. Religious festivals, then, on the streets of México de afuera expressed not only religious feelings but the highly charged politics of church and state in Mexico. Opponents of the Mexican government's anti-clericalism helped organize such manifestations of piety to bring attention to what they considered to be the atheistic and bolshevistic tendencies of the revolutionary government. I will return to the political aspects of the Church and the Faith when it is time to discuss the political culture of Mexican Los Angeles; for now I will make some comments about the meaning of these articulations of belief.

In June 1928 an estimated 10,000 Mexicans took part in the Church-sponsored La Fiesta de Corpus Cristi. Believers marched from Nuestra Señora de Guadalupe Church in Belvedere to La Soledad. Participants included several consequential Mexican prelates "who live in California in exile." But the same year witnessed the first procession in honor of the Holy Mother (see figure 9). In a rather small undertaking at first, members of Hijas de María paraded in adulation of the Virgin. The march soon found a sponsor in José David Orozco, a local travel agency owner and radio personality, who saw the event as an opportunity to further the prayer movement that he had been organizing in support of the religiously persecuted in Mexico. In late 1929 he began forming chapters of la Asociación del Santo Nombre (the Holy Name Society) and by the next year had established about forty chapters in Southern California. Urged on by his uncle, the exiled Archbishop Francisco Orozco y Jiménez, Orozco mixed veneration of the Virgin with antigovernment politics when he persuaded Julio C. Guerrero, patron of Hijas de María, to cede sponsorship of the procession to Santo Nombre.[62]

The year 1934 beheld the most magnificent procession in honor of the Virgin Mother. Heralded as a testimonial to the Catholics persecuted in Mexico, it merged several interests. Two of the event's sponsors, Bishop John J. Cantwell and his wealthiest supporter, oil man Edward Doheny, had a stake in the restoration of the old ways of prerevolutionary Mexico: Cantwell sought to restore the prerogatives of the Church, and Doheny the prerogatives of foreign capital that had so benefited him in the rich fields of Tampico. For Orozco and Santo Nombre the event offered not only an occasion to express support for the Church in Mexico, but also the opportunity to promote what Orozco called, in an interview with historian Francisco Balderrama, "Mexican consciousness." Aware that the discrimination against Mexicans and the antipathy of the americanos to Mexican culture would likely produce a sense of inferiority, Orozco understood Santo Nombre as a way to resuscitate la raza's ethnic pride. Thus the shouts of "Viva Cristo Rey" (the slogan of the pro-Church faction in Mexico); "the rosary beads slipping through rugged fingers, the hymn to Our Lady of Guadalupe on a thousand lips;" and the affirmation and presencing of Mexicanness on the streets of Los Angeles, all merged in this stunning procession of 40,000 people. Members of non-Latino Catholic organizations numbered among the marchers, but the heart of the parade, and the overwhelming majority, consisted of Mexicans.[63]

Of course, different observers of the phenomenon, then and now, take different meanings from it: exaltation of the Mother of our Savior; mother worship based upon unfulfilled childhood desires; the deflection of political and class tensions via powerfully charged religious iconog-

Figure 9. A parade in Los Angeles in honor of the Virgin of
Guadalupe. (Courtesy Shades of L.A. Archives, Los Angeles
Public Library.)

raphy; a model of womanhood some rail at and others revere; a symbol
of the oppression of, and a comfort for, the indigenous people of the
new world; a metaphor for mestizaje; a female representation of the divine. La Virgen de Guadalupe is all of these and more; She is a complicated and ambiguous figure, no matter how She "is given."

Catholic doctrine affirms a communion of saints uniting "the faithful
on earth, the souls in purgatory, and the saints in heaven in the organic
unity of the same mystical body under Christ its head, and in a constant
interchange of supernatural offices." From this doctrine emerges the ongoing and vital association between those on earth and those whose
souls have passed on. Rituals such as those surrounding the Virgin Mary
and the other saints can activate that relationship and bring about the in-
tercession of the saints either with God or with events on earth, and bring

about miracles, the most inspiring events for the creation and strengthening of religious feeling. (Santa Teresa, the spirit woman at the Fiesta
Days street pavers' strike, allegedly had the power to tap into this supernatural process.) To have the idea that some people or icons are sacred
is one thing, but to believe that the holy actually have power to inter-
vene in the operation of the profane world—phenomena that have been
witnessed and testified to—manifests what some would call True Belief. The many miracles associated with the Virgin Mary, in particular,
have presented positive proof of these convictions.[64] And this understanding of the spirit world is why a prayer movement for the persecuted in
Mexico, by convening the communion of those on earth and those in
heaven, could have positive effect there. What might have seemed like a
transnational migration of spirits, then, was actually a reconvening in
Los Angeles of the old relationship between the Mexican believers and
the saints.

For the 1929 march *La Opinión* displayed the Virgin's picture on
the front page: She was "the Only and True Queen." "In Mexico," the
article expounded, "one of the most powerful spiritual bonds is, undoubtedly, the veneration that all of the Mexicans—except the non-
believers—feel for the Virgin of Guadalupe, Indian Virgin, of our raza,
of our color."[65] Those who performed rituals around Her figure, either
prayers, votive candle offerings, pilgrimages, or processions, hoped that
their actions would invoke Her intervention in this dolorous world,
either in their lives or on behalf of those whom they cared about or
had an interest in. The immigrants transported to the new land these
old rituals, but only those of the universal saints, like Mary. Many of
the lesser spirits, peculiar to specific places in Mexico, were left behind.
Mary, along with Her Son, was the One whom the Mexicans from diverse places had in common.

Politically, such manifestations of religion reanimated the fights over
the role of belief in people's lives and over the relationship of church
and state. Recall the Liberales who lived communally, farmed fruit, and
published an incendiary newspaper about the need for revolution. One
of their followers spoke in the Plaza in the era of World War I, saying
that "that old Roman Church opposite us is a nest of deceivers." A decade before, another had referred to "the clergy, this impenitent traitor,
this servant of Rome, and irreconcilable enemy of free nations." And
another pronounced, "Religion, whatever the denomination with which
we are presented, is the most terrible enemy of woman." The *libre pen-*

sadores, or freethinkers, also took to Plaza pulpits, in this case to chastise religion.[66]

Naturally, the Mexican government did not take kindly to the efforts of Orozco and others to organize opposition to its policies, and the Los Angeles consuls monitored the activities of the exiled clerics. George Sánchez notes that Consul Alejandro Martínez charged that the organizers of the 1934 procession were the "traditional enemies of the economic, social, and cultural progress of Mexico."[67] Neither the religionists nor the secularists found sanctuary from their customary nemeses in México de afuera.

Spiritually, the Virgin of Guadalupe reanimated parts of the landscape in feminine ways, ones surely associated with people's emotional yearnings. An article in *La Opinión* affirmed how "in the folds of her cloak, covered with roses, have remained hidden so many longings, so many aspirations, so many dreams, and so much love of country." Though the writer emphasizes the condition of the Mexican nation, there seems little doubt that the fact that She "had come to be the Mexican symbol" is bound up with potent and complicated notions of mother. I suspect, though, that males and females have related to Her differently.[68]

Bonifacio Ortega, the street paver quoted above, unmistakably reveals his association of the Holy Mother with his own mother—both women give protection. La Virgen becomes mother to men who live in solitude, who are orphaned, in the strange, new land. Then, too, for boys whom adoring mothers have raised, adoring la Virgen in turn allows the adult male to continue to focus on an objet d'amour who is undemanding, forgiving, and unconditionally loving. Yet la Virgen is safely distant, should mother be perceived, as she often is, as devouring. Rituals surrounding the Virgin Mary allow men to fulfill their yearnings for the loss of the love of their mothers once they have had to join the macho world of male society.

For women, la Virgen is clearly she who nurtures the nurturers. Since females are responsible for the physical and emotional maintenance of the Mexican home, and solicitude toward women is rarely expected from males, mothers and elder daughters can be very much by themselves in their caring endeavors. Such is, of course, a situation hardly unique to Mexican households, nor is it one universally characteristic of them, but evidence of nurturance on the part of males generally, and Mexican men in particular, is plainly lacking. With Her, perhaps, immigrant women would not feel that new sensation of loneliness.

If, as I have suggested earlier, language limited peasant women's ability to articulate both their frustrations and their yearnings, then the Virgin and Her Child likely provided a window into those emotions. I wonder to what extent on Sundays, while the men played with their bats and balls, Mexican women saw in this Virgen Morena the most perfect love, a model for all human relationships—the mutually adoring mother and boy child. The Christ child was the only one above the state and its soldiers, above the fathers and husbands and their prerogatives, the only one conceived without the *palo,* the man's stick that penetrated her when she consented to her wifely duty. And there has been much in this regard with which to identify in the figure of la Virgen. Gazing at Her beautiful and sorrowful face at the procession, in church, or on a candlelit altar in the corner of a humble abode, a Mexican woman had an intimate with whom to share actual or projected sorrow. With her baby at her breast, Mary asserted that most profound presence of superiority over men and the state. Then Mary, too, had lost her precious son to the profane (male) world of temporal power, lust, and bloodletting.

Bert Colima was one of those mothers' sons of México de afuera (see figure 10). When "el Mexicano de Whittier" knocked Bobby Corbett down with a crashing right to the jaw and then knocked him out with a blow to the solar plexus, the fans at Hollywood Boxing Stadium on June 20, 1924, "were on their chairs shouting their heads off." "The Whittier Flash" to the Anglo press and "el ídolo de Whittier" to the Mexican press, Colima "was recognized as the best middleweight on the Coast" during the 1920s, according to one fight expert, "and his bouts with such men as Oakland Jimmy Duffy were regarded as ring classics." *La Opinión* exulted that "in his ten years [in the ring] he . . . maintained Mexican supremacy in the 160 pound division, and . . . never lost his fame as the biggest ticket attraction for the [boxing] aficionados of our raza." Colima fought Anglos, blacks, and Mexicans; sometimes he *fué noqueado* (was knocked out), but mostly *el noqueó* (he knocked out) his opponent. In those days the referees did not stop one-sided fights or contests in which one of the combatants had become defenseless.[69] They deferred to the shrilly expressed will of the crowd for a knockout: another mother's son left outstretched and bleeding on the canvas.

No events so consistently excited the appetites of so many Mexican men as the fights, and, in my view, nothing provides a better lens through which to view men and their passions. The Mexican boxers quickly became an important presence in the arenas of California and

Figure 10. Bert Colima (the boxer on the right) squares off for photographers against Mickey Walker, the welterweight champion, before their fight. Colima lost. Behind Walker stands Jack Dempsey, his chief second. (Courtesy UPI/Corbis-Bettmann.)

provided a central means by which men's ethnic consciousness was formed. Associated as it was with big cities and immigrants, boxing and its brutality had been an easy target for the urban reform movements and Victorian women's purity crusades of the Progressive Era. James J. Jeffries's knockout of Gus Ruhlin in San Francisco for the heavyweight championship in November 1901 established California, somewhat insulated from genteel reform, as the "undisputed boxing capital of the world," at least until New York legalized prize fights in 1920. The year 1924 was an important one for Los Angeles fight fans: three locals, Fidel LaBarba, Jack Fields, and Joe Salas, won medals at the Paris Olympic Games. LaBarba, the U.S. amateur flyweight champ, won a gold medal in that division, and Fields defeated Salas, national featherweight amateur champion, for the gold in his class. Joe Salas from México de afuera, in other words, won a silver medal for the United States in the

1924 Olympics, and Fidel LaBarba, an Italian and no gringo Protestant, won a gold.[70]

The involvement of underworld figures, fixed fights, racial politics, the physical destruction of many fighters, and a generally corrupt atmosphere of smoky, urine-stained men and auditoriums all characterized what some have called "the sweet science" and "the manly art of self defense." But he who became the champion got to rise above this miasma and muck, and described heroism for men—an indomitable individual, contemptuous of weakness and submission, who through aggression and fearlessness conquers his opponents. Such characteristics immediately suggest questions about the relationship between boxing and life, about which imitates which. But even if "boxing is only like boxing," it is nonetheless a text like the processions for the Virgin of Guadalupe, a series of stories that we can read to find out about the participants, and about ourselves.[71]

While there may be a certain purity to the stark scene of two men going mano a mano in the ring, these were manufactured dramas. "To Dutch Meyers," noted our fight expert, "must be given credit for developing the biggest individual favorite during the days of the four round game in the southern part of the state. Meyers, an old friend and pal of Bert Colima brought him along to the point where his every appearance meant a packed house."[72] Promoters arranged these fights for maximum appeal, of course. This meant that they exploited ethnicity, revenge, and the promise of brutality to increase ticket sales. Aficionados of the sport, almost inevitably deeply steeped in the history of famous bouts, have appreciated both the remarkable skill levels that individual boxers have achieved, as well as the physical aesthetics of the ebb and flow of a bout. It has always been, though, the blood and the knockout and, as with la Virgen, the opportunity both to transcend the mundane and to identify with the fighters that have provided the primary appeal of the big fights.

As in the eastern part of the country, boxers in California were often ethnically identified. "Joey Silver, Jew from San Francisco, won by technical knock out over the Mexican, Young González, from El Paso" was a typical entry in *La Opinión*'s sports section. So was "Colima noqueó al negro Wolcott Langford." After "Colima Noqueó Anoche a Tiger Bob Robinson en el 1er. Round," the many Mexicans in attendance at Culver City Stadium enthusiastically applauded Colima, who on this occasion demonstrated much confidence and ability in his defense and in his delivery of blows: "y un punch considerable." Again, through identification with pan-Mexican figures such as Colima—who was briefly middleweight champ of Mexico—village men from various parts of the republic could see themselves more and more as Mexicans.[73]

Such identifications, though, have their complexities. Put in ethnic terms, the matches separated people who may well have had, if not some notions of brotherhood, at least some common interests and consciousness regarding their economic station in life. One time when Bert Colima was defeated, it was because "Ace Hudkins fought very dirty," as the headline blared: "The North American destroyed Colima with head butts." "It was," La Opinión concluded, "one of the dirtiest fights we have ever seen in the rings of California." To the extent that boxing has provided a paradigm for manhood, it has also contributed to different groups' constructions of other groups: macho, crafty, slick, intelligent, strong-chinned, and dirty are adjectives that come immediately to mind. While boxing arguably has provided a relatively safe outlet for such tribal loyalties, its diverse styles, often ethnically associated, and the way promoters and the press have amplified them, have "reinforced the emotional perception, if not the intellectual idea, that men are different physically and psychologically because they belong to different races." Any fight fan knows that "No fighters in the world are more dedicated to the raw violence of the business than Mexicans."[74]

Boxing gave youths a particular and Mexican notion of manhood to think about, or, more likely, a demeanor to imitate. "Two or three Mexicans have become famous boxers and gotten rich, like Colima, Fuente, and the like," noted a Los Angeles playground director in 1926. "Nearly every Mexican boy has the ambition to be a great boxer. This is the main thing that he thinks about until he gets married and has to go to work digging ditches or working for the railroad." A commentator of the time affirmed that the sport manifested "manliness and heroism." Frankie García provides one among many examples of the boxer as family man. A member of the Los Angeles Athletic Club, García came to fame with a sensational knockout of a fighter known simply as Tamachula in the International Amateur Championships held in San Francisco in 1917. This flyweight turned pro and "is one of the cleanest boxers in the country and one of the hardest right hand hitters, if not the hardest in his class. During his time in the ring Frankie has saved enough money to provide a nice home for his folks and family. He is the proud father of a fine little son, who he claims some day will be the champion of the world in his class." Mexicans rooted themselves in a variety of ways in the new land, and usually with family values.[75]

Almost every boxer has aspired to be a big winner, if not a champion. What was said about Colima in the previous paragraphs clearly marks him as a admirable man. After one of his several suspensions for fouls, Colima sought to open an athletic club "near the inhabitants of Pico" to instruct youths in boxing. Press clippings make it clear that this great boxer, not quite a champion, and others like him, were men to be emulated in México de afuera. But since nearly all fights must have a loser, many youthful fighters proved their fortitude by being able to take a punch, by enduring beatings. To go down, and recall that knockouts were frequent then, evidenced weakness and depicted violation. "Young guys who had the guts to face an unknown opponent used this golden opportunity to become known," noted the sister of one whose dreams were literally KO'd in the first round: "Many were unprepared for the hard blows and soon began to bleed from the mouth or nose. If nothing else Mexican-American vatos had pride; they hung on until the last round."[76] We see here how, consistent with virtually all cultures in which men engage in combat sports, Mexican culture, as its men defined and experienced it, came to associate physical prowess (in victory or defeat) with the quality of character for its men.

Boxing has provided a path to success for young men, one that affirmed in a public arena these masculine values of aggressiveness, forcefulness, and immunity to pain. La Asociación Deportiva Hispano-Americana, for example, feted Colima as guest of honor at its *Baile Deportiva* (dance) held at the Masonic Temple in May 1927. (The middle-class gente danced to the Dixieland Mosby Bluesblowers, José Arias y los Monarcas del Jazz, and the Verdugo Imperials.) After European champion Paulino Uzcúdum won the Latin American championship in Mexico City in January 1928, this heavyweight received an "entusiasta recepción" at Teatro Hidalgo. *La Opinión* adopted this man, actually a Basque, as a "gran boxeador de la Raza," and "Bert Colima personally gave him the welcoming" at this headline-grabbing event.[77] To be a contender, like Colima or Uzcúdum in their respective divisions, was for a working-class youth a way to be somebody.

Fame, fortune, ethnic identification, and the grisly, macabre beauty all have been parts of boxing. But anyone who has ever been to see boxing knows that there is something awfully berserk about the whole thing. It is not merely the violent intensity and desperation necessary

to win evidenced in the several times Colima was knocked out or suspended for fouls (probably head butts and low blows). Only a very hungry young man would get into the ring with someone trying to beat him
senseless. Hungry for what? For the blood and the pain? To be known
as a forceful or durable man? To "have been a contender" and to live
on in fight fans' memories? What demons have inspired these bare-
chested, muscular young men to inflict and experience the pain? Dreams
of fame, of poor nobodies becoming somebodies, surely pushed the men
to the bright lights of the ring. Fighters, though, keep on when they are
beaten; so many content themselves with being losers and allow themselves to be knocked out. There is exhilaration when the punches come,
and especially when the blood comes. I think it is that stinging pain and
good red blood that affirm that the young man is really alive.

The boxers allow the spectators to fear and to pity, and the promise
or threat of the knockout elicits some animal panic. This is the cli-
max that fight fans crave; and both the fear and pity are resolved when
the victor walks away, the vanquished gets back up, and two new combatants enter the arena. The dread and excitement about the fact that
something quite carnal is happening start again as a new fight com-
mences. The viewer, by the second bout, is a participant in this homo-
erotic spectacle, an adjunct now in this yearning for some sensation,
in this loathsome attempt to feel alive. To feel this passion, "to know
with" (the etymology of the word "passion") the fighters, served the
emotional needs of the men of México de afuera.[78]

SAFETY

While Mexicans successfully re-created much of the familiar, they were
still, let us recall, a people unfastened from their customary attachments. When the oscillations of the capitalist labor market brought unemployment, or if fate brought illness, injury, or death, supportive networks of kin and community were not so readily available in this new
land peopled largely with strangers. Nor could government be expected
to respond to the misfortunes of immigrants who did not vote. In this
context, then, and among every immigrant group, strategies for communal aid arose virtually naturally and spontaneously. The *mutualista*
(mutual-aid society) provided Mexicans not only with insurance against
calamity but also with an important social and cultural mooring wherever outposts of México de afuera were established.

La Sociedad Hispano-Americana de Beneficia Mutua dated from at least 1875 in Los Angeles. The largest and most prominent mutualista was the Alianza Hispano-Americana, which Mexican elites in Tucson had founded in 1894. By 1917 it had expanded to 85 chapters throughout the Southwest, and by 1913 it had become more simply a fraternal organization offering its members an insurance policy with a $1,200 benefit, a rich assortment of rituals, and often *funciones de gala,* such as the *fiesta de beneficiencia,* "charity," held at Teatro Zendejas in November 1919. The Alianza enrolled only those with employment steady enough to pay premiums. As the attractions of Main Street and consumerism began to challenge the appeal of the lodges' esoteric rituals, the Alianza continually had to organize more chapters among working-class raza to maintain solvency. Subscribing to the insurance program was an important way for a patriarch to demonstrate that he cared for his family, or at least this was how the Alianza appealed for membership.[79]

In the workings of the Alianza and the several other similar organizations, we find more than simple insurance and mutual aid. While many of the topics discussed previously have hinted broadly at the rise of Mexican national feeling in México de afuera, none so explicitly fomented such sentiments as the various Mexican sociedades organized in Los Angeles and the rest of the Southwest. Some were mutual-aid societies, others were protective leagues, others were charity societies, and yet others existed solely to honor and glorify la madre patria. A sociedad, then, expressed the obligation of the elites or the middle class to morally and materially elevate the rest of la raza. For example, attorney Emilio Garmendia, "organizador supremo de la Liga Protectora Latina," explained to La Sociedad Alegría, a youth group "de ambos sexos," how the league "imparted charity to infirm members and to the relatives of those who had died, etc., [and he made] reference to the social improvement being pursued among all classes of Mexicans living in the United States." Similarly, in a call to found a charity society, the upper-class *El Heraldo de México* explained how it would be "for the good of the needy, [and] the satisfaction of the conscience and good name of our class of Mexicans."[80] In other words, forming a sociedad was a way for elites—who so resented how the americanos simply lumped them with the chicanada, whom they disdained as contemptibly vulgar—to accomplish several purposes. Simultaneously they could act honorably; maintain social cohesion across classes in México de afuera; ensure proper and traditional Mexican behavior patterns among the youth; and fix up, morally and materially, the lower classes so that the "buen nombre de la raza" could be maintained and augmented.

For various reasons, the office of the Mexican consul played a principal role with regard to several of these concerns. First and foremost, the Mexican government actively sought to maintain the allegiance of its sons and daughters residing temporarily (presumably) in México de afuera. After all, those working in the United States were Mexico's most vital and strongest people, its most valuable natural resource. Beyond the issue of the southern republic's wounded pride over losing one-tenth of its population to the United States, the bleeding nation could ill afford to lose the most important component in any of its rebuilding plans after the Revolution—its workers in their physical prime.

By the late 1920s the consul typically led patriotic *festejos*. The big Cinco de Mayo celebration of 1928 "was organized by the Confederación de Sociedades Mexicanas, over which the Consul of Mexico, Sr. F. Alfonso Pesqueira, presides. . . . The formalities were presided over by the Vice Consul, Sr. Quiñones." The previous year Pesqueira had convened the many *comisiones honoríficas* to coordinate their primary function, which was "ultimately to pursue the worthy praise of, but also to maintain alive and constant the memory and love of, Mexico, and to serve as the channel through which Mexicans of every little location can gain access to the local consul when matters of simple protection or mediation arise." The consul either organized or participated in the founding of the comisiones, such as the time when Pesqueira traveled to Bakersfield in August 1929 to found a comisión honorífica whose first event would be a celebration of Diez y Seis de Septiémbre. While professionals and the middle class largely comprised these patriotic assemblies in the urban center, a broader-based association could prevail in such colonias. Still, though, as these expressions of Mexican nationalism blossomed in the new land, the consulate saw them all as functioning with the same intent. Ultimately, it strove to secure loyalty to the Mexican government as then constituted, a regime trying to consolidate its rule at home, where the specter of Church and peasant revolution consistently threatened, and a regime trying to retain the allegiance of its industrious sojourners in México de afuera.[81]

While nationalism seemed reborn in the new land among the recent immigrants, the various sociedades for a variety of reasons, achieved neither harmony nor cross-class unity. Actually, they often proved rather contentious. Patriotic celebrations, wherever they may be, get entangled first with what it means to be a patriot, and then most of them provide an opportunity for enterprising individuals to sell things to the flag wavers. Both of these excite quarreling. For its conservative readers, the aristocratic *El Heraldo de México* on September 16, 1921, ran the headline "We Glorify Our Heroes!" These were Hidalgo, Guerrero, Morelos, and Iturbide, the main figures of the independence effort. At that time, of course, the rural and urban proletarian masses looked much more to such contemporary heroes as Villa, Zapata, Flores Magón, and the others who espoused various forms of peasant communalism, socialism, or anarchism. *El Heraldo* considered these social revolutionaries worse than abhorrent, calling even the moderate Francisco Madero "a forerunner of Bolshevism," and the constitution of 1917 simply "Bolshiviki." Status-conscious Mexicans who sought to "renew the efforts of *El Comité Mexicano de Festejos Civicos*" in February 1919 were "trying to give lustre to the Mexican national celebrations in the foreign land" via "the lofty men who have given you liberty."[82] That is, many of the ones the masses thought were the rich pigs who had been exploiting them for so long. In other words, Mexicans with a strong sense of national pride celebrated very different heroes and revolutions, and fancy parades were not going to bridge those differences.

The purity of their Mexicanness proved pivotal as well. As historians George Sánchez and Ricardo Romo have pointed out, conservative nationalists roundly criticized the Alianza Hispano-Americano for having too many americanos on its board, for focusing too narrowly on being an insurance company to the exclusion of concern for the social needs and uplift of the raza, and for commercializing its events by promoting its insurance product. Since, too, these celebrations aimed to excite love for the mother country, those who declared the most extreme affection tended to presume their special, even exclusive, authenticity. Remember, though, that Mexico expressed not so much the unconditional love of a mother for her children as the fickle, provisional love of a destitute father. Competing to see whose patriotism could exceed whose struck a faint but certainly dissonant chord among those who had fled their ill-faring homeland in that era of Mexican history. In 1926 leaders of the Mexican community of Los Angeles founded the Confederación de Sociedades Mexicanas. (Daniel Venegas, president of the Confederation of Mexican Chambers of Commerce, served as the first president.) Acknowledging the dissension, its leaders sought "to unite the Mexican elements previously in conflict." Ultimately, though, these genuine divisions weakened the sociedades' efforts for "effective work for the educational, cultural, and social improvement of the Mexicans residing in California."[83]

They did better at simple charity. One such organization, the Cruz Azul (Blue Cross), provided often crucial relief for Mexicans who suffered disasters of either the natural sort or of the labor market. Elena de la Ilata efficaciously led the organization from its founding in 1920; though the consul in 1931 claimed the credit both for its success and for directing it. Ilata and the six or eight consuls of the 1920s and early 1930s likely proceeded in tandem. Raising money through various means, Cruz Azul tried to provide on-the-spot aid in emergency situations. This relief included clothing and shelter during colonia floods, repatriation back to Mexico when economic downturns pushed workers out of the labor market, and medical assistance. An all-women's organization, Cruz Azul epitomized the remarkable ability of the financially disfavored to express kindness to those even less fortunate. That their efforts amounted to no more than the proverbial drop in the bucket for the often destitute raza should go without saying. In the two years after Ilata's death in 1931, interest and monetary support waned, and Consul Martínez disbanded the Cruz Azul in 1933.[84]

The Depression even more dramatically intensified Mexican indigence. Of course all donor agencies grew strapped for funds as fewer and fewer people had money to contribute. Thus in 1931 Consul Rafael de la Colina organized the Comité de Beneficencia Mexicana to coordinate and systematize the relief effort that the conditions of México de afuera so needed. A successful fundraiser at the downtown Philharmonic Auditorium featuring Mexican stars of the stage and screen kicked off the sociedad. Again, thirty to sixty local merchants and professionals were the activists in the organization that provided food for the destitute and helped fund those who wished to return to Mexico. And, though the Depression pushed more out of el norte than did the consuls' efforts to sustain patriotism, indeed about one-third of the 150,000 Mexicans in Los Angeles did repatriate in the early years of the Depression.[85]

Residents of México de afuera built themselves a series of safety nets that amounted to new attachments to the new place. Creating a rich institutional life, the patriotic societies and mutualistas—the structural underpinnings of this immigrant culture—encouraged them to continue as Mexicans at the same time that it rooted them in el norte. These institutions were another way Mexicans presenced themselves on the landscape and how people make history. History is never made on a blank slate, of course, nor are people simply free to act. Thus what we would now call ethnic and national identity, both in the forms of institutions and in daily conduct, proved more than a legacy from the past of the cultural baggage carried al norte: it reemerged in America as one more way to negotiate the unfamiliar, sometimes difficult or hostile, new place. Why Mexicans had come to this new land in the first place—a question that readers have likely already posed—and what Mexican history bequeathed to its erstwhile sons and daughters are questions to which we shall now turn.

Born by the River

*The Great Migration from
Mexico to Southern California*

My sight follows
the river upstream
until it bends.
Beyond the bend is more river
and, soon, the mountains.
We shall arrive,
to see, soon.

    Simon Ortiz, in Woven Stone

The Fiesta Days of 1903 do more than provide us with a meaningful and ironic human drama. The parade visually contrasted a profound difference between the Spanish, Mexican, and American tenures upon the land of California: "Among the floats will be those showing the desert soil when it has been left without irrigation, with the cactus and other bushes that grow without water." Although the merchants' efforts to paint Los Angeles in "the romantic coloring of the land of the troubadour" dominated the theatrics of it, the fiesta principally "is intended to present to the public, and President Roosevelt in particular, the possibilities of the western country when irrigation is applied to its soil." Subsequent floats displayed "the grand results achieved by the careful use of water to the seemingly barren soil of California and the great wastes of the West." The sequence of the parade visually reflected the American conception of history.[1]

"The magic power of irrigation," which the local papers celebrated, repeated the same theme as had Roosevelt when he spoke of "The men who with axe in the forests and pick in the mountains and plow on the prairies pushed to completion the dominion of our people over the American wilderness." Linear progress, most apparently reflected for Roosevelt "in wresting from barbarism and adding to civilization the territory out of which we have made these beautiful States," provided the primary theme for Providentially inspired American history. "Yesterday and today," exclaimed Roosevelt at his first stop in the Los Angeles area, "I have been traveling through what is literally a garden of the Lord." The inclusion of more and more lands, and more and more people, into white Protestant American notions of civilization "should be forever a subject of just and national pride," Roosevelt wrote of his country's dealings with former Spanish colonies.[2] Few achievements in this progressive juggernaut could surpass the success of pouring water on the arid lands to make them bloom with grains, fruits, and vegetables.

Very little self-reflection went into this westering venture. Workers, capitalists, and petty proprietors engaged in monumental and vehement battles over the distribution of the West's mineral and agricultural wealth, but they agreed about the appropriateness and virtue of what they called development and progress for self, race, and country. The resistance came from nature: as when, between 1861 and 1864, a devastating drought followed calamitous floods, ending cattle production in the southern counties of California. Or it came from the peoples on the land, like the Indians, or from the Mexicans who put down their picks and shovels on the tracks being laid for Fiesta Days. Often mere nuisances, sometimes powerful challenges to the racial presumptions and hierarchies of Anglo expansion and capitalism, sometimes achieving short-term or, occasionally, structural reforms, such defiances inevitably accompanied the American economic mission.

THE MAGIC POWER OF IRRIGATION

Irrigation explains much about the immigration of Mexicans to the United States. It is a curious and eventful thing indeed, this pouring of water upon the land. It made the deserts bloom, but it sometimes made new deserts of the places from which irrigation waters had been taken; it promised to redeem the land, but too much water often dredged up salts that harmed the land; it pledged yeoman farms, but it created great capitalist ventures and concentrated wealth and power for those who could control the water; it vowed independence for those who tilled the soil, but it brought forth a huge agricultural proletariat dependent upon wages. A discussion of irrigation may appear to be a digression, but we cannot understand the changes in the human landscape, the presence of so many Mexicans, if we do not understand the changes in the land itself.

The Reclamation Act of 1902 first committed the federal government to large-scale irrigation projects in the arid lands of the West and Southwest. No one pondered much about from what these deserts were being re-claimed, but such lack of reflection was all part of how the Americans reconceived and renamed the land, and, moreover, enabled them to proceed confidently. For example, the process of remaking clearly delineated a new distinction between marketable agricultural commodities and the natural flora. The latter became as "waste" or "weeds"; indigenous plants were now growth out of place. Championed by Senator Francis Newlands from Nevada and Theodore Roosevelt, the Reclamation Act, for all its rhetoric about the family farm, reflected American faith in expansion, the increase of wealth, and grand technological schemes. Expansion could be fostered only "if the waters that now run to waste were saved and used for irrigation," proclaimed Roosevelt.[3] This was a prosperous, confident, industrious, retentive culture that sought to make over the peoples and landscapes of the world within the conceptions of pietistic Protestant capitalism. The Fiesta Days floats, which celebrated the forthcoming victory over "the great wastes of the West," conveyed the explicit message that no lands or peoples should go unused.

The water gushing from the irrigation pipes in the Imperial Valley, or any of the later project areas, visually contrasted with the aridity of Mexico. Federal irrigation projects in Mexico did not effectively commence until after World War II; and they occurred largely in the north, where the landscape was more amenable, rather than in the mountainous south or in the area of greatest exodus, the hilly central plateau.[4] The water projects north of the border contributed as much to pulling people from the south as any other factor, and probably more. On both sides of the border large areas of land have either inadequate or inconsistent rainfall. In many parts of California, Arizona, Texas, and Mexico what could be a long growing season but for lack of water makes irrigation projects all the more compelling.

Building dams, sluices, floodgates, and canals requires a number of things, some tangible and some not. Among these are a strong government willing and able to put aside its oratory about the evils of government intervention in the economy, large amounts of capital, a waning trust in Creation's immutableness and a waxing faith in technology, potential markets for the watered lands' produce and transportation to get it there, and a readily available source of labor power both for construction and for the new industrial farms. All of these factors the United States had more or less, and mostly more. For reasons having to do with politics and economic structure, a want of these factors in strong measure in Mexico meant that Mexico watered its lands much less. Again, lack of irrigation actually only symptomatized Mexico's troubles in economic development and in the drain of some of its population, but the contrast between the sister republics is useful and significant.

Let us briefly turn to two projects that opened the fields for Mexican immigrants and illustrate some of the human and natural changes that the pouring of water brought to the landscapes of California and other parts of the Southwest. The reader must bear in mind that these immensely complicated issues will quite obviously be oversimplified and that this necessary digression into the matter of irrigation will propel us well into the twentieth century, beyond the time frame of this narrative of Mexicans in Los Angeles and Southern California. But, as regards the latter caveat, such chronological overlapping and interweaving likely reflect how history is.

The procurement of water and the politics surrounding such activity contain many moments in which great men acted boldly and supplied the greatest amount of water for the greatest number of people. The very same acts sometimes illustrate as well the adage that "behind every great fortune is a great crime." Which rival stand one takes on the issue depends upon where one sits along the river: the word "rival" derives from the Latin *rivalis,* "one living near or using the same stream as another." Few episodes in history better illustrate these notions about the relationship between historical judgments and one's objective position along the river than Los Angeles's acquisition of water from the Owens Valley in the decade following Roosevelt's visit to Fiesta Days.

Under the shadow of the Sierra Nevada about 250 miles northeast of Los Angeles lies the Owens Valley, a dry but formerly fertile narrow strip through which the Owens River used to run. Around it a classic American drama played out. Small, prosperous farms lined the river, and there fruit trees, wheat, corn, and clover and grass for grazing grew. Meanwhile, rivaling the efforts of the Owens white yeomanry, a partnership composed of Harrison Gray Otis, Harry Chandler (the owner of the *Los Angeles Times* and Otis's son-in-law), Joseph Sartori (a banker), Henry Huntington, E. H. Harriman, E. T. Earl, and M. H. Sherman quietly in 1904 began buying acreage—which eventually totaled 108,000 acres—in the dry and rather worthless San Fernando Valley. It was they who approached the Los Angeles Water Department (of which Sherman was a member) with the idea of building an aqueduct from the Owens

Valley to Los Angeles. The planners used the words "profit" and "control" with some facility. The city had enough water from artesian wells and the Los Angeles River for its 102,000 people, but spendthrift use and irrigation, particularly for all the orange groves, began to make some people nervous about the future of the potentially parched city.

And here is "the story of a dream that came true; of an idea audaciously conceived and splendidly realized," as the boomers put it.[5] In 1903 the Reclamation Service's chief engineer for California, J. B. Lippincott, went to the Owens Valley and announced a broad reclamation project that would put an additional 200,000 acres under the plow. He gained the gleeful farmers' trust, uncovered important information about the water resources, and even persuaded some of the farmers to cede priority claims on their water. In the following year Fred Eaton, the former mayor of Los Angeles, appeared in the valley and, complete with Reclamation Service maps and surveys, represented himself as Lippincott's agent charged with leasing options on water for the United States government. This he did in checkerboard fashion, acquiring alternating parcels on both sides of the river. Quickly he bought or leased much riparian land in the valley, and then the plot began to percolate: Lippincott announced that the (fictitious) reclamation project had been canceled, and then he quit the Reclamation Service and hired on with the Los Angeles Water Department, which, it turned out, had been paying him a salary all along. In July 1905 the *Los Angeles Times* trumpeted the story of the planned aqueduct for which the city would need to float $25 million in bonds. Mysteriously a water shortage happened, accompanied by prohibitions against watering lawns and gardens—actually much water was disappearing down sewers—and the citizens of Los Angeles overwhelmingly voted for the water bonds in September 1905. Los Angeles would have the water of the Owens Valley but with the consequence, farmers quickly realized, that the valley would again become a desert.

"It gurgled and splashed its cheerful message of good health, great wealth, long life and plenteous prosperity to Los Angeles and its people," reported the *Times* upon the water's arrival. But Los Angeles did not get the water, at least not for a while. Upon completion of the aqueduct in 1913 it came to the north end of the San Fernando Valley (see figure 11). The previously cheap and dusty lands there skyrocketed in value from $5 to $20 per acre up to $500 to $1,000 per acre. The syndicate made about $100 million dollars. Irrigated acreage increased from

Figure 11. The opening of the Los Angeles Aqueduct at Owensmouth. Note that the San Fernando Valley was nearly a desert. (Courtesy Seaver Center for Western History Research, Natural History Museum of Los Angeles County.)

3,000 acres at the time of the arrival of the water to 75,000 acres in 1918. The "men of vision," under the leadership of chief engineer William Mulholland, created tens of thousands of new acreage for agriculture. The soil's thirst for water quenched, the land then thirsted for thousands of low-wage, itinerant workers to harvest its new plenty.

In history there is often what we might call "the natural unfolding of events." I do not think that the fabulous episode of the Owens Valley plot can be categorized as such. Nor does it exactly qualify as a noble achievement of great men, notwithstanding their remarkable and effective planning and execution, which promised at St. Francis Dam Number 1 only "some spilling in extreme cases."[6] But then, so many contingent factors must be present for a particular historical outcome. The Imperial Valley, in southeastern California around the Mexican border, became a notable industrial agricultural center most essentially because the magnificent Colorado River, energetic cutter of so many awe-inspiring canyons, deposited so much silt there on its way to the Gulf of California. The first farmers, Yuma, Cocopa, and Kamia Indian peoples, found in it an extraordinary place to plant, but only along the edges of the river when it flooded. All humans have altered their environments, but those most inclined to do so, and most technocratic, realized that if water could be spread all over the rich alluvium, then the monetary return from the soil, if transported to market, would bring remarkable affluence. Americans, though, have always been divided over which they liked best, an arcadian democracy of small freeholders or the dramatic triumph of a great land baron. In the West, massive irrigation projects assured the prevalence of the latter.

After several irrigation schemes and a nearly catastrophic man-made flood in 1905, which halted production until 1907, the farmers of the valley founded the Imperial Irrigation District (IID) in 1911. They carried with them ambivalence and confusion, common to American farmers everywhere, about labor and wealth. They resisted the mounting influence of E. H. Harriman, whose Southern Pacific Railroad carried their produce to market and whose crews had been instrumental in controlling the flood for which the railroad company received control of the water distribution system. (The IID used its power to assess property and raised enough funds to buy out Harriman's interests in 1916.) The farmers resented the fact that they had to pay not only for the levees that restrained the river on their side of the border, but also for the present canal (the Alamo, of all names), which meandered for fifty miles through Mexico. Harry Chandler, owner of the *Los Angeles Times* and a sponsor and celebrant of the Fiesta Days, actually possessed most of the land there. That he leased it to Mexicans, Japanese, and especially Chinese, or else employed them all as coolie labor on his own haciendas, intensified the farmers' indignation. To save themselves from their various rivals and to maintain their status as independent freeholders, Imperial Valley farmers appealed to the Reclamation Service to build them a new waterway that would traverse only California. This All-American Canal would free them from the threat of robber baron control, guarantee the supply of water, and deliver them from the assorted irritating entanglements with Mexico. The Reclamation Service, always eager to find water to dam up and move around to justify its ever-bloating bureaucracy, gladly accepted. The legislation of January 1920 enabling the construction of a new canal, under the Reclamation Act and its amendments, affirmed preferential treatment for veterans and small farmers; in fact it limited new lands that received water to no "more than 160 acres."[7]

When yeoman ideology met up with the practice of farming, the ideology's integrity was usually the first to go. Alexis de Tocqueville noticed in the 1830s that "In the United States a man builds a house in which to spend his old age, and he sells it before the roof is on; he plants a garden and lets it just as the trees are coming into bearing; he brings a field into tillage and leaves other men to gather the crops." And so it went in the Imperial Valley. There temperatures in summer typically surpass 100 degrees and can reach 120. The crops grown there, lettuce, melons, vegetables, and cotton, all require much stooping and bending to cultivate and harvest. And those crops, which the Southern Pacific hauled to national market, brought much money, which in turn dramatically enhanced the value of that irrigated, fertile land. Yeoman families had not moved to the valley to swelter in the heat, to become slaves to the soil, or to bequeath their children a life of ceaseless toil. Thus it made sense for a farm family to find someone else to do the work, an Indian or a Mexican most likely, or simply to cash out the appreciated value of their land or rent it for a good monthly income and move to a cooler place. By 1927 tenants operated the clear preponderance of Imperial Valley's nearly 4,800 farms. "It is strange to see with what feverish ardor the Americans pursue their own welfare," de Tocqueville had mused, "and to watch the vague dread that constantly torments them lest they should not have chosen the shortest path which may lead to it."[8]

Not only the acquisitiveness and impatience of American farmers, but also the logic of the technology of large-scale irrigation militated against a hardworking, independent yeomanry. Here we see something of a "natural unfolding" of history as regards our issues at hand. Complex, large-scale irrigation is simply more proficient and convenient with large-scale spreads than it is with numerous little ones. Agribusiness elites always dominated the IID's board of directors, allegedly organized to enable local people to control their own water. The irrigation district hired managers whose worldview assumed efficiency (measured in acrefeet of water), comprehensive control of nature, and high return on the dollar. Small farmers and tenants, usually struggling and on the brink of bankruptcy, often disorganized, and rarely scientific, did not fathom these concepts of technocratic agriculture. Wealthy individuals and corporations certainly did. Thus an alliance of the large owners and the technocrats rather naturally unfolded, and irrigation favored the large field or the corporate farm or both. By the late 1930s Imperial Valley water essentially functioned for the private use of agribusiness farms in the valley. These grand spreads needed workers.[9]

With different particulars, but strikingly similar outcomes and remarkable consensus, this tale of the Owens and Colorado Rivers has been repeated throughout California and the arid West. In the San Joaquin Valley, where the electric pump initially came into play, the Central Valley Project of the late 1930s and 1940s, the most grandiose project in Reclamation Service history, moved Sacramento River water into the service of agribusiness, creating what is arguably the preeminent agricultural center in the world. The natural and human costs of such projects rarely figured in the popular enthusiasm for the awe-inspiring undertakings. Occasionally, the water took its revenge.

In March 1928 the St. Francis Dam broke. Just north of the San Fernando Valley, the waters from the Owens River stored behind the newly constructed dam burst it apart, sending a tidal wave initially 200 feet high through the San Francisquito and Santa Clara Valleys. Estimates on the number the "wild waters" killed range from 385 to 450. Nobody knows for sure because so many of the dead were Mexican pickers and workmen, people whom neither history nor local authorities kept much track of. The nine desultory investigations conducted surmised that the rock abutting the dam was too porous to hold and that the reservoir had been filled too fast. Perhaps. But it is clear that humans in their greed and conceit often do not pay the water the respect it is due. Some people say that "you can feel the anger in water behind a dam." Sometimes the water breaks free.[10]

In yet other words, there is no such thing as technological transformation in the land without social consequences. Maybe some few changes have turned out elementally good and some few have proved unabashedly bad. Such verdicts usually have most to do with taking credit or assigning blame for the outcome and thereby obscure more about historical change than they clarify. Judgments depend, again, more on where one sits along the river than on any tenets of moral philosophy. Sometimes things evolve almost imperceptibly; sometimes they explode like the St. Francis Dam. Such dramatic ruptures, though, isolate and illuminate the social consequences of men's alterations of nature and the economy. There is no better example of this, and none more pertinent to our story here, than the Mexican Revolution.

"AND JUST LIKE THAT RIVER I'VE BEEN RUNNING EVER SINCE": THE ORIGINS OF MEXICAN MIGRATION

Like my account of irrigation, an analysis of why Mexicans migrated to the United States, or why Europeans, Asians, and others did so, requires a careful connecting of a variety of factors. Yet different historians, especially when condensing much into a few pages, will select different threads from the historical record to interweave into an explanation of a certain occurrence. Historians mostly agree that deprivation in Mexico, the dislocation and violence of the Revolution (1911–20), and the opportunity to work in the north provided the "push and pull" for Mexican immigration to the United States. Much less consensus exists about the nature of the poverty in Mexico, the responses of peasants and workers to the appearance of European and American capital there, and what motivates people to take an action such as revolution or migration.

The life history, related in the early 1930s, of "Mrs. G." and her family, who migrated to the south central Los Angeles community of Watts (named for the old Indian village of Tajuata), illustrates the challenge of this uncertainty:

> I can remember our house in Zacatecas. It was adobe and hadn't any windows. We lived on a small rancho. My mother died when I was a baby and I was brought up with my brothers and sisters. One day, one of my brothers had to go away to market and I had to help my brother to plant. He plowed with oxen and a wooden plow. I dropped the corn after he plowed. I was very little, but I can remember how tired I was. The soil was very rich and we had plenty to eat when it rained. I remember once when it didn't rain and everyone was hungry, a great deal worse than the depression here. Everyone deserted their house and went away.[11]

Was her family's difficulty the privation of a windowless adobe or the hard work? No. The family continued satisfactorily, even with the happenstance of the mother's death. Did the shortcomings of their rudimentary technology push them out? Apparently not. These people seem to have been largely self-sufficient. Was the "tyranny of the corn," that is, dependence on one crop that demanded consistent rain and wore out the soil, responsible for this family's migration, as it had been for relocations since pre-Columbian times? In part, yes. Would an irrigation project have saved the ranchito? Not likely. In Mexico, as in the United States, irrigation has benefited the large landholders. Did the family dream of an affluent life in the United States? Such a dream does not seem to figure in her account. Quite starkly and quite modestly, they "went away" simply to survive.

We are about to attribute Mrs. G.'s presence in Southern California to notions about which she would have little awareness or conception. In doing so, we take a historical actor and subjectivate her to our purposes and agenda. She and her family did not know about theories of imperialism or class and caste; nor of the capitalization of railroads and aqueducts, or of the structure of a labor market. Nor did they think much about the profound consequences for their lives of the long, difficult, and imposing history of Mexico. They believed in the ideal, if not the reality, that the old people knew the most truth about life—about how men and women should be, about how children should be, and about how and what they should become. They knew about corn and pigs and barter, and who actually controlled local political and economic power; they lived in awe and fear of nature and the spirit world, which they often conflated; their sense of history revolved around elaborate accounts of their forebears and of who was related to whom. Quite starkly and quite modestly they knew about survival, at most on a year-to-year basis. So why *did* Mrs. G. and her family wind up in south central Los Angeles?

Individuals and families moved for their own reasons, of course. But we can recognize several factors that thrust people toward the migrant stream. In the late nineteenth century, Mexico transfigured its philosophy and practice of land tenure. The former Spanish colony had always held contradictory impulses toward large estates and free villages. On the hacienda, the *patrón* kept his *peones* bound to his lands by means of debt or other obligations, and though he worked them often mercilessly, he at least guaranteed their livelihoods with produce from the land. In the pueblos the *ejido,* "common lands," provided much of the peasantry's sustenance. That both the hacienda and the pueblos emphasized self-sufficiency hindered the industrializing republic's ability to generate agricultural surpluses either for export or for the cities. The Ley Lerdo of 1856 sought to transform village lands into private property, which, according to the regnant liberal ideology of the nineteenth century, would guarantee individual initiative and thus a more energetic system of commercial agriculture. Villages that for whatever reason failed to privatize their lands could have their lands appropriated by individuals who promised to make them more productive. Then, during the regime of Porfirio Díaz (1876–1911), several laws, first promulgated in 1883, allowed companies to subdivide and occupy public lands. These enterprises received one-third of the land at once and could buy the rest very cheaply. Peasants had occupied much of these public lands for generations, and they quickly found themselves ejected from lands they considered theirs by right of use and tradition. The outcome was a stunning transferal of Mexican lands into the hands of foreign capitalists and an equally staggering immiseration of the Mexican *campesinaje,* not to mention desperate peasant revolts.[12]

Theoretically, this process could have worked to industrialize and bring prosperity and stability to Mexico. Those thrown off the land could have moved to factory centers, where the input of foreign capital could have given them jobs. Then they could have had enough money to buy both the produce of the newly productive agribusinesses as well as the products of the new manufacturers. But this was not at all the outcome of the Porfiriato (as the regime of Díaz was known) in large part because of the consequences of foreign control. The quantity of such ownership is striking, but the quality of it for Mexican peasants and workers is the most meaningful. American corporations, consortiums, and individuals owned over 100 million acres, some held for speculation and some actually producing. This acreage amounted to more than 22 percent of Mexico's land surface. The Hearst family owned 6.6 to 7.5 million acres in several states; Texaco, 4.7 million; Continental Rubber Company, 3.8 million; Harry Chandler over 1 million; R. Vick, 1.5 million in Sonora; the Henry Muller heirs, over 2.5 million, 1.25 million acres on one ranch; the American International Land and Mining Company, 1.2 million acres; and on and on. The Mexican government sold many of these lands cheaply, some they simply conceded, and some these "investors" simply took. Statistics showed that the program was succeeding. During the Porfiriato, exports of rubber, chili, henequen, cacao, coffee, peas, tobacco, and vanilla all increased substantially, and exports of other products such as corn, wheat, rice, and other vegetables showed ample growth. The new wages the campesinos received for their labors on these lands betokened another positive economic indicator.[13]

The poor of rural Mexico, the vast majority of the population, experienced this separation of land and labor on a continuum that ranged from despair to rage. Wages do not satisfy people either accustomed to or aspiring to self-sufficiency on land under their control—the goal of peasants worldwide. By 1910 no less than 90 percent of rural Mexicans did not possess land, and in some states that figure reached 99 percent. Moreover, a drop in the mortality rate increased the population of Mexico between 1875 and 1910 by more than 50 percent, from 9.5 million to 15.2 million. Thus both the supply of laborers and the demand for food were increasing, a situation that boded ill for the ability of wage labor to compensate suitably for the loss of the people's lands. Quantitative gains in the domestic supply of foodstuffs proved quite modest, and after 1907 food production declined. In other words, the Porfirian political economy had the outcome of taking land from people and making them hungry. Wages went down and prices went up—the cost of beans and corn increased by about 50 percent in the twenty-five years after Díaz came to power—and there were more people.[14]

It is meaningful in the great scope of things that the population figure of 15 million in 1910 still fell far short of the estimated 26 million who had inhabited pre-conquest Mexico. The land could feed all the people.

The village of Naranja in central Michoacán exemplifies and elucidates this situation well. For generations there, Tarrascan Indian people farmed chilies, squash, beans, and corn, which, patted into tortillas, formed the key component of their diet. Farmers alternated the first three crops with wheat, which not only produced two good crops annually, but eliminated the need for fallowing or fertilizer beyond animal dung. Some of the bean crop they sold in the nearest town, but mostly the people of this independent village ate what they grew. Much of their productive lives centered around a marshy lake that harbored or attracted a vast array of animal life. The clams and roots women and children dug from the lake constituted part of their daily meals, as did edible reptiles. In the surrounding area, villagers gathered fruit, grasses, acorns, and cactus to supplement the staples. Most everyone kept chickens and, occasionally, a pig. This diet revolved around the environment that the people inhabited.

In the 1880s two Spanish brothers realized that under the marsh lay soil of extraordinary fertility. They engaged in the appropriate negotiations both with the government for surveying, drainage, and acquisition of the titles and with corrupt local leaders for even more land. By 1900 the marsh had been drained, the new soil had been planted, and prodigious quantities of corn began to pile up in the new granaries; and most Naranjeños now depended on the new landlords for wages. But this compensation could not buy them adequate food. Their housing decayed; their clothes became shoddy, and they went barefoot. They were, in a word, destitute. Many of the men migrated for work, some even to the United States, including Primo Tapia, who went to Los Angeles and actually met up with the Liberales. Indeed, the Porfirian strategy brought "development" to Naranja, if this is measured by the quantity of corn and revenue produced. But the people had very little to eat.[15]

This is not to say that Mexicans had not suffered before, but now the world market drew so much of the country's agricultural produce away. While many starved, statistics showed that Mexico still exported livestock, guayule (raw rubber from a shrub of the same name), grains, and vegetables to the United States and actually imported corn. In other words, many Mexican campesinos, often on lands that they or their ancestors had once farmed for subsistence, harvested crops for export in exchange for wages that were utterly inadequate to support their families. These were the relatively fortunate ones; the rest wandered, burdened relatives, or merely idled hungrily. Imagine, too, the devastation that a crash in the international sugar market in the last years of the Porfiriato brought to plantation workers in Morelos: No market for their

produce, no job. This sort of loss of control over the value of one's product—and sugar is only one example—powerfully contrasted the old subsistence ways, whether on a hacienda or a ranchito, with the new commercial agricultural production that depended on the remote, obscure,
and unpredictable world market for success. Such were the complications that foreign control, or export-oriented Mexican growers, brought
to the routinely shaky agricultural scene in Mexico.

Any fluctuation can be devastating for people living close to starva-
tion. Agricultural people have always been vulnerable to the weather
(those with irrigation much less so). While Mexico often shows good
averages, rainfall varies considerably year to year. Drought came between 1907 and 1910 and partially or completely destroyed the corn
crops of Durango, Chihuahua, Coahuila, Zacatecas, and Aguascalientes.
The price of corn increased by 38 percent and that of wheat by 20 percent in those parched years. Famine ravaged the central and northern
states. Sometimes people migrated: many to the cities, although Porfirian economics had created few jobs there, and some few to the United
States. Sometimes they simply resigned themselves to these painful and
sorrowful times for the rural poor of Mexico. Sometimes they began to
think even more about revolution.[16]

The cities could not compensate for the crisis in the Mexican country-
side. Here a comparison with the economic development of the United
States is illuminating. In the latter, on the northeastern seaboard and the
manufacturing belt of the Midwest, industrial centers that saw large investments of capital soaked up much of the exodus from the farmlands
of both the United States and Europe. That this did not happen effectively in Mexico again evidences the problems with reliance on foreigners for capital accumulation. In this case the mines and railroads provide the best illustrations. Envision for a moment the process initiated
when iron ore was extracted from the mines of northern Michigan and
Minnesota. Miners labored in the iron ore fields; then shippers on the
Great Lakes floated it down to the great steel centers of Chicago/Gary,
Pittsburgh, Cleveland, and so on; there the ore met up with the product
of yet other mines, namely, the coal that fired the great blast furnaces.
The steel produced became everything from trains and rails to building
beams and, later, automobiles, appliances, and airplanes. Each of these
industries called forth all manner of other production such as tires, upholstered seats, and Fiesta Days floats; the proficient railroad system
(built with much British capital but controlled by American captains of
industry) distributed all these things throughout the country; and then
all these products entered the realm of wholesale and retail sales. At

each point in the process workers got a pay envelope. The bosses were rarely kind, and the work was often harsh, alienating, dangerous, or boring. Eventually, though, their union activity increased wages until in many cases workers could support a family decently; that is, they could effectively consume their products and those of other workers, including the foodstuffs of the irrigated valleys of California. In this way American workers and capitalists, with much rancor between them to be sure, built an American economy.

Now when capitalists from the outside invest and exercise control the story usually differs remarkably. Unless consumption in the country (like the United States or England) with lots of capital increases dramatically, or new industries such as the automobile spring up, profits have a hard time finding investment outlets that will produce commodities for which there will be effective demand. Capitalism is always overproducing profit and goods: it must pursue new outlets for profits and goods in a place like Mexico, where Díaz's *scientíficos* optimistically opened the doors to foreign investors. Thus American railroad barons, the "Big Four"—E. H. Harriman, James Stillman of National City Bank, Jacob Schiff, and William Rockefeller—came to hold the lion's share of the 80 percent of Mexico's railroad stock that American capitalists owned overall. Toward the end of the Porfiriato, American capitalists accounted for the ownership of 81 percent of the capitalization of Mexico's mines, and the British owned 14.5 percent. French bankers controlled 45.7 percent of the banking assets in Mexico. French investors concentrated their efforts on commerce, retail sales, and textiles. By 1910 the Waters-Pierce Company, affiliated with Standard Oil, controlled 90 percent of the illuminating oil market and all the gasoline.[17] These statistics are quite remarkable in themselves, but the consequences of such ownership are the issue here.

The configuration of the Mexican railway system is instructive. In the heyday of foreign development, essentially all roads led in and out of the country. Foreign businessmen built the railroads to go to the United States and to the ports to facilitate an import-export economy. This sharply contrasted to the United States rail system, which connected the nation's extractive and manufacturing centers with one another and with the expanding markets of its great cities. Statistics often give the appearance of success in such situations: Mexico's exports increased consistently by about 6 percent per year in the years before 1911. The problems, though, have to do with stagnation, the export of profits, and vulnerability to international markets. For example, oil and minerals left Mexico as raw materials and returned as finished products.

Although this benefited importers and exporters (hence the shape of the railroad system), Mexican workers did not gain the benefit of all of the jobs in between the extraction of raw materials and the sale of the final product. No steel industry, for example, arose in Mexico to make all those rails and cars. No steelworkers and no nationalist steel manufacturing bourgeoisie resulted from the railroad's increased demands for finished steel products. New technology in mining and smelting allowed employers to lay off 40 percent of their carriers and 25 percent of their pickmen in Mexico.[18] Fewer jobs, an oversupply of workers, sparser wage packets, all truncated the demand for goods, few of which Mexico produced anyway.

All capitalists invest to make profits, and foreign ones, naturally, like to take theirs home. Thus profits generated in Mexico did not become new capital (understood simply as productive machinery, facilities, and so on that put people to work) in the host country except as the means by which technology replaced workers. (Significantly, such capital goods as the air compression drills in the mines and the power looms in the textile mills, both of which displaced workers, were not made in Mexico.) We see here how the Porfirian strategy of attracting capital by throwing the doors open to outsiders did not result in the economic development of Mexico in ways that would spur the creation of either investment capital or jobs.

Dislocation attributable to this reorganization of the economy further agitated the Mexican masses. Technological advancement always displaces artisans. Transporters, weavers, and candle makers, anyone who made things that relatively efficient machines suddenly made more cheaply or replaced altogether, not only suffered financially but lost social status as well. Thirty thousand skilled and respected artisans found themselves with nothing more to offer than their labor essentially as unskilled proletarians. They competed in a job market crowded with a growing population and hundreds of thousands of de-landed peasants.

No national economy, no matter how autonomous, escaped the fluctuations of the business cycle in the decades before and after the turn of the twentieth century. But an economy dependent on the world market for investment capital and sale of its exports particularly suffers crises in world financial and commodities markets. For example, in order to maintain an influx of investment during the banking crises in the United States and Western European (1902–3 and 1899–1904, respectively), Mexico devalued the peso by 50 percent. While the notably cheaper peso promoted purchases of Mexican goods and businesses by outsiders with harder currencies, it ravaged the buying power of Mexicans. Their wages were worth less while the prices of imported goods and foods rose. Here we see clearly the hardship that involvement in the world economy brought to people. Life was often difficult in a village like Naranja before capitalist development, but a family could always fall back on what the land and the marsh freely gave for subsistence. Now, in 1905, in a place like the American-owned mines of Cananea, Sonora, miners continued to receive their wages in Mexican money or company script while the cost of their staples, largely from the United States, abruptly doubled. This situation of dependency and vulnerability repeated itself throughout Mexico wherever people had become part of the volatile market economy.[19] These new phenomena, which the elders' wisdom could not fathom, severed the people's ties to their customary spot and sent them to some new place.

The overproduction crises and the increasingly interconnected world market constrained the capitalists' acquisitiveness. Still, though, capitalists and their markets initiated historical changes. They, and recall that this was a diverse and rivalrous North Atlantic assembly of businessmen, pressed new ways upon the Mexican landscape, ones that have yet to improve the lives of most of the people. Beginning with the arrival of Cortés in 1519, Mexico found itself swimming against the several tides of European and, later, American imperialism. Porfiriato elites, with a mix of faith in free trade and a penchant for corruption, surely prompted capital penetration of Mexico, and then attempted to mediate the disruptions and conflicts that were the outcome. As when the Aztecs' many enemies allied with Cortés, such bonds of domination are inevitably the outcome of historical processes, albeit ones where power—military, economic, or even those intangible forces behind a society's cultural momentum—proves unequal. Thus did Mexican peasants act in a history in which circumstances not much of their own choosing emphatically compelled their actions. If this account seems to give Mexicans an unfavorable share in the making of history at the turn of the twentieth century, let us recall that the word "imperialism" derives from the Latin *imperare*, "to command." Imperialism it was, and command Mexicans it did.

LAND AND DEATH

The literature on why people spurn their employers, patrones, fathers, or chiefs and embrace the means of rebellion, be they weapons, a union, or passive resistance, is as rich as it is inconclusive. People throw down their shovels, harvest bags, kitchen tools, plows, or machines—all means of getting a family's subsistence—in exchange for the terribly uncertain benefits of rebellion for a variety of reasons. Whether because their very survival was so deeply threatened, because their rising expectations were dashed, or because there were a whole array of very personal and particular causes having most to do with the ironies and contingencies of each individual's life—fate, that is—Mexicans engaged themselves in violent revolution during the period from 1911 to 1920.

Much attention is paid to the headiness of revolutions, to their promising ideologies and their exhilarating organization of previously alienated and oppressed peoples. True social revolutions, like the one in Mexico, are truly horrific as well. One side or the other cuts off food supplies, burns agricultural lands, floods mines, and cruelly besieges towns and cities in the service of higher principles; both zealous sides take few prisoners. Maybe this violence is why men's notions and practices of revolution, their inspiring ideologies and transcendent visions of justice notwithstanding, prove not to change much in the lives of ordinary people: hierarchies backed by the threat of brutality remain the basis of order after the revolution. In Mexico, the chaos and agony of the years of upheaval only intensified many Mexicans' preference for migration. And then, afterward, the Revolution made some important changes, but many people would remain without a dependable means of subsistence.

People and groups joined the Mexican Revolution out of different concerns and in the context of various interests. Francisco Madero, a mix of nationalist grand landowner, naive democrat, and Enlightenment liberal, ignited the various and generally volatile situations in Porfirian Mexico by mounting in 1910 a campaign to have a genuine election instead of more years of Díaz. Arrested and thrown in jail, he then escaped to the United States, from whence he called for insurrection in 1911. He assumed power in the chaos of the revolt he catalyzed and sparked.

Others, like many of those once independent of the capitalist market because they owned some tools or had a skill, or some entitlement to land, wound up proletarianized: they found a voice for their discontent with capitalism in the young intellectuals of the original supporters of liberal (variously understood) revolution, in the Partido Liberal Mexicano and its leader, Ricardo Flores Magón. By 1910 they formally espoused anarchism, as did the workers of Mexico City organized into the Casa Obrera Mundial. Still others, most of the elites and the Church, preferred the old ways of oligarchy and dogma about land tenure and the Faith. Victoriano Huerta, with the support of the American ambassador, briefly reasserted the power of these elites in a coup of 1913, and had Madero murdered.

This coup helped catalyze the extraordinary División del Norte made up largely of campesinos, artisans, and miners. Under the famous Pancho Villa, often in units of extended families, people marched and fought east and west, expropriating great landowners. They briefly and dramatically went north and raided Columbus, New Mexico, but ultimately aimed to fight their way to the capital. In the south, campesinos rallied to the standard of Emiliano Zapata and fought for what they considered their rightful access to land.

Then, too, the provincial elites, skilled workers, small business owners, and the tiny middle class, including the intelligentsia, referred to themselves as Constitutionalists and united behind Álvaro Obregón and Venustiano Carranza. The Wilson administration gave them critical aid, including in 1914 the occupation of the port of Veracruz, which allowed the Americans to determine who would and would not get arms. Under the leadership of Obregón, the generals who led the Constitutionalists assumed power in 1915. After much bloodshed in the suppression of the Villistas and Zapatistas, Obregón, who had Carranza assassinated, emerged in charge of a thoroughly devastated Mexico.[20]

In spite of Octavio Paz's famous notion that "The Mexican's indifference towards death is fostered by his indifference towards life," the chaos and brutality of the Revolution were harrowing and appalling.[21] The Revolution responded directly to the insufferable social, economic, and political conditions that the Porfiriato brought forth. It demanded, and it was destined, to happen. And the Revolution was a big fight in which the suffering of the people and the land far outdistanced any of the heroics. A million people died, countless more suffered grievously in various ways because of the killing and disruption, and plenty were launched into the migratory streams (see figures 12 and 13). In Jalisco, for example, crops diminished by 70 percent in 1913, which caused a 100 percent increase in food prices. Villa's forces confiscated whole trainloads of food to send north, and people simply ceased planting in this climate of fear and chaos. Jalisco had once produced agricultural surpluses, but revolution put it near famine. Moreover, the violence did not cease even after national political stabilization began in 1920, the formal end of the Revolution.

Armed bands, whose allegiance to various leaders and movements

Figure 12. The Mexican Revolution cost the lives of one million people. (Courtesy Department of Special Collections, University Research Library, University of California, Los Angeles.)

Figure 13. Some of the first refugees crossing the border, April 1913. (Courtesy Department of Special Collections, University Research Library, University of California, Los Angeles.)

ranged from genuine to feigned, continued to maraud in the country-side, demanding material support from the campesinos, killing oppo-nents, and impressing young men into their ranks. Involvement in this continuing violence combined political ideology, land tenure disputes, religious beliefs and the political power of the Church, clan loyalties, and fate. As the anti-clerical government tried to give out some of the lands expropriated during the Revolution, landlords, usually invoking Church teachings, countered such efforts with their "white guards," pri-vate bands of thugs, to terrorize peasants. *Agraristas*, peasants who sup-ported a return to the old ejidal ways, fought back. The years 1926 to 1929 marked the Cristero Revolt, in which priests and their devotees raged against the godless, allegedly communistic government that had affirmed secular education, threatened more expropriation of lands, and curtailed the power of the clergy in general. Many villages lived in con-stant fear of the continual terrorism and reprisals. Both sides sacked and burned agricultural lands and appropriated foodstuffs, which discour-aged planting: so many continued in poverty and hunger. Firing squads, summary hangings, and rapes could await anyone even suspected of sup-porting the other side, that is, either the Church or the federal govern-ment. The viciousness of these fights typified those sorts of local wars in which kinsman fights kinsman first over deeply held beliefs regarding land and religion and then, all the more fervently, for revenge.

There are many ways to look upon this violence and disruption: we can see heroism and sacrifice in support of a more just economic and political system or senseless efforts to upset the natural hierarchies or fu-tile killing that actually did not improve matters in Mexico very much, or we can focus on the human misery that the fights brought to so many innocent people. It depends on what we want to arouse in our readers or listeners, on the purpose(s) of the narrator. And here we only seek to un-derstand how and why people picked up and went to the United States: the consequences for Mexico were much more profound.

MIGRATION

All this pain and disorder cast many into the migrant streams. "People are too poor here," stated one who had returned in the early 1930s to his village in Jalisco; "all the time they want to fight, and they take all you have in taxes." Another, who made three trips from Jalisco for work in the United States (the railroads of Texas, agriculture in South-ern California, and a steel mill in Chicago), said in 1917 that he made the journey "because of the Carranza and Villa revolution, and paper money, poor business here, and robberies and fights, and also to see the country." "Here we work like burros, from sun to sun," stated another from the same village who hoped to emigrate; "and they say there is good order in the United States." One of many *corridos*, "folk ballads," composed about the exodus from "our adored country" queried, "but what are we supposed to do / if our country is in ruins?" "For I am not to blame / that I abandon my homeland thus." "The fault is that of poverty / which keeps us all in want," went another.[22]

We see here that people migrated not to find some new prosperity, or what we often call a brighter future. The purpose of their actions was survival. Our analysis so far has emphasized the cause and effect of an outcome, such as the presence of Mrs. G's family in Southern California, and eventually we will see the evolution of Mexicans in the new place. But rural peasants would not understand their actions in this linear way. Those who left the country village did so in order that they and their families would be able to continue. Most of their concepts of the future could not encompass the notion that they would have some new life. "I went five times," stated a chili merchant from Pénjamo, Guanajuato, in the early 1930s. "When I came back, I would stay twenty four days, a year, two years, seven months, así." Going back and forth was a strategy to have the old ways carry on or, in the case of the Mexicans who had experienced the Porfiriato and the Revolution, how to have the old ways, well idealized, resume. "Next month I'm going to Mexicali, I think, and try to get back into the United States," stated another from Purépero, an anti-agrarista village in Michoacán. "I have a cousin near Wilmington, California, and he said that my boss there [a Japanese truck farmer] says I can get work again where I was before." The historical and moral worldview of the peasant affirms not progress as industrial and commodity cultures understand it but rather a "rebecoming" of the peasantry's old, communally independent practices and relationships.[23] Indeed, as we have seen with the coming of market capitalism, progress is what wrecked the old ways.

Sometimes a large percentage of a village cleared out because the market, violence, or drought had made life there untenable. About 40 to 50 percent of the men of Purépero had been to the United States, largely to work in the foundries of Torrance and Pittsburg, California. In the Tarrascan village of Etúcuaro, Michoacán, where the ejido had prevailed and people fought for its return, 90 percent of the men had sojourned al norte for work. "Most of the men here," stated the schoolmaster at Etúcuaro, "who have been to the United States went there for only a few years, leaving their families here and sending money back." Even this strategy, which so often successfully buttressed an imperiled family, brought forth many unintended consequences for a Mexican family's life. "Everyone has known someone who has been," says Richard Rodriguez. "Everyone knows someone who never came back."[24]

Such migration also unbound other elements of society. In Mexico the economic structure included not only peasants and large landholders, but artisans such as shoemakers, barbers, and musicians; professionals such as teachers, lawyers, and doctors; and petty proprietors such as grocers, innkeepers, cantina owners, and transporters. As towns and cities emptied to various degrees, those of this middling sort had fewer customers for their services and products. As is typical, then, of most such migrations, these people journeyed in search of new customers, or they followed their old ones. While we are witnessing a migration overwhelmingly of peasants in search of wage work, the dynamics of the process meant that these other elements of the Mexican social and economic structure would follow their fellow villagers. Thus the chatter and smells of the bars, shops, and restaurants in the new place, wherever that might be, differed little from those of the old place.

Most moved within Mexico, but the train system that served the import-export economy carried migration to the United States as well. The completion of the Mexican Central Railroad in 1884 connected Mexico City with El Paso, Texas. That it stopped at several places in the central plateau of Mexico especially facilitated the northward movement of people from Jalisco, Michoacán, and Guanajuato, the states that contributed the most to the expanding rivers of migration. The steel brutes, who had blown apart so much in their way, now caught up all manner of people in their powerful south-to-north draft. In the early years of railroad migration a young man could swap a good horse or a few pigs for the $20 to $25 that the ticket from Jalisco or Guanajuato would cost, which did not include incidental expenses, or he could get a high-interest loan. This cost would about double in the 1920s. Accordingly, only people with a little bit of property could get north; others could afford to migrate only within Mexico. Workers on the Mexican Central were often the ones who went to El Paso. As the changes in the Mexican economy pressed more and more to labor for wages on the railroads in the north of Mexico, these workers heard their fellows' stories about the even higher wages in the United States. Thus the Mexican Central constantly had to recruit workers from the southern and central parts of the country to replace the ones who went farther north to the United States.[25]

The farther north one traveled the higher the wages. In Jalisco before the Revolution agricultural workers received 12 cents per day, though they got an allotment of maize; and 15 cents per day was the maximum pay. Section hands on the Mexican National Railway earned 50 cents per day and a little more in the northern part of the country. The Mexican Central paid 75 to 80 cents per day around Chihuahua and a dollar per day at Ciudad Juarez on the border, almost what one would make in the United States. In the less populous north of Mexico, wages were roughly double what they were in the interior, which explains in part why so many immigrants came from the central part of Mexico rather than the part contiguous to the United States.

The news of wages traveled in a variety of ways. Returning villagers were an obvious source, but the ways in which history was unfolding, and chance encounters, also fueled the enthusiasm for migration. For example, consider the relationship between the Yaqui Wars and villagers of Arandas going to California. In northern Mexico the Yaqui Indians had been fighting first the Spanish and then the Mexicans for autonomy over their homeland and way of life, a fight that included raiding (see figure 14). The land policies of the Porfiriato intensified pressure on Yaqui lands as Sonoran *hacendados* and American speculators sought to increase and solidify their holdings. While the Yaquis' titles from Spanish days may have been legitimate, "this most rich zone is not properly exploited by the Indians, and progress requires that it be," noted Dr. Manuel Balbás, a surgeon for the Mexican army in the rebellions at the turn of the century and a formulator of the hacendado point of view. The Yaquis, excellent and dedicated fighters, were continually revolting, and they established themselves as the unyielding and hated enemies of the hacendados and the Mexican government. Some Yaquis went to southern Arizona to work in the mines and railroads, and there these energetic workers became essential in the local economy. "The best labor we get from Mexico is the Yaqui Indians," stated the governor of Arizona. But the goal of Yaqui life was to fight Mexicans and maintain their homeland: "They come up here," explained the governor, "fraternize with the Mexicans, and then buy arms and go back home to shoot Mexicans." Getting anyone to fight Yaquis was immensely difficult even in those days of human displacement, and so the Mexican government impressed prisoners into this counterinsurgency effort. To bring this story back around to our discussion of why people emigrated, I would like to

Figure 14. Yaqui Indians ready to fight the Mexican army. (Courtesy Department of Special Collections, University Research Library, University of California, Los Angeles.)

point out that the first of many of the men to leave the village of Arandas, Jalisco, for the United States claimed that he had heard from such prisoners that "the United States was a good place to work." He and his brother first went to Kansas via El Paso for six months in 1905 and then in 1907 to Fresno, California, via El Paso, both times to work on the railroad.[26] Through such curious but indeed closely connected concatenations, peasants departed for the north to become workers.

The greatest wave of migration north occurred in the 1920s, the decade that followed the destruction and dislocation of the Revolution. It was a time when Mexico urgently needed its most able-bodied people to rebuild the war-torn nation. But Mexico's efforts to stem migration proved ineffectual. Little land was redistributed to the peasantry, the Church's and the landlords' cavilings notwithstanding. The little that was came with neither irrigation nor machinery to make it more than marginally productive. "We get big peaches from these trees," declared a man who had repatriated in the 1930s, "but the trouble is that it is so dry here. If only we had irrigation." Neither appeals to patriotism nor newspaper accounts of the racism and discrimination (and lynchings in Texas) that Mexican emigrants experienced in the United States had much effect. Wages did not improve much after the Revolution. Urban workers averaged about two pesos per day, or the equivalent of a dollar, and rural peasants only one peso. The best paid Mexican workers, miners, earned only the equivalent of $1.25 per day, and the poorest from 35 to 40 cents per day. So many migrated that the interior states that had been sending the greatest number of Mexico's most vigorous workers to the United States actually lost population. And in the north, even with its higher wages, people began to cross into the United States for work in the fields and on the railroads. Although one could do a lot better in Sonora, where the population had grown 30 percent between 1900 and 1930, than in Jalisco, more improvement waited on the other side of the border, where wages roughly doubled the relatively high pay received in the north of Mexico. By going north a young man could simultaneously escape the troubles of Mexico and, by making money to send back to the village, assist in the inconsistently successful efforts to maintain the viability of the old ways. And all that money came back, all that good, hard money. It may have been crumpled bills or just money orders, but it gleamed like gold in a desolate village. (Actually, according to Manuel Gamio's calculations, an annual average of 10 million dollars in money orders alone went back to Mexico in the 1920s.)[27] The money advertised so forcefully for el norte, for a young man to go there and get more of it, or for a family to go where it appeared there would always be enough of it.

EL NORTE

Laborers were wanted in the north, usually people of color, to whom notions of liberty and equality need not be applied. In the great Euro-American tradition of searching out economical workers, employers in Los Angeles and throughout the Southwest maintained contracts with, for example, the L. H. Manning Company and the Home Supply Labor Agency, representatives of the Southern Pacific Railroad, to bring workers from south of the border. Each had agencies in El Paso that dispatched representatives to Mexico to tell people of the high wages awaiting them in Los Angeles. These *enganchistas* (from *enganchar*, "to hook or snare") would then contract with Mexicans to come north and work. "In 1913, an agent [a Mexican] from the Santa Fe railroad came to Arandas and took three or four of us by auto to the railroad, and north," stated a Jalisqueño who had spent many years in the United States. "I did not pay anything to go to the frontier; they paid all." In the last nine months of 1907 one agency alone supplied the railroads with 6,474 workers, and six El Paso agencies supplied 16,479 during a similar period in 1908. The deal was that the railroad would transport them to the places where they were needed and then provide them free transportation back to the border when their term of employment had been completed. Then, they would go back to Mexico, or maybe take another contract, or maybe they would not have gone back to the border at all, but rather sojourned for a while longer in the new place.[28]

Typically then, a young Mexican male took the train to the border at Ciudad Juarez/El Paso intending to work for a while in el norte. Perhaps he had worked briefly on the Mexican Central and accustomed himself to wage labor; or perhaps timorously or even gleefully, likely with a mix of several emotions, he had taken the long walk to a train station in central Mexico; or perhaps he had contracted with an enganchista and arrived bound to work. Just as certainly sometimes whole families came with the hope that the men would get enough work to feed the children and free the family from its bondage to the often parched land. In the new place the family could be delivered from the destitution and meanness of the new market capitalist ways and from the commotion and privation of ceaselessly violent revolution. By any of numerous ways, and really from virtually every village in Mexico (but especially from those of Michoacán, Guanajuato, and Jalisco), Mexicans were coming north to work, and to continue.

A variety of statistics have been tossed about to quantify this migration. It should already be clear that the frequency with which individuals crossed back and forth would confound attempts at enumeration then and now. Thus Mexico, whose law required registration of both emigrants and immigrants, recorded that far more returned than ever left in the first place. Not until the Quota Act of 1924 was there an effort or the means for the United States to count immigrants from Mexico. The census of 1920 included Mexicans in the "white" population; that of 1930 established a separate category of "Mexican," which lumped together those Mexicans born in the United States with those born in Mexico; and by 1940, largely at the urging of Mexicans themselves, the census had them included as "white" again. Only the Rio Grande and the imaginary border line from El Paso to the Pacific Ocean, and God, were privy to all of the crossings. At any rate, the census of 1930 tabulated that there were nearly a million and a half Mexicans in the United States. The Mexican government put the figure at more like two million because it included undocumented people. We can say that well over a million—a Great Migration indeed—came in the first three decades of the century (lack of jobs during the Depression meant that very few came in the 1930s) and were in place long enough to either be counted or appear in the impressionistic evidence that others used for their calculations.[29]

We cannot, however, let this northern vista obscure the fact that in the first three decades of the twentieth century, Mexico lost 10 percent of its population. Moreover, these several million people who either stayed in the north or crossed back and forth largely constituted the most vital workers, those in their physical prime, and they helped to build the Southwest of the United States rather than to rebuild and develop imperial- and war-ravaged Mexico. We can understand, then, Mexico's ambivalence about all of this migration. For a variety of reasons, Mexico could not simply let its young manhood flee: its national pride, still grievously wounded from the Mexican-American War; the turmoil created when tens of thousands of indigents suddenly returned to the homeland when depressions such as the one in 1921 summarily cast Mexican workers out of the United States; the "Americanization" that the repatriates evidenced; and its need for strong arms to help it develop. Actually, in some areas, so many left that food crops were sometimes not planted, and those that were planted were not harvested, to the great alarm of authorities, especially in Jalisco, Tamaulipas, and Nuevo Leon. (It may be surmised that given how many under- or unemployed workers there were in Mexico, we are actually witnessing some upward pressure on wages in response to the numbers emigrating al norte, and some lessening of dependence on the patrones. This may be what some of the elites in fact griped about.) On the other hand, Mexico needed the dollars that its erstwhile sons sent back—nearly a million per month during the 1920s—to pump up both the national and the local economies (as economists would say) or to help the people continue (as the campesinos would have appreciated). Many Mexican politicians and intellectuals grudgingly understood that so often young men and numerous families had little choice but to watch their loved ones starve, turn to semi-political banditry, or emigrate.

The Mexican Congress passed a law in 1926 that forbade workers to emigrate unless they had a written contract, validated by a local government authority, guaranteeing their wages, hours, and housing. The law also required the American employer or agent to place on deposit an amount equal to the cost of a return trip should employment be terminated in the United States. State governors and the nationalist press propagandized about harsh and doleful situations in the north that so often disappointed the émigrés. They publicized the news of the mean-ness of working and living conditions and the destitution that so often resulted from a naive journey to the north. Stories of gringo discrimi-nation and brutality, especially in Texas, where indeed an average of one Mexican was lynched per week in the xenophobic times following World War I, circulated through the press and state government broad-sides. Mexico's efforts had little effect, though: despairing campesinos ignored these unenforceable laws, brazen enganchistas carried on their nefarious trade, and not until 1925 did the United States establish a (rather ineffective) border patrol.[30]

From the point of view of Mexico, then, several matters surface: we see in these paths not taken, or effectually blocked, more than irony and failure. Only outlined here are the remarkable complexities of national economic development and the power relationship that existed (and still exists) between Mexico and the United States. It is truly a many-stranded web of causes, rooted in locales ranging from the smallest vil-lage to national economic and political policies and actions. Mexico was hardly passive in these matters of expanding its wealth to feed adequately its people and in the emigration of its sons and daughters. Rather, a mul-tifarious tangle of factors rendered it vulnerable and ineffective.

"LIKE SWALLOWS AT THE OLD MISSION": THE MEXICAN WORKER IN THE UNITED STATES

Surging, but flowing only quietly upon the landscape, they came, borne by the rivers of migration. Debouching into the North American job market, Mexicans came to the sugar beet fields of the northwest, Col-orado, and Michigan; by the thousands to the Calumet steel mills along the shores of Lake Michigan; to out-of-the-way railroad sections through-out the West; to the mines of New Mexico, Arizona, and Colorado; to the grain fields of the Great Plains; to the winter gardens of South Texas; and even to farms along the eastern seaboard, especially in New York and Pennsylvania. As African Americans fled the South for rela-tively friendlier northern cities, Mexicans took some of their places in southern agriculture all the way to Florida; and migration would soon make Los Angeles the second largest Mexican city in the world.

How we name, categorize, define, and analyze this historical circum-stance depends upon how and from where we focus our gaze on the his-torical process. I provided above a bit of the Mexican focus on the emigration of so many of its people. American capitalism, from its perspective, had expanded its labor pool south and got plenty of unskilled, itinerant, and tractable workers who worked for very low pay. We have, in other words, a migration for work rather than an immigration in which people would have intended a permanent transfer of residence. Such talk of labor markets may shroud, though, poignant human dramas. We will also see families forever separated, wives occasionally abandoned, lonely graves far from the home village, and subtle to flagrant to brutal racist treatment. And we will see youth forging new models of behavior, the perils and opportunities of new educational systems, interethnic solidarity in labor and political organizations, and the joy and anguish of family life in the new land. Of course the most frequently articulated view, then as well as now, expresses white Americans' discomfort and fears about the presence of allegedly unassimilable, peculiar, and threatening immigrants in their neighborhoods, schools, and job markets. This story means much more than capital penetration, wage differentials, and economic opportunity and exploitation.

Octavio Paz suffered his people's, or rather his men's, dismay and anxiety about being *hijos de la chingada,* that is, children of the sexual violation of Indian women by European men, as personified in the figures of Hernando Cortés and his Aztec mistress, La Malinche. Similarly, Mexicans already in the United States referred to the recent migrants as *pelados,* "stripped ones." (*Pelar* means "to pull out or cut the hair of"; and *pelado,* more literally "a de-haired one," is what a destitute person often is called in Mexico.) There is much talk these days in the social sciences about "liminality," or a condition "neither here nor there . . . [but] betwixt and between the positions assigned and arrayed by law, custom, convention, and ceremonial." Such people, like the Mexican migrants, "possessing nothing," exist on the fringes and boundaries of society. (The word "liminality" is related to the Latin terms *limen,* "threshold," and *limes,* "border," particularly a border fortification.) I am not sure whether "pelados" or "liminal" best describes many of the migrants, but both terms portray in a usefully evocative way these folks with little genuine presence upon the landscape. "I don't know where they come from," stated one grower. "They just keep coming, year after year. When the work is finished, I do not know where they go."[31] People appeared in the new place stripped of identity and history, if not in their own self-conceptions, then certainly in the eyes of those already there. They lived concealed on the margins of society, but on the threshold of unanticipated and unintended new lives.

They may have been pelados and liminal, but these floating proletarians were hardly marginal to the economic development of the Southwest and California. Agriculture, with its long history of "dusky workmen," and the railroads, burgeoning in the economic expansion of the United States, provided the primary arenas of employment and reinforced the historical presumptions about a racially segmented labor force. Like the factors pushing people from Mexico, the issue of labor demand in the rapidly changing economy of California and the Southwest is complicated. Broadly speaking a powerful and alluring vacuum drew up suffering people from south of the border, whose attachments to place, kin, and master had been loosened or snapped. Such figurative language aside, several sweeping generalizations can be made.

Industrialization in the United States made demands on the labor supply in the form of wage inducements such that native agricultural workers, whether sons and daughters of petty proprietors or wage laborers, fled to the cities, to its lights and its (only relatively) higher wages. With irrigation and the rise of large-scale farms, though, demand for agricultural labor increased in some places, hot desert ones, that is. Because of the heat, the low wages, the presence of colored workers, and the lure of the cities, Euro-American workers, even those cast from the increasingly mechanized countryside of the Midwest, certainly did not gravitate to the sweltering farms or tracks of the Southwest and California.

The white, middle-class American standard of living had come to assume lettuce in winter, melons in spring, and grapes in the summer, a wonder and a joy without doubt. Irrigation and the railroad car, especially refrigerated ones, defeated the seasons that had previously promised fresh vegetables and fruits only at nature's harvest time, late summer and early fall. Some examples: lettuce production increased from 7.8 million crates in 1921 to 17.4 million crates in 1926; over the same time period, asparagus rose from 3.3 million to 7.6 million crates; cantaloupes went from 11.55 million crates to 14 million. Between 1915 and 1926 the orange crop grew from 21.2 million boxes to 33.9 million; lemons swelled from 880,000 boxes in 1899 to 6.6 million in 1919; canned soups and fruits increased from 51.7 and 9.5 million cases, respectively, in 1914 to 101 and 25.9 million cases, respectively, in 1925.[32] Such statistics reflect grand changes in eating habits and in consumer expectations. What the management of land and water had so ingeniously brought to American tables, though, concomitantly brought forth the problem of finding people to do the work of husbanding the soil, the work upon which this man-made rescheduling of nature was based.

Mexicans largely worked those newly bounteous fields. It is remarkable that the Mexican migrant worker was simultaneously so intrinsically involved in changes in the intimate americano family practices of eating and yet remained so obscured upon the landscape.

Demand for the products of Mexican labor derived not only from the changing expectations at American tables, but from the consequences of the battlefields of Europe as well. World War I raised dramatically the demand for agricultural and industrial goods and, thus, increased the promise of big profits. The war drafted able-bodied men into the army and effectively closed off the immigration of workers from Europe. In line with the many profound changes that wars have brought to the home front, World War I powerfully intensified demand for Mexican labor. At first, as non-Mexican workers fled the railroads and fields for higher-paying jobs in war industries in the cities or entered the military, the rise in the number of Mexicans on the railroads was the most noticeable. But as agricultural employment dropped (5 percent between 1916 and 1918) and demand for foodstuffs soared, places like the Imperial Valley thirsted insatiably for Mexican workers. However, the Immigration Act of February 1917 forbade the entry of aliens who could not read (either English or their own language) and of laborers under contract and charged an $8 head tax. In spite of the utter lack of any enforcement mechanisms, Southwestern employers had an immediate tantrum. The secretary of labor suspended these bars to Mexican immigration because of the labor shortage of the war emergency, but only for work "in agricultural pursuits, maintenance of way on railroads, or lignite coal mining." These Department of Labor regulations stipulated further that "of course none should be admitted who can not be returned immediately that necessity arises." At least 80,000 came under contract, of which about 30 percent left no record of actually repatriating. Certainly many more came and were eagerly accepted into a wide variety of jobs in the profitable war boom. The Great War firmly established the expectation that Mexicans would provide rail maintenance labor.

This war also instituted another labor practice as regards Mexicans. The year 1920 marked the peak for Mexican railroad and industrial employment. But a bust, the abrupt and penetrating recession of 1921, followed the war boom. From those highest crests of employment in 1920, employers in the Southwest cut their Mexican workforces in the railroads and industrial plants by a whopping 72 percent and 63 percent, respectively. Steady advances in the economy had nearly restored the old levels by 1923, but these actions established the policy that Mexicans were, if not always the last hired, certainly the first fired.[33]

"We do not see how agricultural, industrial, and railroad interests can get along without the Mexican," stated one California railroad official in the 1920s. In 1909 Mexicans constituted 17.1 percent of the workers on nine western railroads, but by 1928–29 they were 59.5 percent. The percentage of Anglo Americans remained very much the same, 31.3; the Asians, Greeks, and Italians disappeared from the tracks partly because of immigration restrictions, partly because they switched to urban jobs, and partly because railroad bosses liked Mexicans better. Mexicans, moreover, did very specific tasks on *el traque*. From the Atchison, Topeka, and Santa Fe to the Southern Pacific to the Pacific Electric, Mexicans worked only on "pick-and-shovel" jobs (as section hands, as yard gang workers, or on maintenance and construction were known) and on ones whose requirements for workers varied immensely on a seasonal, monthly, even weekly basis. They worked under native white, European-born, or sometimes Japanese foremen, a position to which the railroad companies simply never advanced Mexican workers. "This extra gang is for that work," the general solicitor for the AT&SF stated to the U.S. Senate in 1928, referring to what was mostly repair work. "It is here today and yonder to-morrow." And he continued, "The variance in labor employment for that purpose is very much greater . . . as is demonstrated by the fact that during normal times we had employed for the purpose of extra gang work 5,447 men, which increased in peak times to 10,486 men . . . all Mexicans." At about the same time the Los Angeles Railway Company, of whose 4,000 employees 1,200 were Mexicans, affirmed that "the Mexican is the best labor we can get; sticks to it, plugs along, best return on the dollar." This is why in Mrs. G.'s community of Watts "The first [Mexicans] in greatest numbers," reported a researcher in 1933, "were the four hundred cholos brought in as contract laborers to work on the tracts [*sic*] in 1902, but others soon followed in the revolutionary days."[34]

The California Immigration Commission of 1910 bluntly reported that Mexican railroad workers generally earned 25 percent less than non-Mexicans. On the Southern Pacific just north of Los Angeles, a 1908 study noted the following wages "to be in force for ordinary section hands: Greeks, $1.60; Japanese, $1.45, and Mexicans, $1.25 a day." "Foremen said," according to this Bureau of Labor researcher, "that Mexicans did as much work as men of either of the other nationalities, and that the discrimination in wages was due to arbitrary orders issued from headquarters by men who had no practical knowledge of the efficiency of different kinds of laborers."[35]

The railroads and commercial agriculture came to exist in a symbiotic relationship. Freight cars hauled farm goods to market, and fees for that service made up a large part of railroad revenues. But many farms got their workers from the railroads too. Because farmers perceived a serious labor shortage, they could pay a little more than the railroads and thus attracted the cheap arms and hands that the railroads had already recruited, amassed, and transported to their towns. Many Mexicans came to work in the fields more directly, but many drifted over from el traque as well. Of course it has been in agriculture where the whole culture of "dusky workmen" originated in California, but several other features of farming created a demand for a certain type of employee.

Irrigation's scale needed gangs of hirelings engaged in the largely undifferentiated routines of planting, hoeing, and harvesting. Even more important, the sheer variety of crops grown at all different seasons required workers who could move from one job to another. "The conditions are such that wise men of experience contend that fruit culture and truck farming would become unprofitable without Chinese and Japanese help," reported the *Pacific Rural Press* in 1902. "A number have confessed that they would be forced out of the business if they were deprived of this class of employees." The California Fruit Growers Convention of December 1902 observed, "The unprecedented scarcity of orchard help during the past season has been noted in every fruit district of the State." A contemporary report on the convention then went on to outline farm labor history and reveal the weird ideas about race that had been twisted into it:

> When fruit growing was begun as a California industry many Chinese were here and they were employed in the fields. Then the Exclusion law went into effect, and from emigration, death and other causes the Chinese became less numerous . . . The Chinaman had his faults, but the Japanese were worse . . . Chinese and Japanese are not ideal workers. They lack interest; they lack intelligence.

A decade later the same publication would proclaim,

> One of the greatest problems that confronts the California rancher and stockman and the large estates is, How are we going to hold our white labor? Every year it becomes more scarce and the person who can solve the problem will go down in California history as a genius of the first water.

Mexicans had been working the fields for a good while, of course, but they often remained within the enclaves of the old pastoralist economy. In the twentieth century, though, Mexico would supply for agriculture what it had for the railroads.[36]

Statements of those representing agricultural interests in California and the West indicate that they perceived little choice in these matters. In 1902 the president of the Woodland Chamber of Commerce noted, "farm hands have become migratory . . . as the character of employment demands." In 1928 Fred H. Bixby, a representative of the California Cattle Raiser's Association and resident of Long Beach, in southern Los Angeles County, said,

> The man who is producing is not the small man who has twenty acres. He can handle his stuff. It is the big producers who produce the big acreages of cotton, wheat, and beets; those are the men that the brunt of the whole production falls upon. We have 3,700 acres of [sugar] beets. If I do not get Mexicans to thin those beets and to hoe those beets and to top those beets, I am through with the beet business. We have no Chinamen; we have not the Japs. The Hindu is worthless; the Filipino is nothing, and the white man will not do the work.

An executive of an Imperial Valley company affirmed, "Large scale production would be impossible without Mexican field labor. Without the Mexicans, costs would be increased 50 per cent." "We would prefer white agricultural labor and we recognize the social problem incident to the importation of Mexicans," stated the chair of the agricultural committee of the Fresno Chamber of Commerce in 1926. "We are loath to burden our State with this type of immigration, but after a complete survey of all possibilities, it seems that we have no choice in the matter," he lamented, indicating that "The Mexican seems to be our only available supply." "We are totally dependent at the present time upon Mexico for agricultural and industrial common or casual labor," affirmed Dr. George Clements, manager and avowed "Mexican expert" of the Los Angeles Chamber of Commerce's Agricultural Department in the 1920s and 1930s. The logic of technology and scale made these ideologues of economic freedom dependent on and captive to their own market system.[37]

This notion of market existed not so much as an instrument of economic liberty, but rather as a device for development, change, capital accumulation and concentration, and control of workers and materials. In the United States, as in Mexico, some associated the advent of the market with freedom and prosperity, whereas others equated it with subjection to new burdens and new suffering. We are beginning to see in this narrative how employers neither spoke nor acted in sync with free market ideology as regards the fields of California. Free-market ideology, like "the old fashioned hired man," according to George Clements, "is a thing of past." Clements elaborated to the Fresno Agricultural Conference of March 1926: "There is no place for him [the hired man], and the farmer who does not wake up to the realization that there is a caste in labor on the farm, is sharing too much of his dollar with labor. . . . We are not husbandmen. We are not farmers. We are producing a product to sell." Back then everyone knew that this was a caste system in which those in the lower orders should not and would not progress and that the remuneration for Mexicans' labors had little to do either with the value of what they produced or the actual going rate for white labor.[38]

Like the railroads and the farmers, other employers in Los Angeles favored Mexicans as workers for a variety of reasons. "They compare favorably with all other cheap labor, in fact are much better than any other labor, including cheap white labor," stated a superintendent of maintenance and construction of a street railroad company just before World War I. "They make good laborers for track and concrete work or any place where ordinary manual labor is required," he continued. "We have no objections to Mexican labor, they being the best to be had in this part of the country." A rancher near Los Angeles noted that they are "very good labor if watched . . . much better than the IWW white element in Southern California." "They are as good common labor as you can get in this part of the country," echoed an assistant manager of a large construction company in Los Angeles. An asphalt contractor in Los Angeles stated in 1907, "'cholos' are better workers than Japanese, Chinese, or Negroes." Referring to the desert, a railroad boss stated in 1926, "A white man cannot work there; a negro will not work there. We have no other source of labor available. We must have Mexican labor if our tracks are going to be maintained." In the late 1920s employers surveyed by the College of Agriculture of the University of California overwhelmingly preferred Mexican labor to Filipino, Japanese, Chinese, and so on, because it was "available" and "dependable," because there was "not enough white help," or "because Mexicans work at tasks repugnant to whites." A farmer in Ventura declared in 1928, "I never go near the white man's employment agency, because they will not go into the country, and if they go into the country they are no good. . . . The Mexican is better than the white man."[39]

White Americans of the West based much of their racial beliefs on the vague idea that various traits were in the blood of different ethnic groups. "As workers, the Mexicans are stronger physically than the Japanese, more tractable and more easily managed," stated a national study of immigration in 1912; "they are, nevertheless, though unprogressive, intelligent enough to work fairly well under supervision." "Mexican labor [is] satisfactory when placed in occupations fitted for," a California employer attested. "They apparently fit well on jobs not requiring any great degree of mentality, and they do not object to dirt."[40]

Except for the good red blood that flowed from Mexican boxers, Mexican blood was threatening, and helped define Mexicans as other in the minds of Anglo Americans. Presumptions about blood also delineated the boundaries between Mexican workers and the Anglos who hired them. The managing editor of the California Farm Bureau monthly publications, who had moved to California from Washington, told a congressional hearing in 1930 that "I labored in the fields; my mother labored in the field; my sisters labored in the field, and with the exception of very few farms in Western Washington . . . we have what I consider peasant farms. For him, the conjugal family was the primary and most meaningful unit of reference. Life was hard for this clan no doubt: "By 'peasant farm,'" he clarified, "I mean a place where a man has to labor so cheaply that in order to exist, his children and his wife must labor in the field, and I was raised on that kind of farm." Life was easier now: "And I live in California to-day and I am making money to-day in California and I am sending some of it up there to help my folks who live on those peasant farms in the State of Washington, where they don't have Mexican help."[41]

There is so much contained in this statement. The consanguineous family demarcated his world. The others, the Mexicans, who undoubtedly had the same feelings of affection for their abandoned families at home, and whose blood did not naturally predispose them to peasant labor, did not exist as sentient humans, but only as objects whose utility was to bring relief from toil and even leisure to the white families. The presence of a pool of cheap labor, available through the market mechanism, brought him prosperity and ease, which he shared with the rest of his blood relations. He understood the possible threat of pollution that the presence of such others presented to his people's conjugal families, but responded, "I say to you that I am a good American citizen." He reassured the congressional committee that the Mexicans "would go back to Mexico." This pro-family stance would eventually serve to justify such antisocial behavior as the squeezing of wages and the vicious strike repression for which the Central Valley became so famous, or even, one could argue, to justify the adulteration of America as a white man's country.[42]

The system worked for the big farmers and for many of the little ones too. The family farmer quoted above had 6 to 10 Mexican helpers on his ranch at all times and up to 75 at harvest. This typified the demands of the large-scale, irrigated agriculture of the twentieth century. Mexicans picked navel oranges in the first months of the year and Valencias in late spring and early summer. They cultivated cantaloupes in February and March. January and February have been the peak months in Imperial for the lettuce harvest. In May Mexicans moved northward from the Imperial Valley "following the fruit." Those who had stayed in Imperial to harvest the cantaloupes in May and June joined those who had been working in the citrus groves to converge on the Central Valley for more thinning and picking during the busiest months, June through August. In late August the grape harvest, which lasted through late September, demanded workers, rather skilled ones actually. After that, peas, walnuts, and some citrus occupied some of this floating rural proletariat, but at this point in the year many were accustomed to wintering in and around Los Angeles. The winter months were ones of unemployment for many, and daily work, except at peak harvest times, remained unusual. In the late 1930s the fields of Los Angeles County, remarkably productive of agricultural goods in their own right, required 7,175 workers in June and only 2,300 in December. The results of estimates and surveys varied, but five to eight months of paid work constituted the norm for migrant agricultural workers in California; the rest of the time was spent in idleness, looking for work, or traveling back to Mexico. "This peculiar feature in our labor demands has in the past created a great nomadic labor supply," explained George Clements. "At first they were the Chinese, then when we drove them out they were blanket men [white tramps]. Following that the Japanese coolie came. Still later we employed the Mexican who supplied all the qualities of the Chinaman and endeared himself to the heart of the agricultural people."[43]

The migration of Mexicans to work in the fields, railroads, and factories of the north happened in a more complicated context than simply market demand. A variety of forces pulled on all of the players in this historical drama and in a variety of ways. Just as the market severed the Mexican campesinos' ties to ancestral place, it impelled employers of unskilled labor in California to adopt certain labor practices. But just as in Mexico, where emotional or ideological considerations such as attachment to locality and kin hindered outright accession to the exhortations of the market, such concerns as those regarding racial purity and the threat that either unprogressive or revolutionary Mexicans posed to the social order rendered white America emphatically divided over the importation of cheap workers from south of the border.

"The existence or the adoption of such indifference toward racial intermixture in this country would lead us perilously near the brink of mongrelism, a danger we have been struggling to avoid in recent years," warned one congressional report in 1930. "Yet," it concluded, "the continued flow of Mexican immigrants into this country can have no other biological result." The presence of Mexicans posed a threat to white conjugal families and to the collective solidarity of those families. Exactly how Mexicans might penetrate the bastion of the white clans was never articulated, though California law did not legally prohibit intermarriage between whites and Mexicans, as it did between whites and Asian or African Americans.[44]

Mostly, though, objections to "the cry for more peons" stemmed from the resentment of the advantages gained by large farms "whose mass production techniques with cheap labor is playing havoc with the small farmer;" from the "overplus [of labor] with its consequent shortage of price" that disadvantaged citizen workers; and from the threat that Mexicans' living conditions and culture allegedly presented to the American social body. This polemicist's evocative statement that "equally serious is the anomaly of leaving our southern border wide open while we are trying to preserve our 'American stock'" does, however, suggest that several of the above concerns combined in the minds of the nativists.[45]

The American Federation of Labor (AFL) led the fight for limiting Mexican immigration. The AFL affirmed the principle of restriction partly because "the maintenance of the nation depended upon the maintenance of racial purity and strength," claimed its president, Samuel Gompers, and because such wage workers "have been a constant menace to labor organization and have been directly and indirectly instrumental in weakening the unions and threatening their influence." This latter notion derived from some very real and problematic episodes in American labor history. For example, in the Great Steel Strike of 1919 and in the packinghouse workers' effort of two years later, the Mexicans who had been working in the plants generally joined these famous walkouts. But then, along with many African Americans, other Mexicans, such as the 900 that Inland Steel recruited largely from el traque, acted as the strikebreakers who played key roles in the devastating defeats that the unions suffered.[46]

The National Origins Act of 1924 succeeded in establishing quotas for immigration from Europe, but the Western Hemisphere was exempted. The AFL mounted an effort to include Mexicans in the quota, arguing in 1927, "Low wages, long hours, low standards of living on the part of Mexicans, means that the Mexicans are wresting the Southwest from Americans." The AFL's efforts failed because of the diplomatic difficulty of excluding Mexicans and not Canadians, and because of the effective counterefforts of employers. The AFL then initiated its own negotiations with the largest Mexican union, the Confederación Regional Obrera Mexicana (CROM), to get it to pressure its own government to mandate restriction of emigration from Mexico. The CROM, however, insisted that the AFL recruit Mexican workers on the American side. Upon the rock of the AFL's racism and exclusionary organizing and the CROM's diminishing influence in the government in the wake of the assassination of Álvaro Obregón (July 1928), for which the union was falsely blamed, this effort at "labor diplomacy" foundered.[47]

The hostility that Mexicans encountered as they moved onto the land that was once Mexico is simultaneously ironic, offensive, and indicative of much about the Anglo-American society that they were confronting. The legacy of the Mexican-American War awaited Mexican immigrants as they arrived in the north. The inheritance of history denoted them as a defeated and inferior people for whom unskilled labor was their only fitting role, a notion that distinguished Mexicans' experience from that of other immigrants to the United States.

For other reasons, too, Americans found Mexican lifeways objectionable. Here we get into the dangerous matter of characterizing cultures in ways that reduce their complexities and stereotype them and the people that make them up. But cultures do differ, which is why they can be interesting and antagonistic or both. Cultural traits, often inferred, projected, or exaggerated, often justify relations of domination. Americans usually perceived Mexicans as "dirty."

IDEAS ABOUT MEXICANS

Issues of class and locale must be considered here. Americans saw working-class Mexicans, ones who labored on the tracks, in the fields, or in other menial travails. These people, obviously, worked in "the dirt," and like all such people were often "dirty." Furthermore, because they received so little reward for their hard labors, they generally lived in squalid conditions, ones that were "dirty." White Americans used that word to describe everyone who worked in the soil in a servile way without regard to ethnicity. So did upper- and middle-class Mexicans. "Dirty" in several ways actually described the particular class of Mexicans that white Americans mostly encountered, but they ascribed this trait to all Mexicans and assumed that such "dirtiness" was "in the blood." Protestant Americans, moreover, fondly repeated such axioms as "cleanliness is next to godliness" and then judged people accordingly. Those of the middle and upper classes associated goodness and health with the absence of filth and dirt. For agricultural people, and, if Octavio Paz is to be believed, for Mexicans in particular, it is from dirt, known as soil, that good food comes, and it is filth, known as dung, that makes soil healthy and fertile.

"Mexicans do not know what sanitation is" came as an observation from San Bernardino (just east of Los Angeles County). "The personal hygiene of these people is deplorable," droned a social work researcher in 1935. "Many do not have the facilities for cleanliness of the body, but if they did, the majority would still be dirty." The connection between privation and dirt was circular and self-perpetuating. A California state report pointed to a simple but profound truth about the Plaza district, "Grinding poverty, which makes the inhabitants struggle for the poor food they get, does not leave much money for soap and brooms and clean rags." In 1922 another researcher noted regarding Mexican shacks in Pasadena, "Some are ill-kept and some are spick and span." Still, many white Americans attributed dirtiness as essential to the Mexican character and then argued for their exclusion.[48]

Working Mexicans, central to the "peculiar features" of the economy's labor demands, were simply out of place in the ideal typical Anglo-American conception of society. Mexicans, the ones the Americans largely saw, allegedly had not "progressed" to Protestant notions of asceticism, antisepsis, and control of the body's passions. Anglo Californians understood the Mexicans as revolutionary in this context: they were wild men who responded to sensations "in the blood," not political ideologies or material conditions. Their rebelliousness derived from their lower intelligence and moral constitution. The Mexican Revolution, then, did not correspond to the images most Americans held about their own ancestors' efforts of 1776; thus the turbulence in Mexico did not qualify as a worthy revolution, and Mexican politics were not taken

seriously. The *Los Angeles Times* attributed "Plans for a general upris-
ing of the Mexican population of Southern California, the seizure and
holding of the land by force of arms, following a programme of terror-
ization by pistol and bomb assassinations, together with wholesale jail
deliveries" to propagandists speaking "to a mass meeting of lower class
Mexicans." An ardent advocate of restriction, Congressman John C. Box
of east Texas claimed, "Mexico is by far the most bolshevistic country
in the Western Hemisphere," which provided even more reason why
they "constitute a bad element to have imported into the United States."[49]

These views complicated the notion that Mexicans were docile or, as
one academic expert put it, "hacienda-minded." "But, despite their good
qualities, they are, we must remember, illiterate and grossly mis-informed
about the United States," stated the *New York Times,* quoting a Protestant minister from Southern California. "Accordingly, for instance,
I.W.W. [the Industrial Workers of the World, an anarchist organization]
agitators find it comparatively easy to play upon their ignorance and
convince them the United States is a tyrannical country." Mexicans were
either dupes or hell-raisers in this estimation of their political activities.
Pancho Villa's celebrated raid on Columbus, New Mexico, in March
1916 touched off all manner of hysteria in Los Angeles and elsewhere,
as did reports of German influence among Mexicans following disclo-
sure of the famous Zimmermann telegram, in which Germany allegedly
promised return of the Southwest to Mexico in exchange for the latter's
support in World War I. Thus, in the fertile but twisted imaginations of
some restrictionists, Mexicans, naturally docile but acting under the influence of smart but devious enemies of various political stripes, threatened to form a fifth column undermining American democracy, capitalism, and world prominence.[50]

White Americans at the Fiesta Days heard Theodore Roosevelt extol
reason and self-control, traits central to their definition of their society.
This has much to do with why they identified themselves as civilized,
their many frenzies notwithstanding. It also helps to explain their fas-
cination with those they considered savage or barbaric. They saw such
people as stuck in the first, and utterly distasteful, stages of historical
evolution on the way to civilization. Indians served this thought-system
most usually and effectively around the turn of the twentieth century, but
depictions of lusty and violent Mexicans unable to control their passions
excited anxieties among the American populace as well. A 1907 study of
Los Angeles affirmed that Mexicans were "a peaceable, hard-working
people," "with the exception of the quick use of the knife after drinking

cheap wine." An interviewee from two decades later confidently thought himself sufficiently competent to speak for his people when he said, "On the question of crime there is likewise almost complete concurrence that the Mexicans commit more offenses against law and order, both petty and serious, than do the native whites or negroes."[51]

Such impulsiveness exhibited itself in other actions of the body, ones with possible consequences for the American internal empire: "It must be clear that the continuation of such a birth rate (or even considerably less) in California, New Mexico, Arizona, Texas, Utah, and Colorado," went congressional testimony in favor of restriction, "will in a comparatively short time change the complexion of the population of those States, and bring about a hyphenized, politically unstabilized, Latinized majority throughout the Southwest." Moving their bodies across the border, "The recent Mexican immigrants are making a reconquest of the Southwest." In these times when the principle of conquest still figured in white Americans' understanding of their relationship to Mexico, Mexican immigration threatened "almost to revise the essential consequences of the Mexican War." In the imagery that the nativists presented, Mexican bodies seemed to die, to be born, and to move suddenly, dramatically, and threateningly.[52]

The Mexicans had their defenders. Harry Chandler, son-in-law of the scion of the *Los Angeles Times,* a great landowner in Mexico, and an officer or director of twenty-five California corporations, argued in a 1930 congressional hearing, "a certain number of Mexican laborers are helpful to all our industries, and I do not believe they produce real social problems." He sought to placate Anglo-American fears, explaining how

> in the first place, the peon who comes there [Los Angeles] is an innocent, friendly, kindly individual. He has in him 85 percent Indian blood on the average and every American who knows anything about Indian characteristics can measure from that the Mexican peon who comes to work in the United States. They are not enterprising, of course, like other races.

Contrast this languid blood with the alternative, which the indefatigable Dr. Clements authoritatively presented:

> When the sob sisters of America, particularly those of California, could not get rid of the Mexican in any other way, the Filipino was brought in to displace him, the most worthless, unscrupulous, shiftless, diseased, semibarbarian that has ever come to our shores, who has done more in the last ten years to make a polyglot problem out of the population undertow than any other people we have ever brought to us—even the Negro.

When this army of laborers remained in reserve and often indigent during the winter months, there was plenty of whining about "the Mexican problem." When harvest time came, though, the yammerings about a shortage of labor and the wonders of the Mexicans, who were "industrious, simple-minded, peaceful, farmer folk," drowned out the strident voices of nervous nativists.[53]

Anyway, "the Mexican laborer," Clements reminded California Governor C. C. Young in 1927, "is an alien possible of deportation should he become indigent or a social menace." But such force was not usually necessary because of the Mexicans' nature. "My experience of the Mexican is that he is a 'homer,'" stated the chair of the agricultural committee of the Fresno Chamber of Commerce, responding to charges that the Mexicans menaced white society. "Like the pigeon he goes back to roost." One U.S. senator wondered, "After they get here and mix in with our people, how are you going to send them back?" Responded a rancher from Ventura, who represented the California State Grange and Farmers Union, "They go back naturally." The wonders of Mexicans as workers continued: "There was there in Mexico, or in immigration from Mexico, a reservoir which we could draw from to get those men," stated a railroad man, "and when we were through with them they went back into the reservoir of labor." Another employer, in a remarkable combination of nineteenth-century history, California Pastoral, and the demands of the twentieth-century capitalist labor market, stated that the Mexicans "are like swallows at the old mission. They come and go about the same time every year."[54]

It is important to point out here that the American arguments on both sides of the immigration issue used race to make their case. Mexicans were threatening because of racial characteristics contended the exclusionists, and non-threatening because of yet other attributes carried "in the blood," according to the many employers who favored them. Mexican workers were docile because they were Indian, deportable because they were "aliens," and adaptable to working conditions "not requiring any degree of mentality" because somehow as a race "they do not object to dirt."[55] The whole discussion revolved around the traits each side considered to be essential in the Mexican biological makeup.

In the minds of Los Angeles's industrial leaders, the economy demanded a strata of underemployed workers like the Mexicans. Those who controlled land and machines connected their resources with human labor and rationalized their enterprise in a fashion most conducive to control and discipline—with a racially identifiable group. Then, too, opponents of the presence of Mexican immigrants took on a similarly twisted view of those whose kin had only recently inhabited the American Southwest. Thus we see how prevailing racist ideas derived not only from the exigencies of labor demands, anxieties regarding the conjugal family, and the inheritance of history, but from the very arguments in which these people engaged.

The market, and history and fate, threw Mexicans and Americans together on a plain to which they had all arrived only recently, on a frontier often seething if not always with tension, at least with complexities about who belonged where. Americans did not recognize, or care to notice, the great European-style cultural achievements of Mexico City; nor could Mexicans know of and acknowledge the peaceful, tolerant, and interracial American traditions embodied in Unitarianism, Abolition, and the movements involved in the formation of such organizations as the NAACP and the ACLU. In other words, both sides were positioned to look through only a few windows in forming an overall view of the other's lifeways.

Yet here they were together on the landscape of Southern California. Both people, and no doubt we should include the Asian sojourners, felt a sometimes contradictory mix of entitlement and wonderment about being there, and antipathy and wonderment about each other. Both had some knowledge of why they were there, which was mixed up with how their received wisdom explained their presence. Neither can withstand the scrutiny of our smug view from nearly a century later. But Mexicans were in the place of their ancestors, borne there by the historical currents of Mexico, America, and the world. How they would work and change there shall be the subjects of the following chapters.

CHAPTER THREE

"Like Swallows at the Old Mission"

Mexicans and the Politics of the Labor Market

Confused and Amazed Again
  by this life we lead:
The rat-tat-tat of hammers,
and crops fat and willing as our own children
to give us nothing or everything.
  I am amazed by life's bottom layer of people,
  with our fingers in dirt
  plying our very soul thick with rain and sun,
  combed by winds, dress up with seasons,
  where we slowly fall in despair,
  then blossom up and out like water pushing
  and pushing, swirling in mud,
  we heavy with things to do.

> *Jimmy Santiago Baca, from*
> Immigrants in Our Own Land

Progress Is the Life of Law.

> *Los Angeles City School District certificate*
> *given to 1927 night school graduates*

For all of California's flux and apparent newness, a historical legacy as veiled as it was weighty awaited the Mexicans who migrated there. California had always been a distant, often disorganized, and obscure outpost of first Spain's and then Mexico's far-flung territories, but patterns established there about who should work powerfully constrained the lives of Mexicans who sojourned in the long-faded footsteps of the priests and soldiers who first conquered the now rapidly evolving Golden State. Its Indian and Hispanic past instituted numerous presumptions and routines about race and labor, ones that explain much about the curious and mystifying spectacle of "the dusky workmen" laying the tracks for the Fiesta Days parade, which introduced the present narrative. In chapter 1 we saw how Mexicans began to presence themselves on the landscape of Los Angeles, and in chapter 2 how people in Mexico found themselves pulled into the intense historical, political, and social currents associated with the Porfiriato and the Mexican Revolution. We have, in other words, an excellent illustration of the old adage that people "make their own history, but . . . they do not make it under circumstances chosen by themselves, but under circumstances directly encountered, given and transmitted from the past."[1] Now we shall see more of how various aspects of the Southern California society, especially the place's historical legacy, its economic structure, and the efforts of social reformers and educators to "Americanize" the new immigrants, conditioned the lives of Mexicans. We shall analyze, in other words, the constraining context in which people made history.

DUSKY WORKMEN—A BRIEF HISTORY

The true saga of Indian, Spanish, and Mexican California proves more interesting and meaningful than the arcadian, self-justifying inventions of the newest Californians on display at the Fiesta Days. It is a rather complex history, one with high ideals, much grief, and a legacy of hard feelings, but a few words about it here will help make more explicable the variety of events around the electric railway tracks. First of all, the Spanish priests, who founded their first mission in Alta California at San Diego in 1769, took it upon themselves to discipline not only the Indians' spirits but their bodies as well. The padres strove to narrow Indian spirituality, work practices, and sexuality into the confines of Catholicism, peasant feudal production, and Christian marriage. It is pointless to calculate which priestly endeavor failed most dismally; disease proved the only victor anyway. Failing as Christians, Indian neophytes, their bodies tortured, labored in the missions and were often rented out to the presidios. More often than not, those who avoided the outposts of Christianity either became desperados living on the fringes of Spanish and Mexican frontier towns or hired themselves out to the town settlers. Such *pobladores* (settlers) were *mestizos*, people of a biological mix that was to some degree—depending on the time, place, and perception—mostly Indian and a cultural mix that was mostly Spanish. No matter what their situation, though, Indians did most of the work, rather sullenly, though, in their pain and anger. Later, when the Mexican government secularized the missions in the 1830s, Indians attached themselves to the emerging big ranchos. They continued as the usual workers on the coastal California landscape.

Through marriage, war, and debt, English-speaking outsiders took over the ranchos from the socially aspiring rancheros. The mestizo Californios were now made into Spaniards for the Fiesta Days. These spoils of conquest, formalized in the Treaty of Guadalupe Hidalgo, which ended the Mexican-American War of 1846–48, came complete with labor forces of Indians. On the ranchos, unlike in the missions, they could come and go, but the alcohol with which the ranchers often paid them bound so many of them to their employers, and so many to a highway of death. Almost completely deprived of any means of subsistence, many of the California Indians, and some few of the mestizos from the lower classes of California, took to a life of raiding, which included a measure of rebellion, for their maintenance. Such actions classed them, and by implication many of their people, as criminals.

With too few of what then were called *cholos,* or Mexicans of the poorer and rougher sort, and the Indian population tragically diminishing, California employers looked to the Chinese for cheap labor. This sufficed for a while in the 1870s and 1880s, but legislation restricted their immigration, and nativist riots quickly confined them to Chinatowns. By this time, the pattern established during the first decades of old California had sustained itself through Mexican independence (1821) and the American conquest and had permeated through all levels of Anglo-American economic undertakings. The railroads, emerging agribusiness, ranches, households, vineyards, and road and building construction all used the half-paid labor of unskilled (actually de-skilled) Indian, Mexican, and Chinese people.

By 1900 employers perceived that the area south of the border held the most constant, reliable, and boundless source of unskilled workers of the type to which they had become so accustomed. Their market economic system, which they associated with freedom, rewarded those owners of land and machines with the cheapest labor costs. In fact competition determined that each and every employer have the lowest possible labor costs or be forced out of business. Their racism mixed notions of superiority about physical appearances as well as about other cultures' relations to the spirit world, to technology and "progress," and to the body and pleasure. California civilization has as one of its bases the provisioning of its tables and the serving of its households by, for the most part, Mexicans. This confident superiority buttressed Anglo-American feelings of entitlement to the superexploitation of the others' labor and provided justification for the whole construction.[2]

It is a more involved story, of course; we have not yet even broached the matter of the creation of the mythical Spanish California, and we have just seen how complicated the issue of why Mexicans migrated north has been. But, basically, this legacy of conquest is why, when the Pacific Electric set out to build what would become a fine interurban railway system in Los Angeles, the track workers would be Mexicans, and why the language described them in such dehumanizing ways. Those who variously acted against the Pacific Electric Railway as it prepared for Roosevelt's visit were products of nearly a century and a half of Spanish, Mexican, and American California history.

INDUSTRIAL LOS ANGELES—ANOTHER BRIEF HISTORY

The concept of "the labor market," often portrayed as free of values and the past, replaced consciousness of this history. "When people engage the land, its resources, technology, and human labor in the cause of production, they inevitably produce more than either their subsistence or commodities. They produce a particular structure of human society, which we may best term the social relations."[3] As liminal as Mexicans might have been in typical chronicles of the place, their positioning in the productive system profoundly affected the evolution of the social relations of Southern California. Mexican labor is clearly associated with the particular direction industrial Los Angeles took as regards unions and other labor-management issues, the structure of the labor market and how "free" it has been, and the fantasy construction of the nature and meaning of the term "Mexican" and of California history. The context of the political economy of Los Angeles; its nature as a city with service, agriculture, and fledgling heavy industries all existing side by side; and market competition; all prove central to an understanding of how various people created the prevailing social relations.

Harrison Gray Otis, publisher of the then-conservative *Los Angeles Times*, stands as the captain of Los Angeles's economic development and the acknowledged leader of the city's employer class through the 1920s. As early as the turn of the twentieth century, Otis and his compatriots committed themselves to a vision of Los Angeles as an industrial metropolis that would completely erase the actual landscape of the missions, rancheros, and ranchers. No longer would the boom and bust of real estate wingdings suffice for development. Nor would the city's industry be confined to flour mills, carpentry shops, and slaughterhouses—all small in scale and limited to the home market for consumption. Not simple dreamers but optimistic and spirited industrialists with the competitive skills necessary to bring themselves fulfillment in the market place, Otis and company realized that the city lacked important ingredients required of an industrial center, and they set out to alter the situation. A sparse population meant few workers and small local consumer demand to exploit. In spite of the two transcontinental railroads, isolation made it difficult to produce goods for a wider market. By turns, the need for water, a deep-water harbor, and such municipal necessities as fire and police protection, sanitation, education, and transportation could be, and were, taken care of by the diligence of these civic leaders. "The Los Angeles Chamber of Commerce, with over 1500 members," puffed a 1908 Southern Pacific Company brochure, "neglects no project of public importance." Between 1880 and 1920, the Chamber of Commerce promotion made Los Angeles the best-publicized city in the country. And the glossy pictures of orange trees, winter flowers, and open space brought many, often as not midwesterners, to Southern California.[4]

Yet the biggest problem still remained. San Francisco, with its gold rush–induced forty-year head start, dominated industrial production on the West Coast. Otis and company decided that absolute control over Los Angeles's workforce could offset San Francisco's competitive advantage. For reasons of both capital accumulation and discipline of the labor supply, Los Angeles employers strove to eliminate any and all interference with their comprehensive control of labor. In 1892 Otis's *Times* and the city's other newspapers demolished the printing trade union after a bitter strike of two years, and established the open shop in Los Angeles. Between 1890 and 1910 employers achieved a 20 to 30 percent wage differential between Los Angeles and San Francisco. In some industries, the southerners' advantage approached 40 percent.[5] Lower wages meant higher profits and a more appealing climate for investment.

This wage squeeze pressed trade unionists into an organizational drive that exploded into national notoriety with the lethal bombing of the *Times* building in 1910. The twenty deaths shocked the city and the nation, turned public opinion against the union drive, and ended the strong chance for the election of a pro-labor socialist as mayor of Los Angeles. The business class now took the offensive and firmly established the open shop.[6] Between the far-reaching consequences of this event, and the wage squeeze that the local, state, and national markets produced, we have the two central themes of pre–World War II Los Angeles labor relations: the open shop (that is, no unions) and the attempt to forge from the residents of México de afuera a labor force that functioned outside of the standard workings of the uncertain labor market.

"Industrial freedom" became the favorite slogan of the *Los Angeles Times* and the Otis clique. They espoused the ideology of competitive capitalism unfettered by any restraints or privileges. "Every employee," claimed Otis, "has a right to be free to work when he will for any employer and for such a wage as the two, standing face to face, may agree upon." The ideology was not the practice. Employers united in such organizations as the famous and powerful Merchants and Manufacturers Association, which concerned itself mostly with "labor relations," and in the Chamber of Commerce, whose less spectacular but equally important job with respect to unions was "one of coordination and concentration . . . of the direct fighting tool [of the Merchants and Manufacturers]." Agricultural capitalists parodied this free-market ideology, for example in a 1912 grower publication in which they opposed any restriction in the hours of labor:

> But when the work is wholesome and the competition is fair, as they are in the industries of this State so far as we know them, it is tyranny to limit the hours a woman shall work, just as it is tyranny to do the same thing for a man. Both men and women have a right to sell their time; whose right is it to limit the amount of salable commodity, under reasonable conditions?

Only a few years later the same publication reported that in "Sutter county [in northern California] fruit growers feel like they have been paying too much for fruit harvest laborers. . . . Some growers have come together and agreed to pay not over 30 to 35 cents per hour (where the previous rate was 40 cents)." The ideology of freedom bound one side of the market and freed the other. In other words, as the Southern California Restaurant Association granted, employers favored "the continuance of the open shop and the right of the owners and operators to control and guard their own invested capital and continue their own business as in their own judgment seems best."[7] In Los Angeles, industrial freedom did not mean free competition or the abolition of privilege. It meant control of the economy and relations between employers and employees as the former saw fit, an ideology that became amplified when applied to Mexicans migrating to the United States.

At its founding in 1781, Los Angeles was a little farming and ranching pueblo, of course, but it continued as an agricultural city at least until World War II, in spite of its rapid urbanization and industrialization. In human terms this meant that 17.5 percent of the population lived in rural areas of the county in 1930 and that 7.6 percent of those gainfully employed in the county worked in agriculture. These figures compare to 8.8 percent in transportation, 7.3 percent in construction, 19.0 percent in manufacturing (much of which was related to agriculture), and only 2.3 percent in the important area of oil and gas production. In 1935 Los Angeles contained an astounding 13,549 farms and ranches totaling 619,769 acres, or 23.5 percent of the county's land area. Of this total, between 261,000 and 339,000 acres were devoted to crops. In 1938 the total value of agricultural production in Los Angeles County amounted to $76,367,153, compared with only $22,774,975 in Imperial County and only $23,666,744 in Orange County. Los Angeles was important not only as a transportation hub for the surrounding agricultural counties, but as an important producer of agricultural products in its own right in the era before the farms became the suburbs.[8]

THE WAGES OF WORK

Farm labor only paid 25 to 35 cents per hour, and then the demand for it fluctuated vastly, as we saw in chapter 2.[9] "This peculiar feature" of agriculture, a product of the seasons and the competitive market, meant not only that the human needs of agricultural laborers took second place to those of the employers, but that gang and contract labor prevailed in the fields as well as on the railroad. A mexicano or americano received a contract to plant, hoe, or harvest a field or orchard. This contractor then paid each worker, usually by the quantity picked. He even bought gangs of workers from the *enganchistas* who recruited them in Mexico. The more this "patron" squeezed from his workers, the more money he made. This hiring of groups of Mexicans (or Asians) rather than individuals was well established at the turn of the century.

This type of agricultural and railroad labor not only segregated Mexicans into colonias, but also turned Los Angeles into the winter homes of the seasonally unemployed Mexican agricultural workers from all over the state. The depression of 1907–8 first drew attention to this phenomenon. Paul Taylor calculated: "In February, probably 80 percent or more of the Mexican population of the state is found there." They had to be accessible to the fields and the railroad yards but also sequestered away, or, in Carey McWilliams's words, "invariably on 'the other side' of something: a railroad track, a bridge, a river, or a highway." Thus hidden away from white society, the Mexicans would come and go to work in the fields, food would appear in the grocery stores, and people would travel on the roads and rails, and no one outside the Mexican community would question the situation. And, importantly, this segregation further encouraged the perception of Mexicans as "other."[10]

This spectacle of Mexicans digging, picking, canning, cleaning, hauling away, and so on defined them in Anglo eyes as a homogeneous group set socially and institutionally apart from the rest of society. It is more than ironic that the people who did so much of the work and figured so centrally in production were also so invisible to the rest of society when they were not working, except occasionally as "the Mexican problem." What they did on these jobs, when Anglo society saw them, reflected and reinforced both the labor and social structures of the Southwest. As they lived often in segregated colonias, it was not Mexicans' social and cultural lives so much as their more visible work lives that defined them for the public. We may say, then, that Mexican liminality as regards dwelling on the landscape paralleled their liminality in the job market. To use yet another metaphor, the overwhelming majority of Mexicans participated in the secondary labor market. Low wages, harsh working conditions, supervision that was intense or arbitrary or both, little opportunity for advancement, and insecurity of employment all characterize work in this bottom sector of what has been called a dual labor market.

Construction work on roads, railways, and buildings illustrates these notions most clearly. As we saw in chapter 1, when Mexicans did not work as gang laborers on major projects, they were usually "helpers" under the supervision of whites. In other words, when they did have contact with primary-strata journeymen, usually in construction, they worked in obviously inferior positions carrying things for the white workers and then cleaning up. From Texas to California, they carried most of the hods (troughs hoisted on the shoulder to carry bricks, mortar, and so on), shoveled the ditches, excavated the roads, conveyed away the dirt, and then went away when they were supposed to. And in Los Angeles in the era we are discussing here, Mexican construction workers had to count on about a month and a half of unemployment per year.[11]

Fruit and vegetable canning, an urban agriculture-related occupation in which California led the nation in production, provides an archetype of the job structure into which Mexicans were to fit as unskilled itinerant labor with little chance of promotion to either skilled or supervisory positions. Again, this is not so much an anomaly in a fair system as part of the essence of how the racially hierarchical system functioned. In 1928 Mexicans comprised 23.5 percent of those employed in Los Angeles canneries, and, of these, nearly 90 percent were women. One cannot conceive of more inconsistent employment. Let us assume that 100 was the average number of workers employed steadily for the whole year during the mid-1930s in a medium-size plant. If typical of statewide figures, that plant would employ only 16 workers in a typical December week, 18 in a January week, and 354 in an August week (when deciduous fruits were packed). (For comparison, the number of rubber workers deviated only 1.5 percent above or below the yearly average.) Statewide, 60,000 to 70,000 found late-summer jobs in California canneries, whereas only 10,000 to 13,000 did so in winter. Average time of employment amounted to a mere ten to eleven weeks per year.[12]

Cannery workers still managed somehow to live on their meager earnings. With wages averaging $26.64 per week for men and $16.55 per week for women, 75 percent of the women and 50 percent of the men earned less than $300 per year. Cannery workers were not transients. By the time that the Mexican population stabilized after the great migrations of the pre-Depression decades, they included few out-of-state workers, and average residence in California was a full fifteen years.[13]

Cannery workers, like other seasonal workers, often did not find work in other industries when the job was over either. A 1937 California Unemployment Reserves Commission study found that only 1 percent of the male workers surveyed found employment outside the canneries, and only 10 percent worked the entire year in the canneries. It remains to be determined if Mexicans comprised much of this 10 percent. Fully 70 percent of the male cannery workers found either only casual employment or none at all; 19 percent attended school. It was simply part of the Mexican work experience to be underemployed or unemployed some part of the year.[14]

Patterns of female employment expectations meshed with what George Clements called the "demands of our casual labor," which the cannery industry illustrates. As Mexicans urbanized, they adapted their old division of the public world for men, and the domestic for women, into the ideal of the sexual division of labor into wage earner and housewife. Certainly, however, one would expect that poor women's labors would no more be confined to the home in the city than in the country, where peasant women worked the fields when they had to. But women's labor was still in the home, and wage work, because it took place in the public world, was not appropriate for women. As much as husbands or wives or both may have desired to have the women stay home (where they had more than enough to do), husbands' meager wages could not support such a situation. Mostly, women worked outside the home because they were poor. Cannery work supplemented the family's unfit income; women worked there to strengthen their families. Sixty-one percent of the women in the California Unemployment Reserves Commission study worked only in the canneries or in the home and claimed that they did not want to work outside these two areas. In a 1933 University of California study of a San Diego sample of 100 Mexican families, the husbands of those women who worked outside the home had a yearly average income $300 lower than those who did not. In other words, if the husband's income bought the family's expected subsistence, the wife did not work outside the home.[15] In many cases, though, Mexican men's position in the labor market pressured women out of the house and children out of school to supplement the family income with wage labor. (The often explosive consequences of this are discussed in the following chapter.)

According to the 1930 census, 60 percent of Mexican families in Los Angeles had only one wage earner. This figure may not tell us much because those women who worked usually engaged in irregular, part-time employment to supplement their husbands' or fathers' inadequate wages. In other words, their work patterns, especially in a situation like the canneries, cannot be accurately reflected in a static census statistic. The above-mentioned study in the San Diego area showed that of a hundred married women, "forty four were gainfully occupied at some time in the year. . . . Thirty two worked in canneries at cleaning and packing fish. Four of them worked full time during part of the year; the others worked broken time." Here, at least, "in no case did the canneries provide full-time, year-round jobs."[16]

The United States is increasingly a place of service industries, and Los Angeles emerged as the first service metropolis. In 1930 service industries and trade employed 62 percent of the area's workers. Manufacturing (including building) and extractive industries (including agriculture) employed 37 percent of them. Manufacturing as a percentage of the economy grew during the 1930s, in large part because of the establishment of branch plants by eastern manufacturers. Yet, even by the late 1930s, Los Angeles employed 9 percent more in trade than the U.S. average and 5.4 percent more in service, and it lagged 5.1 percent behind the national average in manufacturing employment. In 1929 Los Angeles, with a relatively high per capita income, ranked fifth in population but only ninth in volume of manufacturing. Los Angeles had a slightly higher population than either Detroit or Pittsburgh, but only one-half the manufacturing wage earners of Pittsburgh and two-fifths the wage earners of Detroit, despite the efforts of city leaders to attract major industry.[17]

This situation structured but did not determine the work lives of Mexicans in Los Angeles, as we shall see in the following chapter. Certainly, though, the nature of the Los Angeles economy remains central to an understanding of the employment of Mexicans. Where conditions of monopoly or near-monopoly prevail, increases in production costs such as wages, rents, interest, or the price of capital goods can be passed on to the consumer in the form of higher prices. The competitive sector, on the other hand, is just that—competitive. It is much more difficult to pass on cost increases in the context of competition. Since costs for land and machinery are rather fixed, it is always profits and wages that must be squeezed. Marginal profit rates mean that more businesses come and go, leading to less stability in employment in competitive businesses, relative to the more monopolized heavy industry sector. Labor is the variable factor of production. Workers can be temporarily laid off, paid less (especially if there is a surplus of them), and worked longer or faster. These considerations made labor in these overabundant service and competitive sectors more arduous, tedious, and fast-paced than industrial labor.

Low pay, underemployment, seasonality, and bad working conditions characterized employment in such competitive-sector businesses as construction, the manufacture of clothing and accessories, restaurants, service stations, and the laundry trade. Since these labor-intensive enterprises required little capital investment, they proliferated rapidly. Newcomers to an industry entered by underpricing those already there. Markets tended to be local, unstable, and seasonal, yielding little opportunity or incentive to stabilize production and employment. No wonder Clements, the Chamber of Commerce, and employers found Mexicans so much to their liking. The racial power relations that prevailed assured a ready, tractable, and necessarily cheap labor supply. *La costura,* "the garment trade," further illustrates how Mexicans were adapted, whether they wanted to be or not, to the demands of California's labor market. Textiles actually expanded its total employment during the 1920s and 1930s, though it was a volatile, competitive industry prone to a great deal of turnover. Mexican women comprised three-fourths of the women's clothing workers. About 3,000 sewed garments in the mid-1920s, when the industry centered in New York and Chicago, but 7,834 did so in 1929, as more and more companies had opened up local factories. The unpredictable demand of the Depression years put employment levels in flux, but 8,000 stitched in 1933, and 15,890 (of which about 12,000 were mexicanas) filled the burgeoning West Coast demand for dresses and blouses in 1939.[18]

A label might have manufactured an entire garment in its own shop or contracted all or part of the sewing to an outside shop. It has been there that conditions have been most rugged: the "jobber" must come in with a low bid, then sweat his employees to produce the work at a cost less than his bid, and then slough off workers until he has got a new contract. Often "the 'Open-Door System' prevailed" in the garment district. A union organizer described how "Women hunting jobs were given 'the freedom of the building.' Doors leading to staircases were left unlocked, so that they could take the elevator to the top floor, ask at each shop if there was work, walk down to the next floor, and repeat the performance until, if lucky, they found a few days employment for the price offered." María Flóres related, "I come in the morning, punch my card, work for an hour, punch the card again. I wait for two hours, get another bundle, punch card, finish bundle, punch card again. Then I wait some more the whole day that way." No doubt, the natural working of the competitive market in the garment industry compelled such labor practices, but to María Flóres it was inhumane—in her words, "what the boss makes us do." It may be a bit redundant to note, as the union organizer did, that "Garment factory owners regarded their employees as casual workers, in the same class as migrants who harvested fruit and vegetable products," but it further establishes our points about Mexicans and the nature of the labor market. Even after the union came, an important topic of the fifth chapter, women's clothing workers earned $20.00 per week, the lowest in the state except for hotel and restaurant workers. In 1935, before unionization, wages averaged between $13.00 and $17.00 per week, at a time when the state minimum wage was $18.90 per week.[19]

The many Mexican laundry and dry-cleaning workers suffered the effects of working in the competitive sector, as did restaurant workers. The California Department of Industrial Relations fielded many complaints about the former industry, "which has always paid low wages" for long hours. The same department claimed that the hotels and restaurants were "productive of more complaints than any other industry . . . due probably to the fact that there is a great turnover in restaurant ownership, as well as labor turnover."[20]

The heady surge in the economy of Los Angeles during the 1920s proved as shallow as it initially was phenomenal. "The growth and business activity of the County from 1920 to 1930," reported the Los Angeles Bureau of Municipal Research, "was impelled by new oil discoveries in the Los Angeles basin, land speculation, promotive building, and the lavish use of credit for public works, all of which only provided temporary employment."[21] It was just the old boom and bust, and, actually, famous oil and water scandals. As in Nathanael West's and Raymond Chandler's fabled literary portrayals of Los Angeles in this era, Mexicans—the backbone of the agriculture and service economy—are simply hidden from view.

Almost incongruously, the Depression years saw transformation in the economy as eastern manufacturers, enticed by favorable fuel and transportation costs, opportune tax rates on capital investments, and above all, the open shop and proximity to the huge local markets for automobile-related products, established branch plants in the city. This "most significant trend," a UCLA economist of the 1930s noted, "is attributable in no small degree to the success of the local chamber of commerce." Exclaimed the Los Angeles Times, "Capitalists back of the new industries here have stated frankly that they came here rather than to another coast city because of the American Plan, or open-shop system of employer-employee relationship for which Los Angeles has become famed the country across." In the years between 1929 and 1936 plants that General Motors, Ford, Willis-Overland, Studebaker, Goodyear, Goodrich, Firestone, and U.S. Rubber built achieved a stunning world ranking for Los Angeles, second only to that of Detroit and Akron in auto assembly and tire assembly, respectively.[22]

The New Deal also pumped up the Pacific Coast economy. Big-time California capitalists like A. P. Giannini (Bank of America) and Henry J. Kaiser concretely supported the Roosevelt administration even when their East Coast cohorts began to oppose further reform measures. Thus the federal government rewarded California (and Washington and Texas) with projects that essentially built the infrastructure for further development—Boulder (later Hoover) Dam, the Bay Bridge in San Francisco, more irrigation projects, shipyards, and so on. Along with the branch plants, these New Deal–fueled enterprises stoked additional economic development.[23]

But until enlistment and the draft for World War II begot a shortage of able-bodied men, jobs in those plants and technical undertakings were usually only for primary-sector (white) workers. When heavy industry like steel mills or light manufacturing like furniture shops did employ Mexicans, it was only in particular ways, ones corresponding to our discussion of the secondary labor market. All of the tasks in the steel mills and foundries were hot and gritty, but the skilled positions of core maker and molder paid the best and had the most status. Mexicans rarely worked there; more often they toiled in the cleaning rooms or the foundries, where the molten metal could elevate the air temperature to 130 degrees. Before the union and the war, they owed their jobs to a foreman under whom they worked much as they would have on the railroad tracks—in an undifferentiated gang for long hours, for short pay, and with little hope of advancement.

In furniture, cabinet work, and woodworking, ethnicity also corresponded to workers' positioning on the shop floor. A total of 5,904 worked in the furniture industry in 1929, 3,225 in 1933, and 5,888 in 1939, earning Los Angeles the fourth-place position in furniture manufacturing centers in the United States. Although several large producers dominated the industry, the average establishment was a small one typically employing 25 workers. Since setting up a new shop required only a small capitalization, many shops came and went. Usually, ambitious upholsterers founded the new businesses. There was some seasonality to the work—10 percent more or less than the median at different times of the year—but there was considerable instability to the work owing to the nature of the industry and the economy. Wages for the industry ranged from a low of $1.50 for a ten- to twelve-hour day in an unorganized shop in 1932 to 35 cents per hour in 1934 to 50 cents to $1.25 per hour after the United Furniture Workers local gained strength in 1938. Again, Mexican workers found themselves segregated in the furniture shops. Whites from the South usually dominated the skilled woodworking trades, Jews the upholstering, and Mexicans the finishing and unskilled labor. A few, though, moved up to upholstering, especially after World War II, when blacks entering at the bottom pushed some Mexicans up the ladder.[24]

Likely, our points here about the positioning of Mexicans in the secondary labor market have been established. But let it be added that Mexicans drove trucks and comprised 10 percent of the major Teamsters' local even before the big drives of the mid-1930s. A similar percentage poured and smoothed cement rather than simply hauling equipment and supplies at construction sites. Many had grimy jobs in local packinghouses. Mexicans, many of them skilled craftsmen imported from Mexico to supervise the making of the intricate and delicate patterns, created much of the ceramic tile in the area; their less skilled brethren hauled those tiles and made lots of bricks. Mexicans did much work as maids and janitors; and many were "helpers" in lumberyards, at building sites, and at typical small manufactories around Southern California.[25]

Why the Mexican immigrant "endeared himself to the heart" of employers should now be readily apparent from this impressionistic but statistically validated overview of the most important and representative workplaces of Mexicans. The same employment and work patterns repeated themselves over and over again in numerous areas of the economic structure. The new city fathers fancied Mexicans to be politically impotent, (initially) unorganized at the workplace, second-class (at best), and temporary. Mexicans would neither threaten the dominant society by intruding into its enjoyment of the ongoing spoils of the Mexican-American War nor even protest their situation. But Mexicans were not marginal workers. They occupied a central position in the economy in which competitive, service, and seasonal enterprises were at the heart.

THE NEED TO RE-FORM THE MEXICANS

No one is perfect, however; and employers and social reformers saw a need to re-form the Mexicans. The Mexicans did not always come and go. Sometimes they nested in their homeland's former frontier, in the city their ancestors founded in 1781. Several concerns underlay the various reform efforts. One was antagonism toward Mexican lifeways: "The Mexican peon," wrote sociologist Emory Bogardus, Los Angeles's academic Mexican expert, "is hacienda-minded. He has not been taught to save." Fear of conflict between Mexican workers on the one side and their employers and the Anglo community on the other inspired the need for reform as well. More urgently and ominously, Clements understood and feared that "The Mexican laborer, if he only realized it, has California agriculture and industry in the hollow of his hand." Then, too, more humanitarian, if not less narcissistic, Americans saw in such immigrants an opportunity to supplement and complete the American social and political order. If Mexicans would assimilate, that is, become "capable, efficient Christian citizens of the United States," it would help validate Americans and their culture. Thus almost all of the reformers could agree that Mexicans needed to be taught to "accept and practice those ideals, customs, methods of living, skills and knowledge that have come to be accepted as representative of the best in American life."[26]

The need to uplift these threatening people appeared all the more acute in the context of the Mexican Revolution. Demonstrating that people can hold quite inconsistent images of others, Anglo Angelenos also envisaged Mexican uprisings, and this fear obviously contradicted the image of hacienda-minded Mexicans. Such thinking, though, should not be a surprising idea, given that the Revolution continued to fire the passions of Mexicans north of the border for whom the homeland's politics still mattered overwhelmingly. Especially as anarchist refugees of the Partido Liberal Mexicano (PLM) made Los Angeles their headquarters after 1910, the threat of Mexican insurrection burgeoned in the minds of those prone to conspiratorial fantasies. The anarchists remained in the city through the 1920s, and one finds local police and reformers quite concerned with speakers in the Plaza "making many fiery and sometimes vile accusations against religion and capitalism." Although police violence often met the PLM, Anglo reformers and Mexican pastors concerned themselves with "ever wisely meeting the 'Red' enemy at the gate and answering the shallow arguments of these propagandists of anarchy." Now, somehow, the allegedly docile Mexicans became violent and dangerous in the Anglo mind. Now that they had collected so much of the land and productive resources that had once belonged to Mexico, anything that smacked of collectivism terrified Anglo-American Protestants. They guarded their hordes tenaciously with a mixture of force and reform. Animosity born of fear intensified as charges of German subversion accompanied descriptions of Mexican labor or community organization during World War I, when the labor shortage intensified and more Mexicans were imported. The *Los Angeles Times* spent several months fanning fears of a Villista "outbreak" in Los Angeles, especially after the infamous raid of March 1916 on Columbus, New Mexico, by Pancho Villa's forces. Bizarre fears surfaced: local Villistas (an unlikely grouping) reportedly planned to bomb the Los Angeles Federal Building or touch off a local insurrection. Such was the context in which reformers and employers sought to bridge "the chasms of distrust" and have the Mexican workers "partake in the common interests of life."[27]

Indeed, it would have been difficult to avoid conflict between a noncapitalist culture on the one hand and a culture that saw the market, accumulation, and Anglo supremacy as givens on the other. Importantly, Los Angeles did not have a political machine like those in East Coast cities to integrate Catholic immigrants into the American electoral system. More fundamentally, America, overwhelmingly peopled by settlers from other lands, has never been institutionally or emotionally predisposed to multiculturalism. Its goal has always been to transform the individual, to make her or him into an "American." Immigrants could be helped not by strengthening their sense of personal worth through reaffirming their culture, but by subjugating them to the apparently successful ways of the dominant culture. Thinking this way, Protestant reformers—some emphasizing religion and others, more secular fields like home economics—targeted, with the active support of such employer organizations as the California Fruit Growers' Exchange, activities that would benefit and re-form the Mexican communities of Los Angeles.[28]

"In general," stated the Los Angeles Commission on Religion in the late 1920s, "the united purpose of all denominations doing work among the Mexicans is to spread the spirit of Christ through personal commitment and devotion to Him, and to raise the standards socially, educationally and morally among Mexican people." Both the religious and secular Protestant missionaries centered their efforts around the settlement house, made most famous in Chicago under the leadership of Jane Addams. A 1907 booster of Los Angeles and the settlement house cheerfully defined it as follows:

> It is a home in an industrial center, where employer and employed, educated and uneducated, rich and poor, can meet on friendly terms; come to an understanding of the human element that vitalizes them all, and so remove the narrow prejudice that ignorance begets and that keeps men asunder. The Settlement has for its fundamental basis the Fatherhood of God and brotherhood of man. These are eternal.

The capitalist property owners and the middle class for whom society and the economy functioned acceptably found the notion of a harmonious national community agreeable. For some workers and some of the intelligentsia, such a notion served only to paper over the conflicts innate to a system in which the few controlled nearly all of the resources and the opportunity. Mexican conservatives understood that such phrases as "narrow prejudice" probably referred to traditional Mexican ways and beliefs.[29]

Like their counterparts in the famous Chicago settlements, from which came such Los Angeles reformers as Catherine Higgins, the Protestant reformers had a triple purpose: to raise the living standards of immigrants, to acculturate them to "American" ways, and to provide young Protestant women with a useful and fulfilling life outside of marriage, patriarchal rhetoric notwithstanding. The demand for cheap labor and Yankee Protestant anxieties about unwashed Catholic immigrants had thrown these strangers together, and fostering internal controls over the foreigners' threatening ways would gently resolve the resulting cultural conflict, though certainly in favor of the prevalent culture. Unlike the vigilantes of the 1850s, who had lynched and terrorized Mexicans into submission, and the twentieth-century police, these reformers sought to break down Mexican culture nonviolently. Settlement reform in Los Angeles presented the same ambiguous issue as it did in Chicago, where Jane Addams sought to give young, middle-class Anglo women, otherwise trapped in their homes, meaningful activity by marshaling their talents and energy into elevating apparently "backward" immigrants to the ascendant culture's ways.[30]

Reformers observed the often miserable conditions in which Mexicans lived and did provide much important assistance, especially medical care, that was unavailable to Mexicans elsewhere. By the early 1920s the Protestant churches, especially the Methodist-Episcopal, had already invested more than $350,000 in property, buildings, and equipment to carry on their religious and social work among Mexicans just in Los Angeles, and another $260,000 waited to be expended in the Methodist coffers. In 1915 the Methodist-Episcopal Church set up the All Nations Foundation on East Sixth Street in the downtown area. From the beginning All Nations provided varied services, including an employment agency, a craft shop, a music department, health clubs and medical care, choral clubs, sewing clubs for the girls and sports clubs for the boys, "a Children's Home to provide Christian training for Mexican orphans," and a Christian training school for older youths. Its boys club alone claimed 1,040 members in 1933. In 1935 All Nations expanded to Boyle Heights, where it founded the Hollenbeck Center. The Catholic Church, on the other hand, offered Los Angeles Mexicans little in the way of social services until after World War II. Nor could the Mexican charity societies even come close to such funding for beneficent efforts.[31] Attention to infant mortality and the plight of Mexican children combined genuine maternal concern for babies, and fear of people who threatened to spread contagion. But Protestant reformers were interested in saving more than souls and babies, no doubt a factor in the urgency that we saw in the sociedades' efforts to maintain the cultural fidelity of the mexicanos de afuera.

Indeed, the expanding Southern California economy, its agricultural, industrial, and service sectors, simply called forth a growing number of Mexicans. Merton Hill, a reformer in the late 1920s, claimed, "the greatest problem confronting Southern California today is that of dealing with the Mexican element that is forming year by year a larger proportion of the population." Mexican immigration did not impress these guardians of the Anglo way of life as positively as it did employers. Hill urgently continued: "According to present tendencies the time is not far distant when every other child in the elementary schools will be Mexican. The Mexican families . . . import their native standards of living. How shall this element be taken care of? Can the Mexicans be raised to the American standards of Life? . . . And finally, can the Mexican people be assimilated into the American population?" To a typical reform-minded student of the situation in 1914, "the Mexicans are a child-like race without the generations of civilization and culture back of them which support the people of the United States." In the eyes of the Protestant reformers, this situation called for an intense educational program that would train every Mexican woman in "economical house management including lessons in sewing, cooking, and thrift." Every man would learn "thrift [of course], gardening, and the principles of American government."[32]

Certainly the efforts both to re-form and to re-educate Mexicans and to elevate them socially and economically overlapped not only in content but in motivation. The education system, on a statewide basis, attempted assimilation as a public policy. For example, in 1919 Georgiana Carden, raised in Oakland and Chico, with a genuine sympathy for the dismal plight of the Mexican agricultural workers, which she had observed firsthand, took charge of migrant education in the California school system. The schools Carden established generally failed because of the inability of migrant children to stay in one place and the reluctance of local school boards to accept, let alone welcome, brown-skinned children. This was true even where cooperation from the growers, as Carden noted, "could not have been better." There were some short-term successes: at the huge Tagus Ranch near Fresno, the manager cooperated with Carden and actually established a school on the ranch itself. Carden sought to reform too the "selfish spirit" of local school boards through personal exhortation, and she vowed to enforce the attendance law even if she had "to truck them [the Mexican students] myself." She advocated better housing and schools as an inducement for stabilizing the family while the father moved with the fruit. *Papá* would be a more efficient worker and better integrated into the wage economy, and *los niños* would be weaned away from a culture the reformers considered stultifying. Though in the end futilely, Carden sought to elevate the less fortunate to Yankee conventions by extending to them the key to individual success in her particular culture—the spirit of market calculation extended even to the migrant family.[33]

Progressive ideas about education infused the settlement houses of Los Angeles. With some sophistry and much naiveté, Americans have often thought that education would solve the social problems of poverty, racism, crime, violence, and cultural conflict. This has unfairly burdened educators, and, as should be apparent from this work, schooling could not counter the historical legacy of exclusion and exploitation bequeathed such people as the Mexicans of Southern California. Educators, furthermore, sometimes shared Clements's opinions about Mexican indigence. An assistant supervisor in the Department of Compulsory Education who did special work among Mexicans attributed poverty to the "original raciality of the Mexicans' Mongolian descent." Although solutions to the Mexican problem could not come from such analyses, educators proceeded nevertheless. The Mexicans would have to be changed for society's benefit and safety, and for their own good. "Their morals are a menace to our civilization, they are illiterate, ignorant and inefficient and have few firm religious beliefs," our student of these "childlike individuals" stated in a 1928 article in the *Los Angeles School Journal* titled "The Mexican Problem in the Schools." "Yet those problems may be largely summarized in the one word—ignorance." The guardians of Anglo-American culture needed education to remedy the Mexican problem as powerfully as employers needed Mexican labor.[34]

Ignorance would fall to "a system which makes the school house at once the center of educational progress, economic direction, home improvement, social development, moral influence, ethical upbringing, hygienic institutions and an ever ready bureau of general advice," continued the article. To replace the parents as their children's figures of authority became part of the neighborhood school's design. This was necessary because "American ideals which are held out to them in our educational institutions are drowned in the environment of their Mexican homes which are surrounded with the traditional atmosphere of Mexican thought." These locals of the allegedly inferior culture would naturally want to come into the school ("after all, they are entertained at school, as if it were a fool's paradise"), but attendance was also compulsory. School administrators proceeded with confidence in their mission. The niceties they offered the Mexican children, neophyte americanos, would draw them to the school, but then, "Leaving city appearances of wealth and luxury behind they turn their little faces homeward to meet penury, filth and often hunger." The educators' job of assimilating the Mexican children was an uphill task because "what mental elevation they indulged in at school is crushed in the family circle."[35]

Educator John Dewey would have solved this dilemma by having every student in Los Angeles study and experience literature, industry, the arts, biology, and history because "it is the office of the school environment . . . to see that each individual gets an opportunity to escape from the limitation of the social group in which he was born." In Los Angeles itself, however, public education stressed vocational education for Mexicans, as did most immigrant and working-class schools, because the business of America's schools was business. In the 1920s three of Los Angeles's thirty-one high schools offered virtually all of the city's vocational courses, and two of these schools were predominantly Mexican. Ever vigilant and calculating about their labor needs, representatives of the Chamber of Commerce formed a committee with school board officials to resolve vocational education issues, which met regularly beginning in 1922, though it is unclear for how long. "Teachers and business people are alike in building the future," stated an 1923 article in the *Los Angeles School Journal*. "Such cooperation as exists in Los Angeles is a long step toward an amalgamation of education and life."[36]

In Los Angeles's early years as an American city, schooling was rudimentary and bilingual. In the 1880s the schools celebrated both American holidays and Mexican Independence Day. But by the years around World War I the practice of, and Anglo community pressure for, segregation had become considerable, especially in rural areas of the county. In 1913 the Pasadena PTA suggested to the school board that a separate Mexican school would be in order, and the board responded with a well-equipped school for Mexican children. In 1914 the schools in the agricultural Orange County community of Santa Ana responded to similar insistence and put Mexican kids in separate classrooms, a practice that foreshadowed a more thoroughly segregated system there. In Orange County, and virtually all of the other agricultural communities, the material consequence of segregated Mexican schools meant decided inferiority in equipment, buildings, staffing, services, and performance of the students. In the late 1920s Lexington, the Mexican school in El Monte (which was 20 percent Japanese), enrolled 39 to 45 students in its early grades, whereas the school for Anglos had 23 to 32 in its early grades. Although Mexicans made up about 40 percent of students in the segregated grades one through four, they numbered only 17 percent in the nominally integrated grades five through eight, and, as the drop-out rate accelerated, only 7.7 percent of those who graduated from eighth grade. At Owensmouth, in the San Fernando Valley, the Los Angeles school board at first resisted community determination to segregate Mexican children. But then, in 1923, when the Chamber of Commerce, Merchant's Association, Women's Club, PTA, and American Legion post donated the land for a separate school, the board caved in. Usually, though, the Los Angeles board resisted de jure segregation. The superintendent said that a 1931 bill in the state legislature to legalize segregation was "un-American," and the board president averred that the schools should serve "the children of all residents of race, color or creed." Most of the pressure for segregation emanated from a fearful, lumpen middle class trying to thwart the enlightened liberals' efforts to elevate the Mexicans. Although the americanos were not of one mind about the matter, school boards in areas surrounding Los Angeles usually and quickly acquiesced to their voting taxpayers' demands.[37]

Proponents of segregation usually argued that it served to bring attention to Mexicans' special problems, that Mexicans would "acquire confidence in their abilities" if they were not mixed with advanced students, and especially that it would help them learn English. Really, though, such arguments masked Anglos fears about their children mingling with Mexicans; parents worried that their children would "catch diseases" and the like. A retired teacher from just east of Los Angeles stated, "I attended every one of those [meetings] about segregated schools. . . . We spent our time listening to citizens' delegations and parents' petitions, all to the effect that they didn't want their children in the same schools with dirty, ignorant foreigners."[38] Realistically, too, Mexican children were not going to learn English or "American" ways surrounded by only Spanish speakers and a few Japanese kids.

This is not to say that urban Los Angeles districts aimed for nothing but little melting pot schools. Reflecting both policy and residential patterns, much de facto segregation prevailed. Los Angeles founded "neighborhood schools" in the early 1920s that served the children of Mexican districts: enrollments reached 80 percent or more Mexican in the barrios. These schools primarily functioned within the overall concept of Americanization, especially in teaching English. But it is impossible to conclude that such segregation characterized the overall educational experience of Mexican children. In the following chapter the reader will encounter a brief volley of statistics showing that Mexicans attended a variety of schools, ranging from some in which their numbers were minuscule to others where they represented the overwhelming majority.

Like all "systems," American society has acted to reproduce itself.

Thus the primary instrument of social reproduction, the public school, endeavored to socialize and specialize its charges, especially its immigrant ones. The public school promised to create social order out of the apparent and fearful chaos of the United States' immigrant metropolises. Alien children learning English nicely ordered in a classroom under the tutelage of a trained pedagogical specialist proved attractive to anxious Protestants. Thus these neighborhood and Mexican schools sought not to make of the Mexicans full-fledged Americans, but to fit them into the United States by deleting their objectionable traits (especially their language) and tailoring their skills to correspond to what would be useful for them as workers and to industry. And these schools did all of this with their particular notions about hierarchies of the races and individual intelligence and about the advancement through history that different cultures had or had not made.

Integrationists and segregationists, in other words, often had the same goal—"Americanization"—but differed on how to achieve it. This is why, besides residential patterns, both strategies could exist simultaneously. And why some Mexican students sat in ethnically mixed classrooms and others did not. The common places, though—the playgrounds, sports fields, home economics and shop classes, eating areas, and homerooms—were surely remarkable arenas for rubbing elbows, for comparing fashions, for wondering about other people, for just looking.

SCIENCE AND MEXICANS

In much the same way that it had validated nineteenth-century social hierarchies, science, in the form of the intelligence test, arrived on the scene and helped to resolve this messy dispute over where to put Mexican students. This whole notion of intelligence proved intriguing and useful for social scientists in the decades after the turn of the century. It related not only to certain individuals' and groups' capacities for learning, but also to social and political hierarchies because it created a sense of the mentally superior few and the inferior many. "Intelligence" and "the intelligent" replaced the earlier Anglo-American notions of "hard work" and "the people" as what explained, respectively, economic success and who should rule politics. Intelligence was innate to a person and, significantly, inheritable, that is, passed down from generation to generation. It was also measurable: hence the famous "Intelligence Quotient," or IQ, test.

Although Alfred Binet originated the IQ test at the Sorbonne in France at the turn of the twentieth century, its American application germinated quite close to this area of México de afuera, at Stanford University. Binet, who understood that intelligence was multifaceted and actually not quantifiable, intended that his scales should be used only to identify the specific shortcomings of children making inadequate progress in school, with the goal of giving them special attention. Ironically, and with great consequences, Stanford professor Lewis M. Terman, primary popularizer of the IQ test in American schools, transformed the test into an instrument for identifying, numerically measuring, and categorizing levels of intelligence on a much larger scale. Portentously, Terman's Stanford-Binet test, marketed to thousands of school districts for millions of dollars in the decades after World War I, promised to measure cognitive ability so that school administrators could effectively sort students into curricula appropriate to their intelligence levels. The outcome would be efficient training of students for the society: those who performed poorly on these objective tests would best not waste their or society's time and resources on an advanced or a multifaceted education. The educational system would simply direct people with different intellectual capacities to their appropriate station in life—owners, managers, professionals, and political elites on the one hand and workers and political subordinates on the other.

We should not be surprised at all to learn that Professor Terman mixed profoundly racial thinking with his science. In 1916, noting the frequency with which certain children scored between 70 and 80, he explained,

> Among laboring men and servant girls there are thousands like them. . . . The tests have told the truth. These boys are uneducable beyond the merest rudiments of training. No amount of school instruction will ever make them intelligent voters or capable citizens. They represent the level of intelligence which is very, very common among Spanish-Indian and Mexican families of the Southwest and also among negroes. Their dullness seems to be racial, or at least inherent in the family stocks from which they came. . . . Children of this group should be segregated in special classes and be given instruction which is concrete and practical. They cannot master abstractions, but they can often be made efficient workers, able to look out for themselves.

Thus did Terman set the stage for Mexican children's interaction with the IQ test.[39]

Other scholars extended the vision. One West Coast professor, writing in 1924, stood "firmly on the ground that the cause of school difficulties must be found in the more innate intellectual differences." He affirmed that Mexicans tended to score in the high seventies on "very scientific" IQ tests, though he hedged on the degree to which the environment or natural ability was responsible. Either way "the truth remains that the mass of the Southern European immigrants of Southern Italian, Portuguese and Spanish extraction, and the Mexican immigrant from our neighboring republic bring us retarded material which the public schools have to handle." "Then," because of the issue of heredity, "the educational policy, even with the restriction of immigration, would have to continue in a modified form to care for the on-coming generations from these inferior stocks."[40]

A report that the Los Angeles City Schools' Department of Psychology and Educational Research published in 1931, a study typical of ones done in other places in the United States with non-Anglo children, found that Mexicans scored IQs 14 points below those of whites and that 48 percent scored below 90, which qualified them for programs designed for what were variously termed the "retarded" or "slow learners." Such systematic studies suffuse academic and school journals of the 1920s and 1930s.[41]

Now, indeed, one finds much diversity within humankind regarding cognitive abilities, just as one does regarding muscularity and the emotions. There is, however, overwhelming evidence that the so-called races that compose the human family have the same intellectual and moral capacities. There are, in other words, explanations more logical than race for why Mexican kids scored poorly on the IQ tests. The inability of a non–English speaker to read and understand the tests is the first consideration that comes to mind, but factors related to socioeconomic background (such as the availability and use of books in the home), the gearing of the test toward the information certain cultures believe to be important, and what sort of knowledge different parents have instilled in their children also explain such discrepancies. Anyway, it is inherent in the use of such rank-order norms that half of the students will always be "below average"—the outcome, in other words, is predetermined. The cultural biases in the trivial test tasks decide which peoples will be on the bottom end. But in the context of the emerging American reverence for science in the era, the IQ test provided conclusive proof of the inferiority of non–Northern European peoples, a mind-set with profound consequences for Mexican students in the Southwest.

The fuzzy and contradictory thinking here emerged from efforts to invoke science to confirm and explain a social hierarchy that derived not from the natural evolution of the species, but from the human-constructed evolution of such history as that of "the dusky workmen." It was not so much bad science as it was a dubious and shady effort to legitimate the social order via the public's increasing credulity about conclusions that bore the imprimatur of science. This notion of "retarded," a defining one in the school careers of non-assimilated Mexican students, must be seen in this well-muddled framework.

School authorities placed Mexican students in special classes for the retarded, delinquent, and so on three times out of proportion to their numbers. Doing so proceeded from the same logic as segregating them: what administrators initially and often reluctantly did to placate Anglo community members, they regularly did by the late 1920s for what they considered sound pedagogical purposes. The IQ test warranted and sanctioned these actions. The word "retarded," though, has carried ambiguous connotations. The district superintendent of the El Monte schools quite plausibly explained in 1930 that it referred to "a pupil who fails to make normal progress" and that the causes may include "illness, irregular attendance, lack of native ability, entering school late, lack of parental interest, and physical handicaps." But, then, an entire group may be retarded, for these reasons: "First, a language handicap. . . . Second, poor or faulty instruction on the part of the teacher. . . . Third, seasonal labor may take many from place to place. . . . Fourth, lack of native ability on the part of certain races and classes of pupils." Thus nearly all Mexican schoolchildren in grades one through four in El Monte were classified as "retarded."[42]

The efforts to educate the Mexicans proceeded in confused, contradictory ways. On the one hand, it was a good idea for Mexican children to be exposed to as much of the American circumstance as possible. On the other hand, sequestering them in vocational classes and "Mexican schools" negated the original assimilationist goal of sending them to the common school. On no account were Mexican children to receive an education that prepared them for participation in the American political system, Progressive Era reforms having swept away such nineteenth-century notions as "training for citizenship" for the masses of ordinary kids whom the public schools had come to serve. "Democracy" for the Progressive Era school reformers, and for those who followed, implied that everyone should have the opportunity to apply their talents for the good of industrial society and to maintain social order and etiquette by internalized and voluntary allegiance to law and (Yankee Protestant) convention. Participation in, and the practice of, politics were for the "intelligent," for the "better stocks," who knew what was

best both for the commonweal and for those "certain races" less culturally and economically advanced than they.

The teachers and administrators of the Mexican students of Southern California combined an impressive, sometimes contradictory, series
of assumptions as they approached their Mexican students. We must
always first be aware of their optimism and assurance about their vision of a socially and economically efficient society: it was one in which
reigned hierarchies based on race and gender, which scientific tests validated. Many of the school men and women then proceeded with a willingness to help their students fit into this system. This they did with their
own culture's confidence, test results, and ethnocentrism, particularly in
its assumptions about the role that Mexicans would play in the Southwest. A girl should be taught "household economics while she is still in
the grades," stated the principal of a Mexican school in Santa Ana, "and
this course should be of such a practical nature as can be made to apply
to the needs and economic condition of a home where there is a large
family to be supported on a laboring man's irregular daily wage." The
schools sought to substitute their own authority for that of the girl's
mother: "The Mexican mother is so tied down with her many babies
and the regular round of housework," the principal continued, "and she
contacts American homes so little that she has no opportunity to learn
American methods of cooking, sewing, buying, and housekeeping, so that
she is entirely incapable of helping her growing daughter to gain this
knowledge."[43]

Mexican mothers knew how to sew and cook as well as any woman
from the lower classes. The problem was, in the schools' collective mind-
set, that they sewed the wrong way—for ornamentation—and cooked
the wrong food. Likely, the intricacies of buying food in the marketplace perplexed people accustomed to producing or bartering for their
subsistence. The Santa Ana school principal proffered the Mexican girls
some important help. But what we see here is the de-skilling of Mexican women, intended or not, and then re-skilling them as housewives
whose function was to support a laboring man and his children on an
irregular daily wage: in other words, to reproduce the cheap labor supply efficiently. "It seems to me," stated a teacher, "that all or most all of
[a Mexican girl's] junior high school training should be directed toward
making her a better wife, mother, and homemaker." Obviously, many
Mexicans lived in dismal poverty and the schools would solve, or salve,
any potential tension that might have resulted by retraining the future
mothers of Mexican America. "They need most, as I see it," stated a

Los Angeles teacher, "the following: hygiene and sanitation, child care, home economy."[44] The Mexicans presumably occupied a dead end in the labor market, but the schools, through training in efficiency, would make their lives bearable, or at least less repugnant to Protestant sensibilities.

In 1915 the California legislature prodded the schools to take a more active role in these matters when it passed the Home Teacher Act. In an experimental program in 1917 the Los Angeles school board established a program, with funding from the State Commission of Immigration and Housing, to teach foreign-born women English, sewing, preserving, Americanization, and such specifics as the "proper care of milk." According to the commission, "with women in her poor home there are few points of contact with educational opportunity." Such a measure, then, sought not only to elevate poor immigrant women and their families but to include them in American civil society, or from another point of view, further extend over them the power of the state: visiting teachers would "connect these mothers with the public schools and our civic life."[45] Likely in tune with Victorian notions of women's greater "sensibility" (understood as sensitivity to sensory stimuli), authorities foresaw that mothers would be most open to ingesting the ways of the reformers.

Anglo young women who were recent or near-graduates of the Los Angeles State Normal School taught the classes at either a local school or a settlement house and supplemented that instruction with home visits. Ann Street Elementary School in 1919 offered such classes five nights per week. The teachers emphasized English, but they offered a movie on Friday nights and sometimes dances with a jazz band. The local recreation center organized a Mexican Club and the Alegría Club, which assisted in the task of Americanization and held weekly dances as well. The home teacher, Miss Kate Bassett, brought lessons in English, family relations, hygiene, and children's proper diet into homes in the Plaza district. All of these efforts focused on immigrant women as the ones most likely to reflect and effect cultural change.[46]

Educators, reformers, and businessmen agreed about the solution to the Mexican problem. Of course the intractability of children and the enlightenment or dedication of many teachers subverted them, but reformers' prescriptions are nonetheless revealing. "Girls should be trained to become neat and efficient house servants," and "the industrial high school" was the highest level the reformers mentioned to which a Mexican youth could aspire. The most important English words for Mexicans to learn in Merton Hill's proposed Americanization schools also reveal the mind-set in which the Protestant reformers founded them, at least in agricultural areas: "to pick," "to prune," "box," "branch," "clippers or pruning knife." Americanization included neither social mobility nor training for citizenship—sometimes the professed essences of the American educational myth—as it reflected educators' assumptions about how and where allegedly culturally backward people should be integrated into the society and the labor market. A poem in *El Mexicano,* a reformer magazine published in Southern California, reflected the aspirations the reformers had for Mexicans:

America we come to you.
We seek what you can give—
Yes, come and kneel before the Cross,
and 'neath its shadow live.[47]

MEXICANS ON AMERICANIZATION

Mexicans of the era who commented publicly on these matters shrewdly questioned the motivation behind Americanization. In 1920 *El Heraldo de México,* with graciousness befitting its aristocratic demeanor, presciently told how "Courtesy of various educational, political, economic, and social institutions in the United States, our humble editorial department many times has received stylish and well presented pamphlets which deal with a difficult and thorny point which is worthy of study by anyone who values seeing in the events of the present the signs of what will happen in the future." The arrival of shiny brochures proposing Americanization at the offices of this stridently Mexican nationalist, conservative, and Catholic newspaper no doubt piqued some passion. Courteously, however, *El Heraldo* stated editorially "that such movements arise from impulses that are patriotic and humanitarian, elevating and generous. But this is true only in certain aspects, because if one wants, or if one has thought of, the notion that 'everyone' should think the same, feel the same, work the same, and speak the same, the issue suddenly changes." "What is behind all this?" they mused. "Ill will? Misunderstanding? Mutual ignorance about what the two countries and their peoples value? Racial antagonism? Ethnic, physiological, psychological, social, or developmental differences? Perhaps it is a little of all of these," the editorial diplomatically concluded.[48]

After seven more years of Americanization programs, and with a keener view of the picture, an editorial in *La Opinión* of 1927 understood that "organizations like [the House of Neighborly Services] . . .

which work to improve the Mexicans, act not out of humanitarianism, but for Americanism; neither a feeling of charity nor cultivation guide them but only provincial conformity; they acknowledge as given that Mexicans living here will live near them for their whole lives and they want to bring them closer to their level and make them more fully useful." Americanization, then, has always been a matter of dispute, as these polemics from México de afuera demonstrate.[49]

La Opinión heard how the message of Americanization came broadcasted in assorted ways and from several towers and how it evidenced different impulses. A tract more gentle in tone than some of those discussed above elicited this editorial response: "Do not think that it is simply a sheeting of insults for our nationality. Included are some painful truths, and in all of it we note a humanitarian trend to help us and to raise us to a level which, according to their manner of understanding things, corresponds neither to the century nor to the means of the immigrants whose health we are here toasting." In this pamphlet, "some exaggerations, some flimsy interpretations, have slipped through; but there is not this biliously hostile tone as in the other cases where we have been discussed." Speaking only to those of México de afuera, the editorial then disclosed, "If when the American calls us irremediably inferior, we become indignant; when, like in the [brochure's] paragraph just transcribed, [he] refers to us as likely capable of abilities not reached in our own country and offers to help us reach them, we become sad, a wave of shame rises to our face." To comprehend this statement, we must understand both the general context of the extensive turmoil in Mexico, and the specific one of the bloody Cristero Revolt, which the editorial spoke of: "While they [the Americans] go gathering resources to offer the children of peons an ample education, in Mexico we close our schools under the pretext that they are making religious fanatics." "We exalt our pride, [and] our love of country that we should like to see strong, cultivated, and healthy," but the American educators' assessments of the need for uplift through education punctured tender tissue: "the estimations of this school master have painfully taken away our dignity; and nevertheless we cannot protest, because he has not stated falsehoods."[50] The transmission and reception of educational reform have been fraught with many difficult emotions and opinions.

Yet, until recently, accounts written from the middle-class Protestant perspective, which simply congratulated these endeavors to elevate needy immigrants from cultures considered substandard, held sway over discussions of the matter. The public debate between the two cultures has been a bit like the sports described in a 1942 study of Los Angeles high schools: "The athletic contests that take place between the 'Mexican' schools and the 'American' schools become almost international competitions for the honor of the race."[51] Such matters are inescapably more complex.

MEXICANS AND THE SOCIAL WORK BUREAUCRACY

No doubt most reformers and educators proceeded ignorantly and disdainfully of Mexican culture. Rarely did they critically examine their motives for undertaking reform work; thus their actions and words often bespoke more about them and what they found distasteful (boxing and spicy food, for example) than about their objects of redemption. Moreover, educators' goals for Mexicans in Los Angeles reflected broader liberal sentiments about the role of education in America. As president of Princeton University, Woodrow Wilson earnestly advised the Federation of High School Teachers: "We want one class of persons to have a liberal education and we want another class of persons, a very much larger class of necessity in every society, to forgo the privilege of a liberal education and fit themselves to perform specific manual tasks." In the 1920s what was good for business was good not only for America but for Mexican immigrants as well. Many reformers and educators engaged in social engineering that reflected the interests of business and helped mesh the needs of industry for a rationally stratified labor force with notions of ethnicity, race, and the rectification of immigrant cultures. Sometimes reformers' compassion for the Mexicans took them in unexpected directions, as when the Methodist Church spoke out against police violence at a strike of Mexican pickers in Venice, California, in 1936. This action prompted the police chief to claim the Methodists had "been captured by the Communist Party" and to write the Merchants and Manufacturers Association, "[I] ask you to withdraw your support from the Methodist Church, and to urge your friends, relatives, and employees to do likewise."[52] Then, too, the reformers brought the Mexicans good and useful things, ones that would make their lives, and especially their children's, much better. But these matters of the children and family life of México de afuera will be the subject of the next chapter.

Again, the point must be made that being Mexican had little more to do with these problems to which the reformers attended than did the fact that they were poor people. The point could also be made that if Mexicans had been paid enough to buy their own milk and more salubrious living quarters, they would not have needed such assistance.

There are other difficulties with charity. For one thing, when times are flush people have more money to give to charity, but there is less need. Thus private benevolence seems to suffice. But when times are bad economically there is much less to give, and much greater need. And, indeed, one does not find evidence of any such service organizations assisting Mexicans during the Depression. (Then scarce private and public resources went to "Americans," who had suddenly become more needy.) Charity also suggests the need for pity and rescue. In order to get material support for these sorts of undertakings, which have as much to do with reformers' needs for meaningful activities, the expansion of their worldviews and lifeways, and the elimination of behaviors they find offensive as they do with benevolence, social workers must establish the need for such projects. Their appeals usually have revolved around proving that suffering is worthy of pity. Thus to get private charity or government social services one must appear pitiable, which may make one an object not only of compassion but also of scorn. Becoming pitiful is also part of the process by which one becomes a subject of the authority of social agencies.

In this way middle-class reformers, especially the social workers and school people, sought to replace the old sovereigns (the Church, the Porfiriato, the family patriarchs) with the "professionals" and their institutions—the school, the relief agency, the local government bureaucracy. Such bureaucratization is one of the principal transformations that have brought forth what we usually call "modern life." An ideally legal, rational, and scientific system has been replacing the personalistic and enchanted world of the pre-modern societies. For those who had moved to México de afuera, their interaction with these agencies simultaneously bewildered and attracted them.

The experts mixed pity with an understanding of hygiene; they knew about the value of milk and how to counter tuberculosis and how to help more babies live. But the experts' knowledge had the power to come around and subjugate Mexicans in new ways to the state and various social agencies. I suspect that the Victorian definition of Mexican women as pitiful actually connected with Mexican images about "the wronged woman," associated with veneration of the Virgin of Guadalupe and often based in reality. By no means did all Mexicans relent:

some maintained their opposition to political, economic, and even religious authority; others simply remained oblivious to such cultural intrusions; and there is nothing mutually exclusive about going to the clinic and maintaining allegiance to Mexican culture. Indeed, some Mexicans, described in the showy language of *El Heraldo*, came under the sway of the social agencies of America, "who, like a mother hen, outstretches her wings first to cover her own baby chicks, but who is now trying to cover the baby chicks of another hen."[53]

Again, matters appear to unfold in a confusing and contradictory manner. We have here the fervently anti-statist culture of the Americans, in rhetoric if not always in deed, ardently bringing in its state agencies first to inspect and then to become involved in the private lives of its residents. Certainly the private actions of Mexicans, and other poor people, had social consequences—health services, population pressures, contagion, and labor strikes all have public costs, for better or for worse. Another function of racism, though, and presuppositions about class is that they have allowed the state to contradict its expressed values about laissez-faire and cultural pluralism in order to regulate the poor and to engineer working people's lives to the benefit of industry. Almost all governments have derived legitimacy from punishing people who have committed harmful acts toward persons and property. With racial thinking that designated the Mexican as contagious, revolutionary, retarded, or otherwise dangerous, however, governments could have rights over Mexicans based not on anything that they actually had done, but on their potential to harm society. Since these ominous traits seemed in the americano mind to be part of the Mexicans' nature—in their blood— social agencies aimed programs and sanctions at them to counter a putative threat rather than any actual transgressions of law. In the old ways, the state attended mostly to criminal acts. This is one way the modern state, with its rhetoric of life, liberty, and the pursuit of happiness, imposes in new ways on individuals whose alleged menace to society derives not from their deeds but from characteristics, sometimes real but usually imagined, of their nature.[54]

It is difficult to gauge the success of the reformers with respect to Americanization. Certainly the efforts in the area of health and infant mortality, in cooperation with county health agencies, achieved meaningful success. Thousands of Mexicans, especially the youth, had some interaction with the Protestant missions and settlements. But how much these organizations succeeded in Protestantizing Mexicans cannot be told precisely and concretely. (There is no evidence that the boys' enthusiasm for boxing waned.) Certainly Catholicism remained the primary influence in Mexicans' spiritual lives, in spite of the coldness of the Church and anti-clerical sentiment remaining from the Mexican Revolution.

When a Mexican male did become Protestant, he allegedly became "socially and economically . . . a changed man. He no longer squanders his pay in drink and gambling and therefore is now able to dress better and to provide more adequately for the care of his family," at least according to one Mexican Baptist minister. We do not know how many became so transformed, but from the impressions gained from the comments of reformers, it appears that Mexican culture and religion proved stronger. (*El Heraldo* noted in 1920 about that greatest of Protestant victories over Catholic immigrant cultures—Prohibition—that "since the vigorous enforcement of the prohibition against alcohol, the Mexican workers have gained in efficiency and the majority of them earn from five dollars and up." The functioning of the labor market would quickly betray their optimism when it drove wages down, but we see here the interconnections between reform of immigrant cultural habits, evangelizing, and the economy.) "Protestant Mexicans," the above-mentioned minister-reformer stated on the basis of information from Vernon McCombs, the guiding light of Mexican missionary work, "are drawn chiefly from the middle class." Mexican anthropologist Manuel Gamio noted both that "Protestantism [in Mexico] flourishes principally among the middle classes" and that "an opportunity for assuming successful roles in the immigrant community [was] presented to the more educated Mexican by evangelical Protestantism" in the United States. The Baptists, who founded eight Mexican churches by 1932, had the most success in Los Angeles, and the Methodists followed with five churches, and then came various Pentecostal sects. (It was largely the latter's members that attended the Misión Mexicana Aimee Semple McPherson.) Conversion distanced Protestant Mexicans from the rest of the mexicanos de afuera. Often called "allelujahs," their enthusiastic church services were objects of at least curiosity, if not outright derision. It appears that the Protestants had major success only with Mexican children, with those who either achieved or aspired to middle-class status, and with those that many Mexicans thought of as strange.[55]

Efforts at missionization tend to fail. This apparent fact of life stems from both the resilience of the culture that faces conversion and the ambivalence of the converters about the heathens. Mexicans no doubt heard the condescension in their uplifters' voices. They also heard the meanness of those in the dominant culture who wanted not to transform the

Mexicans but to exclude them. Many Mexicans, thus, feared getting too close to these aspects of americano culture. Surely, the americanos' culture held some attraction: it was powerful in war and the control of production; it had a lot of comforts and "things"; and, tussles with the law notwithstanding, the United States was a much more peaceful place than Mexico. Yet, admission to American society (which was rarely actually forthcoming anyway) would cost the Mexicans' beliefs, culture, and familial authority. The male adults, at least, usually responded with apathy to the Americanization efforts and to the schools. The educational institutions did not bring Mexicans into the Anglo materialist world so much as did American popular culture, a complex subject to which we shall turn in the following chapter.

The efforts at Americanization, while providing many benefits to Los Angeles Mexicans in the areas of health and social services, also paralleled and reinforced the integration and control of Mexican workers in the economic structure by attempting to inculcate in them a Protestant worldview, albeit usually unsuccessfully. Americanization and education provided the nexus between the industrial demands for control that George Clements outlined and the demands for social control by Anglo culture over the threatening "alien" culture of the Mexican workers. Together they created the backdrop against which those who dominated Los Angeles perceived Mexican labor.

Nevertheless, education and Americanization proved insufficient. Force would be used to maintain the social and economic hierarchy that Anglo Americans acquired from their California predecessors through the mechanisms of war (1846–48) and then sealed through terror in the decades immediately following. Time and time again the Los Angeles police arrested Mexican political activists, particularly if they were associated with anarchists. We must remember that at this time Los Angeles immigrants found Mexican politics much more compelling than issues north of the border. In June 1911 the office of *Regeneración* was raided and the PLM leadership was arrested for neither the first nor the last time. On Christmas Day 1913 in La Placita, police agents assassinated IWW activist Rafael Adame. Three Plaza speakers were jailed in the Cinco de Mayo celebrations of 1917. At the time of Villa's raid, the chief of police tripled the patrol in Sonoratown and outlawed the sale of alcohol and guns to Mexicans. In the northern part of the state, Mexicans, among myriad others, revolted against an employer who advertised for more workers than he needed to keep wages down and on whose ranch working children lived "in unspeakably filthy condition."

Here, in the famous Wheatland riot of August 1913, Governor Hiram Johnson crushed the IWW-led strikers with five militia units. The agricultural strikes that hit the southern counties in 1919 (San Gabriel), 1928 (Imperial Valley), and in 1935 and 1936 (Orange County and Venice)—to name only those about which we will hear more later—underwent similar military solutions. Typically charging bolshevism, the courts issued injunctions against picketing and interfering with strikebreakers, and then the police clubbed the strikers and arrested the militants and held them until the crops were harvested.[56] Often suasion and necessity proved insufficient to bind Mexicans to the labor markets. Then the force and the violence, which always lurked behind that market, reforged the chains that indentured workers of color in the fields and factories of California, where the ideology of "industrial freedom" prevailed.

ADIÓS JOSÉ Y MARÍA: THE REPATRIATION DRIVES OF 1931

Then, in a magnificent reversal of everything that had emerged from the history of Mexican California, those who so complimented, if not in many aspects created, the American standard of living by putting inexpensive fruits and vegetables on the nation's tables, cheaply building the transportation system, and so on, now stood blamed for undermining that standard of living and were then banished back, south of the border. Whites in Southern California were themselves often cast from the ranks of the employed during the Depression, but they usually responded with the explanation that Mexicans took jobs that rightly belonged to "Americans." After the market so dramatically foundered in its allocation of goods and jobs in late 1929, Anglo Americans came to blame Mexicans rather than the innate fluctuations of the economic system for their misery. Gringos from Herbert Hoover and his secretary of labor to the publishers of the *Los Angeles Times* to the local coordinator of unemployment relief, Charles P. Visel, all urged the repatriation of Mexicans. "If we were rid of the aliens who have entered the country illegally since 1931 . . . ," explained County Supervisor John R. Quinn,

> our present unemployment problem would shrink to the proportions of a relatively unimportant flat spot in business. In ridding ourselves of the criminally undesirable alien we will put an end to a large part of our crime and law enforcement problem, probably saving many good American lives and certainly millions of dollars for law enforcement against people who have no business in this country.

(Yet, while Labor Secretary Doak thought that deportation had the added benefit of "hastening the day when our population shall be more homogeneous," the Chamber of Commerce demurred from adding to the hysteria that threatened its labor supply.) The press often referred to Mexicans, regardless of their resident status, simply as "aliens," and sensationalized Mexican crime.[57]

Many residents of México de afuera, tied to Los Angeles primarily by the jobs there, began packing for a return to the interior. Such had been the practice during downturns like the one in 1921, when nearly 100,000 from México de afuera returned; a trickle back could even be detected as the economy started slowing in 1927. Since, as we have seen, labor migration formed so many of the colonias of México de afuera, it makes sense that the colonias would experience some depopulation when the demand for labor dramatically diminished. Mexican authorities such as Consul Rafael de la Colina even welcomed the opportunity to encourage Mexico's evanescent sons and daughters to return home to the mother country. Colina helped the Comité de Beneficencia Mexicana to organize a gala, which included Ramon Novarro, Virginia Fabregas, and Will Rogers, at the Philharmonic Auditorium in February 1931. The successful benefit raised money to relieve destitute elements of the Los Angeles colonia and earthquake victims in Oaxaca and to buy transportation for those of la raza who wished to return south of the border. Perhaps 1,500 boarded trains for Mexico in April and May with tickets that the comité had funded.[58]

No doubt similarities existed between the decision to go back and the one to come up in the first place. People acted to survive and to continue in a context in which their own degree of choice and volition varied greatly. People without access to means of subsistence, in México de afuera or the interior, cannot be considered free to act in history. People in such predicaments have indeed been those most like "the swallows at the old mission," caught in the sometimes convulsive, sometimes clement, current of forces well beyond their control or even comprehension. Many repatriated in 1917 when rumors flew that male sojourners were eligible for the draft, although actually only those very few who had taken out "first papers" for citizenship faced service. In the early 1930s case workers at relief agencies often suggested that an applicant might be more content in Mexico, or threatened the cutting of relief or even deportation. In 1931 the state of California passed legislation forbidding contractors from employing Mexicans and other "aliens" on public jobs, although such pick and shovel work had long been their acknowledged domain. Municipalities passed ordinances restricting work on public improvements to citizens. Informal nativist pressures encouraged preferential hiring for "Americans"; unemployment always had dogged Mexicans, and during the Depression more and more people competed for fewer and fewer jobs. The conglomeration of all these factors persuaded or convinced or forced many Mexicans to repatriate.[59]

For those who wanted to go, repatriation was a free ride back to the interior, but for others it involved arrest and forceful deportation. Most fell in between, with ambivalent and contradictory emotions prevailing. For families whose members had rooted themselves, to widely varying degrees, in the new place, repatriation became a dramatic human saga. As in the irrigated mono-crop fields of the Southwest, where the natural flora had become weeds, Mexicans whose labors had built those fields in their homeland's former territories now had to be weeded out.

The *desocupados* and *cesantes,* whom the police called vagrants, sometimes found themselves swept up from the Plaza or Pershing Square and jailed, even during the allegedly prosperous 1920s. In January 1931, however, local and federal authorities initiated a coordinated effort to round up and deport "illegals." Welfare costs would be lowered, jobs would be preserved for Americans, and the (newly) white complexion of Los Angeles, and other sites where México de afuera had been growing, would be restored. The year 1931 was a fearful one for la raza in Los Angeles: the racial thinking that motivated the dragnets meant that anyone who looked Mexican to the authorities could be snared, regardless of his or her rootedness in the north or affinity for old Mexico. Public places that Mexicans customarily frequented became dangerous. Recall the vagaries of establishing residence in the days before the border patrol and the immigration acts: although those who had established residence technically had little to fear, hyperbole in both the Spanish- and English-language presses fanned the fears of all of la gente: "11 Mexicanos Presos en un Aparatoso Raid a la Placita" blared the headline of La Opinión on February 27, 1931. (Police also detained five Chinese and a Japanese.) Nine of the Mexicans were released. Parallel raids in El Monte and East Los Angeles, which produced much excitement in the press, afforded a similarly meager weeding of deportables. The significance most likely lies in the fact that authorities detained and questioned 3,000 to 4,000 people in February and March 1931. Residents of México de afuera were singled out for discriminatory treatment based on their being Mexican, and streets in Mexican districts—to the terrific alarm of merchants—were cleared of pedestrian traffic. The preposterousness of the actions, that they culled only 259 illegal aliens, and merchants' protests convinced the authorities to suspend the raids on March 7.[60]

The nasty commotion of the raids should not overshadow the equivocality of the issue. Several forces from several directions pulled on those who considered repatriation: official Mexican government policy supported reversing the migration of its most productive workers, especially those who had assimilated some Yankee work habits. The land of the gringos, its relative peace and material comforts notwithstanding, grew increasingly alien and forbidding. There have been strong hints in this narrative, ones that will further unfold, that children and youth much preferred the abundance and personal freedoms in the north, that mothers cherished the milk and schools for their children, but that fathers often resented the challenges to their customary authority that cultural aspects of city life presented. This often profound ambivalence of those in México de afuera about repatriating matched in complexity the above-mentioned issue about people's autonomy as they acted in history. Thus, citing government statistics that 13,332 from Los Angeles County returned to Mexico on sixteen trains between March 1931 and April 1934 obscures more than it illuminates.[61]

In any case, if we include those who left on their own, more like 35,000, or one-third of the Mexicans in Los Angeles, repatriated to Mexico. Mexicans loaded on trains (from the Southern Pacific, ironically, with whom the consulate had arranged a discount on the fare to El Paso) and headed south to solve the problems of the Depression. Local governments paid their fares to the border, where Mexico, glad to welcome its erstwhile sons and daughters home, provided transportation to their hometowns. The savings in relief costs were joyfully counted, while families were split, most painfully when children and teenagers born and rooted in the United States accompanied their less-attached fathers back to Mexico. Repatriation neither ended the Depression, nor engaged energetic, industrious workers in the cause of rebuilding Mexico, nor brought happiness to those who replanted themselves in la madre patria.

The market may well have pushed people out of the north, but it did not guide them back to those places in Mexico where they could most effectively put to use their labor. Considerations of place and kin prevailed, and people moved back to the old villages, where subsistence was no easier than it had been when they had first left. Some few made the labor migration system work: they turned their savings into capital. "Now I own a house and two trucks," said a *repatriado* in Jalisco; "I was a laborer here, and never could have bought trucks here." Others took their cash and purchased land, farm animals, tools, or businesses that could earn them a living. For the most part, though, periods of unemployment and expenditures for food, clothing, and the "things" and pleasures of the americano city had dissipated their money. A family or an individual might have arrived back in the old village with a phonograph, nice clothes, or even an automobile. These things were not capital, though, and could not be put to productive or effective use. These few commodities wore out and could not be fixed in undeveloped Mexico. So people came back north. "Repatriation was a tragicomic affair," Carey McWilliams sagely noted: "tragic in the hardships occasioned; comic because most of the Mexicans eventually returned to Los Angeles, having had a trip to Mexico at the expense of the county." The labor market needed some adjusting outside of its "natural workings," and many Mexicans had to get on the trains.[62]

CALIFORNIA PASTORAL AND RACIAL THINKING

While the Mexicans boarded the trains at Union Pacific Station just off the old Plaza, the cultural and economic elites of Los Angeles readied for the celebration of the 150th anniversary of the founding of the city. Organizers of the festivities—none had Spanish surnames—recalled the re-created Spanish past, and phone operators at City Hall cheerily answered "Buenos Días" for the occasion.[63] It is often said that Anglo Americans, owing to their activist attitude toward the present and the future, care little for history. Like the Fiesta Days, celebrations of the little Spanish pueblo's founding in 1781 attest to an actually intense and heartfelt interest in history. This pursuit never considered a candid exploration of the past, but instead proceeded from a curious set of emotional needs of the present. It may seem a bit incongruous to place this discussion of the remaking of California history and racial thinking here, but the central features of Anglo-Angeleno thought about Mexican people and culture are important. How, in other words, their understanding of history, culture, and race framed their interactions with Mexicans in the City of the Angels.

Actually, there was a lot of Spanish-named stuff around the city. Housing subdivisions built in the 1920s and streets carried names like Casas de Vista Gloriosa, New Granada, Rancho Malibu La Costa, or even the Streets of Old Monterey. One commentator wrote in 1931 about Olvera Street right off the Plaza: "It has been referred to as a 'bit of Old Mexico' in the heart of Los Angeles, but it is serves as more than a mere novelty; it is part of a movement to preserve the beauty of the olden days of California and a step toward the improvement of the district surrounding the Plaza." She allowed, though, that some Mexicans had criticized it "because it is not a replica of any street in Mexico." Whether it be for the promotion of tourism or the sale of "candied fruits, orange juice, candies, clothing, furniture, and many other California products . . . almost invariably there will be something Spanish mentioned in the advertisement. It may be a large picture of a dancing señorita or a tiny picture of one of the missions but it is there because it represents one of the most important attractions of the state." "Then of course there are the Mission Play at San Gabriel and the Ramona Pageant at San Joaquin and Hemet."[64]

The creation of Old California, like the Old South, provided those in the present with "a legend of incalculable potentialities."[65] For one thing it kept hidden the contradiction, obvious to us now, between saying foul things about Mexicans and deporting them from Los Angeles, on the one hand, and celebrating those mestizo Mexicans' ancestors, who first came to the Río Porciúncula and founded Los Angeles, on the other. Then, too, it allowed Californians to pursue and worship their dollars with typical capitalist disregard for human attachments. California "Pastoral" also gave the sojourners from the East a rootedness in their new land.

An Anglo immigrant to the place first probed the bathos of the "fantasy heritage" of the "Spanish" Southwest and California. The remarkable Carey McWilliams, who left Denver in 1922 to attend the University of Southern California, unmasked the "schizoid" nature of the Spanish and Mexican-Indian past.*[66] What the progenitors of the myth liked in California's past they deemed Spanish; what they found disagreeable, unsuitable, or uncomfortable in the past or present they deemed Mexican. Thus the patrician dons of the rancho era of California history became Spanish (they were largely mestizo ex–army officers), while those defeated in the war that won California for the United States, the impoverished and unhygienic colonias, and the problem of Spanish speak-

---

*Not enough can be said about Carey McWilliams's efforts, as we would say today, "to speak truth to the lies" commonly told about Mexicans and other minorities. His writings have been crucial in recasting the ideas of many americanos about Mexicans and field workers. Dr. Clements hated McWilliams and said of his pathbreaking *Factories in the Field:* it is "so grossly incorrect and misleading that it has no historical value whatever. It should be returned to the garbage can from whence it emanated."

ers in the schools were called Mexican. The reconstruction of California's history centered around the genteel rancheros, whose fiestas the americanos now imitated, and the resuscitation of the missions, which purveyed the appropriate relationship between European civilization and non-whites. Each notion had important bearing upon Mexican Los Angeles in at least the first six decades of the twentieth century.

Rituals such as the *Rancheros Visitadores* and the Fiesta Days simultaneously fed the emotional needs of some Anglo Protestants and cheated Mexicans of their historical legacy upon the Southern California landscape. Both ceremonies celebrate the non-market social relations that often actually prevailed in old California. Saints' days, Mexican national holidays, and especially a daughter's wedding always occasioned a fiesta in which elites shared bounteous quantities of food and drink with relatives, friends, and their laborers. Ideally, consideration of the patriarchal family influenced an individual's actions. The dictates of the Faith, not those of the market, were to guide one's deeds. La gente spent (and in Spanish the infinitive *gastar* means both "to spend" and "to waste") time in visiting. As surely as patriarchy, racism toward the Indians, and hierarchies of power corrupted Californio social relations, these organic and ethereal connections fulfilled part of human nature. Market relations, especially as regards labor, have swept away these economically wasteful attachments and replaced them with the presumptions of *homo economicus.* Then "economic man," often lonely, hungers for the rest of what it means to be human. The creation of California Pastoral in the decades around the turn of the century fed this subconscious craving of the Americans in capitalist Southern California.[67] Perhaps it was gratifying; maybe it was pathetic; and no doubt many americanos considered such celebrations boring or primitive and simply ignored them. But there has not been, nor should there be, any law against myth-making.

This curious relationship with the past, though, had important consequences for Mexican Southern California. It in large part explains why the Mexican immigrants stood as such pelados upon the landscape. It might have seemed from the first chapter here that Mexicans freshly presenced themselves in Los Angeles. Indeed, it is now time for us to rethink some of that episode. Actually, their ancestors had seeded widely in the place; the fantasy history of California had simply cut the new immigrant sprouts at their historical roots. Mexicans were not presencing anew, but presencing again. But being so truncated in the history of the area made it harder for Mexicans to feel much entitlement to what was really not the new land. Or to make claims on the place that was theirs at least as much as it was the Americans'.

And thus for the Americans, only Spanish Californios occupied the land with any validity. And thus Mexicans could be shooed away when the economy contracted.

The train station stands right across from the Plaza of the once inconsequential little pueblo. In the late eighteenth century the missions a few leagues to the east and to the northwest of the town, San Gabriel and San Fernando, and those tens of leagues away, San Buenaventura, Santa Barbara, San Juan Capistrano (from whence came and went the real swallows), and San Luis Rey, had much greater prominence, both for Spain's plans for this distant frontier and in the everyday workings of the place. At first the Americans saw in the missions popery, servitude, and monopoly of land that independent freeholders could put to much more productive use. In many ways they were accurate in their interpretations, but as we saw in the section above about the dusky workmen, the Americans quickly effected their own peculiar notions about faith, control of labor, and land tenure. After 1848 the mission buildings decayed. "A thoughtful man," wrote Charles Nordoff in 1873, "cannot visit these and other old missions . . . without feeling a deep respect for the good men who erected these now ruined churches." The Catholic padres had "gathered around them communities of savages, and patiently taught them not only to worship in a Christian church, but also the habit of labor, the arts of agriculture, and some useful trades." To "the old Dominican [they were Franciscan] friars in a noble work," he continued in a statement challenging in candor the one about the "swallows at the old mission," "Southern California is to-day indebted for a valuable laboring force." In 1888 Charles Fletcher Loomis founded an organization eventually known as the Landmarks Club, which undertook the restoration of the missions. The beautiful old buildings quickly became centerpieces for the promotion of tourism, but they enjoyed a spiritual rebirth as well. My precious *Ramona* figured most prominently in all this as well.[68]

One ad in the *Los Angeles Times* of 1919 trumpeted, "The Classic of the Century, *The Mission Play,* by John Steven McGroarty . . . Sublime with the Soul of California. Joyous with the Music and Songs and Dances of Spain. Gorgeous with Barbaric Indian Splendor. The largest and greatest Dramatic Organization in the World—at—Old San Gabriel Mission." Anglo Californians fed on this mythology until California history became so fatuous that one of its eminent chroniclers could write in 1952:

> It is said that the Indians eagerly looked forward to taking part in this per-
> formance in which the scene of the Nativity was represented. . . . The bells
> rang merrily calling the neophytes. . . . From the choir loft came the clear,
> melodious voices of the Indians, their singing mingling with the sweet, haunt-
> ing music of flutes, violins, bass-viols, and trumpets rendering the old hymns
> and chants taught them by the padres.

Such accounts utterly obfuscated Indian-mission history.[69] A point here,
though, is the exceptional resonance with the rhetoric of the school reformers of the 1920s. Substituting "Mexicans" for "Indians" should
demonstrate the ways in which the re-creation of history served the
Anglo-American approaches to, and designs for, the Mexicans of that
time. We see here, too, the numerous sources from which we must select to draw together our story of Mexicans in twentieth-century Southern California.

Mission history scripted the Americans to view their own mission
with the Mexicans as one in which they would bring the primitives civilization—genuine faith, discipline, and training for work. The neophytes,
though, could never become the equals of the missionaries; they could
only become "useful" within the advanced system. The Los Angeles
Chamber of Commerce's George Clements, a medical doctor, waxed eru-
ditely in a 1927 letter to the governor, "Biologically, the Mexican alien
offers no complications," and he compared the Mexican worker to "the
Porto Rican Negro." The latter "is a hybrid possessing all the bad qualities of his progenitors yet few of the physical identification marks of
the Ethiopian race, being a thin lipped, freckled faced, red-haired and in
many cases light eyed negro, [who] offers a biological menace which we
would hate to contemplate." More than simply reflecting obsolete scientific notions of the nineteenth century, Clements's statements, partly
buffoonish and partly vicious, encapsulated the business class's notions
of Mexicans as workers and as people:

> The Mexican is an Indian and must be considered so. He is undergoing ac-
> tive evolution and we must always take this thought into consideration in
> dealing with him. His wants are few and his habits, while docile, are not in
> harmony with Western Civilization, and he so recognized it and was willing
> to abide by it. To pay him an exorbitant salary only meant to cater to his ex-
> travagance; to pay him a living wage and add to his future comforts seemed
> to be the only way in which to handle him.

It is remarkable that this view, wherein science again attempts to legitimate the social and productive hierarchies, could be articulated as late
as 1939, the date of this memo.[70]

Such thinking meshed quickly and easily with that of the school system and its strategies for dealing with the Mexicans. An assistant supervisor in the Department of Compulsory Education (a mainstay of the IQ test), who had performed special work among Mexicans, worried in the *Los Angeles School Journal* of 1928 about Mexican poverty, and then traced it to the "original raciality of the Mexicans," that is, their "Mongolian descent." "The infusion of Spanish blood into Aztec and Maya veins," he continued, "has latinized later generations since the sixteenth century. The mixture of the two is fundamentally responsible for the carefree, if not indolent, characteristic of the race."[71] We have here not only an unclouded example of how what was "in the blood" explained culture and hierarchy for Americans in positions of authority vis-à-vis Mexicans, but more evidence that affinity for the IQ test has been inversely proportional to the intelligence applied to such social issues as Mexican education.

This Indian history motif often appeared in American racialist explanations about Mexicans' nature. C. M. Goethe, president of the Immigration Study Commission, argued that Spanish guns had destroyed the "intellectual class" of the Aztecs, the warriors, that is, leaving "only the peon slaves, attached to the soil owned by the priestly and warrior castes, which persisted. They were docile then, and they remain docile today." Relying not on impressionistic evidence, he continued, "Intelligence tests made of California school children have shown that the Mexican children are markedly low powered in intellect."[72]

Such convictions, though, derived neither simply from the scientific studies of Clements, the Chamber of Commerce, the Los Angeles school board, or the immigration commissions nor from a conscious justification for exploiting cheap labor on racial grounds. As it did with IQ tests, science, and in this case the history of Indian-European relations in the missions, verified social and economic hierarchies. The scientific method had been reversed: the conclusion, racial hierarchies, came first; and then the hypotheses and evidence—physical and cultural traits, IQs, and an invented history—were assembled in such a manner as to prove the conclusion. Now the economic needs of Anglo enterprise could be met in a way that would appear to be a natural outcome of science, history, and social evolution: the position of the Mexican worker was the one best for all concerned. Knowing and accepting where one fit in this ranking system promised its effective and harmonious functioning.

Recall that in 1903 the Los Angeles Public Library circulated more copies of Theodore Roosevelt's *This Strenuous Life* than any other volume. Now we are ready to hear about the second most sought-after book. Again, according to Miss Darrow, it was "anything by Booker T. Washington, with *Up from Slavery* preferred." This volume by the African Americans' champion of self-help and accommodation reaffirmed for the whites that the American system rewarded those who worked diligently, that hierarchies were therefore natural ones, and that the problems between the races would work themselves out, eventually. The important thing, then, was for people to know their place, and to act accordingly. Washington sought "to dignify and glorify common labor" for his people and affirmed that "agitation of questions of social equality is the extremest folly." Booker T. Washington was a good colored man, in contrast to, for example, those Filipinos: "Many of their people," according to *This Strenuous Life,* "are utterly unfit for self-government, and show no sign of becoming fit." The president did not make himself clear about whether such people's problems owed to "Spanish tyranny," or to the fact that "Their population includes half-caste and native Christians, warlike Moslems, and wild pagans," something dimly "in the blood." Either way he prescribed "wise supervision, at once firm and beneficent," a notion to which Booker T. Washington adhered. All this fabulous racial thinking extended from the history of the missions, to the fields of the Imperial, San Gabriel, and San Fernando Valleys, to America's imperial mission in the Philippines, to the street railway workers at the Fiesta Days. Mexicans needed "a helping and kindly hand," according to a 1928 electric railway industry magazine, if they "were to be counted upon to supply the all-necessary element of brawn so essential in the great building program of this 'world's largest inter-urban system.'"[73]

People were not equal, in other words, as regards their productive vigor, their need for material comforts, their participation in politics, and their moral, intellectual, and leadership capacities. Those most capable people, from Theodore Roosevelt to George Clements to the schoolmen, should lead and guide those with less capacity, and these latter people should submit, work hard, and not try to rise above the natural limits of their abilities. Thus most, but certainly not all, Anglo Americans understood an Indian revolt at a mission, minority demands for political or educational equality, or a labor strike of Mexicans as an attempt to violate the natural order. Such challenges exhibited either such people's inferior judgment or some devilish subversive force leading them astray. The labor structure of Los Angeles and the rest of the Southwest appeared, then, as a natural reflection of California history and of scientific ideas about race as each was understood at the time. It is within this context that we can best understand much about labor in the Southwest and California—who does it, for how much, and why people then resent those who do the work. It also explains why city bureaucrats in 1931 could instruct phone operators to answer "Buenos días" in honor of the anniversary at the same time as they said "¡Adiós!" to the founders' successors from Mexico.

THE MEXICAN LABOR FORCE OF LOS ANGELES

Lots of real Mexicans lived in Southern California, though. Mexicans officially numbered 167,024, or 13.5 percent of Los Angeles County's population of 1,238,048 in 1930. Most of them lived in the central and eastern areas of the city. Urban occupations employed the most by 1930, although close proximity to the fields of eastern Los Angeles meant that many also worked in agriculture at least some of the time. They worked in the garment factories, furniture shops, and myriad other small manufacturing plants in the southern part of the downtown area. Mexicans also lived farther east, in two areas of the San Gabriel Valley, where they labored mostly in agriculture: those in the northern San Gabriel Valley worked the citrus groves of Pasadena, and those in eastern San Gabriel tilled the truck farms around El Monte. Mexicans also lived in the San Fernando Valley, north and west of downtown, where they labored primarily in agriculture, as did those in West Los Angeles in the Culver City and Venice areas. South of downtown some Mexicans still lived in the Watts area. In the Harbor areas Mexicans found employment in occasional harbor jobs and in lumber.[74]

Recently, Chicano historians have statistically validated what most had acknowledged as "Mexican work" all along: dead-end, low paying occupations and harsh working conditions. Richard Griswold del Castillo studied late-nineteenth-century Los Angeles, the era before the big migrations, and concluded, "During the American era, the Mexican American occupational structure was stagnant, with little opportunity for significant upward social mobility." Albert Camarillo has arrived at similar conclusions in his study of Mexicans in Santa Barbara. For the early 1900s, Camarillo shows that "Chicanos remained immobilized within the lowest occupational categories," illustrating "the continuity that existed from the time Chicanos were first incorporated into the labor market during the late nineteenth century." Camarillo found 64.2 percent of Mexicans working in "low blue collar" jobs in 1910, 68.6 percent in 1920, and 68.3 percent in 1930. In addition, Camarillo cites a California labor commissioner who found working "conditions even worse than reported" and "so many children in the orchards that the schools were all but depopulated." Ricardo Romo sampled Los Angeles marriage records for 1917 and 1918 and found that 76.1 percent of Mexicans had semi-skilled or unskilled jobs, though the figures for the third generation were better. This figure compares to 24.7 percent of Anglos who worked in such lowly occupations according to the census of 1920. Using city directories, Pedro Castillo found that 77.5 percent of Mexicans in 1910 and 79.6 percent in 1920 worked in low blue-collar occupations, whereas only 24.7 percent of Anglos did in the latter sample year.[75]

My own study of marriage records for 1936 in the Los Angeles Hall of Records and from the city directories for 1929 and 1934 also attempted to determine what percentage of Los Angeles's total Mexican population in the 1930s worked in unskilled, skilled, and white-collar occupations.[76] Marriage records indicate that 77.5 percent of the men and 85.4 percent of the women (mainly dressmakers and housekeepers) worked in unskilled or semi-skilled jobs.[77] Of the men, only 9.5 percent worked in skilled jobs, and virtually no women did so. Still, about 13.7 percent of all Mexicans could claim white-collar status. We must remember that most of the women workers were without children. Childbearing and child rearing obviously have an effect on female work patterns. The figures from the city directories do not differ significantly from those from the marriage records. The 83.3 percent of Mexicans who worked in unskilled jobs compares to only 21 percent of Anglos for 1929, while the 84.4 percent from the 1934 sample compares to 18.8 percent of Anglos working in the lower echelons of the Los Angeles job market.[78]

This was not really new information. One Los Angeles area colonia surveyed in 1912 had among its 803 male inhabitants two musicians, three cement workers, one blacksmith, one teamster, and one grocer. The other 795 were simply "laborers." In a sample for 1934 and 1935 of ninety-nine Mexican families in Los Angeles, researchers in 1939 found that 56 percent of the families had a semi-skilled wage worker as the chief earner, 29 percent an unskilled worker (85 percent together), 8 percent a skilled worker, and 7 percent a clerical worker. These figures compare to 45 percent of Anglo families who had a clerical worker as chief earner, 17 percent a skilled worker, 28 percent a semi-skilled worker, and 10 percent an unskilled worker. Romo notes how a 1920 study of Mexicans' occupations done by the Interchurch World Movement "was amazingly close" to his own.[79]

All these numbers raise some interesting issues about our relationship to the past. Our pursuit of statistics derives from a concern about what they tell us about our historical subjects as producers, certainly the most important predictor of their status, success, and levels of comfort. Statistics lack precision, of course. In the case at hand we must remember that people moved around a lot, from job to job and place to place. Lots of Mexicans spent only the winter months in the city; they may or may not have been counted in the census or city directory. Even more significant, such data do not include many of the thousands of Mexicans who lived and worked north of the border without the knowledge of the immigration authorities. Estimates range as high as 30 percent of the total for this group. A lot of the time, enumerators did not bother with people they perceived as insignificant. Nonetheless the figures speak clearly to us: though there existed a group of skilled workers and a significant number of white-collar and even middle-class workers, Mexicans overwhelmingly worked at unskilled or semi-skilled occupations. A tautology will actually make this point most clearly: Mexicans worked almost exclusively at "Mexican work." This work, though, efficiently filled important niches in the economy. This picture of Mexicans in the labor market does not arise from a tour de force in the manipulation of statistics or from methodological luck or from fate. Rather, we observe the reality of the market for labor as it meshed with the ability of one country to command the resources, especially the human ones, of another (imperialism) and with its people's constructions of the way the people of that other country had been, should be, and are (racism).

So often these matters seem part of the natural order, but we can usually rely on history to deny immutability. Sometimes fate brings new ways, but more often changes in how production happens—frequently connected with the arrival of foreigners or their capital or both, as we saw in the case of Mexico—alter people's practices. Capitalism can never be static; what we might call "structural changes in the organization of production" always occur. Recall here some of the developments in the economy of Southern California that we saw earlier in this chapter—automobile-associated branch plants moving to the Pacific Coast, garment manufactories producing for a local economy, and the uneven but ever upward thrust of building. In other words, in the history of the American economy of the middle four decades of the twentieth century, tenders of assembly lines and machines replaced gang-style or common laborers as the most typical non-agricultural workers. These changes most directly affected mainstream, or primary-sector, workers, but some minority workers, too, found new opportunities in the new factories. Employers still appreciated Mexicans as casual and gang laborers, but demand for workers who could keenly and precisely attend to industrial production tasks drew a few of the sons and daughters, typically, of Mexican immigrants into new jobs, ones usually called semi-skilled.

No doubt, job prospects for Mexicans were not good in the periods cited above. "Good," of course, is a relative term. Within this lowest strata of the evolving labor structure, Mexicans acted to improve their life and work situations. Steadiness and regularity of work appear to be the most important considerations in job selection—to the extent one could do so—for Mexicans in Southern California. Thus, while Mexicans overwhelmingly worked in the harsh, dead-end, low-paying, and most seasonally volatile areas of the economy, distinctions existed within this secondary sector of the labor market. Other, more informal factors, such as family contacts and personal relationships with employers and foremen, stabilized employment for some Mexican workers in Los Angeles. Urban and industrial work, which the business cycle and seasonal demand too often made undependable, was certainly far less fitful, not to mention less wandering, than agricultural work. Undoubtedly, the length of time spent north of the border contributed to the accumulation of those various factors producing stable work. Camarillo suggests that Mexicans born in the United States fared better on Santa Barbara's street-paving crews than those born in Mexico, though by no means as well as Anglo workers. Ricardo Romo shows that although second-generation Mexican men managed only slightly better than recent immigrants in the job market, many third-generation men achieved the status of skilled jobs. For the years 1917 and 1918, "over 29 percent worked in skilled occupations, while no more than 13 percent of the first-generation group held similar positions." Romo continues that "only 47.7 percent of third-generation laborers were unskilled laborers, as compared to 71 percent of the first generation."[80] Many of these no doubt participated in the evolution of American production's labor needs away from gang labor and toward machine tending. These workers had various skill levels, but they all appear to have achieved a significant measure of stability in their work, and some upward mobility, certainly relative to the patterns of gang labor that prevailed in agriculture and on the railroads. Greater geographic and social stability followed as a consequence. This achievement, a form of social mobility, set some Mexican workers off from the rest, at least as much, I would suggest, as skill levels did. The skill categorization presented in the quantitative data above gives us a picture of an integral and crucial aspect of the structure of the Mexican workforce. But this view of the variation in the stability of work gives us an impression of another factor as crucial to the Mexican work experience as labor market segmentation.

Work stability certainly figured importantly in status and material differences among Mexican workers in Los Angeles. In El Monte, for example, most lived in the impoverished Hick's Camp, but recall those who dwelled there "in comfortable homes . . . where the houses and yards are well kept." Mexican home ownership was not unusual in Los Angeles in the 1920s and 1930s. In 1919, 15.4 percent of Mexicans owned their own homes in the downtown district, where the average rate among the rest of the population was 23.4 percent. In Maravilla Park on the near east side, a 1925 survey reported that out of 317 houses inspected 199 were owner occupied. Among the total "some were made into rather nice habitations, but most of them are hopeless. Fully half are poorly lighted and ventilated. Screens are sorely needed." According to a special census taken in 1933, 18.6 percent of Mexican families in Los Angeles lived in homes they owned, as opposed to only 4.8 percent and 8.6 percent for Japanese and Chinese families, respectively. Also, a 1939 study of ninety-nine Mexican families found a fairly wide divergence in annual income. Of these families, twenty-one had incomes between $500 and $900, thirty-five between $900 and $1,200, twenty-four between $1,200 and $1,500, and seven over $1,800. For those between $500 and $1,500, the average number gainfully employed per family did not vary significantly—1.43 to 1.34 to 1.58. To achieve a family income over $1,800, however, required an average of 3.28 wage earners in the family. The average family net income amounted to $1,204 per year.[81] The skill differences of the chief earners cannot by themselves account for this wide variation in mean income and home ownership. The fact that some Mexicans found consistent and steady work explains this wide divergence in annual earnings, which in turn brought different families different levels of consumption, home ownership, and physical and psychological security.

Given the greater stability and higher wages, urban industrial work constituted a step up the social ladder for the Mexican worker within the secondary sector of the labor market. Many urban workers began as agricultural ones in Los Angeles proper, or in outlying areas such as Palmdale or San Fernando. Usually recent migrants went first to the fields and then to better and steadier urban jobs. For example, Manuel Hernández came from Mexico in 1926 to the fields around Los Angeles. Then, in 1934, he and his family moved to a small steel mill community in the city, and he became an industrial laborer. Similarly, Camarillo finds that recent migrants dominated agricultural work in Santa Barbara. One finds this pattern repeated in other industrial centers. In the Chicago-Gary region of the Midwest, the same advantages of industrial work drew Mexicans from the sugar-beet fields to the city. In Detroit, the higher wages of the factory attracted Mexicans from the farms as well as from the railroad tracks.[82]

Importantly, though, agricultural labor still figured in urban Mexicans' lives. The Plaza Employment Office on North Main Street contracted with Mexicans for labor outside of the city and often failed to deliver on the number of hours or days of labor it promised. Women and especially older children from the community in which Manuel Hernández lived would often "go to the fruit" to earn extra money, as would whole families in times of strikes at the steel mill. "The walnut season," recalled one of Camarillo's informants from Santa Barbara, who migrated from the city to the field for thirty to forty days, "was the only time of the year us poor people could get a little ahead." Another, the sister of the victim of the first round knock-out mentioned in chapter 1, noted that for Mexicans in Pacoima, "Picking fruit entre familia was what folks did come June, July, and August." She added an important reminder lest we take this discussion of political economy too seriously: "I had heard that Mexicans were a cheap source of labor. Mostly we were poor folks who welcomed the extra money earned in the summer."[83]

Indeed, the evident preference of Mexican workers for industrial work over agricultural, and the fact that length of residence north of the border related to the achievement of urban work, show that Mexican workers perceived an important and clear-cut difference between different jobs within the secondary labor market. While little social mobility up and out of the low-wage sector occurred before unionization and World War II, Mexican workers' wages, comfort, and status improved relatively and diversified as some found steadier, usually urban, jobs. Such mobility, of course, was hardly the be-all and end-all; work went on being harsh and a mere instrument for continuing in the north. We see here the importance of the economic structure in the work lives of Mexicans in the United States generally. To be sure understanding this structure is necessary, but it hardly completes our task.

People exist in society not only in relation to their factory, whether in the field or in the city, but in relation to their families, their neighbors, their enemies, and their gods. These exist in people's private realms, an area largely closed to historians, who are generally concerned with external circumstances. Yet, to fully understand the meaning of the Mexican work experience, we must see how work affected this private realm, just as we did with the Indians who underwent missionization and who worked on the ranchos. If we are to know the meaning of the Mexican experience in the United States, we must understand the perceptions of that structure and its consequences for a people's sensibilities.

Consistent with the prevailing patterns of conquest and control since 1769, life and labor confused some into passivity and self-blame. Just as surely this new life and labor angered others into active resistance: witness the tenacity and solidarity with which Mexicans participated in and led union and civil rights struggles, the subjects of a following chapter. Sentiments of both assertiveness and apathy motivated many, if not most, of the Mexicans who only supported their more militant leaders depending on the time and circumstances. Most of the time most of la gente proceeded to act in ways that allowed them to continue in the new land. They generated culture from the material conditions of their lives, in other words. So far, in this chapter, Mexicans have been only the objects of history, rather like the swallows at the old mission indeed. Soon, however, they will become the subjects of history in our narrative, influencing its direction as much as history influenced them.

"Our Children Get So Different Here"

Parents and Children in
México de Afuera

She wants me not to wear the "rebozo," but I cannot go with
nothing on the head. She is getting American ways; she will
not wear the earrings that hang on her ears. They are not the
same kind that the American girls wear in their ears. Oh! Our
children get so different here.

> *A mother of México de afuera, in Mary Lanigan's*
> *"Second Generation Mexicans in Belvedere"*

Much had already been pre-arranged for Mexican immigrants. If nothing else, we have seen in this narrative how various aspects of the
American economy, Mexican and Anglo culture and history, and, actually, society as a whole were orchestrated to script Mexican lives along
a particular course. In powerful ways indeed, all these historical legacies oversaw and controlled life in the colonias. But the dramas that
we will soon witness reveal and confirm how these powerful structures
generated as much change and conflict as they contained. And such factors as fate, human nature, and contingency assured that people would
play out their roles in unforeseeable ways.[1]

In spite of both the voluntary and enforced segregation that prevailed
in Los Angeles, Mexicans lived in an American city where they found
themselves exposed to American popular culture. In the new land, even
with low wages, they could buy commodified things of great iconic value.
Seductive images encountered in movie houses and in fashion advertising offered compelling new models of behavior for Mexican youth. Mexican children and teenagers attended schools where they saw their Anglo classmates and felt at least ambivalent about how they looked.

Specifically, we are about to see how the Mexican family provided a
mooring and a shelter for people in the new land at the same time that

it arose as an arena of generational conflict. The youth often gravitated toward certain aspects of americano popular culture learned from the movies, fashion images, and their Anglo peers at school. Many of these notions began to root the youth in Southern California and marked the first steps toward cultural transformations that often distressed their Mexican parents. In addition to their lives as workers and their existence as an often despised racial and cultural group, these various conflicts, adaptations, assimilations, and compromises show both how Mexicans used their culture to assuage or counter the harshness of life in a place often perceived as hostile and how they forged a new and syncretic culture—that is, an immigrant culture blended and merged from two others, but nevertheless distinct from each—from their customary ways and the demands of life in a new land.

Not all dissolved in the move from rural or village Mexico to metropolitan Los Angeles, of course. Life in México de afuera provided the familiar sounds, tastes, and sights—solace in a place still strange and often threatening. The youth of both sexes and the single men ventured out more than others did. To Main and Spring Streets they went, where not only the doors of the Mexican theaters opened to them. There, and even in their east side neighborhoods, the doors of the americano movie theaters beckoned them to pass through into the "palaces of daydreams." Shop windows and magazines displayed new ways to look to the young women. Main Street had two burlesque houses (one Mexican and one American), where the young men watched eagerly but quietly. Cheap and sleazy picture shows catered to the lurid side of the male immigrants' imaginations; there sometimes the shadowy men in the audience seemed to put their heads in one another's laps. The many beer parlors, although often ethnically owned and identified, displayed remarkable diversity in their imbibing, often nodding, patrons.[2] Most likely we must ascribe these things not to the United States but to the metropolis; these new sensations were common to twentieth-century cities throughout Europe and the Americas.

Homogeneity in work can hide the diversity in how Mexicans negotiated the other areas of life in México de afuera. We will see here how parents and children, and women and men, experienced the perils and opportunities of American popular culture in often very different ways. The new lifeways began a dialectic between the weakening of the patriarchal family, efforts to reaffirm it in the face of unfamiliar consequences of people's new lives, and adaptation to those new ways. Instead of looking mostly inward to the family and the community to satisfy their myriad emotional and physical needs, people in the metropolis began to look outward to impersonal urban institutions and popular conventions. The family was relieved of many burdensome functions, but it lost some of its most important adhesives as well. Such an unfamiliar situation proved a fertile ground for tensions to grow between family members. The fruits of these tensions tasted variously tart, sweet, exotic, and rotten. The experience of this variety ranged from dismaying to thrilling.

Social scientists once customarily referred to this process simply as assimilation and "progress" and used consumption patterns to measure people's departure from traditional cultures. More recently the concept of modernity has been used to denote both the assertion of individual prerogatives as regards physical appearance, marriage, and one's life work and the assumption of autonomy in matters of political and religious beliefs. Even more recently the discovery of the tenacity of traditional cultures in the face of the values of individualistic, liberal capitalism has been taken as testimony of resistance to the commodification of modern life. All such notions are value laden and usually couch both one's values about the worth of ethnic cultures and one's views about whether or not the trajectory of history aims toward the increase of human freedom or the destruction of the sustaining and organic bonds of pre-industrial cultures. Such judgments aside, there can be no doubt but that Mexican immigrants, outside of the important realm of work, proceeded with their received wisdom and responded to such external stimuli. The resulting tensions affected families the most.

It is remarkable and fortunate that we have a record of this experience told in the words of Mexican immigrants themselves. In the interwar period, graduate students at the University of Southern California wrote a series of master's theses on the Mexicans of Los Angeles. Usually humane, generally critical of Mexican culture, and sometimes strikingly ethnocentric, these studies garnered much of their data from actual interviews with the "problem immigrants." Seeking to assimilate the Mexicans, these students have helped give those Mexicans of the 1920s and 1930s their distinctive history by transforming their spoken story into the printed word.

MEXICAN YOUTH AND NEW IMAGES: AN INTRODUCTION

It may have been México de afuera, but new seeds were sprouting in the new place. Parents quickly became aware that their little flowers were growing thorny stems. One daughter stated:

American girls go to parties and dances. They go alone, too. Their mothers don't go with them either as ours do. Mexican people are queer that way. The girls laugh at us when our mother goes with us. They don't have to have their mothers with them all the time. I'm not ashamed of my mother but girls don't take them. My mother doesn't understand us.

A mother affirmed the nature of this conflict in the 1920s, acknowledging:

My Maria goes to the dances when I let her. She is a pretty good girl. She wants to go all of the time to have a good time. I know. I was a girl once. I do not let her go very often. They are not good dances. I go with her when she goes. She does not say anything, but I know that she wishes I do not go with her. There are other girls who are there with other girls and boys. They do not always have a brother or a mother with them. She sees these girls alone.

New models of behavior prevailed north of the border, ones that emphasized individual prerogatives over the those of the patriarchal family. Eighteen-year-old Henrietta complained in 1932:

I never had any fun since I was sixteen years old. As soon as I was sixteen my father began to watch me and would not let me go anywhere or have any friends come home. He was born in old Mexico but he has been here long enough to know how people do things. The way it is with the Mexicans, the bigger a girl is, the farther they pull her into the house.

Wage labor encouraged these breaks with the parents, especially the fathers. "I am working and earning my own living," Henry, age seventeen, argued persuasively, if not fruitfully. "I am no kid. I think I should be able to stay out until ten o'clock at night without having to give an account of myself."[3]

We are not witnessing here the success of the Protestant settlement houses or the public schools in having young Mexicans imbibe American ways. Certainly, those new authorities encouraged the estrangement of youth from the ways of their parents. Yet most likely, young Mexicans assimilated these attitudes to a greater extent through the medium of American popular culture, particularly fashion and the movies.

EL FLAPPERISMO

In March 1928 *La Opinión* published an article with the header "El Flapperismo Ha Hecho Iguales Las Mujeres" (Flapperdom Has Made

All Women the Same). The paper attributed the comments, with dateline New York, to Helena Rubenstein. The editors clearly approved of Rubenstein's view that "With her short hair, with her painted cheeks and lips, with her skirts to her knees, they all seem the same. One no longer finds the true attraction and beauty with which women should be possessed." This typified complaints made generally about the flapper. Then, too, her figure evoked much attention: La Opinión often presented americana models, emblematic of "the New Woman," in bathing suits. One issue from June 1929 explained that such attire "would be the scandal of our grandmothers without any doubt. In these fast moving times we generally stifle the age-old and irreproachable sense of female modesty in favor of comfort and hygiene" (the bare backs gave "a healthy sun bath.")[4] These sentiments actually masked all manner of profound ambivalence about the flapper. Whether the culture based its ideal female on the model of la Virgen de Guadalupe or Queen Victoria, the notion that a woman could use physical allure to be an active participant, even initiator, in romantic occasions met with powerful repulsion, and attraction.

Mexico had a thriving film industry to expose its youth to the magic of the silver screen. Several important stars developed there and then made their way north to the international movie capital, Hollywood. Often their accents prohibited their transition to the talkies, but at least Ramon Novarro, Gilbert Roland, Lupe Velez, and Dolores del Río will forever be associated with the glorious early days of Hollywood (see figures 15–17). Ambiguous days, though, days when there was ample space, demand, and opportunity for Latino stars, but when none could portray positive Mexican characters because none existed; they were usually cast as generically exotic romantic figures.[5]

Far more emerges from the figures of Lupe Velez and Dolores del Río than we have been aware of, or shall even surface from these pages. La Opinión called del Río "nuestra estrella máxima de la pantalla." In November 1928 a "Fiesta Mexicana . . . a royal event of homage and welcoming from the Mexican Colony" was held for her after her "Triumphal Return from Europe." Los Angeles Mexicans had in the aristocratic del Río not only a compelling story in its own right, but a star whose beauty, fame, talent, and charisma equaled those of any other. And she provided an appealing model of womanhood, one that expressed the range of feminine possibility more fully than the usual well-known dichotomy. Of course, the movie star as archetype has been a problematic figure in the twentieth century; too many fans are starstruck.

Figure 15. Dolores del Río in *Evangelina*, 1929. (Courtesy
John Springer/Corbis-Bettmann.)

An excerpt in translation from an article in *La Opinión* will help readers imagine the Hollywood scene in México de afuera: "the most sensational movie of the year: 'Evangelina,' based on the poem by Longfel-
low and directed by Edwin Carewe. Two Mexicans who have reached
prominence on the screen have the principal parts in the production: she,
the sublime [*excelsa*] Dolores del Río; he, Ernesto Guillén, best known
in the cinema world by the pseudonym of Donald Reed." Such spectacle could happen only in America, and only in Hollywood. On Mexican
Independence Day 1927, *La Opinión* included Dolores del Río among
"five Mexicans who give prestige to la Raza."[6]

Figure 16. La Excelsa Dolores del Río.
(Courtesy Herald Examiner Collection,
Los Angeles Public Library.)

While Dolores del Río typified the "grand dame" of the silver screen, red-haired Lupe Velez, "la inquieta e inquietante" (the restless and disturbing) Lupe Velez, embodied "the genuine sort of sensual actress, vehemently without artifice or falseness." She was born into an elite family in San Luis Potosí and took to acting after her father was wounded in the Revolution and her mother's stage career foundered because of the turmoil. First known in the United States as the "The Wild Cat of Mexico" and later famous as the "Mexican Spitfire," she initially gained renown in the 1927 movie *The Gaucho,* in which she played the jealous lover of Douglas Fairbanks. Indeed, she provided quite a restless and disturbing figure for movie fans. The news of November 1929 about her romance with Gary Cooper—according to *La Opinión,* "the only man with whom she had been in love in her whole life"—and her illnesses and speeding tickets (for "following her natural impulses") regularly made movie section headlines. She was, well, a "fast woman." Luella Parsons, whose syndicated column appeared regularly in translation in *La Opinión*'s *Página Cinematográfico,* referred to her as a "Spanish beauty," an identity that Velez seemed at times to cultivate. *La Opinión*

Figure 17. María Alba and Dolores del Río, 1928. Like
many Mexican movie stars in Hollywood, Alba's accent
kept her out of the talkies. (Courtesy Herald Examiner
Collection, Los Angeles Public Library.)

took umbrage not only at how "our Lupe Velez . . . had been mistak-
enly called 'Spanish,'" but also at how the "simpática artista mexicana"
herself seemed to connive in misleading fans about her identity.[7]

Such stars became popular not only on the screen but also at well-
publicized events, especially at the openings of their films. In June 1928
Lupe Velez appeared at the downtown United Artists theater "in person
with her lively dances and songs at the first showing at popular prices
of the Douglas Fairbanks film 'El Gaucho.'" Dolores del Río appeared
from time to time at least at Teatro Hidalgo. Lupita Tovar, "the new
Mexican star from Fox," introduced the El Paso Shoe Store baseball
team in their Cinco de Mayo (1929) championship game against Pacific
Electric. But many of these Mexican stars faded: "Lupe is one of the few

of our stars who has been saved from the shipwreck occasioned by the talking picture." (Lupita Tovar starred in 1931 in the first talkie produced in Mexico, *Santa*.) Hollywood could accept the pretty faces of exotic Latinas, but not their Spanish-accented voices.[8]

Film buffs in México de afuera clamored for movies in Spanish (an episode to which we will return), and while American stars received significant mention, Mexican stars were all the rage in *La Opinión*. What did it mean, though, that of thirty-seven young mexicanas of the All Nations Foundations settlement house who listed a favorite actress in 1929 in a social worker's survey, six liked Billie Dove, three liked Greta Garbo and Dolores del Río, and four liked Mary Pickford, Clara Bow, and Lupe Velez?[9] Obviously their preferences were as manufactured and capricious as the popularity of the actresses, themselves products of the star system. Their choices indicate adolescent tastes nonetheless. Billie Dove was publicized as "The American Beauty." Mary Pickford, "the gamine," epitomized the poor waif who struggled valiantly against the injustices of repressive and moralistic elders. Always the child-woman, she made spontaneous and unladylike demands that her adoring female fans found gratifying. Clara Bow (the "It Girl") often played "the star-kissed working girl who with considerable aplomb leaps out of the slums and into her hero's heart." An independent woman, she beguiled men on and off the screen. *La Opinión* divulged how this "inquieta flapper," "Princesa del 'It,'" "played poker, drank liquor, and gave jewels to her friends." Femme fatale Greta Garbo portrayed a woman who attracted men through her mysteriousness but remained "divinely untouchable." And then there was Lupe Velez. This is not to say that young mexicanas aspired to flapperdom or that the sensuality of these stars was all that attracted mexicanas to the cinema. But virtually all of those surveyed from the settlement house went at least once a week, and about half went from two to six times. A United States Department of Labor study of 1934–36 found that "the largest proportion of the expenditures for items under the heading of recreation by Mexican families [in Los Angeles] was for movies." It would appear from this study and from these interviews that Mexicans found their favored entertainments in the "palaces of daydreams."[10]

There they saw all sorts of new images, which they then used to fill in, or even replace, some of the tiles that the move to urban Los Angeles chipped from their cultural mosaics. It is easier to know what movies they saw, at least in 1929, than to know what they saw in them. Of course their favorites surely came and went. Five of the thirty-two who

listed the "best movie you ever saw" picked *Singing Fool,* a hugely successful Al Jolson movie. The sentimental plot revolved around a singing waiter who became a Broadway star and then disastrously involved
himself with a soubrette who caused his ruin when she left him for a
racketeer. The movie ended happily when the cigarette girl in Blackie
Joe's Cafe saved him and they left for California. Most likely, though,
the singing (including Jolson in his famous blackface) and dancing provided the primary appeal. Three liked *The Fair Co-ed,* a college sports
capers comedy. The rest of those surveyed preferred a variety of pictures, ranging from the sleazy *Road to Ruin* to the moralistic *Why Be
Good* to the romantic comedy *The Cardboard Lover* to the predictable
(but surprisingly underrepresented) *Ramona.*[11]

In many ways such movies became the new stories of the new place
for Mexican immigrants. We saw in chapter 1 how the new localities,
especially the Boxcarvilles and colonias, had few stories of either the be-
haviorally or morally proscriptive sort, or about how to live a virtuous
life. Movies filled this gap in complicated and tension-producing ways.
To some degree the movie images provided a bridge to americano culture and how its participants acted, what they valued, and new possibilities within it. Responses varied from ridicule to a desire to emulate.
The purveyors of popular culture wielded the means of description, and
they constructed stunning and seductive images in the pictures of clothing on the silver screen, especially to portray how people should be. But
these images have so often been unconnected to any sort of material
or actual reality: life on the silver screen, especially in the 1920s and
1930s, has not been about, or corresponded to, real life. Dolores del
Río's *Evangelina* and *The Pagan*—"un fracaso [failure] definativo" saved
only by Ramon Novarro "Singing Love Laden Songs of the South Sea
Isles"—provide more examples of these new stories that had no connection to the actual world that Mexicans inhabited.[12] Thus when we
refer to the americano ways that became attractive in the movie palaces downtown, we must remember *which* americano ways we are discussing—not the real ones, mostly. There were such new twists in the
scripts by which Mexicans would act in history.

On the screen they saw new models of adult, particularly female,
behavior. Schools, dances, the settlement house, and the youthful col-
lectivities forged in the streets meant that many young people were directing their activities outward, away from their families. The movies,
in spite of their often as not being family affairs, served to heighten the
sense of estrangement already appearing between children and their parents. It is unlikely that young mexicanas simply aspired to be Billie Dove,

Clara Bow, or Lupe Velez. One nineteen-year-old informant, however, claimed that he "knew a girl who was very nice and she saw one of the pictures starring Clara Bow. . . . This girl wanted to dress like Clara Bow because she thought Clara Bow looked pretty swell. The result was that she started to wear her dress to above her knees and to paint her face until it looked like a clown's, and to adopt all the filthy ways that Clara Bow has in the films."[13] Likely he blamed too much on one movie star, but certainly young women saw new and tempting ways to be on the silver screen, which no doubt had a potent allure of its own. In their formative years, girls saw images to which they could aspire, at least in fantasy. In any event, the new and enticing visions would make them feel ambivalent about the ways in which the old culture had scripted their lives. All of the stars noted above portrayed women who acted in the public world and flaunted their sensuality in ways that simultaneously both objectified them and made them active participants in romance and courtship.

The threatening fantasy image that the stars presented materialized in the figure of Dolores del Río and her stormy divorce from her Mexican husband in 1929. "Dolores Del Rio Habla Sobre Los Hombres Y El Amor" blared a headline of October 1929 on the *Página Cinematográfica*. In this interview, apparently carried throughout the Spanish-language press in the United States, she explained, "The most important contribution which the United States had made for the progress and the happiness of the world was the quality of its husbands." They "consider their wives companions in their daily activities." The American husband was "tender, noble, and loyal," though, "surely, in the matter of romance, he had much to learn from the latino." Not so influenced by tradition, the American husband was less apt to view a wife "through the prism of antiquated criteria." Her conclusions about American men could only have been based on, at best, some impressionistic evidence. Perhaps she has engaged in some latina romanticizing herself here; perhaps her knowledge of americano husbands derived from the movies. (She would, though, marry Cedric Gibbons, who was in charge of Metro-Goldwyn-Mayer's sets and costumes, in March 1930.) More likely, her comments reflect one (very public) Mexican woman's yearning for an egalitarian relationship, one in which a woman could live with a man and in society freed from Mexican patriarchal culture's prescriptions for a woman's proper role.[14]

The disapproval of *el flapperismo* actually had less to do with its alleged homogenization of women than with its strong suggestion that a woman could act independently of a man and outside the acceptable role—virgin or wife/mother—that culture and religion ordained. Citing Anita Loos as its authority, one *La Opinión* editorial railed at "Women who Pursue Men." They not only lost their femininity and attractiveness to men but also threatened "a pronounced anarchy, not only as regards what we might call the principles, but in practice." Several apparently disparate notions need connecting here. The authoritarian family provides the basis and paradigm for such hierarchical societies as Mexico's, at least in the eras of colonialism and Porfirio Díaz. The patriarchal archetype of command and control has justified and modeled the political rule of elite families. Then, because they both identify with elite patriarchs and derive some benefits from their privilege even within poor families, the practice of patriarchy has tied the men of the lower classes into the social-political system. Such family cultures tend overwhelmingly to adulate women as mothers. In an extraordinary piece in November 1928 another *La Opinión* editorial expounded on why Mexicans did not become citizens of the United States: "Not from ignorance, rusticity, not pride, or lack of confidence," but because of the "intervention of the Mexican woman." The author explained how

> To honor the woman of our raza is for us not only what we owe her when she affords us satisfaction by doing her duties. She should constitute a sacred cult to which we should be devoted at all times . . . Across the pages of our history we see her always abnegating and sweet, deeply Christian, and devotedly patriotic, worthy of our reverence and affection, because while such remarkable virtues exist in her, while she continues as the manager of homes and of the indestructible seeds of love and of loyalty and of kindness and of the faith, Mexico can be confident of its destiny, expect days of glory, and fortify itself in the vision that it will be women who illuminate the path on which will march the generations to which we will leave the future of our country.

This remarkable construction of womanhood simultaneously idolizes Mexican women and prescribes severely their role and aspirations; they are concurrently honored, assigned responsibility for the future of the Mexican nation, and confined to the house.[15] Add to this the dictates of pre-marital chastity and post-nuptial sexual passivity and inhibition and we have the male-constructed model for womanhood, one upon which "the future of our country" depends. In other words, the active New Woman, be she Lupe Velez or Clara Bow, menaced not only men's expectations and entitlements and the family as most social conservatives understood it, but the society and its future built on those families as well. And indeed, all kinds of trouble would soon arise.

FAMILIES AND THE NEW IMAGES

Although people experienced the movies in individualized ways, they attended in groups in the 1920s and 1930s. (In the era before the movie palaces, only immigrant men attended roughly made films, which were often about the Mexican Revolution.) Most of the young women surveyed went with their parents or their brothers and sisters. Felipe Montes, who came from Guanajuato and owned a barbershop on Main Street, told Manuel Gamio, "I don't enjoy the movies and the theaters here but I go to take my wife. She likes the American movies especially." Not unusually, though, adolescents went with girlfriends, boyfriends, or even alone.[16] The daughters gazed upon the screen and saw what the dominant culture apparently valued. They might even have aspired to become that way, at least in a daydream lasting as far as the movie palace's door. The mothers, though, surely saw what they were not. Las madres were socialized to maintain, and to stay within, the family realm. In the old ways, a woman ideally attracted a man through her display of obedience and good housewifery, not her sexual allure. These times confused everyone in the new and strange society of metropolitan Southern California, which the movies, with all their seductive appeal, intensified and epitomized.

These daughters and sons of La Malinche were, of course, deeply the products of their parents and of their cultural history. They had inherited the expectation that obedience to their parents was the greatest virtue. But they related just as profoundly to urban popular culture, which they encountered in the movie houses and shops of Southern California. Again, there would be cultural mestizaje, which would beget new ways from the commingling of the old. We can now understand and sympathize with both a daughter and her mother, who lamented:

> My Lupe says she will bob her beautiful hair if I say, "yes," or if I say, "no." What makes her like that? She knows that her father will beat her if she does not mind us. Since we have been in the United States she has always been a good girl, until now when she says that she will do what she wants. She says that we are funny and that we want her to be funny and like the old people, too. Do you think that the girls will laugh at her in the school if she has long hair? The nurse says for us to let her cut her hair, that it will be good for the hair. Lupe says it is her hair and she will cut it if she wants to. She is young and she will not listen to the ones who know more than she does.

Much is contained in this statement from the late 1920s. We know "What makes her like that." She wants her hair bobbed like that of the flappers on the screen and in the picture windows of the shops and like that of other girls she sees at school. The authority of the school has been inserted between parents and children, in this case over what is healthy for the hair. Lupe sought to act outside of the patriarchal domain in ways that americano popular culture suggested. She was not unusual. Sobbed another mother, "My Josefa" (who apparently saved for herself some of the money she earned picking walnuts with her family)

> came to the home last night and she have her hair short. She have the beautiful hair and she will cut it off her head. I have try all her life to take care of it and have it to shine. She knows that I like her hair and she knows I will not want her to have the cut hair. She take the money that she have from the nuts and go to the barber herself. I am sad. She have only one day with it off, but yet I cannot speak with her. My heart she hurt right here.

In the new milieu customary concepts of womanhood engaged threatening new images and ideals. Another, whose daughter bobbed her hair, said, "I told her not to but she did as she pleases. She thinks she looks nice, but she looks like a fool. If she wore it that way in Mexico she would be laughed at." Mothers and fathers looked for security to the familiar and comforting past—when girls wore their hair long and obeyed the high-handed and peremptory dictates of their elders. Said Fernando Sánchez, a Los Angeles typesetter, "I follow my Mexican customs and I won't change them for the anything in the world. I haven't let my sisters cut their hair nor go around like the girls here with all kinds of boys and I have also accustomed my sons to respect me in every way." The sons' simple maleness guaranteed them entry to the public world, however difficult that new urban landscape might be. For the daughters this access proved far more problematic.[17]

Images in clothing loom crucially significant in these tensions as well. In the old country—and this has been true for all immigrants, particularly ones from rural areas—the quantity and quality of cloth one wore bespoke one's social status. The voluminous, intricately woven, and decorated fabrics elites wore visually demonstrated how much wealth and labor they commanded, and that they did not do manual work. Only they donned hats and lace. The peasantry, on the other hand, wore loose, "untailored" clothing appropriate for movement and physical labor. In America, however, an equality of appearances was being born. Control of land and machines produced the social distinctions and hard working conditions that Mexicans experienced in Los Angeles. Yet, machines, often the same ones, produced inexpensive clothing, including lace and hats, and almost anyone who found regular employment at even a low wage could afford at least one of these. The Department of Labor study cited above noted, "The most striking differences between the distribution of expenditures by the Los Angeles Mexican families and by other families of similar income in Los Angeles [controlling for family size] is the relatively large proportion spent for clothing (13.5 percent as compared with 9.8 percent)." (A dress in Los Angeles during the Depression could be bought for $3, though $5 was the more usual price.) We cannot minimize the significance that such display worn upon the body, and the images on the screen, had for Mexican immigrants to the city. Conditions they had taken for granted in the old country could now be perceived as deprived. An impoverished young mexicana, she and her family burdened by work, could dress—a little—like an elite from the old country. Being able to do what was once unthinkable, even unimaginable, now became common practice for many Mexican girls and women in America. Politically, this meant that while great disparities of wealth, power, and status prevailed, or even intensified, a rough parity of appearances emerged as one donned a cheap hat or lace blouse. One did not wear the disparaged mark of a peasant anymore.[18]

Political ramifications arose in the household as well. Hair potently symbolized these troubles and so too did the rebozo, the shawl that Mexican women traditionally wore. "Maria wears silly things on her head," stated a mother. "I even saw her in church with head uncovered. I was very much ashamed." And Maria opined, "Mama thinks she'd catch cold without that old thing around her head. I beg her not to wear it when she comes to the P.T.A. meetings at school." The mother quoted above about chaperoning her daughter at dances said that "She wants me not to wear the 'rebozo,' but I cannot go with nothing on the head. She is getting American ways; she will not wear the earrings that hang on her ears. They are not the same kind that the American girls wear in their ears. Oh! Our children get so different here." The precise meaning of these intrusions into the customary ways of Mexican immigrant families varied with the degree to which the young people manifested their newly acquired tastes and the degree to which the parents resisted, of course. The following statement nicely illustrates the predicament:

> My daughter says that I am a funny one to wear this [rebozo]. I think it is pretty, don't you? She does not like it . . . I do not like to wear a hat because I cannot. But I do not want the Americans to laugh at my [daughter]. Why do they laugh at her and not at me? She *must* go with me to town. I cannot speak the English and she must be with me.

We can easily visualize this scene of mother and daughter walking to the grocery store. The rebozo covers the elder's head, and the daughter sheepishly walks first a little ahead, then a little behind, glancing furtively to see if anyone spots them. A 1932 study noted that while mothers appeared publicly with the rebozo, "The girl's dress is a cheap copy of the models made stylish by movie stars and actresses."[19]

Exercising their liberty to choose their dress, within the confines of their meager wages and the new authorities of fashion and advertising, made their migration (to any metropolis, actually) all the more worthwhile. It provided an escape from, and a commodified reward for, their dreary labors. These were important roots that the younger generation of these allegedly temporary immigrants were sinking down in Los Angeles. Furthermore, although the "natives" (surely a curious term in la Ciudad de la Reina de los Angeles) despised these working-class immigrants, their adoption of the styles of dress displayed in movies, magazines, and stores enabled them to feel some belonging in the repulsive-attractive culture into whose midst they had journeyed. A Mexican newspaper editor and former consul representative observed,

> Here in Los Angeles I have known many fellow-countrymen who because they were markedly dark or they couldn't speak English even when they were decent people have been made victims of contempt and humiliations. They have been denied admission into some public places, especially in the bathing places and swimming pools and in some dance halls.
>
> On the other hand the Mexicans, I am referring to the immigrants in general, who come to this country are dazzled and attracted by certain comforts which they get and that is why they live here for an indefinite period of time, even when they don't change their nationality.

It is as ironic as it is significant that those in the dominant culture tended to condemn or ridicule these facsimiles of their ways, terming such immigrant dress "cheap," "gaudy," and so on. Even so, that one inexpensive lace blouse or hat and those cheap imitations of Billy Dove's, Clara Bow's, and Lupe Velez's jewelry all appeared to bridge the gap between the rich and poor, the glamorous and the previously shoddy.[20]

As we are becoming increasingly aware, historical changes happened upon, and were reflected in, the body; these young Mexicanas prove no exception. Of course, human beings of both sexes, all cultures, castes, and classes have decorated themselves throughout history. Sartorial appearance always tells much about a person, whether we are discussing the austerely dressed product of the Protestant ethic, the luxurious clothing of a seigneurial elite, or the loose garb of a peasant laborer.

Film stars, movie and fashion mags, and the enveloping environment of the city with its storefront adornments and advertising showing people what they should look like, all contributed to the idea that people were on display. How one displayed oneself—from clothing to gestures to makeup and hairstyle—communicated to others who one was. Unlike in the old villages, where everyone knew, or was even related to, almost everyone else, in the anonymous city personal images identified and defined an individual. Never mind that everyone looked rather the same, since the fashion industry and its advertising told people how they should appear. "Looks" became crucial and the object of terrific concern. This is why what might be perceived as a relatively minor aspect of the Mexican experience in Southern California actually involved so much family passion and must be seen as a decisive aspect of immigrant life. The body had previously been an instrument for work, reproduction, and occasional pleasures. Now it served all these purposes, but for identity and allure as well. As a young mexicana cast away tradition in dress, she became trapped in new forms of sexual objectification. She received a variety of powerful suggestions from consumer culture, no doubt taken to heart with great individual variance, about how to look and act in order to attract a husband. In her parents' customary consciousness of womanhood, only "those women" dressed that way. Parents were distraught, if not aghast, over their children's new tastes. New *lloronas* cried for their lost children.

WISE GUYS

Boys went to the movies a lot too, of course, and they had their favorites. In a 1933 survey of 103 young males (overwhelmingly Mexicans, but including a few Japanese) at All Nations Foundation, James Cagney, Tom Mix, and Joe E. Brown emerged as the most popular movie stars. The tough guy, the cowboy, and the comedian no doubt would have topped the lists of most working-class boys. They liked detective, mystery, war, comic, and gangster movies. Fifty-seven claimed a favorite, which, it should be noted again, would change over only a short time. The greatest of gangster films, *Scarface* (1932), led the list with seven votes; while *Forty-Second Street*, featuring songs and dancing girls, and *Wings*, about aerial warfare, came in second with four votes each. Their favorite actress, by the way, was Joan Blondell, followed by Jean Harlow, Joan Crawford, and Mae West.[21]

The hugely popular *Scarface* epitomized the appeal of the gangster to the downtrodden of the Depression. Usually portrayed as immigrant Italians, the gangsters had fast cars and fast women, made fast money, and assaulted and insulted authority. The gaudily dressed star of this film, Paul Muni, did all these things in a maniacal, brutish, and arrogant manner. The audience witnessed the murders of twenty-eight people, and the sign of the cross accompanied each one. It is a film about vulgar and aberrant figures who, in the context of the Depression, conceivably became folk heroes to many. When the boys were asked if they imitated things they saw in the movies, three-fifths said that they did. They wanted to be like cowboys and "to make wise-cracks."[22]

Nor was the importance of images of dress lost on either male youths or the dominant culture. Their most famous attire, the zoot suit, figured most prominently in Anglo perceptions of Mexicans in the later years of the Depression and the war years, when the craze swept through East Los Angeles. Forbidden access to americano culture—which simultaneously repelled, rebuffed, and allured them—and insulted, ignored, or patronized in the schools (not to mention problematic in their own homes), young Mexicans donned their "drapes." Did the gaudy attire that the likes of Paul Muni flaunted in *Scarface* and other gangster movies influence the dress of Mexican youngsters? Did any of those seven who liked *Scarface* in the 1933 study become *pachucos*? Unfortunately the voices of the zoot-suiters have not emerged from the sources with regard to what their clothing meant to them or from where or whom they got the idea of adopting such dress.

By the early war years groups, sometimes gangs, of Mexican youths strutted this attire. Surely the baggy trousers and oversized coat of the pachuco symbolized passive defiance of Anglo-American culture, and the models for such expressive attiring of the self were frequently encountered in the movie palaces. The zoot suit, which Malcolm X later wore in Harlem and rebellious English youths wore in London, showed that a young man was neither of his parents' culture nor of the americanos'. For both cultures, clothing was functional, adapted for work or warmth. The former used it for work, and the latter to convey austerity, particularly during World War II. The zoot suit looked a bit like an Anglo business suit, but utterly exaggerated. The former quality unnerved the wearer's parents, and the latter one infuriated the americanos. The zoot suit affronted the cultures between which a young man was caught. But it also announced that, although such a youngster was not an American, he was not exactly simply a mexicano either. Then, too, he was certainly not a "Mexican-American." Such a youth was involved early on in the process by which Chicanos were coming into being.[23]

Rather than trying to label or define the zoot-suiter, it is more worthwhile to try to see what he was doing when he dressed this way. He was creating an identity, one that can be understood only in this historical context. The youngster mocked the racist society that often scorned him, repudiated the rural folkways of his parents, and rejected the advice of the sociedades about bringing honor to the raza. With their "reat pleats," such working-class youth collectively donned an identity that disavowed both their working-class and their subservient status. There is so much to be read in this matter of dress.[24]

MARRIAGE AND FAMILY

The family, no doubt, is a pillar of resistance to oppression, a source of pleasure, a haven in a world that treats working people, especially those of color, with disdain. It may well be that the concept of *respeto y honor,* the guiding principle of child-parent relations and Mexican family life, is the most appropriate and necessary attitude to hold toward all beings and the earth. Then, too, the family is a source of pain and oppression in its own right. Within the family, even a poor man has access to some of the psychic and material rewards of the upper class when he has unpaid domestic servants in the form of his wife and daughters, who, without wages or income, have no option but to be his *familia.* The tradition upon which Mexican fathers called derived as much from ideology as from history. A creation of power relations, *respeto y honor* buttressed male authority over women and children. It has conveyed with it fear of the patriarch as well.

Most parents carry in their unconscious baggage wounds from childhood suffered at the hands of their own authoritarian parents, particularly, but hardly always, their fathers. The conveyance of culture from one generation to another means that members of the receiving generation must internalize their parents' aspirations and suppress their own; they must live out ancestral commands. Because their own parents are so "honored," many of them must redirect (or "split off," as psychologists would put it) upon their own children the anger that results from this self-repression. This subconscious process provides them a safe outlet for their own distantly repressed filial rage, allows them to pass on their earliest humiliations and to regain that power they lost to their own parents. These notions would be true particularly in the context of the emotional discipline required of Mexican parents who were attempting to make a better life for their families in the north. Of course, their children's new garb and social aspirations provided a ready object for Mexican parents' wrath. But parents say that this was the way their own parents treated them, and that they were honorable people. Thus they can identify with, or at least mimic, their own paternal oppressors, suppress their own rage, and act it out upon their own children. The body and its new appearances carried the messages of their children's rebellions, and thus fathers occasionally delivered punishment upon those bodies. This is why Lupe's "father will beat her if she does not mind us." Parents of all cultures are not always so honorable and so deserving of all the respect they might wish, and children sense this.[25]

It is not surprising that the changes in family ways broached so far would influence forcefully the very process of making families. Indeed, the desire to choose one's own spouse and sometimes to escape a tyrannical family literally and figuratively increased the distance between Mexican parents and children in Southern California. In the patriarchal family, where the father rules over production and his wife, children, and servants, if there are any, it follows that his rule includes such important matters as familial alliances—marriages, of course. One simply did not engage in such matters outside the considerations of the clan, whose expectations may or may not have coincided with the wishes of the betrothed. But in the city, individualized wage labor replaced the family economy and broke the connection between production and family. This dynamic delegitimated patriarchal authority, and individualized wages encouraged the desire and ability of young people to make their own choices about such matters. The heroes of popular culture, the stars of the silver screen, provided compelling models: they attracted a spouse through their appearance and their own exertions. Elopement became a common resolution to the conflict between old and new patterns of courtship.

"My father would not let Joe come to the house," stated "Concha" in 1928. "He said when it was time for me to get married, he would have something to say about who my husband would be. So Joe and I fixed that. I ran off with him." Explained another, "My mother have forgive me now for the running away, because she like Lucas now. You know I run away because she never let the fellers come to the house." She continued, "She think it is bad for girls to have friends with the boys. She never tells me why. I saw the American girls have boys, and I like to have the good times too." In this case, the young mexicana resolutely escaped what she perceived as arbitrary authority, an act that Lucas's independent wages facilitated. She recounted, "You know my mother is poor, and I have to quit school to go to work in the Kress. One day Lucas say he have much money and he want me to marry with him. I love Lucas and I say 'Yes.' We went to Riverside and got married in the 'court.'" Another girl told the story of Petra and her mother:

> We sure felt sorry for Petra. She had run away and gotten married a few days ago because she loved Manuel and did not want to leave him just because her family told her to. Her mother would not forgive her because she had disobeyed her. Petra went to the train to tell her family good-bye and her mother wouldn't even speak to her. She stood by the train window and she was crying and she reached up her arms to her mother, but her mother wouldn't pay any attention to her. Suddenly, just as the train began to move, her mother began to cry and she reached out her arms and said, 'Oh, Petra! Petra!' And the train pulled off and the saddest thing at the depot was poor Petra standing there with Manuel's arms around her, crying and crying.

Of course, such flights in the cause of love have been resorted to since time immemorial. Yet, as one student of the situation stated in 1932, "This method of escape has become more or less common." The historical record contains many more such tales. When the couple returned, the family and community usually accepted them back, though such episodes increased parental vigilance over the younger daughters.[26]

"Men are bad. We don't dare to let our daughters go out without us," as one mother expressed it. "If we do, everybody thinks they are bad too." There was certainly some reason for such statements. "Well, my sister run away too, because my mother no let the fellers come to the house," explained the sibling of a fallen one. Fathers and fearful mothers assumed the innocence of their children and yet presumed their potential for depravity. "Our mother does not tell her girls the things they should know. Before I was married she no tell me things." Her younger sister ran away with a forty-six-year-old man when they were all working the apricots. The police were called, and the runaways caught; the man was put in jail, and the girl in a detention home. "Now she have 'ashamed' and she no want to go again to the school. The sad thing is she is no longer a girl. . . . The girls go to the camps and there is no one to look after them and they do things they should not do. There are always bad mans hanging around to do harm to the girls."[27]

New authorities challenged the family patriarch as arbiter of correct behavior on the part of women and children. Some were subtle, such as cinematic and fashionable images, and some were more overt, such as the school and the workaday world of foremen, clocks, and the labor market. The objection of numerous fathers to their daughters' attending public school combined several aspects of this dynamic. The school competed with the fathers for their children's sensibilities and allegiance—both, I would submit, with equally unexamined assumptions about what was best for them. Whether we refer to courtship rituals or the new directions in which the education system was leading Mexican children, vigilance over youth, especially girls, protected them from "bad mans" and the threatening ways of the surrounding and intrusive culture of Anglo America.

Fathers, to unfathomable but various degrees, acted to reverse these assaults on their received wisdom about such matters as morals and manners. "When I came to the United States, I wanted to go to school. My father wouldn't let me because boys and girls went to the same school," recalled one mother. "So I didn't have a chance to learn to read and write and do numbers." In the early 1930s, when she was interviewed at age twenty-two, she recalled running away with Perez, who "went to school and can do all those numbers," to get married at age fourteen after her father had forcefully prevented her marriage to an americano. "My father said it wasn't right for boys and girls to go to one school. I had to stay home and keep house and cook. When I went out, my mother went with me." To her father, apparently, women were not to be granted access to the public world or emancipated, only passed on to other men. As in the old country, daughters were trained for housewifery so they could attract a good husband. Her desertion of the family authority did not bring her joy: "My girl Theresa wants to go out but Perez won't let her, not even to a Christmas party," she stated. "She says she's going to marry an American and do as she pleases. She cries all night. Perez says if she won't stop, she'll see what she'll get."[28]

We cannot explain this behavior simply by some peculiarity of Mexican men and their behavior toward women and children. Indeed, evidence suggests that they abused women and children with about the same frequency as other men of their status did. They lived in the United States, after all, to work, not to find some new culture. "I don't like the customs of this country anyway," stated one man who worked in a brickyard in Los Angeles and in the fields of San Bernardino. "Although my children are already grown up I don't want their children to be *pochos*. That is why we are all going [back to Mexico] so that their children will be born over there and they will be brought up good Mexicans," he concluded.[29] Parents simply looked to their customary assumptions and ways to negotiate the bewildering complexities of their lives in the city. This is why the entreaties of the new individualist and consumer culture proved

less compelling to them than to their children. It is true of all such rural
people, daughters with fathers accustomed to ruling over the family economy only complicating this picture of family life in the new metropolis.
On the other hand, the children surely had deep roots in Mexico, but
they grew up in the American city. They had much less need and affinity
for those ways that protected their parents, and they had new models of
behavior that seductively and potently challenged parental authority.
Those children and their behavior would have to be watched, lest the new
environment influence them in ways that challenged the rule of the fathers or brought into question the very culture that held together the bodies and souls of the men and women who toiled so endlessly for their
families' livelihoods.

Sometimes women looked forward to the personal freedom that liberal social relations might bring to them, sometimes backward to the
familiar old ways, and sometimes heavenward in flight from "a heartless world," aching in their "soul of soulless conditions." One mother
wailed, "The Mexican girls seeing American girls with freedom, they
want it too, so they go where they like. They do not mind their parents;
this terrible freedom. But what can we Mexican mothers do?" Another
mother ruminated about these new relationships between women and
men in the late 1920s:

> The husband of my daughter is so good a man. And to the little girls! He
> will do anything for all of us. He wants to make my daughter happy but she
> is mean with him. He wants to buy her the dress. He is very poor and he
> cannot have much money for it. She says that in the US that the women go
> to the store and buy the dress themselves. They do not wait at home for the
> man to bring them home a dress. She does not like the dress when he brings
> it home to her. He works so hard for his money and he wants her to have the
> pretty dress, and then she says the bad things and will not wear the dress.

These were surely perplexing times. Women received new models of behavior that encouraged their independence from harsh, as well as gen-
tler, if not insightful, patriarchs. Confusion and pain, as well as affection
and shelter, emerged in the Mexican families of Southern California.
"My wife does not want to stay at home and take care of the baby," affirmed a husband. "She learned how to make money in a beauty parlor
and now she wants to start a beauty parlor and make money."[30]

Manuel Gamio retells the story of Wenceslao Orozco, a carpenter
"who still keeps the view that the man is the one to decide things and
that the woman ought to obey; so that he wants to take his son to Mexico because here the old women want to run things and a poor man has

to wash the dishes while the wife goes to the 'show.'" One woman gave herself an emancipation present upon her marriage, symbolic of her hope for an egalitarian relationship: "The first thing I did was to bob my hair. My father would not permit it and I have wanted to for a long time. I will show my husband that he will not boss me the way my father has done all of us."[31]

While each of these family episodes depicts poignant human dramas— ones provocative of so much in our historical imaginations—they also illustrate some sweeping notions about how families come to take the forms they do. The view that introduced this chapter, that cultural and historical structures create as much conflict and change as they contain, should now be amply illustrated. The circumstances of the girls and young women in particular have uncannily close parallels to the situation at the St. Francis Dam, which we saw in the second chapter: it is as if we could feel the anger in the young women behind the patriarchal walls, and sometimes the anger breaks free. Such strife, like the bursting of a dam, is not always creative, but the havoc and confusion do generate new forms on the familial landscape.

Then, too, family patterns owe much to such structural considerations as the conditions of work. Chapter 3 introduced us to how household formats changed in response to a wage economy. In the pre-industrial family economy, women, children, and (among the wealthy) servants participated as producers under the direction of the patriarch. Now, in modern times, women (wives) function to reproduce the primary wage earners (husbands) and re-produce the future workforce (children). The state, via the education system, has played an important role in all this. We could have a discourse about which is more important here, structure or culture; better we should acknowledge that they are dynamically related. These family stories have surely made it more apparent that two things are true: first, people, with their yearnings, habits, and passions, make families the way they are, and second, cultural ideologies, historical legacies, and the structures of production have powerfully shaped their subconscious endeavors and narrowly constrained their intentional efforts.

REAL MEXICAN MOVIES

Regardless of time and place, those for whom such changes have felt most threatening have usually relied on religion, patriotism, or cultural nationalism to buttress their defense of the conventions, especially the prerogatives of patriarchy and class privilege, that they have liked. One mellifluous word, apparently imported from Mexico proper, which also felt the reverberations of American movies, expresses how tradition-minded people in México de afuera responded to the ordeals of modern culture. That word is *desmexicanización.* Here, of course, we enter the dangerous waters of modernity. The modern era, from which we may be exiting now, has numerous characteristics that people are eager to label as good or bad. Indeed, "liberty, equality, and fraternity," each guided by reason, have their downsides. These include heartlessness, lack of reciprocity, loneliness, the commodification of life, and the despiritu-alization of the world. The historical actors cited above and immediately following have been arguing enough about the relative merits of these matters, so that I will only say that in the transition some things are gained and some things are lost, but much is changed. Thus, I think it important to distinguish between Americanization, associated with the assimilation of Anglo-Protestant lifeways, and modernization, which is identified with the rise of individualism and materialism. Both, though, were called desmexicanización.

Hollywood movies did portray Mexicans, but almost always in an insulting manner. Before 1918 many of the films about Mexicans had the word "greaser" in the title, and they usually depicted good Americans saving virtuous women from bad Mexicans. In these films the Mexicans were usually greedy, thieving, treacherous, bumbling, and, well, greasy. The Mexican government pressured the Wilson administration to urge upon Hollywood more kindly portrayals of Mexicans. For a while the studios replaced greasers with savage Indians and vile Huns. After the war the portrayal of Mexicans as villainous recommenced. The Mexican government first banned movies with negative images and then, joined by Panama, threatened to bar all movies from offending studios. The name "greaser" disappeared, but the character reappeared, without, though, an explicitly stated nationality. When there were positive roles for Mexican stars, they were usually some sort of exotic, but non-Mexican, character. In *Evangeline,* Dolores del Río and Donald Reed play Acadian lovers who are separated by the French and Indian War. In *The Pagan,* filmed in the South Pacific, Ramon Novarro plays a "handsome islander [who] devotes his days to singing and his nights to romance."[32]

An article from Mexico reprinted on the society page of *La Opinión* expressed alarm at how "Pictures spoken in English will contribute to the faulty drawing of our imprint of nationalism." Mexican critics dreaded both the derogatory portrayal of Mexicans and the celebration of American culture and its language. English-language movies portended "a pacific and deeply resonating conquest." The author referred to "an alien language that would provoke disasters of *desmexicanización*." These words came in support of a group in Los Angeles led by Ernesto Romero, whom the consul had appointed, that sought "to form a society consisting of all of the cultured elements of the Spanish speaking people who reside in the United States of America, whose object would be to raise the consciousness of the North American producers about the necessity of establishing the Spanish language in the sound cinema worthy of our public, [and] without the barbarisms of language or mystification of our customs and psychology which have prevailed until now." This critique referred to both the poorly dubbed English-language films that Hollywood produced as well as the over 100 movies made in Spanish for pan-Latino audiences in the 1930s but featuring fractured Spanish, an impossible array of dialects and accents, and foolish or even insulting subject matter.[33]

La Asociación Cultural America-Española, composed of "artists, intellectuals, movie technicians, and those others interested," met in February 1930 with the Association of Moving Picture Producers to insist upon *películas hispanoparlantes*. The two groups agreed to "a plan which would include the cooperation and help of this association [America-Española] to obtain the services of the best artistic and technical elements, the most authentic information pertaining to the issues of dress, customs, social environment, and language in support of the producers, and the manner in which the Spanish-speaking actors and actresses with stage experience will be selected in all of the movie studios of Hollywood will be explored."[34]

While this group continued agitating, the independent Hollywood Spanish Pictures Company released in March 1930 the musical review *Charros, Gauchos y Manolas* and the short *Un Fotografo Distraído*, both "totally spoken in Spanish." The former revolved around a bohemian painter imagining great scenes of Mexico City, then Buenos Aires, and then Seville. After a premier at Teatro México, the "World Debut" took place at the Million Dollar Theater on Broadway with such stars as Gloria Swanson, Norma Talmadge, Ruth Roland, and Gilbert Roland in attendance. According to one reviewer, though, "the film is not a very admirable production like the ones which Fox, Warner Brothers, and others have launched at the market." "At any rate," he continued, "it is an effort which represents an unknown aspect among elements of our raza: the spirit of enterprise."[35]

November of 1930 saw the "first film from Paramount completely spoken in Spanish," *El Cuerpo del Delito*. "The best Hispanic artists in Hollywood are taking part in this admirable film . . . Antonio Moreno, Barry Norton, Ramon Pereda, Andres de Segurola, and Maria Alva." Paramount made Spanish-language versions of a few of their films, such as *East Is West*. *Oriente y Ocidente* featured Lupe Velez speaking Spanish and played at Teatro Hidalgo. "Finally," though, in January 1931 Paramount announced that from its studios would come a film that *La Opinión* affirmed would have "Original Story Lines for Our Cinema." Now there would be films made from original scripts written in Spanish "for those who love our own customs and traditions [to be] conveyed on the screen." These movies did not turn out well. *La Opinión*'s movie reviewer reckoned that "falta de libretto," or the shortage of worthy original Spanish scripts, and the lack of Hispanics in positions in the studios to supervise productions that had themes relevant to Latino audiences, accounted for the failure.[36] The abundance of talented Mexican playwrights and stage technicians in Los Angeles (which we saw in chapter 1) makes questionable such explanations. More likely, Hollywood studios simply had more energy and capital to support English-language films.

Guardians of Mexican culture in Los Angeles knew that both the cultural content and the language of the new metropolis's movies had the potential to capture the consciousness of the youth. Synchronized sound simply amplified the threat. Stage productions articulated the cultural elites' critiques and fears. Desmexicanización meant not only the loss of Mexican culture, but its replacement with an inferior one. Recall that people migrated not because they thought that American culture was better, but because life in their homeland had become untenable. Two of Gabriel Navarro's stage revistas, which often actually celebrated Hollywood nightlife, *La ciudad de irás y no volverás* and *La ciudad do los extras,* provided two of many examples of theater that satirized the assimilation of americano ways, criticized the loss of the language among youth, and disparaged the denial of Mexican identity in favor of Spanish.

At least those involved in the theater knew well the peril that movies presented, but these voices of cultural retrenchment were quieted as repatriation and the Depression dramatically shrank audiences, which in turn darkened more and more stages. "The ones who stay in Los Angeles," noted *La Opinión* in August 1934, "are those who have not been able to leave the city or those who don't want to. The former are trying to deal with their most pressing problems, rather than with entertainment. The latter frankly prefer American spectacles." The rich theater life and the Spanish-language cinema succumbed to the same forces: "The old people are few. The young people have learned English and can go to a first-class theater that offers first-class variety, plus a movie, and orchestra etc., for a minuscule charge, something that our theaters cannot do."[37]

AMBIVALENCE ABOUT LIFE IN AMERICA

Mexicans who experienced uncertainty about life in the United States, particularly about whether or not to stay, often expressed their doubt and resentment in the context of the changes that they blamed on, or credited to, *americano* culture. "I want to go back to Mexico where my sisters and brothers live," stated one woman. "They are good for me. Here my children are no comfort. I think I should never have come in the first place. My [daughter] ran away and got married." A martyr to the changes in family behavior and an idealizer of the old country, she continued, "That was a bad thing for her to do to her mother who had always been so good for her. She married with a good man, yes, but she ran away to do it. In Mexico she would not have run away." Misfortune followed her family north, where "the girls do those things. If they do not like what the parents tell them they go and do as they like anyway." Another woman, who migrated from Zacatecas when she was one year old, envied these latter qualities, acceded to the new authorities, and wanted to stay in the United States. She wrote to the local school for advice on how to deal with her husband's family, compared to whom she was better educated. Her statement illuminates the poignancy and complexity of her immigration experience. She said of her in-laws, "I can't stand their dirty ways and awful ways of living. All my friends disapprove of the type of family I fell into." She continued, "My husband's step-father knows I have had a good education and that I am smarter than all of them so they have decided to force me to go to Mexico." For this woman who had grown to maturity in the metropolis there awaited an untenable situation: "Many of my friends went back to Mexico only to be laughed at for wearing short dresses until they had to use them for underclothes. Now they are in rags and have no shoes.

Please advise me before I make a false step." Obviously, these two immigrant women—one a mother and the other a daughter—had entirely different attitudes about life in America and whether or not to stay.[38]

So many factors influenced their estimations of life in the north. Obviously, the turmoil and poverty of Mexico and the higher wages in the United States affected the immigrants' views. Then, too, a variety of very personal reasons entered the picture. The family and its fortunes south of the border no doubt had meaning. It does seem, though, that such material considerations as the availability of commodities, the culture of individual prerogatives, and the issue of education for children rose to the forefront as Mexicans decided on which side of the border to live.

Women and men differed in their estimations of life in the north. We have already seen how men were more likely than women to object to changes in expectations about male-female roles. Economic opportunity made the north more attractive to both. One man, who repatriated to Pénjamo in Guanajuato and had saved enough money from working eight years in the orange groves to buy a small plot and grow guavas and lemons, told a sociology student from USC, "Yes, we don't have the tools and facilities we had in California . . . I don't like it here very much because I can't make anything." Asked if he would prefer Pénjamo, he said, "Yes, if I could make money here, I'd like it here . . . mi tierra, mas bonita. But I want to go back there and make something. There is no chance here." "I don't like the town, customs . . . anything," said another. "You can't make anything here. In Los Angeles I always had some money in my pocket; used to make it selling papers and giving shoe shines. Here we are always broke." "I'd rather be there anytime," a youth born and raised in the north attested; "those [burros] are the machines here. Nothing but donkeys around here." The convenience and allure of cars meant a lot, especially to men. The bad roads of Mexican towns blew out the tires of the vehicles that repatriates brought back, and in Mexico tires and gasoline cost three to four times as much as in the United States.[39]

Stoves and washing machines loomed especially large when women compared their lives north and south of the border. "There [in the United States] they have *mas comodidadas* than here," stated a repatriada. "Electric light is very expensive here. We don't use electric lights in the house— just candles. We have to use charcoal for cooking. There, even the poor houses have baths and running water, but here no." She bathed now "In a little tub of water in the middle of the patio exposed to the four winds." While indeed appliances have sometimes created a domestic trap for women, the washing machine has brought relief from lighting fires under tubs of water and the backaches from rubbing clothes on wash-boards or rocks by the rivers. Researchers' conversations with male re-patriates showed little concern for such labor-saving devices. In the north many women had washing machines, sometimes purchased collectively by several families. "It's better here," explained a woman on the east side of Los Angeles, "there [in Mexico] we hardly had anything. We slept on the floor on serapes. Here we have a washing machine, there not even tubs, we washed at the river."[40]

Women could appreciate the remaking of family ties when they relo-cated back, south of the border, but the move also heightened the con-trasts regarding individual prerogatives. "I never go to dances here. You can't go out with boys," said a repatriada. "If you do everyone starts talking, and you are regarded as a lost person." A professional man con-curred: "The women learn American customs. The women want more liberty, but the husbands don't want it." "Here [in East Los Angeles]," said another in the post–World War II era, "even a woman can work and make money—there is better food."[41]

Life back in Mexico did bring welcome relief from the discrimina-tion that prevailed in the north. Whether in the schools, public swim-ming pools, movie theaters, or jobs, second-class treatment in the United States incensed Mexicans who had no reason to believe Anglo-American attitudes about them. The consistency of the work and the money in the north varied, but our informants make it clear that more often than not both were better than in Mexico.[42] For the most part, recent immigrants, who could compare life in the United States with that in Mexico, lived with the discrimination because they could better support their families, in a more peaceful place. The second generation, who did not know the old turmoil of Mexico and who compared their economic and social lives and access to public places to the americanos', would think very differently about life on both sides of the border.

WANTING SCHOOL

School played a dynamic role in Mexicans' opinions about life in the north. Its steadiness and services proved attractive, but then school dis-crimination propelled Mexicans to action in American politics. For par-ents who journeyed to the United States with their families or sent for them after a while, the situation of their children's education influenced their feelings about staying. A laborer father in Los Angeles whose children had taught him to write stated in 1907, "I will never go back to Old Mexico, because I have five children in the public school." Working-class people, native born or immigrant, have generally perceived, correctly or incorrectly, formal schooling as a ticket out of dependency on manual labor for their dreary subsistence. Although hindsight may provide grounds for questioning the accuracy of their perceptions, access to school figured importantly in parents' hopes for their children's futures. "In Mexico the teachers very bad, the children very good. In California, the teachers very good, the children very bad," as one mother cleverly expressed the situation in the early 1920s. School provided, moreover, a way for immigrant children to gain entry into the rest of society, their frequent disillusionment and anger at the white supremacist and authoritarian institutions notwithstanding. We have already seen the distress initiated when the father of the wife of the troublesome Perez would not let her attend school. Her case was not unusual. "When I got here, my parents wouldn't let me go to school because there were boys in the same school so I had to stay in the house and work," stated another woman, who obviously felt left out of the experience. An eighteen-year-old mexicana said, "I feel sorry to give up school and the days seem very long when I have to stay home."[43] A knowledge of the printed word opened up terrific new vistas for sheltered ones' lives. Schools ruled over the printed word, and so people wanted to go there.

The school, as we have seen, widened the gap between parents and children, which increased the ambivalence of the elders about life in the north. "Some children here don't respect their parents," stated a mother who had been a teacher in Mexico, "because their parents haven't an education." There was more involved than simply such drawing of the children away from their parents' culture. The schools profoundly challenged the customary assumptions of Mexican parents, particularly fathers, and sowed the seeds of family discord when, for example, the school system expected girls to attend as much as boys. Literacy statistics from 1914 demonstrate the presumptions about the formal education of boys and girls that Mexican parents carried with them to the north. In this early sample of seventy-five immigrants, 72 percent of the Mexican men but only 22.6 percent of the women could read Spanish.[44] Patriarchal culture, then, often discouraged school learning for girls, as the preceding quotes from mexicanas whose fathers forbade them to attend have already suggested.

Some hard-working fathers perceived their sons' attendance at school as idling, and girls were usually pressured out of school, or forbidden to attend. "I will never forgive my father because it was his fault that I quit school," stated a twenty-five-year-old mother. "I tell him about it yet. It was two months before I was to graduate from the eighth grade and he went to the teacher about me and a boy and it started so much talk that I would not go to school anymore. I was so ashamed. . . . That is the way with the old Mexican people." She clearly felt the loss: "The day the girls in my class went past our doors with their diplomas, I cried my eyes out." She also sensed the enforced dependency of uneducated women: "I never went to high school because of that. What could I do now to take care of my children if my husband died. Wash and iron like the other Mexican women?" The overwhelming majority of Mexican students who dropped out did so because of the necessity of working. Many others flunked out, or the language barrier discouraged them. Still, eleven out of ninety from a survey of the early 1930s dropped out because of their fathers' pressure. The demands of work and family often combined: "My teachers gave me a regular lecture and told me it was wrong to quit, but my father said it is bad enough to worry about something to eat without worrying about school," explained she whose days at home dragged.[45]

LIKING SCHOOL

Recall here our brief discussion of the Mexican immigrants' diet. Fundamentally, not having enough money frustrated Mexicans' efforts to acquire adequate food. A state study of 1916 noted that the Macy Street School in the Plaza district provided clothing for its young students and a "penny lunch" program for its young students. The citywide PTA and the teachers at the school financed the program, the teachers carried it out, and a philanthropic organization provided milk. For a penny, an immigrant child typically received soup of "meat stock, vegetables, and rice . . . and a sweetened bun." After 1917 lunch cost five cents, but children did small jobs around the school for the money. A similar routine at Ann Street School provided lunches for kids too, whether they had the penny or not. The school served americano food, of course, but my point here revolves not around the quantity and quality of the food, which were no doubt beneficial for hungry kids, but around what came with it: milk. "Through the kindness of certain individuals each child is allowed an egg and a quart of milk a day," reported a sociology student in 1920 about the Ann Street district. The recreation center there had a "Mother's Clinic" that distributed pure milk and a "Children's Clinic" with a district nurse and a city physician.[46] But not enough can be made of the fact that milk, especially when it replaces coffee (a diuretic that leeches calcium), forms strong bones and muscles in little children. Not only is calcium essential for bone development and muscle activity, but milk's electrolytes are necessary for cellular growth. Mexican mothers could simply watch the improvement in their children's vitality.

Like most such efforts it all came with a dose of condescension. The women's clubs and clinics at the schools and recreation centers sought to instill the Protestant virtues of thrift and cleanliness. Recall here too the opportunities for contagion raging around the house courts' public toilets, sewage ditches, and contaminated water. Mexicans' understanding of disease varied widely in Los Angeles, but many certainly relied on "folk beliefs," or the mysteries of the spirit world to explain illness. Modern, scientific culture, whether it be in Mexico City or Los Angeles, had begun to understand the relationship between microbes and disease. Thus efforts at sanitation could have profound effects on rates of tuberculosis, cholera, and gastrointestinal ailments, the very infections that killed so many of the babies of the Mexican, and non-Mexican, poor. Anglo nurses ministering to Mexican mothers, with an air of superiority or not, taught those who came into the clinics or had home visits about the relationship between contamination and infection.

Hygiene saved children's lives, and milk made them much healthier. In 1923, when the rate of infant death before one year of age for Mexicans in Los Angeles stood at 250.3 per 1,000, or about one in four, the county initiated an intensive program of maternal and infant hygiene. By 1929 the rate had fallen to 104.5, or about one in ten, and other statistics put the rate at 111.6 in 1935. Although the rate was more than double that of the white population, there can be no doubt about the profound meaning of such a statistic in the lives of families in México de afuera.[47] The mother standing before an altar, a candle illuminating the faces of her baby and the image of the Virgin, could give thanks not only to the Holy Mother but also to the clinic for her little miracle and his or her well-being.

Several different metaphors have already been presented to readers of this narrative to foster their imagination about various matters. Now numerical ones, all derived from Los Angeles school district statistics, are offered to abet thinking about the nature of the schools. Macy Street School in 1916 had a student body 34 percent Mexican, 27 percent Italian, 12 percent Syrian, 9 percent French, and 3 percent Chinese—quite obviously a remarkably polyglot population. As migration increased, the composition of the student body changed: in 1923 the school became 68 percent Mexican, 14 percent Chinese, 8 percent Italian, and 8 percent Syrian.[48] As Mexicans left this more general immigrant quarter of the city for neighborhoods more exclusively Mexican, the children could usually expect a less international assortment of peers, but not always.

A 1936 study of fifteen Hollenbeck area elementary schools showed these proportions of Mexican students: 83 percent of Utah Street School (with 13 percent Russian), 87 percent of Echeandia Street, 73 percent of Bridge Street, 55 percent of Second Street, 29 percent of Breed Street (with 34 percent Jewish), 9 percent of Sheridan Street (with 88 percent Jewish), 70 percent of Euclid Avenue (with 20 percent English speaking), 57 percent of First Street (with 26 percent Japanese), 40 percent of Malabar Street (with 38 percent Jewish), and 22 percent of Lorena Street (with 53 percent English speaking).[49] Readers may want to leave for a moment the question of whether in schools like First, Second, and Malabar Streets the classes were half segregated or half integrated, but there is no doubt that meaningful diversity regarding the segregation of Los Angeles's elementary schools prevailed (see figure 18).

The populations of the two junior highs in the Hollenbeck area reveal both the terrifically significant dropout rate for Mexicans and the remarkably integrated school life experienced by those who remained: Hollenbeck had 38 percent Mexicans, 35 percent Jews, 7 percent Japanese, and 9 percent Russians; and Robert Louis Stevenson had 31 percent Mexicans and 50 percent English speakers. More statistics further evidence these trends: at Roosevelt High School on the East Side, 24 percent were Mexican, 28 percent English speaking, 26 percent Jewish, 7 percent Russian, 6 percent Japanese, 1.5 percent each Armenian, Italian, and German, and 0.5 percent African American. Two years later Jews made up 40 percent, Mexicans 27 percent, Japanese 9 percent, and Russians 5.5 percent, and English speakers had stunningly dropped to 4.5 percent. These statistics attest to remarkable fluidity in the ethnicity of the school experience as well as white flight from the area. Neighboring Garfield High School remained more stable between 1934 and 1936: English speakers went from 71 percent to 59 percent, and Mexicans from 17 to 22 percent; while Japanese, Italian, and Armenian remained at about 2 percent each.[50]

A high dropout rate—reflective in part of the assumption that a junior high education sufficed for Mexicans—provided the only consistency in the experience of Mexican schoolchildren in Southern Califor-

Figure 18. A classroom on the East Side. Was the class half integrated or half segregated? (Courtesy Shades of L.A. Archives, Los Angeles Public Library.)

nia. In striking contrast to these diverse statistics in Los Angeles, Orange County (adjoining to the south) educated Mexicans in fifteen utterly segregated elementary schools. Using the usual arguments about cultural and intellectual retardation and responding to whites' objections about Mexicans in their schools, schoolmen in Orange County established "Mexican schools" to purge immigrants' children of Mexican language and custom and drill them in tasks appropriate to their presumed future roles—as laborers and housewives. Large discrepancies prevailed in the amount of money spent on the American and Mexican schools' physical plants and teachers. According to Gilbert González's research, in places like the La Habra area in 1934 a school district would have 4,000 Spanish-surnamed children in the elementary schools, but only 165 in the high school. Of these only 15 made it to their senior year, and usually fewer than 3 actually graduated. It is so curious, and politically significant, as we shall see in the next chapter, that the discriminatory practices of these school programs in which Americanization played such an important role made Mexicans more aware of being Mexicans. A former principal told how "many times . . . our youngsters would say to me, 'The reason they do it is because we're Mexicans.'"[51]

Children in the agricultural colonias throughout the greater Los Angeles area underwent similarly mean treatment. Recall how americano parents in the San Fernando Valley successfully pressured for segregated elementary schools. In these schools, as in those of Orange County, Mexican kids would be held back because they had failed to pass "tests." Consequently, when they finally graduated from elementary school and had the option of going to an integrated junior high for seventh grade, they would often be too old, too big, and too embarrassed to feel comfortable. Again, eighth grade was the typical dropout point.[52]

From San Fernando we hear about other conflicting issues regarding the body's presentation at school. As is no doubt typical for many adolescent girls, gym class could prove stressful for Mexican students. Mexican mothers sometimes objected to girls' wearing only "short bloomers and no stockings," reported one study. The students varied in their responses to this aspect of physical education in the Los Angeles public schools. "We dress in gym shorts and have lots of fun," said one in 1929. "Trinidad," whose family picked fruit and lived in a shack in the San Fernando Valley, would not dress for gym, explaining how "all the girls laugh at me because I haven't nice underclothes like the rest of them, and I won't undress in front of those girls."[53]

And we must acknowledge and affirm that individual teachers have always made a difference in children's lives. Imagine how one child might take a class from a teacher made miserable by having to teach a room full of students she considered culturally inferior and dirty; kids would feel the meanness of her prejudice, or maybe the teacher would simply ignore them. Another might take a class from a teacher who simply loved all children and teaching; with devotion and intelligence she would enrich all of her students' intelligence and self-worth. Two other Mexican children might attend a class where the teacher had a mission to instill in the students the virtues of Protestant American civilization, and he would measure the students' "progress" against standardized tests; one student would accede to the norms and learn to read books and do numbers, while just as likely the other youngster would withdraw into himself in the face of the aggressive Yankee, and then drop out. The degree of segregation made a difference too. In some school settings all of the children would be mixed together on the playground and in class skits and plays; regardless of the attitude of the teacher, the mingling of their diverse voices and little bodies would forge bonds and solidarity between them. In other scenes a dreary segregated school combined with a dreary teacher to foster dreary children.

Parental attitudes and involvement have always been key to children's achievement in school. We have already seen how many Mexican parents so approved of the idea of the school, regardless of the operation of it. But with at best only a modicum of experience with schools in their own lives, most Mexican parents had only vague conceptions of the functioning of these public schools, which, it must be recalled, commanded prestige and authority for many. Schools did not encourage academic achievement for Mexican kids, but industrial arts in high schools offered a Mexican son the opportunity for a steady, skilled job. Thus did many parents consent to schools' educating and socializing their children.[54]

We must say, then, that Mexican children shared many aspects of the school, but in other ways had widely dissimilar experiences with it. To isolate the most important points: the plans of fathers and schoolmen conspired to have children drop out at around the eighth grade, and yet, at least at Garfield High and Roosevelt High, one-quarter of the seniors were Mexican; Mexicans were to be Americanized—actually only to undergo desmexicanización—but school policy heightened their experience as Mexicans; although schools endeavored to sort them into areas of the economy and society thought appropriate to their cultural or intellectual capacities, at the schools children saw manners of being that encouraged them to participate in American society; at the schools mothers learned about new routines that safeguarded their babies from diseases, and they became subjects of the new clinical ways; and the children often learned how to read in English.

REAL MEXICAN SCHOOLS

Those in México de afuera who articulated their views about the education of the young emphasized two inequities. Desmexicanización and segregation powerfully offended those who believed, the majority of Mexicans obviously, that Mexican culture, language, and people were at least as worthy as any other. Mexican parents of all classes were quite aware that schools that did not admit Mexicans did so because the americanos considered the immigrant children inferior and undesirable. The lower quality of the school facilities simply amplified the message. Especially in the surrounding agricultural counties, various organizations, from La Liga Protectora Mexicana to El Comité de Vecinos de Lemon Grove in Orange County, publicly protested to school boards and city councils about segregation. In January 1930 La Opinión railed at how in Oxnard "Mexicans are considered as Indians and separate schools are adopted."

There "those born in Mexico" were sent to "Indian schools," to the great insult of many Mexicans.[55]

Commentators in México de afuera, parents, and the Mexican consulate strove to counter desmexicanización and the insulting attitudes and practices of the public schools and to maintain the allegiance of the youth to Mexico, via a system of separate Mexican schools. One of these schools, Palo Verde, "like similar ones which exist in various places of California, has come from the combined labor of the Consul of this city and Miss Margarita Robles, delegated by the Ministry of Education [of Mexico], so that the youth who immigrated at an early age to this country and the Mexican children born in the United States will not distance themselves completely from the mother country." Both California and Mexico had certified Robles to teach so that credits could be transferred back to Mexico when and if the expected repatriation came. From 4:30 to 6:30, "after the instruction which the youth and kids received in the American schools, classes are given to raise the patriotic spirit of the students." Interestingly enough, most of the schools in existence by September 1929 were in agricultural areas—Claremont, Campo Hicks (El Monte), Pacoima (San Fernando Valley), Watts, Van Nuys, and so on. Each school averaged 100 students, claimed *La Opinión,* and the urban Belvedere had day classes for children and night classes for adults to preserve and repair their allegiance to Mexican culture.[56]

The political content implied in the courses of study paralleled what we have already seen in such groups as the comisiones honoríficos. The Mexican professionals and business owners who dominated these endeavors stressed individual achievement, national pride based upon the upper-class values of political and familial hierarchies, and distrust and even contempt for the masses, especially those identified culturally or phenotypically as Indians. "To inspire in the students a powerful love for our country . . . they are taught . . . Spanish, national history, patriotic readings, stories of our heroes, Mexican music," and "the responsibilities they have toward Mexico and the United States, while they live in this country."[57] Students would be taught, in rote fashion, the "best" of Mexican culture and history: those aspects that most closely paralleled elite European history—families successful over generations, great leaders, and acquiescent lower classes. Non-conservatives could agree with such a program too. After all, progressives had always been supportive of pushing Mexico in the direction of the modern nation-state that England, France, and the United States epitomized. A coherent national purpose and culture, forceful leaders, and either the discipline or repression of non-European peoples had proved key in those nations' greatness, and were thus appropriate for Mexico.

Sustaining such genuine Mexican schools was no easy task even with the consulate sponsoring a Department of Education with Miss Carmen Ramos in charge of coordination. Mexico had troubles enough educating Mexicans who still lived in Mexico; the state of California ruled in 1928 that it could not accredit Mexican teachers; and the Mexican middle class in Los Angeles gave support more verbal than financial. As resources diminished only three schools—all in agricultural colonias with segregated public schools—with a total of 200 students remained by the end of 1930.[58] Vaguely but genuinely, México de afuera perceived the threat that American schools and popular culture posed to its children. The effort to institute the Mexican schools, like the effort to make Mexican movies, could not command the energy and resources necessary for the creation of such parallel Mexican institutional structures within the new land that simultaneously segregated and enveloped those children.

NEW LANGUAGE

Like the notion that "people make history," the idea that "language shapes consciousness" both states the obvious and contains more depth and complexity than is at first apparent. Written language differs meaningfully from spoken, more so, in key ways, than Spanish differs from English. But just as certainly, that one generation of immigrants spoke Spanish and the next English is not without powerful consequences. The issues at hand, then, are the meaning of the fact that schools pressured children of Spanish speakers to learn English and that, at least as important, many Mexican youngsters came to have a new relationship to literacy and the nature of stories. We shall now unravel more about movies and schools, as emblems of what is usually called "modernity."

So far we have seen several manifestations of the challenges that the metropolitan institutions of the cinema and the schools presented to the old authorities of the Church and the patriarchal family, their striking resiliency notwithstanding. Let us now, though, contrast each's use of language and story. The Catechism dominates the linguistic interaction of the Church and children. Learned via a series of questions to which those receiving instruction respond with rote answers, the Catechism not only teaches the principles of the Faith, but instills an unambiguous sense of right and wrong. "From what do our temptations come?" asks the priest. "Our temptations come either from the devil, our spiritual enemy, or from the world; that is, the wicked persons, places, or things in the world; or from the flesh; that is our body with its strong passions and evil inclinations," answer the pupils. The ritual of asking and responding creates social solidarity and a social identity within the community of believers united in the institution of the Church and, when the catechumens have finished training, through Holy Communion with the Body and Blood of Christ.

For people, at least in Europe and the Americas, who have been socialized in the hierarchical family, familial talking practices have fortified unchallengeable assumptions about authority and social roles, gender roles in particular. Sayings—*dichos*—provide the most lyrical examples of the use of authoritative words that tell children how to be as regards their roles both in general and in particular situations. *A la mujer ni todo el amor ni todo el dinero* (To the woman neither all the love nor all the money); *Al decir las verdades se pierden las amistades* (In telling the truth, friendships are lost); *Cada quien es como Diós los hizo* (We are all the way God made us); and *Los padres que quieren a sus hijos, con más vera los corrigen* (Parents who love their children apply the switch more often) provide dulcet, but rigid and immutable, pronouncements about how to be in the world.[59] And they carry the imprimatur of the ancestors. The language practices of both church and family, then, have forged, affirmed, and elaborated a fixed consciousness about indisputable social structures. This shared understanding of the ways of the world has been part of what has maintained the variously warm, callous, constraining, and redemptive bonds of non-industrial communities.

I include "redemptive" because of how such communities handle those who transgress the assumptions about correct behavior. Obviously, people, for all manner of reasons, violated the norms; this chapter is full of people doing so. And note the typical consequence of, say, cutting one's hair, eloping, or dressing certain ways: offenders are not spoken to; they are cast out from the community either via expulsion (Petra) or given the silent treatment (Josefa). When they have been redeemed (from the Latin *re*, "back," and *emere*, "to get or buy"), they are reintegrated into the community. Thus their trespass has been clarified for them and the community; they have experienced consequences that should dissuade them and others from doing it again; the mores of the group have been reasserted; community solidarity has been reaffirmed; and those who have been so castigated will mature to eagerly castigate the new crop of transgressors.

The elaborate rituals of the sociedades that Mexicans established in

Figure 19. A queen of an honorific society and her court. They appear under the approving male gaze of *heroés mexicanos* and a leader of the society. (Courtesy Shades of L.A. Archives, Los Angeles Public Library.)

the new land functioned to weave youth into the cultural webs that the leadership thought correct. In this milieu a "good" person—one rewarded with initiation, honor, or even selection as queen for a parade or holiday—was one who properly fulfilled his or her expected social role (figure 19). The formality and sartorial splendor that prevailed in the ceremonies and initiations affirmed the notions of hierarchy and authority. The sociedades provided one place where Mexican men still had prestige and control that they used to reaffirm cultural and moral orthodoxy. Conventional male-female roles and morality were understood to be a part of what it meant to be Mexican, to be patriotic, and to have pride in la raza. One club formed in early 1930 sought "to unite the Mexican youth to work to maintain the good name of the raza, and it resolved to accept youths morally and physically able to work for such a noble and elevating ideal."[60] The sociedades had many functions, but they also responded to the apparent and natural unease that the older generation of middle- and upper-class Mexicans felt about the palpable deterioration of the ideals and behaviors, associated with conservative Mexican cultural norms, that avowedly held society together. The rituals insinuated a remaking of a sense of order in the new land, one that subordinated individual desires to the collective needs of la raza and the patriarchal family.

Movies and literacy tendered the new urban dwellers—and let me again emphasize that this process proceeded, albeit unevenly, in all of the cities of the Americas and Europe—the notion of choices about how to be and act. This was what so disturbed the older generation and caused so much generational conflict, especially when so many of options that popular culture and the school environment presented appeared so alarming. Education brought about sea changes too, but in ways more profound than they appeared on the surface. The acquisition of literacy means that one enters the private world of the printed page, a place where an individual reflects upon the messages that the printed words carry. Rereading passages, thinking about the stories, considering oneself in relation to the subject being read about. All these activities combine to make a literate person different from an illiterate person. The printed pages can make language something very different from that used for the Catechism or the dichos. When people interact with printed texts they can wonder, imagine, and engage in self-reflection. Such self-consciousness differs tremendously from a situation in which people interact with language that tells them how to be, how to fill a prescribed role.[61]

It is certainly not the case that all, or even most, Mexican children passed through such a transformation. The information presented above shows clearly that many Mexican kids simply experienced rote learning, even the suppression of language when they were punished for using Spanish, or else they dropped out before they could learn much of anything. But this is another point to be made about the diversity of the educational experience: some graduated from high school literate in English (but the particular language is not the point), able to pore over books, magazines, and newspapers. In other words, they internalized texts and could use language to engage in self-reflection. At least there were all these new stories circulating about the place, ones that usually were disseminated more broadly and blossomed more fully than the old dichos or rote learning about the great heroes. Young people talked about the new movies they saw and maybe about the new things they read about in magazines and books. These new stories provided new guides for living.

Choosing one's own style, courtship and sexual practices, and values and beliefs from those the modern city displays and offers culturally and educationally provides the opportunity for the individuated self. While psychologists associate such a self with emotional health, sociologists tie it to normality, and anthropologists used to see it as a key distinguishing factor between modern people and tribes, it is a much more complex and controversial issue than these fields have allowed. Capitalist popular culture and schooling, with their apparent agendas, have powerfully influenced the development of a self, as we have seen in this chapter. On the negative side, the notion of the modern self thus includes the delusion of autonomy, suspicion of others, a large measure of denial of the difficult organic bonds that humans have with nature, culture, and family, and, quite often, loneliness.

The operation of morals changes too. For people who are illiterate, or nearly so, the sense of right and wrong derives from such rituals as the Catechism and dichos; actions are measured against axioms that are given. Indeed, it could be argued that the old stories that the elders told conferred not so much wisdom as restraint. As one engages in the process of creation of a self individuated from the cultural and familial environment, right and wrong are measured against an ethical sensibility developed through the self-reflection that literacy, and even fanciful movie plots, have brought about. The self, in other words, not the bequeathed culture or the family, becomes the arbitrator of what to be and how to act.[62] This is the deepest meaning of why "children get so different here," and this is what Mexican parents, especially fathers, so recoiled and raged at in the episodes narrated above.

No doubt it is a big question whether we humans, with all of our seedy passions, can develop ethical selves good enough not to create such turmoil and pain, or whether humans genuinely need the external restraints of such authorities as family and church to tell us how to be and keep ourselves and our children from harm.

The Political Passions
of México de Afuera

El Partido Liberal Mexicano has solemnly declared
war against Authority, war against Capital, war
against the Church.

> "*Manifesto a Todos los Trabajadores
> del Mundo,*" Regeneración, *1911*

Our people do not have Bolshevik blood.

> El Heraldo de México, *1919*

"Insult" and "wounded pride" are the first words that come to mind
when describing the Mexican reaction to Americanization. This response
derived in part from the unquestionable facts of American economic superiority and political stability. Consequences of the former included
the presence of so many jobs on the north side of the border that a million Mexicans left their homes for them, and that consumer goods and
entertainments were produced so plentifully there that even working-
class Mexicans could get a few. The latter fact conveyed that death and
violence did not ordinarily accompany civil life in the north. The pundits
of México de afuera had to acknowledge the clearly evidenced deficien-
cies of la madre patria in the first decades of the century. Economic superiority and political stability clearly did not, however, translate into equity
or justice. Discrimination, prejudice, and condescension were everyday
aspects of life for Mexicans when they journeyed out of their homes and
colonias for work, shopping, recreation, or school. This painful and creative tension formed the context in which mexicanos de afuera framed
their political discussions about life in el norte.

But politics would be formulated as well within the weighty historical legacy rendered in chapter 2. The experiences of the Porfiriato, the
Revolution, and the resulting chaos and efforts at political consolidation in Mexico provided the framework in which Mexicans of all stripes

would think about the politics of living in a México de afuera inescapably surrounded by, and interwoven with, America. Fairly quickly, in order to contest their American situation, Mexicans in Los Angeles and elsewhere sometimes even adopted much of the political rhetoric and thinking of the United States. Notions of equal rights, integration, and non-discrimination entered the political discourse and rivaled passions revolving around *tierra y libertad,* "land and liberty," and *¡Viva Cristo Rey!* (the slogan of the violent Catholic faction of the Cristero Revolt). This rhetoric also proclaimed the transformation in political consciousness that reflected the metamorphosis of most Mexicans from being marginal or de-landed peasants in the south to being wage workers who suffered discrimination in the north.

Discussion of the condition of the Mexican worker in México de afuera provides a clear window into how people thought about America. The political analysis that derived from the examination of the condition of Mexican labor folded into Mexicans' perspectives on the colossus of the north. The inferior station of the Mexican worker clearly pricked Mexican national pride. The conservative *El Heraldo de México* attributed the problem both to the characteristics of the Mexicans who migrated and to the attitudes of the Americans: "An ignorant man is a big child," it editorialized, "and the majority of Mexicans who come to this country to get work are composed of big children." Thus "they resign themselves to performing the most common of labors, [and] receive the minimal salaries which correspond to these most physical of tasks." "On the other hand," the article continued, "foremen and other superiors abound who, taking advantage of their ignorance, inflict on them bad treatment, speak to them in deprecating tone, exclude them from contact with Americans, and even establish hateful differences in the wages because the Mexicans are not considered white, even though the work they perform is equal to or better than that of the sons of the country whom they frequently succeed." "The conditions of the agricultural and factory worker must be other than what they are," the author concluded, "with nothing of the hateful distinctions, nothing of the humiliations."[1] The concern for the worker was not simply a humanitarian one; it included this painful sense of general disgrace in the eyes of both Americans and Mexicans.

Yet, *La Opinión* had to admit, "naturally the value of the money earned in the U.S. is much greater than in Mexico, [and] this is what permits the worker to live decently, even with this lowly day work." "And it is that the Mexican works well and cheaply, not disdaining to do work that, because of its poor remuneration, the North American finds flatly repulsive," the paper continued, noting how work in the fields paid $3.50 and in the factories $5.00 per day *como mínimo* (at a minimum). "And on the other hand, we must ask, what agriculturist in Mexico pays his peons seven pesos per day?" Not that the north was simply a place where dollars grew like lettuce in the irrigated dessert: "brought by the mirage of the dollar . . . many times the disenchantment is truly tragic." Unemployment ruined the hopes of so many: "It is true that the wages are in the $3.00 per day range," stated another article, "but one doesn't always work."[2]

Again, the humanitarian concern merged with affronted dignity. Discriminatory vagrancy arrests most prominently offended Mexican sensibilities. The biggest problem with seasonal labor, even more so with day labor, always has been that in some seasons and on many days one did not work. Unemployed people frequently idled in La Placita or some such place. The police considered them vagrants and made sweeping arrests. "The persecution of vagrancy," noted an editorial of January 1928, "is only one particular of this problem whose principal aspect is the excess of a people [Mexican immigrants, that is] in a total population which does not have the wherewithal to receive and sustain them." Two years later, the calls for deportation of Mexicans, who were now blamed for the Depression, would prove particularly galling, the appropriateness of Mexicans voluntarily returning to la madre patria notwithstanding. To be arrested when one was between jobs was both baffling and infuriating, especially because the police targeted only Mexicans. If, as Consul Pesqueira stated in *La Opinión*, "The Mexicans are the Basis of California's Prosperity,"[3] then only their nasty prejudice could explain why the americanos would treat Mexicans so meanly.

It has been a peculiar feature of Mexican nationalism that it has been formed in negative contexts. Whereas the Americans could celebrate great military victories over indigenous and foreign foes (including the Mexicans), Mexican nationalism emerged first from the wounds suffered at the hands of rebellious Anglo Texans, then from the loss of one-third of its land to the American army, then from defeat at the hands of the French in 1864, and then from the loss of so many of its most vital people through emigration to the country that had routed them so soundly in 1846. A headline of May 1927, "10,000 More Mexicans Emigrate in 2 Months," was more than merely disturbing: "The problem of the depopulation of our vast territories is frightful. . . . One could predict that the time will arrive when Mexico is so depopulated that, for the few that remain, no other recourse will remain but to ask for annexation to this country." *La Opinión* perceived that the number who left represented "not only an imaginary numerical factor but a good part [of Mexico's] creative and progressive capacity." Emigration marked collective and personal defeat: "From that moment [of emigration]," declared *El Heraldo* in 1919, "with hope lost of any further economic improvement, [emigrants] flee with their eyes still cast upon la madre patria, where there are those who understand them and those who treat them with affection, even though it be no more than in the bosom of their family."[4]

Even in the best light, this situation boded poorly for Mexicans' national self-esteem. "Mexican emigration is good for both Mexico and the United States" because "when our workers return to their country, they have not only notably improved their work habits, but, even with the simplest peons, they have become accustomed to dressing, wearing shoes, eating, and entertaining themselves as do the American workers."[5] There was simply no escaping the productive, material, and political superiority of the United States.

And there was no escaping the imperiousness of the United States either. In the 1920s, seventy-five years after what Mexico has always considered a conquest of its northern territories, discussion of the Mexican relationship with the United States continued in the shadow of ongoing American foreign policy exploits. The decade of isolationism, the 1920s, witnessed six American military interventions in Central America. These catalyzed Latin American opinion against the United States' hemispheric policy, or what *La Opinión* called *norteamericanismo*. The paper made a big issue of the landing of U.S. Marines in Nicaragua in early 1928, with the goal of neutralizing Augosto Sandino and his forces, who were fighting General Emiliano Chamorro, executor of a recent coup d'état. Sandino emerged as a "bandit to the American Secretary of State, a patriot to his partisans, and a hero for all of the inhabitants of Latin America," and he had "many points in common with the famous Mexican fighter Pancho Villa."* For many Mexicans "the extension of these conquests over the last century" represented norteamericanismo. To this imperial ethos was juxtaposed *panamericanismo,* or the principle of equality among hemispheric nations and multilateral cooperation.[6] Thus the

---

*Villa and Zapata, once the enemies of the generals who took power after the Revolution, had been rehabilitated in the cause of solidifying support for the Mexican state. Indeed, the U.S. Marines chasing after Sandino paralleled General Pershing's 1916 action against Villa. Mexico was among the leaders of the attack against U.S. intervention in Nicaragua at the Sixth Panamerican Conference in Havana in February 1928. Ironically, American occupation of the port of Veracruz in 1914 proved crucial to General Carranza's eventual victory over Villa and Zapata.

thinking of mexicanos de afuera about the United States involved envy and resentment both over matters having to do with material success, emigration, and treatment of immigrants, and over the historical legacy and present practice of imperialism.

For most mexicanos de afuera, however, there was no escaping the everyday discrimination of the workplace and the schools. The experience of discrimination created their political sensibilities much more than the Marines in Nicaragua did. Discrimination may, however, be the wrong word to use here. It implies the violation of the principle of liberty and equality for all human beings. But chapters 2 and 3 elucidated how it was that neither the Mexican nor the American society was designed to realize those principles for anyone but elites, in the former, and whites, in the latter. Indeed, as explained previously, there may even be a relationship in the United States between the lack of freedom that racism created for menial, extravagantly exploited laborers, on the one hand, and the promulgation of notions of democracy and liberty for everyone else, on the other. In other words, it did not occur to very many Anglo Americans in the first decades of the twentieth century that Mexicans, Asians, Africans, Indians, or women were entitled to equal rights or to equal access to the material wealth of the United States. To Anglo Americans, Mexicans did not live under discrimination; they worked and lived in their proper place in the world racial hierarchy.

Indeed, it has certainly been the case that some Mexicans opposed discrimination not in the abstract, but only when it humiliated Mexicans. *La Opinión* complained that theaters in San Bernardino sat Mexicans only "in a certain section, that is in that of the Negroes." There Mexicans "were humiliated in the theatres and movie houses." Several Mexicanos de afuera protested to Consul Pesquiera about the Pasadena Fair Oaks Theatre, "which proceeded to denigrate the Mexican people, because it would not permit their entry except in the Negro section, including even girls and boys, who by their color and features, the Caucasians acknowledged to be pleasant and neat."[7] Here, it was not that discrimination violated the principles of human equality, but that it lumped mexicanos de afuera with those who have been most maligned in the United States, African Americans.

To poor Mexican immigrants from the countryside, the situation they faced in Los Angeles did not feel all that different from the disparagement they had known in the south. A racially defined labor market had only replaced considerations of caste and landlessness. Yet, to Mexicans born in the United States, such prejudice denied them access to equality that popular culture and camaraderies at school were preparing them to assume. To middle- and upper-class Mexicans, who had always presumed superiority over the lower castes, being treated as second class was both unfathomable and intolerable.

In this context diverse mexicanos de afuera created a political culture in which ambiguity toward the United States—strong sentiments of envy and resentment—and disparate experiences of class, gender, and legacies from Mexico all prevailed. Added to this was a huge dose of the political and racial ideologies and passions of the United States and the rest of the world. The evolution of politics presented a remarkable and rich array of ideologies and movements.

FIRST UNIONS

Many, if not most, of the political controversies swirling around México de afuera revolved around the issue of work, especially when a strike action focused attention on the predicaments of labor in the north. Organizational efforts carried their own ideological foundations, and groups with explicit political agendas allied with strikers and attempted to influence the political ideas of the participants. Most basically a strike functions to collectively withdraw labor from the market until wages increase to their market value. Although unions operate within the market system, a sense of deprivation—based on what is perceived as an equitable share of the rewards of production, or more simply on hunger— has usually motivated strikers. The organization of Mexican strikes has ranged from ad hoc to nationally organized, hierarchical unions. The political purposes of Mexican strikes has varied from nil, to bureaucratic integration with the national state, to the complete overthrow of the capitalist system.

The first work stoppages usually were not particularly political, but they sometimes attracted a large number of radical outsiders. The 1903 strike of the track workers preparing for the Fiesta Days, which introduced our narrative, was hardly the only Mexican effort of that year. So often, especially in agriculture, work stoppages protested the contract system, wherein owners of large farms contracted for labor and the contractor made his money by squeezing his workers. In February 1903 Japanese pickers united with Mexicans over this very issue in Oxnard. They formed the Japanese-Mexican Labor Association (JMLA), which, after a month-long strike in March of that year, won independence from the Western Agricultural Contracting Company, so that Mexican and Japanese beet workers could contract directly with the growers. Afterward they formed the Sugar Beet and Farm Laborers Union and applied for membership in the American Federation of Labor. The AFL's president, Samuel Gompers, responded that the "union must guarantee that it will under no circumstances accept membership of any Chinese or Japanese." JMLA secretary J. M. Lizarraras wrote back extolling "our Japanese brothers" and refusing "any other kind of a charter except one which will wipe out race prejudices and recognize our fellow workers as being as good as ourselves."[8]

These were ethnic matters as much as they were strikes of workers. Another Fiesta Days strike occurred in March 1910. This time, however, the Mexicans' walkout initiated a wave of strikes by all unions in response to the employers' aggressive wage squeeze. Though the workers of the Los Angeles Gas Works, the majority of whom were Mexican, won a wage increase in August 1910, most strikes of that year ended in defeat. The bitterness of the workers is generally associated with the fateful bombing of the *Los Angeles Times* building on October 1. Passions from the Mexican Revolution began to fire some of the participants: anarchists apparently played a role in the short-lived Unión de Jornaleros Unidos founded in 1911.[9]

Nothing in the world, or at least the northern hemisphere, seemed the same in 1919. Eastern and Central Europe had been redrawn after the collapse of great empires, and a revolutionary workers' government, which promised to end capitalism, had taken power in Russia. In the United States workers struck the steel and packinghouse industries and closed down the entire city of Seattle. Many Americans associated these strikes with immigrants and communists, often correctly. Not only had the Great War been a disillusioning experience, but now in 1919 it seemed as if working-class revolution threatened civilization itself, at least as property owners understood it. This worldwide tumult affected Mexicans in Los Angeles.

In what must have been very scary or thrilling or inspiring times, that eventful year saw not only the establishment of Soviet power in Russia, and briefly in Bavaria, Hungary, and Seattle, but also a strike in February of Mexican citrus workers in the San Gabriel Valley, located just east of Los Angeles. Though called with a dramatic strike meeting at the Walker Theatre (aka the Teatro México), it proved a relatively minor affair—in retrospect—the pickers struck because of miserable housing conditions and because the market had forced wages below what they could live on. Yet, the names of those arrested and their political affiliations provide a window into what must have been a remarkable revolutionary moment in Mexican history in the United States. The press associated those with Spanish last names, such as Manuel Sastre or "Francisco Zamora . . . one of the leading I.W.W.," with that organization. Those with Jewish last names were the "agitadores Rusos," one of whom allegedly stated that his group was "like a Russian Soviet or committee." The usual array of police power, arrests, stacked juries, and vigilantes forcibly removing organizers from the fields, defeated the strike. But we see here the efforts of two internationally affiliated directors of the class struggle, anarchists and communists (apparently without rivalry in this case), attempting to lead, politicize, and focus the spontaneous, "economist," strike actions of Mexican workers, who, like workers everywhere once their class consciousness had been raised, were understood to be the basis for worldwide revolution.[10]

Obviously, other Mexicans besides those affiliated with the IWW articulated their views about the historical role of Mexican workers and their strike activities in Southern California. The conservative *El Heraldo de México,* which had had more than enough of revolution in Mexico—it referred fondly to "the illustrious President Porfirio Díaz"—agreed with the americano press and simply blamed the San Gabriel strike of 1919 on "Russian agitators . . . who have been working with great energy to establish a strike among the pickers." According to *El Heraldo,* the strike happened only because the troublemakers "told them that they should not work for less than four dollars." The paper's readers could be rather sure of this because "the Mexican is not naturally lawless or inclined towards strikes, being in general agreement with his wages which vary from three to four dollars per day." "Our people do not have Bolshevik blood," the paper affirmed. A year later the paper noted that Mexican workers "do not feel the impulses of rebellion that the recently 'Americanized' ones do."[11]

Big strikes and little ones took place in that momentous year of 1919. Even in small manufactories like a brickyard in Santa Monica where thirty-six Mexicans went out in March for a shorter workday, the ferment raged: "Now they enjoy," noted *El Heraldo* with typical disdain for workers' initiatives, "a work day of three dollars for nine hours of work." In August when about one-third of the platform employees and one-half the carmen of the Los Angeles Railway Company struck, most of the Mexican track workers, as usual, joined the action and championed for themselves an eight-hour day and a wage of $2.72 per hour.

By August 24, no trains moved and workers had begun advocating government ownership of the railroads. The Railroad Brotherhoods threatened to rescind the locals' charters, the employers stonewalled, and the strike petered out.[12]

ON TRANSFORMING WORKERS

It is mostly true that the Mexican masses concerned themselves much more with the task of getting a living than with what we usually call politics. As we saw in the previous chapter, contestations over power, "politics," took place in a variety of locales, perhaps most profoundly in the home. Here, however, politics shall be limited to what men, usually but not always, did in the public arena of newspaper debates, union propagandizing, and electoral politics north and south of the border.

For many radicals worldwide, working-class movements promised the most auspicious rebellion against the established order, though it was the peasant revolutions in Mexico, Russia, and China that most shook the capitalist world order. Still, Europeanized radicals throughout the world reasoned that it would be workers, many of them former peasants for whom capitalist discipline of the factory whistle and the assembly line most assaulted customary lifeways revolving around such things as the seasons and saints' days, who would realize the ideals of liberty, equality, and fraternity. And then, according to the logic of capitalism, which saw labor as the only variable expenditure in the labor-capital equation, with costs for rents and machines more fixed, the market would continually push wages below subsistence levels, and push workers to revolt. The titanic battles between workers and capitalists in the decades under discussion here, in Southern California and the world, advanced and sustained the revolutionaries' case. Radicals generally have seen these "class struggles" as inevitable, and hoped to politicize them in ways that would birth fundamental change.

On the other hand, reformers tend to see these clashes as irrational and hope to solve what they called the "labor question" via reform. Still again, many capitalists see labor strife as a matter for the police or militia and have tried to avoid it with a combination of the "iron fist and the velvet glove" and by promoting the ideology that the market is fair and value-free. The classic conservative view, which usually affirms the bonds of hierarchy over capitalist notions of liberty and the market, prescribes for the wage worker that he, as *El Heraldo de México* put it in 1920, "resigns himself, suffering quietly, whether because of obedience to ancestral commands that he has encrusted in his blood in the form of the singular humility (humility, gentlemen of the dictionary, not 'humiliation'), or because he feels weak and isolated."[13] Workers have always been targets of such propagandizing, but have proved only variously responsive. The strike actions of Mexican workers, especially in the 1920s and 1930s, provided the cauldrons into which all sorts of political potions were poured, and they can be understood only in this world historical context. From the mix emerged a new alchemy of Mexican laborers' declining connection to the established government of Mexico and their increasing association with American working-class institutions.

RADICALS

Those curious people we saw in chapter 1, living communally, carting their fruit to market downtown, and putting together a newspaper, stood in the forefront of the radicals who tried to give direction to workers' strikes. Their roots went deep in the Mexican history that our narrative previously touched upon. Many young Mexican intellectuals perceived that the problems of Mexico associated with the Porfiriato derived from the regime's and the foreigners' corruption of liberalism. In the 1890s one such student, Ricardo Flores Magón, began to criticize the regime for its favoritism toward English and American companies and, particularly, for its crushing of freedom of the press and electoral democracy. Díaz expelled Flores Magón in 1903 and the latter joined numerous other exiles in the southwestern United States, the model of liberalism in their eyes. From there these energetic and idealistic people, Librado Rivera, Ricardo and his brother Enrique Flores Magón, Juan Sarabia, Antonio Villareal, and a few others began to organize for revolution in Mexico. In St. Louis in 1905, Flores Magón and others organized the Partido Liberal Mexicano (PLM), which espoused a vague socialism upholding the sovereignty of the people above all else, though asserting the harmony of classes. Mexicans on both sides of the border flocked to the liberal clubs that the PLM organized, and the circulation of the party's newspaper, *Regeneración,* quickly grew to between 15,000 and 20,000. Most of the party's adherents, like its leaders (journalists, craftsmen, teachers), were petite bourgeoisie or skilled workers, particularly miners. They all were the ones who experienced most profoundly proletarianization at the hands of Yankee and British capital. For example, he who would become the great leader of the Tarascan Indian people, Primo Tapia, from the village of Naranja, Michoacán, whose inhabitants had suffered the destruction of their common lands at the hands of the world market, joined the Liberales in Los Angeles, allegedly lived in their house, and worked at the newspaper office in 1910 and 1911.[14]

In the north they experienced the tribulations of Mexicans living in the United States. As the party leaders moved from Texas, to Missouri, and then finally to Los Angeles in 1907, the American police and agents of the Mexican government constantly harassed them with jailings, confiscations of their printing press, and physical intimidation. This, and that great and mortal flaw of americano liberalism—the racism he saw reflected so profoundly in the super-exploitation of Mexican workers—ended whatever illusions Flores Magón had about liberalism and reformism. Following their arrest in Los Angeles for violation of neutrality laws in 1907, the PLM junta became something of a cause célèbre for Anglo radicals. After the 1907 charges were dropped in response to a strong legal defense movement, the junta was immediately shipped to Arizona in October 1908, convicted of violating neutrality laws in May 1909, and sentenced to eighteen months in jail. Meanwhile, during the summer of 1908, the PLM launched several attacks across the border from Texas, which resulted only in failure and more arrests. Now the PLM was in utter disarray. In this context the writings of such anarchists as Mikhail Bakunin, Enrico Malatesta, Carlos Malato, and Pyotr Kropotkin, plus the presence in PLM circles of the likes of Emma Goldman and Spanish anarchist Florencio Bozora, led Flores Magón in the direction of anarchism. Likely from jail in 1908, but definitively and publicly in the "Manifesto de 23 de Septiembre 1911" published in Los Angeles, Ricardo Flores Magón, the junta, and *Regeneración* proclaimed themselves and their organization for anarchist revolution in Mexico.[15]

These extraordinary people, with a vision as compelling as it was utopian, listened to the misery and aspirations of ordinary people and brought ideology and analysis to their people's rebellions against the rule of capital and the market. Like most anarchists, the PLM vociferously condemned bourgeois society, explicitly declaring "guerra a la Autoridad, guerra al Capital, guerra al Clero," and then sought to strike the match that would ignite revolution in the masses they politicized. They believed that all people really were born with the capacity to "make art out of life," that caste and class derived not from anything in the blood (as both americanos and mexicano elites mostly believed), but from the forces of history. The clergy betrayed the people because they fooled them and kept them from the reason and creativity that were their destiny as human beings.

These Liberales believed that since workers produced the wealth, it belonged to them. Since wealth in Mexico came mainly from the land, it too belonged to the people. This worldview resonated with many people in Mexico and the Southwest who saw capitalism as an interloper that altered patterns, often from an idealized past, of independence and subsistence production. Capital and the bourgeois legal system enslaved people by keeping from them wealth that was morally theirs. Only through propaganda and direct action, not political maneuvering or strategy, would people overturn capitalism. They would then replace this system with self-governing institutions in which local autonomy and cooperation would reign. To these ends the PLM propagandized, mostly in the no less than thirty *Magonista* newspapers published in the United States; instituted their many clandestine and open liberal clubs; and organized workers into unions. This publicity and organization, they believed, would ultimately precipitate *the* general insurrection by means of which the people would take power.[16]

Such an understanding of their thinking explains the otherwise quixotic invasion of Baja California in 1911. From Los Angeles the junta planned the attack that would spark a revolt. While the interracial bands composed of Liberales, Wobblies, Italian anarchists, and assorted adventurers succeeded in taking both Mexicali and Tijuana, Baja California did not erupt in the flames of revolution. The PLM leadership, especially Ricardo Flores Magón, who did not take the field, lost credibility, and splits further shook, jumbled, and assailed the organization.[17]

On matters of culture, PLM ideology proves engaging, controversial, and sometimes contradictory. Ricardo Flores Magón was a Mexican nationalist who railed at foreign domination of his country. Then, too, he preached international solidarity of the "disinherited of the earth." The people were sovereign and capable of lives of reason, love, and beauty, but presently they were ignorant and apathetic. They had to be educated away from culture, "the economic structure of society and the spiritual preoccupations which everywhere put up obstacles to individual liberty and human happiness."[18] It was between 1914 and 1916 that the Flores Magón brothers and several other Liberales rented five acres just north of downtown Los Angeles and attempted, as we saw in chapter 1, to live the communal lives they envisioned for the rest of the world. Ricardo and Enrique Flores Magón dwelled with their *compañeras* María Talavera and Teresa Arteaga in relationships based on love, not bourgeois marriage, an institution that "shackled love." Everyone worked together in the orchard, but the women maintained the household and rolled the newspapers while the men wrote. The subscriptions and fruit they sold downtown could not support *Regeneración,* so several women formed Luz y Vida in November 1915. This all-women PLM chapter held dances and benefits and sold food to support the paper and the propaganda effort.[19]

Ricardo's practice reflected his ideology about women, which he elucidated in his famous essay "A La Mujer," published in September 1910. Quite obviously his ideas provided a striking contrast to the other models of womanhood we have already noticed in México de afuera. On the one hand, the essay claimed, "Humiliated, degraded, bound by chains of tradition to an irrational inferiority, indoctrinated in the affairs of heaven by clerics, but totally ignorant of world problems, she is suddenly caught in the whirlwind of industrial production which above all requires cheap labor to sustain the competition created by the voracious 'princes of capital' who exploit her circumstances." It then asserted that women should "spit in the face of those who refuse to pick up a weapon against oppression." On the other hand, women's "duty is to help man; to be there to encourage him when he vacillates; to stand by his side when he suffers; to lighten his sorrow; to laugh and to sing with him when victory smiles." "When it is motivated by economic insecurity instead of love," Ricardo noted, "marriage is but another form of prostitution." *Regeneración* also printed "La Mujer," an essay of 1910 by Praxedis Guerrero, a junta member and field commander killed in battle in 1911. It claimed, "Religion . . . is the most terrible enemy of woman." Here "feminism" was contrasted with "equality of the sexes." Guerrero associated the former with "a masculine female who is divorced from her sweet mission" and stated that the latter "will enforce equal opportunities without disturbing the natural order between the sexes." *Regeneración* affirmed in 1913, "The man and the woman as equal beings in ability, should be equal in rights and the freedom to act their wills upon their persons and their possessions."[20] What we seem to have here, though, is the anarchists' Rousseauian vision of return to "nature," which is associated with nurturant, mysterious, and superior woman.

What women thought about all this, or how they participated in PLM activities, is more difficult to ascertain. At least one activist, the literary figure Sara Estela Ramírez, whose home in Laredo actually served as the first PLM headquarters upon the Flores Magóns' arrival in Texas, expressed similar Rousseauian notions of womanhood: "woman lives forever and this is the secret of her happiness, life." "Only action is life," and women should "arise radiant and powerful," she wrote. Apparently Mexican women's pro-female ideologies remained essentialist ones in spite of such inflammatory claims as that of the *Los Angeles Times* that María Talavera, the compañera of Ricardo, was a "brilliant and bold woman anarchist who dared more than any of the men" and an "expert assassin." Her own activities, such as organizing socialist support for *Magonistas* in the Los Angeles County jail in 1907, got her arrested on several occasions, and she was only one of numerous women who propagandized for revolution in the American Southwest and the Mexican North. She was among the many tried for violations of the Espionage Act in 1918 in Los Angeles.[21]

Consistent with its discourses on "the disinherited of the earth," and for the tactical reason of rallying the masses to the cause and politicizing them, the PLM sought to organize Mexican workers into unions, often in cooperation with the IWW. In its Fresno Local 66 during 1909 and 1910, the IWW, for example, while unable to create an ongoing union, organized many Mexican migratory agricultural and railroad workers. The legendary Frank Little headed the Fresno organizational efforts and the Mexican IWW organizer, Jesus González-Monroy, was also a PLM activist. In Los Angeles in 1910–11, the IWW exerted influence in strikes of Mexican street railway and gas workers. One PLM activist estimated that at its peak before the war "the Los Angeles local alone had nearly 400 active members in its Latino wing, mostly Mexicans." Primo Tapia organized unskilled Rocky Mountain miners and migratory wheat laborers for the IWW. He fled back to Mexico in early 1920 after he and some village compañeros led a remarkable but unsuccessful effort to organize Mexican beet workers in Nebraska.[22]

After the Mexican generals pushed the anarchists out of post-revolutionary Mexico and Flores Magón died in Leavenworth prison in 1921, Los Angeles involuntarily hosted the remnants of the Liberales. These colorful and certainly provocative speakers in La Placita "make many fiery and sometimes vile accusations against religion and capitalism." In the 1920s reformers concerned with "stopping these 'Reds!'" typically cited "a cross-eyed agitator . . . haranguing some two hundred idle, ignorant Mexicans." That these orators spoke against "Clergy, law, [and] capital" quickly establishes their identity.[23]

These inflammatory words did not fall on deaf ears. The people understood that the Catholic Church, the greatest monopolizer of land, opposed the Mexican Revolution. Many Mexicans, while certainly Catholic, were intensely anti-clerical, a sentiment that the libre pensadores exploited in their tirades at La Placita. Of course, the Church was not without its equally vehement backers. Luis Tenorio, a street paver of the late 1920s, described how "on Sundays I go to the little square to hear some of the fellow workers. That is where I have gotten socialistic ideas and I read the papers which these friends sell." During the same period, construction worker Guillermo Salorio said:

> I am studying books and I now lack very little of being well convinced that God doesn't exist. I first became acquainted with these ideas because I went to the square on Sundays and there heard some of the comrades make some speeches. They said nothing but the truth, that the capital is what steals everything and that money isn't good for anything, that it is necessary for everyone to work. I believe the same in everything and that is why I liked their ideas and I began to read papers and books and go to the IWW hall.

Many Mexican workers in the United States, so long admired for their alleged passivity, often revealed themselves as dangerous revolutionaries.[24]

The victim of savage repression as well as its own ideologies, which failed to promote an ongoing organization, the anarcho-syndicalist tradition in the Southwest had faded by the early 1920s. Nevertheless, Primo Tapia became the leader of the League of Agrarian Communities in Michoacán, an organization that sought the return of the people's ejido lands and saluted the Bolshevik Revolution. Through political and military means, Tapia and his followers succeeded in restoring many of the lands and the communal methods of harvesting the crops. Soon, though, the government quashed the movement and assassinated Primo Tapia in April 1926.[25]

The IWW/PLM tradition of class-conscious, non-discriminatory, industrial unionism hibernated in the north and sometimes awoke, if not to motivate, at least to participate in organization and strikes through the 1920s and 1930s. The PLM's continuing influence resurfaced fleetingly in the Confederación de Uniones de Obreros Mexicanos (CUOM), which was organized in November 1928 in Los Angeles. Around that time the colonias had been buzzing with talk of union, and workers furtively organized work stoppages. No doubt appropriately and inevitably in this context, in 1927 the Confederación de Sociedades Mexicanas, including a variety of colonia and community leaders and the Mexican consul, called for a union of all Mexican workers in the area, rural and urban. Several ideologies and strategies surfaced in the negotiations surrounding the formation of the union. The union that emerged has been characterized as revolutionary, conservative, and reformist.[26] I now suspect that mutualista and colonia leaders for whom "unity constitutes strength" simply hoped for the unification of as many sectors of the Mexican community as possible. All of these political tendencies were represented, all competed for leadership, and different ideologies were ascendant at different times.

Actually it wasn't a union anyway, only a confederation of Mexican workers' organizations—mutualistas, cooperatives, and existing and incipient unions. Ringing the One Big Union bell of the PLM/IWW, the CUOM stated in March 1928:

> That the exploited class, the greater part of which is made up of manual labor, is right in establishing a class struggle in order to effect an economic and moral betterment of its condition, and at last its complete freedom from capitalist tyranny. . . . That the corporations, possessors of the natural and social wealth, being integral parts of the international association of industry, commerce and banking, the disinherited class must also integrate by means of its federation and confederation into a single union all the labor of the world.

While the CUOM modified its program of resistance in order to be "in accord with the rights which the laws of this country concede to native and foreign workers," we see here how PLM/IWW principles made their way into the founding statement. The inclusion of these principles is likely why Consul Alfonso Pesqueira refused to recognize the CUOM for at least two months. The relationship between Mexican workers and the consul was always an uneasy one: the consul represented a Mexican government eager to push such class-conscious revolutionary agitation into the dustbin of history.[27]

In fact, the Mexican government saw in the CUOM, and the 3,000 members it claimed in its 22 locals in Southern California, another opportunity to tie institutionally the workers of México de afuera to the homeland. The Confederación Regional Obrera Mexicana (CROM), the huge union closely tied to the ruling party in Mexico, participated in the founding of CUOM and helped to organize workers into it. Of course this element sought to counter the revolutionary anti-statism of the anarchists. The CUOM pledged "to establish strong ties with organized labor in Mexico."[28]

Leaders of various ideological factions competed for the allegiance of Mexican workers. Right at the time of the formation of the CUOM, organizers for the Federación de Uniones Mexicanas del Oeste, hoping to become "genuinely the 'left' of the 'C.U.O.M.' . . . oriented their efforts toward the industrial neighborhoods of Los Angeles and the port of San Pedro." The Federación had in common with the CUOM the effort to negotiate with the Mexican government to impede emigration to California. There were in California, after all, "presently many unemployed without the least hope of ever getting work."[29]

Not everyone agreed with the notion that the Mexican government, or the CROM, could or should be of assistance to Mexican workers in California. The secretary general of the Agrupación Obrera Mexicana (AOM) declared himself and his organization in favor of "harmony between capital and labor," a position diametrically opposed to that of the CUOM statement quoted above. In order to benefit "both industrialists and workers [the AOM] sought, above all, a total distancing from such organizations as the CROM, of Mexico, considering them causes of enmity." "The solution [to the problem of unemployment] is in the hands of the class affected," AOM declared, and proposed "forming Labor Exchanges, which would be the base for a just workers institution."[30]

None of these organizations met with much success, especially after the Depression hit. Yet there were many Mexican strikes in the early Depression years in which agricultural workers refused the wages that the allegedly hard-pressed growers and the labor market assigned them. Mexican workers believed that their families' subsistence required a certain minimum remuneration, and only a strike could achieve this. Their labor was not some commodity, but their means of supporting their families. That something as impersonal as the market could establish how much money they would be paid was a notion hateful, immoral, or incomprehensible. They could agree with most of what their CUOM or the Communist-affiliated Cannery and Agricultural Workers Industrial Union leaders told them about capitalism, if not always about the Church. Yet a man joined a union and went on strike not from ideology or vision, but from a sense of necessity. This was the same mind-set with which he migrated to the north in the first place, and then took on work as onerous as stoop labor in the sweltering fields. One did what family survival required on a week-to-week, even day-to-day, basis. This meant taking dreadful jobs that paid enough to maintain the family, and then going on strike when the market pushed that pay below what was minimally necessary. From their precarious position in the labor market, their summoning up the courage to challenge their bosses and the police in order to provision their families reveals another facet of Mexican patriarchy—the responsibilities and obligations of family leadership—in the strike actions of Mexican men.

The El Monte strike of June 1933 illustrates this rejection of the commodification of their labor, as did the 36 other agricultural strikes in California that year. The El Monte strike also epitomizes the ideological battle for the hearts and minds of Mexican workers. Antagonistic forces—Consul Alejandro Martínez, mutualista-oriented leaders, and this time even Communists—all vied for supremacy. Again, we should not try and understand the CUOM as reformist or revolutionary, but as an organization that included a wide range of tendencies, and one which was then itself an arena of intense political struggle.

At El Monte, the largely Japanese growers (who were in violation of the state's Alien Land Laws of 1913 and 1920, which forbade Japanese land tenure) calculated the amount they would pay per crate of picked berries based upon the return they expected the Depression market would give them on the produce. They offered 40 cents per crate, which meant that one could make up to 20 cents per hour, though the women and children would make less because they picked more slowly. As picking time approached, a group of twenty Mexican, Anglo, and Japanese pickers demanded what they considered a subsistence wage from the Japanese growers association. When their appeal was rejected, workers at Hick's Camp voted at the Communist-led rally to strike for 25 cents per hour or 65 cents per crate. The growers, at first somewhat conciliatory, countered with 15 cents per hour or 40 cents per crate, and later with 20 cents per hour and 45 cents per crate. But because the berries had to be picked immediately and the spirits of the strikers, most of whom were Mexicans, were high, perhaps unrealistically so, they would not budge.[31]

They stood fast even though during the Depression plenty of unemployed waited to take their jobs and even though they were particularly vulnerable to the economic squeeze that a strike inevitably entails. But then it had always seemed like a depression to Mexicans anyway, and such secondary-market workers had simply accustomed themselves to insecurity, strike or no strike. Kin networks undoubtedly reached out to those in need and put extra plates on the dinner table for striking relatives. This was a working-class community familiar with such obligations and accommodations. Since these strikes were very much community affairs, rooted as they were in the mutualistas, prestige derived from sacrificing oneself and supporting the people's efforts to uplift themselves.

The Mexican strikers were not alone in their efforts either. Typically, those Americans who came to the Mexicans' aid were themselves outcasts from society. Only an unusual gringo supported the Mexicans and was not a Communist, or closely affiliated with the Party, in the years between the world wars. Where the narrow, stodgy, and racist AFL feared to tread, the Party and its corps of seasoned militants often stepped in, and often wound up in jail. "They were in on every protest I saw or heard of," stated one former Red. "If they didn't start things themselves, they were Johnnies-on-the-spot. . . . The Communists brought misery out of hiding in the workers' neighborhoods." In the early 1930s capitalism stood at its economic and ideological nadir. The Communists believed, not without good reason, that it verged on collapse. Thus it was crucial for them to build their own organizations to contest for power against the old and crumbling system. One such labor union was the interracial Cannery and Agricultural Workers Industrial Union (C&AWIU). The C&AWIU belonged to the umbrella Trade Union Unity League (TUUL), which competed with the reformist AFL for the allegiance of American workers.[32]

The El Monte strike happened in the C&AWIU's peak year. The 24 of California's 37 agricultural strikes of 1933 that Communists led accounted for 75 to 80 percent of the strikers (mostly Mexicans). Indeed, in 21 of those 24 strikes, the combination of Mexican solidarity and Red leadership won wage increases. But the vanguard party also pushed such unions to transcend what the Communists considered their reformist nature. Communists understood the need to politicize the rank and file to broaden their aspirations beyond wages and family subsistence. They wanted to be ready to lead all of the TUUL unions into revolutionary motion as the system collapsed in a heap under the pressure of these and other workers' protests against such inherent capitalist ravages as the market and the Depression.

It is difficult, however, to pinpoint precisely the nature of C&AWIU activity in the El Monte strike. The Communists competed with the consul, the anarchists, and the mutualista leaders for the hearts and minds of the workers and the CUOM. Initially the Communist Party had at least a tenuous hold on the CUOM's strike leadership and settlement committee. Likely some belonged to both organizations, though, importantly, the leader of the strike committee, Armando Flores, opposed the Reds. (One historian claims that "fewer than 10 percent of the original 1,500 strikers appear to have joined the CAWIU," but it is hard to say if this is a low or high figure when we recall the this was an explicitly

Communist organization.) Several days after the start of the strike, the sheriffs, who were on good terms with the strikers, lured the settlement committee and the Reds to their station, claiming that the growers were ready to settle. The sheriffs delayed the committee for several hours. In the meantime, Armando Flores called in the Mexican consul, Alejandro Martínez, who denounced the C&AWIU, per his orders from the Mexican government, and succeeded in turning the workers away from the Communists. Upon their return from the sheriffs' station, however, the Communists regained at least some influence.[33]

Then, on June 10, eight C&AWIU organizers were arrested. Again Martínez turned the strikers against the Reds. This time the party, indeed perceived as outsiders, could not reestablish control because of the arrests and because the sheriffs kept other Communists out of the area. It was at this point that the CUOM, which had dwindled to include only about ten small unions, was formally reorganized as the Confederación de Uniones de Campesinos y Obreros Mexicanos (CUCOM) with the help of Vice Consul Ricardo Hill, who along with Martínez, was now the outside leader of the strike. Like the old confederation, the CUCOM carried traces of Magonista anarcho-syndicalist ideology, at least in the baggage of its vice president, William Velarde, an IWW member whose father had organized for the IWW and who had "personal and political ties" with the PLM.[34] We should try to understand the CUCOM not as reformist or revolutionary but as an organization that included a wide range of ideologies and was itself an arena of intense political struggle.

Meanwhile the strike spread to the onion and celery fields of Culver City, Venice, and Santa Monica, on the extreme west end of the city. The strikers' numbers reached 5,000 to 7,000. A contemporary commentator noted "the natural spreading of the strike idea and excitement among the Mexicans." Within six months, the CUCOM numbered from 5,000 to 10,000 members in 30 local unions. The scope of the strike against the largely Japanese growers increased as well. In Mexico the government hoped to make political hay by supporting beleaguered workers in México de afuera: financial support arrived from ex-president Plutarco Calles and from the CROM, which also threatened a boycott of Japanese goods. The Japanese consul, ever and justifiably fearful of arousing anti-Japanese sentiment, entered the picture, negotiating with the Mexican consulate to bring about a settlement. Indeed, the *Los Angeles Times* portrayed the strike as "a wage war . . . between the Japanese truck farmers and the Mexican field workers," and *La*

Opinión referred to "los pizcaderos Mexicanos" and "los cosecheros nipones." (Only the Communists noted that Anglos, often the banks, owned the Japanese farmers' land.)[35]

Actually, the race factor seems to have been negligible, except insofar as nationalism united the Mexican strikers for whom the CUCOM was, as the leaders put it, a "cultural organization" as well as a union. The Los Angeles Chamber of Commerce barged in as well. (They privately acknowledged that "American land owners of the El Monte section . . . are back of the Japanese growers.") The chamber feared that the strike would spread further and that adverse publicity about their Mexican workers would fan the flames in favor of immigration restriction. They, and the Anglo growers in the area, were aghast that the Mexicans would act this way. They believed their own rhetoric about Mexican mentality and passivity. Like the priests who blamed the Devil when Indians ran amok, the gringos explained this Mexican apostasy from docilely accepting the ways of the market with a new devil—the Communists.[36]

All of these groups sought to end the strike amicably, and the berries were rotting. By June 26, behind-the-scenes politicking had increased the growers' offer to a crate rate that would allow a male picker to earn from 20 to 25 cents per hour, a near capitulation to the strikers' demands. But the strikers now felt sufficiently confident to transform this battle initially waged merely to maintain their subsistence against the forces of the market into a general offensive against the growers. Finally, however, with the governor of California involving the State Division of Labor Statistics and Law Enforcement, the two sides along with the Mexican and Japanese consuls, the Chamber of Commerce, and the strike committee, reached a settlement. As the berry-picking season passed, the strikers had to accept $1.50 for a nine-hour day or 20 cents per hour, somewhat less than previous offers.[37] If the Mexican workers had not achieved a resounding financial victory, they had at least won a victory of the spirit. Then, too, the agricultural employers' love affair with cheap, manageable Mexican labor began to turn sour.

The JMLA, the CUOM, and the CUCOM were essentially Mexican organizations, though some Japanese and Filipinos figured importantly. The latter two unions had their roots in the mutualistas and the anarcho-syndicalist segments of the Mexican Revolution. The Communists and the Mexican government, through its consuls, both played key, though antagonistic, roles. The Los Angeles Police Department, and its Red Squad, actually highlighted the tension: one Red Squad officer, revealing that he had no sympathy for strikers and was simply choosing the lesser of two evils, reported to his superior, "[I] told them [the strikers at Venice] that if their Consul was advising and directing them, I was sure they would not get into any trouble, but if they were Communist led and directed, it might lead to trouble for them, such as deportation, etc."[38]

One Anglo former Communist active in the strike, who remembered the leadership of the CUCOM "from the old anarcho-syndicalist unions in Mexico," understood both why the union could organize Mexicans so easily and why the Communists could not more fully connect with the situation. The anarchists "never reached out to the public in general . . . because it was strictly a Mexican union, trade union affair." "Of course," this faithful veteran of the class struggle continued, "we wanted to carry it all the way out. They just weren't for doing it." Devra Weber quotes Vice Consul Ricardo Hill, an anti-Communist critic of capitalism who sought to limit the political scope of the strike, on the other side of the intra-Mexican controversy: "I believe that my duty as a consular officer of Mexico is to protect the interests of my nationals and to represent them in any and all controversies in which their human and constitutional rights are at stake." Within only a few years these ideological antagonisms between anarchists and mutualista leaders would divide and ruin the CUCOM. Nevertheless, it should be clear that it was a thoroughly Mexican organization that fired the spirits of its members for precisely that reason. "The natural spreading of the strike idea and the excitement among the Mexicans" derived from the agricultural workers' shared experience, which only they could communicate to one another and which they did so "naturally."[39]

The effect of the union and its diverse leaders on the strikers' political consciousness remains ambiguous. In its own analysis of the failure of the El Monte strike, the Communist Party noted that "the strikers were more apt to give confidence to the leadership of their own fellow workers in carrying through the decisions of the C. and A.W.I.U." Another organizer in the Imperial Valley noted, "At the most we had 20 to 25 people who signed a card, and they never actually became our conception of the Communist Party member. They drifted away."[40] Most likely, for Mexicans and the rest of the folk throughout the Americas, the appeal of becoming heroic proletarians with a world mission of establishing workers' states could never prove as strong as their aspiration of becoming small freeholders. Were they radical Mexicans who organized themselves based on their anarcho-syndicalist heritage and then procured some help from earnest, sometimes effective, sometimes imprudent "gringo" Bolsheviks? Or were they Mexican pickers who merely sought wages adequate to put food on the table? Or were these Mexicans potential recruits for the Communist revolutionary vanguard? Individually and collectively, these Mexican pickers were all three, at different places, at different moments, for different agendas.

UPLIFT

For yet others in México de afuera, what I have termed "uplift" became the key to a better future. While no ideology is class or organization bound, the credo of uplift clearly belongs to the sociedades and middle class of México de afuera. For such people, advancement derived from virtue and honor rather than from voting or the class struggle. It is meaningful and revealing that in November 1926, the year before it called for the formation of the CUOM, the Confederación de Sociedades Mexicanas also called for a reunification of its *Mesa Directiva,* "board of directors." The goal was more than simply "to unite the Mexican elements previously in conflict; but rather at the same time to labor effectively for the educational, cultural, and social bettering of the Mexicans living in California." This statement discloses what was seen at the time as a huge detriment to Mexicans, namely, all of the disunity that today might be seen as pluralism or diversity, or at least as interesting. Many Mexicans in America, perhaps because so many of them shared similar experiences, have yearned for and presumed the possibility of ideological unity. We have seen throughout this narrative the remarkable variety of Mexican opinions about matters, and the substantial reasons why people disagreed. Now here is disclosed the notion of uplift, of the betterment that "surely the most progressive of the many Mexican organizations in Los Angeles" would lead. The leaders of the Confederación de Sociedades Mexicanas proposed "una casa del mexicano," in which would be housed, under one roof, "a theatre, meeting rooms, and even the Mexican consulate, an employment office, and dancing halls."[41]

The men who sat at the Mesa Directiva imagined more than a mere enclave: their building would be a place on the landscape that was purely Mexican, one where no foreign influences would threaten Mexican society in Los Angeles. Commentary on the word *progresista,* one used in the rhetoric, will help reveal much about "uplift." In the United States of the 1920s, "progressive" denoted advancing into the modern, deracinated world of science, commodities, and technology, and in the 1930s, it suggested pro–working class and anti-racist initiatives and people. In Latin America the word has some of these connotations, but it refers mostly to those elements emancipating themselves from the alleged dead-weight of the Indian and feudal pasts. Virtuous conduct, understood as bodily discipline and cultural refinement—better yet, not being like Indians or peasants—denoted one as progresista. Societies with weighty family ideologies locate the definitions of virtue in the family; this is why family values are usually patriarchal values. Thus the most prominent families, the "best families," are those who have succeeded and who, therefore, have the most virtues. Thus their virtues are the best ones, and thus those most likely to result in "the betterment . . . of the Mexicans." Here, in family sense and logic, lie the origins of uplift and other similar notions of the remedy for societal problems. The radicals discussed above would have argued that the big families as often as not do not live up to their professed values and that this political view either does not acknowledge or seeks to deny the role that power relations in the form of class- and race-based imperialism (and a few might have mentioned issues of gender) have so dramatically played.

We have seen how the late 1920s and early 1930s saw the formation of a number of clubs that sought to counter the demexicanization of the youth. In them those most "morally and physically capable . . . would maintain the good name of la Raza." Such clubs existed within the context of uplift ideology that the mutualistas epitomized. For example, upon its incorporation in March 1917, the Liga Mutualista Mexicana of Los Angeles stated that its goals were not only to provide "mutual assistance" but "meetings, to spread ideas of unity, mutual benefit and progress among the Mexican people; to uphold standards of right living; to instruct in the laws and usages of the United States; to inculcate respect for law, government, and religion; to promulgate ideals of education and advancement."[42]

The practice of uplift thrived in Los Angeles and the surrounding counties mostly because of the importance of the services that the sociedades rendered to la raza, but in part because, after the leaders had appointed themselves as spokesmen for all Mexicans, so too did the americanos. This was because these leaders were articulate, they headed the honorary societies and mutualistas that did not challenge the established production and social arrangements, and they were not like, and sometimes even opposed, their more militant counterparts whom we have met above. Anti-assimilation centered in the sociedades until the

World War II era, at which time the importance of involvement in American institutions and issues became more apparent. These sociedades have survived to the present day even though government welfare policies, such as social security and workmen's compensation, have eclipsed much of their original function.[43]

REAL MEXICAN POLITICS

As has already been made clear, Mexican politics fired the passions of mexicanos de afuera much more than, say, the election of 1924, which pitted Calvin Coolidge against another americano. In 1928 matters became even more electrifying when, in July, President-elect Álvaro Obregón, a former general, was assassinated in Mexico City. All of those who dissented from the consolidation of power in the hands of the generals and the ruling party—and there were many—saw in the chaos a terrific opportunity. And that concentration of objectors who lived in México de afuera especially projected into this opening their deepest wishes for delivering Mexico from whatever it was that had driven them out of their homeland. Thus was born *Vasconcelismo*, the insurgent electoral movement that drew in a contradictory array of people peculiarly united behind the paradoxical figure of José Vasconcelos, who campaigned for the Mexican presidency in 1929. Vasconcelos had been, among other things, minister of education (1921–23), and he opposed his successor in that office, avowed Protestant Moisés Saenz, who attempted to bring to Mexico the modern techniques of American education (tests and all) that we saw in the previous chapter. Vasconcelos had exiled himself to the United States, where, before settling in Los Angeles, he had been a professor at the University of Chicago. A confidant of American businessmen with an interest in Mexico, he supported insurgents in Mexico, including the Cristeros. He is probably best known as the philosopher of *la raza cósmica*, the compelling notion of the specialness of the people derived from the dramatic intermixing of the great Catholic Spanish empire and the great Indian civilizations of the Americas. Emerging from México de afuera, Vasconcelos campaigned around the issue of *antireelecionismo*, or the end of the rule of the generals.[44]

The election of 1929 certainly fired the passions of those Mexicans who took an interest in politics. *La Opinión* supported Vasconcelos and his promises of democracy and civilian rule, but rather calmly and straightforwardly presented opposing candidates' platforms and statements by their supporters. The paper made available to mexicanos de afuera the points of view of not only Vasconcelos but government party candidate Pascual Ortiz-Rubio, Adolfo de la Huerta, Antonio Villareal, Felíx Díaz, Aron Saenz, and even the Communist candidate, Rodriguez Triana. Quickly the field narrowed to Vasconcelos and Ortiz-Rubio, an obscure figure who was really the front man for the "Jefe Máximo," Plutarco Calles. Both Clubes Vasconcelistas, directed by the Centro Anti-reelcionista Pro-Vasconcelos, and Clubes Reforma Pro-Ortiz-Rubio, supported no doubt by the Mexican government, sprang into action to marshal support for their candidates in Los Angeles.[45]

The activities of these political clubs are quite revealing. They met in all manner of places, including the Teatro México. Los Vasconcelistas de California included in their program "extensive nationalistic work in all of the Mexican colonias in the United States, towards the end that the children would live and grow loving their legitimate homeland and speaking Spanish correctly." *La Opinión* represented Vasconcelos's supporters as advocating organizing workers in México de afuera in "locals of our famous CROM to impose, with the help of the government and powerful political formations, upon employers demands similar to those in Mexico." Vasconcelos came off as an odd mix of liberal democrat and socially conservative advocate of indigenous Mexican Catholicism who advocated for the Cristeros. Most of his support derived from the better-off émigrés, but he articulated the grievances of working-class mexicanos de afuera about the discrimination that they experienced at the hands of employers and labor unions and in public facilities. Each of his positions "pursues always one inseparable and organic approach, in its essence or in its tactics: nationalism." For Cinco de Mayo 1929 the Vasconcelistas sponsored the gala Noche de México at the elite Philharmonic Auditorium in downtown Los Angeles.[46]

Activities around Ortiz-Rubio begin to unfurl single-party politics in Mexico itself. Calles and his supporters organized the Partido Nacional Revolucionario (which became the Partido Revolucionario Institucional) for the election of 1929. From Yucatán to Los Angeles, it began the process of consolidating political power by building party machinery, by wrapping itself in the banners of Mexican nationalism and the rhetoric of the Revolution, and by engaging in voting fraud. In Los Angeles, mexicanos de afuera found themselves gaining entrée to such organizations as el club obrero, 'El Martillo' ("the workers club, The Hammer") and a newly formed Partido Liberal Mexicano (which bore no ideological connection to the anarchists), all of which supported Ortiz-Rubio. One meeting publicized "a manifesto forwarded by the PLM in which were

made the most grave and concrete charges against . . . Vasconcelos."
Their rhetoric, without much political substance, seems aimed at the
working class of México de afuera. For Cinco de Mayo 1929, the Con-
federacion de Sociedades Mexicanas and the consul sponsored more proletarian celebrations, which appear all mixed up with pro-Ortiz-Rubio
activity, in La Placita and Lincoln Park. Vasconcelos won *La Opinión*'s
straw poll in México de afuera, but Ortiz-Rubio won the election in
Mexico by the fantastic margin of nearly two million to one hundred
thousand.[47]

The meaning here lies not in the apparent inconsistencies in these
political positions and constituencies, but rather in the change, growth,
and flux that were indicative of the liveliness of the political culture.
Within the sociedades, the CUOM, and the people associated with the
Mexican presidential candidates, we see different political views ascendant at different times and over different issues. These were essentially
Mexican views of matters.

NEW UNIONS

In the summer of 1933 some other Mexicans turned to a different type
of union to counter the effects of their weak position in the labor market. On September 27 Los Angeles dressmakers, largely mexicanas and
1,500 strong, met in Walker's Orange Grove Theatre and voted unani-
mously for a general strike if employers refused the demands that the
local branch of the International Ladies' Garment Workers' Union
(ILGWU) had drawn up. The workers insisted upon union recognition,
the thirty-five-hour work week, a guaranteed minimum wage, a shop
chairman, a price committee elected by each shop, elimination of home-
work, and a grievance procedure.[48]

Now connections between México de afuera and other areas of the
North American continent would be forged. The ILGWU functioned
within the American New Deal coalition. From its stronghold in New
York, the leadership constantly asserted that "the union must provide
information and guidance in matters of health, social security, family,
housing, and political matters." The ILGWU had broadened its vision
to a society of security based upon government leadership of the economy. "There can be no security in an insecure industry," said the general manager of the ILGWU's joint board of the dressmakers' union. "It
is therefore our duty, in the interests of the workers we represent, to

concern ourselves with every phase of our industry and to do everything in our power to put it on a sound and solid basis." The leaders of the 1933 general strike of Los Angeles garment workers stated the short-term goals of this program: according to the union general manager, "We want union recognition so that the union can police the industry and see that evaders are made to come to terms and to see that everyone abides by the [National Recovery Administration] code. . . . That's the all-important reason for this strike." "In very few factories," the general manager continued, "is there any sort of supervisory assistance. No effort is made to guide the workers in the one best method of making any particular style."[49] The bosses were schlemiels, in other words, and if they would not cooperate, then a strike would force them to rationalize the industry and treat their workers fairly. The capriciousness of the market and the short-sighted foolishness of the employers yielded a volatile industry. The ILGWU would bring higher wages and higher profits, as well as stability, to an otherwise unaltered situation of capitalist ownership of the means of production. They sought to keep the system working through the cooperation of workers, capitalists, and the national government. It was the essence of social demoracy come to the Mexican seamstresses of Los Angeles.

Confronting the miserable conditions and unscrupulous employers described in the previous chapter, under which workers, mostly mexicanas, in the garment industry labored, revitalized the ILGWU in Los Angeles. In mid-September 1933 labor organizer Rose Pesotta, a Russian Jew, arrived from New York to initiate a union drive. It wasn't, though, as if an organizer could simply get all of the suffering dressmakers to join the union. In spite of National Recovery Administration (NRA) codes, employers could simply fire anyone suspected of union activity. Then, there was the issue of competition for the allegiance of the workers: the Communists had withdrawn from the old Local No. 65 and had formed their TUUL dual union, the Needle Trades Workers Industrial Union (NTWIU) in 1929. And the difficulty of communication between the Mexican, Italian, Russian, and Anglo women complicated the formation of an effective union local. Nonetheless, the ILGWU initiated a successful propaganda and organizational drive that included meetings, radio talks, and twice-weekly bulletins in Spanish and English. The effort attracted hundreds of workers to the union, and the international chartered a new Local, No. 96, which enrolled over 1,000 workers in a short time.[50]

Employers strengthened their organization as well. The Associated Apparel Manufacturers of Los Angeles, affiliated with the parent open-shop organization, the Merchants and Manufacturers, urged its members to stand firm lest they "be forced to strictly adhere to the minimum-wage laws of California" or even lose their open shop. The association also bound its members (in at least the garment, cabinet, and fixture industries) not to deal with unions or provide raises. The M and M provided valuable anti-strike and informational services, made the signing of such a contract a condition of membership, and promised fines for weak-kneed member employers.[51]

The local NRA office stepped in and proposed a settlement in line with the rest of the United States. This action contented the ILGWU leaders, who were "satisfied with the NRA provisions" and "agreed that there will be no strike in the garment trade." However, union recognition remained a prominent bone of contention between the ILGWU and the employers.[52] As the ILGWU soon discovered, the NRA functioned only to cooperate with employers to buy more time to bust the union. That very entry of the NRA marks the most profound consequence for Mexicans, however. The Mexicans were now involved in the American body politic, whether they intended it or not and whether they liked it or not. President Franklin Roosevelt's New Deal brought labor organizations into the political pluralist process through the National Industrial Recovery Act (which the NRA administered) and later through the Wagner Act. Emerging into the political mainstream, the ILGWU in some respects brought the mexicana rank and file with it.

In open-shop Los Angeles, though, the NRA board, in spite of its stated pretensions, cooperated with the bosses who began discharging workers for union activity. An ILGWU rank-and-file movement steadily mounted, with mexicanas leading the swelling numbers of Local No. 96. Factory owners locked out several shops entirely, and by October 8 there was a genuine strike in progress. Local No. 96 now officially called for a general dressmakers' strike, which the AFL Central Labor Council sanctioned, on October 12.[53]

The strike call brought an immediate response from the mostly mexicana workforce. The ranks of the 2,000 to 3,000 strikers held firm despite many arrests. The militant strikers sang and chanted on the picket lines in front of the dressmaking shops. Parades of unionists and supporters, huge quantities of food, and union label propaganda all assisted in the stirring effort. The massive numbers that the union marshaled on its picket lines made an employer injunction against picketing ineffectual.

Figure 20. The ILGWU float at the 1938 Labor Day parade in Los Angeles.

Rose Pesotta and the Mexican women strikers exuded character and vitality. Pesotta did much to reach the mexicano community. During the strike, the ILGWU did short broadcasts on a Mexican cultural society's radio program until it was shut down after a few days. Then the Mexican women in the union facilitated the purchase of time on a Tijuana station, "El Eco de México," so that at 7:00 each morning "Spanish speaking workers all over Los Angeles learned of the progress of our strike before starting to work each morning." The leadership also produced a four-page, semi-weekly newspaper, *The Organizer,* in Spanish and English. The "Spanish Branch" of the ILGWU had Halloween parties for the children, adult parties featuring professional Mexican singers, and parties "to have members of all unions, regardless of their classification, come and make friends with the Spanish speaking members" (admission was two for 25 cents). Photographs of a Labor Day parade later in the decade show those on the ILGWU's Spanish Branch float attired in Mexican costumes (see figure 20).[54]

Within two weeks, the local NRA office proposed arbitration of the strike issues. The ILGWU leadership quickly accepted. However, the employers, ever unable to see the carrot of cooperation dangling on the NRA stick, did not. On November 4 the "impartial" NRA board granted little and called off the strike, to the chagrin of the ILGWU leadership. The settlement called for recognition (technical at best) of the union, NRA minimum wages, and an equal distribution of work in slack periods. Surprisingly, the membership ratified the agreement by a five to one majority.[55]

The Communists, through their dual Needle Trades Workers' Industrial Union, challenged the theory and the practice of the ILGWU in the general strike of dressmakers. They vociferously denounced the ILGWU for having sold out, first by submitting to arbitration and then by accepting the settlement. Much as with their more disastrous squabbling in Germany about the rise of the Nazi Party, Communists and social democrats lambasted one another so terrifically over the Mexican strike that it is difficult to sort out the political situation. To the Communists, who thought that the Great Depression had struck capitalism a fatal blow, all-out struggle against the bosses would bring a quicker collapse of the economic system, which they would lead through the TUUL unions. To them, "the treacherous class collaboration politics of the AFL and the 'Socialist' misleaders" had lost the strike. The Communists told the garment workers, "Instead of using your splendid struggle to beat the bosses into submission, your officials have handed you over to the mercy of an arbitration board, to the mercy of so-called impartial citizens! . . . Arbitration never gave anything to the workers. Struggle on the picket lines did!"[56]

The social democratic–minded ILGWU leadership saw in the rise of fascism not the death knell of capitalism but a terrible threat to ethnic and racial minorities and to progressive forces generally. To them, the Communists, this "fringe of irresponsibles . . . continued giving the employers all the aid and comfort they were capable of" through their impossiblist rhetoric. Their talk turned away potential comrades in the struggle against fascism and for the personal security that social democracy and the ILGWU would bring to all workers.[57] World politics came to the Mexican immigrants of Southern California by way of Eastern Europe's shtetls, from which came most of the garment employers, ILGWU leaders, and Communists in the needle trades. Pushed out of Mexico by the turmoil associated with the Mexican Revolution, Mexicans in *la costura,* as the needle trades were known, encountered the passions and spin-offs of the Russian Revolution in Southern California.

The efforts of the ILGWU prevailed; Communists got nowhere in the needle trades, nationally or locally. Although most of the ILGWU leadership found the decision of the arbitration board less than satisfactory—Pesotta "felt as if [she] had been struck by a lash"—they did realize that the strike efforts of 1933 laid the foundation for a dressmakers' union in Los Angeles. In 1934 Local No. 96 continued to gain strength in individual shops. The following year several quick strikes, or mere work stoppages, strengthened the union and technically achieved the closed shop.[58]

By 1936 the ILGWU had established itself firmly as the representative of the dressmaking industry's workers. Ricardo Hill sanctioned the ILGWU leadership, recommended which Spanish-speaking organizer be hired, and exhorted the Mexican workers of the ILGWU to accept their leadership. On August 5, 1936, some 3,000 workers engaged in another general strike with accompanying picketing and arrests. Luckily, the ILGWU signed agreements for 2,650 workers in fifty-six firms, gaining a weekly minimum wage of $28 for women and $35 for men on a three-year contract. The general volatility of the garment industry, the presence of migrant workers from the South and Midwest, and the continuing resistance of the intensely competitive factory owners still threatened the ILGWU. In spite of all this, it had nearly managed to establish a closed shop. According to the police (to whom "the Mexican problem" had now been turned over), the union had a membership of about 3,000 when it became a Congress of Industrial Organizations (CIO) union in 1936. (It rejoined the AFL in 1940.)[59]

Obviously, though, the women in la costura won the strikes and established the union. Industrial capitalism had drawn them out of the patriarchal home and into the public world, where they earned a wage and a sense of independence. Their wages allowed them to challenge patriarchy in their dress and brought them new expectations about personal autonomy. But, whereas wage work may have loosened male routine in the home, that rule was thrust upon them again in the workplace. In this context the women went on strike. Pesotta noted that during the 1933 strike "the Mexican girls and women . . . acted almost like seasoned unionists," comportment that should not surprise one with any knowledge of Mexican history. Militancy was becoming part of Mexican culture in the contexts of the continuing agitation around the Mexican Revolution and in the pain of the imposition of the market, which inexpensive fashions could not always mask. In fact, Pesotta noted, "The girls came [to the picket line] dressed in their best dresses, made by themselves, and reflecting the latest styles. Many of them were beauties, and marched on the sidewalks like models in a modiste's salon." Frank López, an organizer for the United Furniture Workers (UFW, a CIO union)

and for the United Cannery, Agricultural, Packinghouse and Allied Workers of America (CIO) and also briefly for the ILGWU, observed a similar militance in the Mexican women. López found the women "essentially much more vocal, militant, and aggressive" than the men, as well
as "highly indignant of any abuses or demeaning attitudes toward them"
within the union. Women in factories dealt speedily and definitely with
a stool pigeon or toady to the boss. Those who betrayed the solidarity
of the group received the "silent treatment," reminiscent of what happened in peasant communities.[60]

Scabs and the police received more than the silent treatment from
garment workers. The 1933 strike saw many scuffles between the striking dressmakers and the odious Red Squad of police captain Red Hynes.
In the strike of August 1936, ILGWU members beat up two female strikebreakers and a blackjack-wielding police lieutenant who attacked their
picket line.[61] The women ignored the prohibitions and scoldings about
proper female deportment made by the men who ruled their families and
workplaces. Patriarchy, and other components of hierarchy, were never
so thoroughly internalized that they permanently crippled human actions for justice. While family obligations and expectations may have
kept women from asserting a more dominant role in their unions, the
gender of these particular unionists did not decrease their militance and
solidarity.

This curious mix of Jewish *geist* and *alma* mexicana was inevitably
problematic. "We get them [into the union]," said Pesotta, "because we
are the only 'Americanos' who take them in as equals." She furthermore "contended that the Mexican dressmakers were normal humans,
who simply needed honest and intelligent guidance." Such a statement
is as positive toward Mexican women (relative to what the rest of American society was saying) as it is paternalistic. Obviously, the "intelligent
guidance" of ILGWU leadership, savvy in the ways of the NRA and the
garment industry, proved crucial in the struggle for reform in la costura.
On the other hand, the union had a very top-down organizational structure. At the local level, among those officers elected to the board of Local No. 96, Mexicans numbered only six out of nineteen, and they held
none of the important positions, in spite of their numerical majority. In
1934 Pesotta and Beatrice Lopez were co-delegates to the ILGWU convention in Chicago. Nationally, though, the union remained in the hands
of the cutters, such as its president, David Dubinsky, and other highly
paid garment workers from the "craft" categories of the industry.[62] Yet,
the leaders were certainly not cynical generals of labor who merely or-

ganized canon fodder for their assaults on goyish capitalism. They came from or witnessed the sweatshops firsthand and did not want other people to have to work like that just because they were weak. They proceeded to achieve power in the industry and lead the rank and file to better wages and working conditions. The ILGWU leaders numbered among those few gringos (and, because the Christian americanos called them bad names too, they were not completely gringos) who concerned themselves genuinely with Mexicans. Their own tribe, after all, had been defeated and scattered. Their motivation, like the Spanish friars' concern for the Indians, was multidimensional. But, unlike the priests, the ILGWU brought useful things and people did not have to convert to anything to get them.

The ILGWU and the Mexicans were the exception with the exceptions. Minority workers and women generally confronted an AFL labor movement that not only had no place for them, but had no concern for them either. It was not that such wage earners had no interest in union organization. Rather, the AFL simply chose to disinterest itself in the situation of unskilled workers, except as the AFL perceived them to be a threat, in which case the skilled tradesmen argued for their exclusion. Occasionally, the local AFL would support with the boycotting of scab-harvested fruits and vegetables. But Los Angeles street paver Luis Tenorio summed up the general practice of the local AFL craft unions:

> I don't belong to any union because they don't want to admit the Mexicans. Once the workers in asphalt, all Mexicans, organized a union, but they wouldn't admit us into the Asphalter's Union of the American Federation of Labor because they said that these same Mexicans were going to take their jobs away from them by accepting lower wages. So our union was broken up.[63]

Tenorio simply restated what almost anyone in the United States who followed labor politics with any sympathy and insight would have affirmed: the exceptionalism of the ILGWU, why the Mexicans did not hold the AFL in very high esteem, and the appeal of independent and radical unions. Some few, usually the most radical mexicanos and americanos, saw and understood this hurtful and mutually destructive foolishness born of fear and loathing of those considered "other."

To the extent that the AFL involved itself in the furniture manufacturing shops, for example, it did so on a fragmented and ineffectual craft basis. In such craft organizations the woodworkers belonged to the carpenters' union, the upholsterers to their union, the finishers to the painters' union, but the helpers, most of whom were Mexican, belonged nowhere. In small shops very few of the Mexicans were organized. Even if they were, a whole shop would be unlikely to strike successfully because of this fractured form of organization. An employer could make a deal with one of the skilled trades, leaving the others out in the cold and defeating the strike. The AFL craft unions left the Mexicans out there all the time anyway, so they would not mind working, especially if paid a little more, to break the exclusionary union's strike. This was the general drama in American labor, with several notable exceptions. It was also the situation of furniture workers in Los Angeles as they confronted the Depression, which dealt their industry a particularly hard blow.

Sometimes unions formed when leaders came in and gave organizational structure to the discontent of the workers. This appears to have been the case with the ILGWU in Los Angeles. Then sometimes unions emerged from the discontent on the shop floor, which experienced unionists who were already there shaped into an organization. This seems to have been the case when a motley but seasoned core of unionists led the formation in 1933 of the Independent Furniture Workers Union (IFWU), which was affiliated with the TUUL. These Communists, Wobblies, and hobos (as itinerant white workers were called back then) organized an industrial union, that is, one to which all categories of workers—upholsterers, woodworkers, and Mexican helpers—could belong without craft, racial, or ethnic distinction.[64]

The dramatic success of the organization of the harbor by the International Longshoremen's Association in 1934 and, no doubt, the ILGWU's valiant battles inspired the IFWU, which organized for a big drive (figure 21), which would culminate in an industry-wide strike on May 1, 1935. On the way to this action, industrial unionism was proving itself effective in the furniture shops. For example, in May 1934 the Sterling Furniture Company cut by 30 percent the wages of workers who put on the outside fabric and those who put in the spring coils. The employees as a whole were helpless until the TUUL Furniture Workers Industrial Union (most likely the IFWU)[65] stepped in. Then, as one of the workers reported, "The union then mobilized all five departments in the plant 100%. There were 51 of us." After threatening to call the Red Squad, the boss appealed to "the upholsterers, whose wages were not touched, saying 'what are you fellows fighting for those Mexican and unskilled workers for? We're not bothering your wages.'" All the

Figure 21. Speaking for the union in La Placita. (Reproduced by permission of The Huntington Library, San Marino, California.)

workers held firm and the wage cuts were rescinded. Communist-tinged industrial unionism attracted workers quickly, if not steadfastly, in the small furniture shops. Witness the entire force of 69 workers who in December 1933 walked out of Soronow Furniture to the TUUL headquarters, where they signed with the union. According to the Los Angeles police, two of the ringleaders were Mexican, F. Soto and H. López. Though scabs easily replaced the Soronow workers, a threatened general strike of furniture workers in July 1934 won a few concessions but did not get recognition for the IFWU. These strikes provided crucial precedents and experience for Mexican and other workers as they prepared to unionize the furniture manufactories of Los Angeles.[66]

The Communists relinquished their influence in the union in early 1935, and the successful efforts of the IFWU earned them the attention of the local AFL. The Central Labor Council of the AFL invited the independent union to join the Brotherhood of Carpenters and Joiners as second-class "B" members without union benefits or convention representation. The IFWU did so in March 1935, becoming Local No. 1561.

The effectiveness of their organization forced the Central Labor Council to recognize and accept the furniture workers, who were not wholly to its liking. The furniture workers were militant, dramatic, and industrially organized, and included Mexicans.[67] Whereas the CUCOM was a Mexican affair and Mexicans made up most of the rank and file of the local ILGWU (as well as a few of the minor leaders), now Mexicans joined the IFWU and Local No. 1561, in which they figured as a minority, albeit a prominent one, in terms of numbers. This meant that some mexicanos de afuera had now integrated themselves into an American institution that was racially mixed. Their non-Mexican compañeros lagged behind them, having neither the vitality derived from the likes of the revolution against the Porfiriato nor the local emboldening of the CUCOM. Yet, during the Depression, there came to be a new spirit of tolerance among some working-class whites, which workers' shared experience of immiseration and struggle brought forth. These two factors will have far broader consequences than one would expect from the inauspicious beginnings of the Independent Furniture Workers' Union.

These outsiders, these Reds, Wobblies, and Mexicans (with no doubt some overlap), who started the furniture workers in motion challenged not only employer prerogatives but the labor movement as it was then established. The local AFL leadership still pursued the union label, rather than the strike, which usually failed to increase, or even maintain, their power. On International Workers Day, May 1, 1935, their troublesome new members from the furniture factories not only struck the entire local industry, but established mass picketing. Furniture workers of all skill levels and ethnicities, approximately 3,000 from 60 plants, participated in these actions. Up to 4,000 pickets blocked buildings and stores, followed furniture trucks carrying scab-made products to their destination, and then picketed the stores selling the non-union furniture. The omnipresent Red Squad both intimidated the strikers and pressured stores to purchase only non-union furniture for "this very important phase of maintaining the Open Shop in Los Angeles."[68]

The combatants compromised on 40 cents per hour for unskilled and 60 cents per hour for skilled workers and achieved union recognition in most of the shops. In January 1936, the union called off the strike but continued to urge a boycott of the products of the ten recalcitrants. Crucial victories remained obscured behind the newspaper headlines concerning the strike. Industrial unionism in the furniture industry brought the upgrading of many Mexican workers. Before the union, Mexicans sat at the bottom of the employment hierarchy, "helpers" who carried wood for the woodworkers, assisted the upholsterers, and swept sawdust. Sometimes, though, helpers performed skilled tasks but did so at helper's wages. In those factories in which the union won a contract, it also won a voice in determining the upgrading of helpers and who would be promoted to the significantly higher paid position of mechanic, the first-class journeymen. After World War II, partly because of the influx of unskilled blacks, but mainly because of the union, Mexican workers comprised 30 percent of the skilled workers and 64 percent of the semi-skilled workers in an industry in which the total workforce was 25 percent skilled and 60 percent semi-skilled. While Anglos still dominated the skilled woodworking sector and Jews the skilled upholstering, Mexicans could now become "first class finishers," undoubtedly an improvement for Mexican furniture workers.[69]

Because of the union, not only did "Mexican" no longer simply mean "helper," but it could mean "leader." During their general strike, the furniture workers elected Frank López vice president of Local 1561. He said, "I did not at that time know how to speak or express myself to any great degree, but in the heat of the strike situation you make do. So I became very vocal. I'd been in the local union maybe about two months or three months . . . and I was put on the slate to be vice-president of the local." The local union acted to include minority workers into the leadership. Frank López "was put on the slate" and rose to importance in the local union: "I didn't know that this was going to be a token thing. I was a very green guy, and we had quite a few Mexicans so I said, 'Why not?' I seemed to develop and as a consequence at the next election I was nominated to be secretary of the local, which was a very important thing [and] no longer a token." In the next election he became organizer, on the paid staff of the union, and Jack Estrada became national secretary from Local 1561. These whose leadership capacities the furniture workers' unions developed were not mere tokens. Rather their elections reflected "reality in so far as the contribution that those individuals could make and the recognition that they had attained" in the labor movement.[70]

From a mix of necessity and vision, the CIO included white, brown, black, and female workers in their new unions, which competed directly with the AFL's. Whereas, for example, Mexican and black workers, excluded from the AFL, helped break the Great Steel Strike of 1919 and the Meatcutters Strike of 1921, fueling racism and arguments for the exclusion of Mexican immigrants, the CIO would now organize those very workers so long ostracized and thus willing to scab. The Steel Workers' Organizing Committee (SWOC) epitomized the organizing spirit of American workers nationally if not so much in Los Angeles.[71]

Mexicans worked in most plants in Los Angeles and constituted the majority in several, especially in the foundries, where the work was unskilled and most arduous. Many factors were entangled with organization in steel. Because there had not been much local activism in the industry, many of the business agents and organizers came not from the shop floor but from the national headquarters in Pittsburgh. While Mexican workers who had been in the United States for some time proved to be the union stalwarts always at the forefront of organization and picketing, newly immigrated Mexicans proved the most difficult to organize. Then, in a lodge such as that of Utility Steel, where Mexican workers held the leadership positions, Anglos could be reluctant to join. It appears that the few skilled Mexican steelworkers worked hardest to forge the union, at least in the foundries, and had a difficult time convincing both their Mexican brethren and their suspicious Anglo fellow workers to sign on. The president of Local 2018 for a year and a half, Tony Ríos, perceived that ethnic factions were more important than political ones in shop floor politics in those years. Besides the Mexicans, black and Italian workers supported him.[72] On the one hand ethnic solidarity born of shared experience moved the Mexicans to action in steel as it had at El Monte and other places. Then, too, another cultural group's shared wisdom about minority group workers who allegedly threatened their livelihoods (and who, when they scabbed, truly did) produced such antagonisms. These ideas did not die easily even in those tumultuous and transforming times.

A Mexican foreman brought an interesting twist to the organization of Mexicans in the steel industry. In the cleaning rooms of the foundries, where Mexicans worked in the unskilled jobs, an organizer often encountered a Mexican foreman with whom many Mexican workers had developed a paternal relationship. In the days before the union, foremen often did the hiring, and they had relatively unchecked power over a worker's life on the shop floor. Unions sought to curb this control but, in the steelworkers' case, often had difficulty swaying a worker from the reign of a countryman to whom he owed his job. Newly immigrated Mexicans were often undocumented. They were those most insecure in their employment and therefore most dependent on the goodwill of those very foremen being challenged by the union. They also had less time on the job to develop a backlog of grievances against the boss. They proved the most difficult to organize. SWOC hired several Mexican workers who took a few days off from the factory to work for the organizing effort.[73]

Mexican workers who had accumulated the most years in a foundry or mill had the most reason to support unionization. Again, in the steel industry, "Mexican" equaled "unskilled worker." Before the union, employers demanded a seven-year apprenticeship before a worker would be upgraded. Rarely in the Depression did one work seven years solidly, and even then a Mexican could not count on promotion to core maker or molder.[74] The historical legacy of "dusky workmen" appeared everywhere in the fields and factories of the Southwest, maintaining the racial stratification of labor. But this very superexploitation pushed Mexican steelworkers to the front of the union struggles that began to transcend that history.

The steel plants of Los Angeles would be unionized, but in a way different from the needle furniture or trades. As organizing drives geared up in the late 1930s, so too did war preparation and sales of war matériel to Europe. As orders for goods came in, businesses could not afford strikes as they could in times when their warehouses were full of unsold goods. While important local battles established SWOC at Columbia Steel, Continental Can, American Can, International Harvester, and a number of small concerns, most plants achieved the union when national contracts were signed in Pittsburgh, especially after "Little Steel" acceded to union and government pressure to make peace with the workers in the light of the war emergency.[75]

Steel unions, especially when Mexican-led, responded to the situation of Mexicans. For example, new contracts prescribed a thirty-three-month apprenticeship period, which enabled many more minority workers to move up. When Tony Ríos assumed the presidency of the Utility Steel Lodge, he immediately filed grievances on the part of eighteen Mexican workers. These eighteen had worked in the plant for up to seventeen years without having been upgraded. All advanced to skilled categories. The tremendous expansion of industry that the war brought probably did the most to advance Mexican workers. But the Steelworkers Union had an important effect on the working lives of Mexican steelworkers in Los Angeles through its willingness to file grievances against discrimination and its establishment of contract clauses responsive to the needs of unskilled Mexican workers.[76]

Unfolding now, it should be becoming clear, is how the institution of the CIO not only began to carry some people out of México de afuera and into the American working class, but how too mexicanos de afuera participated in the transformation of racial and political relations in the United States. Mexican CIO members related to American working-class politics, rather than to the situation in Mexico, in treating with their circumstances both as regards prejudice and as regards politics. Discrimination became something for Mexican CIO members to oppose in principle, not simply because it humiliated la raza or lumped them with blacks. Notions of equality with white and black workers entered into Mexican workers' thinking about the issue of discrimination.

Politically, the CIO conveyed the opposition of Mexicans to their place in the labor hierarchy and to the labor market into American institutional channels, namely, into such New Deal legislation as the National Labor Relations Act (1935). What is more remarkable, and less appreciated, is the vitality and militance that Mexican workers brought to the success of the CIO, which in turn brought a modicum of industrial democracy to the United States. Building a union became another way in which people dwelled more profoundly—with new mind-sets that challenged America's prevailing wisdoms about race and politics—upon the landscape.

Likely no union involving Mexican workers in Southern California is more emblematic of the vision and potential of the CIO and of the ferment of those times than the United Cannery, Agricultural, Packing and Allied Workers of America (UCAPAWA). For a while, until Truman-McCarthyism and the teamsters smashed it, UCAPAWA brought a modicum of justice to that most seasonal of urban occupations, cannery work. UCAPAWA's most stirring moment occurred when it won a victory over one of the largest Los Angeles canneries, the California Sanitary Canning Company, during the harvest season (early fall) of 1939. The incomparable Dorothy Ray Healey, Red hero-villain of many Mexican strikes and a UCAPAWA vice president, coordinated the workers' efforts. The unsafe working conditions, tyrannical foremen who favored some few "pets," and the meanness of the production line where women were often paid by the piece, where they became covered in abominable peach fuzz, and which was often sped up, all created the context for unionization. After a strike of nearly three months, which witnessed picketing of both the plant and the owner's house, a secondary boycott, and intervention by the National Labor Relations Board, UCAPAWA established both itself and higher wages in the canning industry. This victory marked a fundamental change in this industry that symbolized the role of Mexican workers in the industrial structure of all of California. Now the Mexican workers had countered with their union that very market that had wed them to such low-paying and seasonal jobs. The odious piece-rate system remained, but the union gained recognition and, assisted by the labor shortages of World War II, persisted until the war's end and the employer counterattack.[77]

"Cannery culture" buoyed, if not produced, the union. Its story, moreover, shows the dynamic of organization when gender and race figure as significantly as they did in the canneries. As Vicki Ruiz's history of the union shows, UCAPAWA's strength grew from the sense that its members shared a common experience of gender and racially segregated and onerous work. Family and peer relations provided the means by which individual workers made these connections. While familial and ethnic bonds may have directed the loyalties of the cannery women away from the multi-racial union, they also served to enhance the cannery culture that produced that union's solidarity. Importantly, the shared experience at the workplace, and of being women there and in the home, forged links with the Russian Molokan and Jewish women who shared positions along the conveyor belts with the Mexicans. In turn, the union became part of the weave of the fabric of cannery women's lives.[78]

THE CIO AND THE MEXICAN COMMUNITIES

Participation in CUCOM, the ILGWU, the IFWU and UFW, SWOC, and UCAPAWA provided diverse union experiences for the Mexicans of Los Angeles. Each union had its own leadership, constituencies, and organizing strategies and different appeals to Mexican workers. Certainly these were not the only unions to involve Mexicans, but they are representative. (The Mine, Mill and Smelter Workers Union was another important union for Mexican workers, which organized during and after World War II and which Truman-McCarthyism shattered.) All of these organizations countered the market, the means by which Mexicans were bound to the employers who so miserably compensated them for their labor. Mexican workers, often allied with non-Mexicans, fought for and often won what they considered a subsistence wage. That wage was to be the same for Mexicans as for Anglos. Industrial unionism countered not only the market but racism. Perhaps as much as either of these two aspects, unionization represented simple dignity to Mexican workers. Because of the unions, a Mexican was no longer automatically a helper or a gang laborer, though most still were. Mexicans stood up for themselves against those who had dominated them for so long, and often they were victorious. To the extent they had internalized the power relations prevalent between them and their employers, they could now cast them off when they stood on the picket line, when they wore their union button on the shop floor, and when they forced concessions from bosses accustomed to servile workers.[79]

CIO activity centered around Mexicans did not stop with shop issues. Because of the presence of Mexicans in the unions and in the CIO Central Council, the progressive ideology of industrial unionism, and the influence of the Communists, the CIO brought its force to bear on a variety of Mexican matters. The CIO, "unity" its touchstone, did not have a specific strategy or program for Mexicans because it did not wish to make a point of distinguishing between national or ethnic groups. The CIO did not organize any specifically Mexican efforts that were divorced from the broader struggle to empower workers. Yet, in the CIO's eyes, the most deprived workers deserved special emphasis, an unusual view for most unions before or since the heyday of the CIO. For the sake of labor unity, the CIO made special efforts not only to organize minority workers and push for their advancement in the unions but also to assist in the amelioration of problems having to do with housing, health, discrimination, citizenship, youth, education, legal defense, and race riots.

Toward this end, the CIO in Los Angeles organized the Committee to Aid Mexican Workers and conferences on the plight of Mexican workers. It publicized such issues in both Spanish and English in its statewide newspaper, the *Labor Herald,* to educate all workers about them. Through this committee, the CIO encouraged Mexicans to become citizens and facilitated the acquisition of papers so that Mexicans could vote in elections and get jobs in the defense industry. CIO lawyers assisted in these matters. The Committee to Aid Mexican Workers aimed to have local unions with large Mexican memberships issue bulletins in Spanish. Primarily at the behest of Mexicans who had risen to leadership positions in their locals, such as Frank López, Tony Ríos, and Bert Corona, the CIO also undertook the advancement of Mexicans within the unions themselves.[80]

Naturally, there were Mexicans, especially in locals with large Mexican memberships, who rose to leadership positions. Gauging minority ascendancy to public posts is always difficult. Often one cannot distinguish between genuine and co-optive leadership. However, it does appear that the ideology of the CIO, the force of circumstances, and the assertion of Mexicans themselves combined to produce the authentic assumption of positions of responsibility and power by leading Mexicans in the union movement. Sometimes Mexicans provided mere window-dressing, a public posture to attract Mexicans to the union. Yet there can be little doubt that genuine Mexican leadership emerged from the CIO movement. Burt Corona (International Longshore and Warehousemen's Union), Luisa Moreno (UCAPAWA), Frank López and Jaime González (SWOC), Rosendo Rivera (United Electrical Workers and president of the Spanish-Speaking Peoples' Congress), Jess Armenta (United Transport Workers), and many others, all filled leadership positions both in their local unions and in the CIO. Many of these people later assumed leading roles in other Mexican community and political organizations.

Of course, these Mexican leaders, whose culture mandated reciprocity toward those less fortunate or more troubled, involved themselves and the CIO in community issues. While several local authorities issued demented reports on Mexican youth gangs, the CIO submitted programs to the Los Angeles grand jury and the board of education calling for improvement in job training programs, an end to discrimination in hiring, better housing and recreation facilities, and the appointment of public officials able to handle Mexican problems intelligently. In addressing this problem, the CIO did not do so in the usual fashion, that is, by invoking fears about property damage and destruction of social order. Instead, it seems to have understood the situation realistically, and sought to counter not with more police power and intimidation but with jobs and even a Mexican Youth Defense Committee (though one finds little mention of it in the sources), which protested the unwarranted roundups and arrests of Mexican youths.[81]

Neither housing nor transportation nor health care served the needs of Mexicans except as the market and accident sometimes allowed. Policy barred non-citizens from federal public housing. The transit lines ran east and west to get Mexicans to work from out of the barrios, but not north and south to transport them within the barrios. The county hospital had bilingual people in the collections department, but not in admissions. In all these cases, the CIO called attention to the urgency of the problem and pressured those in power to make changes.[82]

Yet, the nature of the CIO limited its effectiveness in these community situations. After all, this organization had closed the door on the open shop in Los Angeles, and this accomplishment did not endear the CIO to the local government authorities, who had often risen to their positions by their identification with the rabidly open-shop business clique that dominated the city. The CIO did not rise to strength in Los Angeles or anyplace else through moral suasion. It took power with its numbers. Then, too, the CIO was often identified with the Communists. Indeed, many Mexican and Anglo CIO leaders, if not the rank and file, associated themselves with the Party, one of very few organizations that transcended white supremacy and sought to better the lives of Mexicans. And, when the war came, the CIO unions, non-Communist and Communist alike, now sought, in line with national policy of de-emphasizing social programs, a "program of action to mobilize the Mexican people in Los Angeles behind the war effort" as the new, most important emphasis.[83]

THE END OF THE ROMANCE WITH MEXICAN LABOR: THE AGRICULTURAL STRIKES OF 1936

Mexicans had been proving more difficult than employers expected, especially in the late 1920s and the 1930s. Indeed, the Mexican workers of Los Angeles and their unions were now jilting the employers who had been so enamored of their labor. Then the heart thrust occurred in the spring of 1936, when Mexican workers struck the fields of Los Angeles and Orange Counties. Newspaper headlines of sensationally violent grower and police opposition to what was simply billed as "Communist agitation" emblazoned the situation on the public's consciousness. These strikes paralleled El Monte in their origins. They began against Japanese growers in Venice. The CUCOM initially organized them and then united with other unions into the Federation of Agricultural Workers Industrial Union. Among the leaders were Lucas Lucio, president of Santa Ana's Comision Honorífica Mexicana; William Velarde, the IWW leader of the CUCOM; and Ricardo Hill, who had recently been appointed consul after returning in August 1935 from a stint in France. The consul affirmed his intention to "intensify as far as possible the work of protection which our consular office has been imparting" and to keep the CUCOM free of various Reds and radicals such as the federation's president, Velarde.[84]

The workers, 93.2 percent of whom were Mexican, were suffering. They earned an average of $12 per week, and 88.3 percent found work only in agriculture, where they could expect only 30.7 weeks of work per year. Their family income averaged $491.12 per year, of which $412.36, or 84 percent, was spent on food alone. In Orange County foremen hired the workers from the ranks of those waiting hopefully at the packinghouses. They worked standing on ladders for hours with a 50- to 60-

pound sack on their backs in temperatures approaching 100 degrees. The orange pickers usually had to furnish their own gloves, snippers, and sack. Seldom did the growers supply water or toilets in the fields. On April 20, 1936, the field workers of western Los Angeles, paid 22 1/2 cents an hour, struck for 30 cents. They were overwhelmingly Mexican, but included some Filipino and Japanese workers as well. Ricardo Hill had been recalled to Mexico because of American protests over his involvement with Mexican union organization. On June 15, with Hill back, the citrus pickers in Orange County put down their clippers too.[85]

At first only about 300 Mexican workers left the celery fields of Venice after the growers' association refused their demands. A total of 2,000 would soon be involved, however. This time, though, the authorities reacted with quick violence to put the Mexicans back in their place. Local officials marshaled nearly 1,500 armed men to break the strike. The LAPD's Red Squad hastened to the scene, where it attacked processions of strikers as they moved from their headquarters to picket the fields. As they retreated to their headquarters, actually only a shack, the police hurled tear gas and then seized and beat up the fleeing strikers. On April 20, picketers were again fired upon; one was shot and another badly burned from receiving a tear-gas canister in the chest. "We're busting up a strike," the leader of a police detail candidly told reporters. "We beat the hell out of some strikers last night, and are going to get some more today." Neither the police nor the newspapers could accurately count how many were arrested and put in overflowing and makeshift jails. No longer was agricultural violence restricted to rural California; it now exploded on the fields adjacent to the highways and golf courses of Los Angeles. The strike lasted only a month and resulted in moderate gains for the workers, but no union recognition.[86]

This situation repeated itself two months later in Orange County, only on a much larger scale, when Hill returned to the scene and energized the CUCOM in September 1935. Lucas Lucio, considered the spokesperson for his people, who had soothed over differences between field workers and growers before, presented CUCOM's demands for better wages to the growers, who promptly rejected them. An ineffectual strike was called, resulting only in pledges to strengthen the CUCOM for next year's battles. In March 1936 the CUCOM/Federation of Agricultural Workers Industrial Union formally demanded of citrus growers and packers a subsistence wage calculated on the basis of what was needed to (barely) survive in a colonia—40 cents per hour for a nine-hour day, an end to the bonus system, and transportation to the fields.

They insisted upon union recognition. The growers refused and girded for a strike, which began in mid-June. Sheriff Logan Jackson, himself a grower, provided armed escorts for scab crews. He and the local press blamed the trouble on Communists, who, at Hill's and the Strike Committee's urging, had been purged from the union. "This is no fight between orchardists and pickers," declared Jackson. "It is a fight between the entire population of Orange County and a bunch of Communists."[87]

This was not the first time, nor would it be the last, that Mexicans had arrayed against them such imbecility together with the violence it called forth and justified. Francisco Balderrama's interviews with a number of those present confirm that Hill urged the strikers "to obey the law" and "to avoid violence," and there is no evidence that the Mexicans did not do so. Sheriff Jackson declared, "It was the strikers themselves who drew first blood so from now on we will meet them on that basis." As with the Mexican-American War, there is disagreement about who fired the first shot in the Orange County Citrus Strike of 1936. But really, was it the side with peasants and their picks and hoes, or the side with technology and its armaments? The police acted like utter hooligans. They hired at $8 per day 28 ne'er-do-wells to attack a meeting of strikers and beat them up and then called this a "vigilante" action. According to the front page of the Times, the "old vigilante days were revived in the orchards of Orange County yesterday as one man lay near death and scores nursed injuries." "Suddenly, late in the night, three or four automobiles loaded with grim faced men" attacked a colonia. "In a few seconds, tear gas bombs hissed into the small building where the assorted strikers were in conclave." Untold numbers of strikers were arrested, asked to post impossible bond, and then given sentences the length of the picking season. The growers brought in hundreds of Filipino workers, and similar numbers of college and high school students, to harvest, incompetently, the citrus crop. Hundreds of armed guards protected them with orders "to shoot to kill." Trucks of goods from supporters of the strike were attacked and dumped. International Labor Defense lawyers were facetiously arrested on traffic violations. The growers of Orange County, and the general americano populace, stated that they were protecting the freedom of those who wanted to work. This violent defense of the free market in labor was utter terrorism to the Mexican strikers who had been suffering that market's consequences for so long.[88]

Hill and Jackson, the latter only when anonymously threatened with dynamite, cooperated for peace in mid-July. Jackson rescinded the shoot-to-kill order, and Ricardo Hill cooled off the colonias. Then, the consul general and former president of Mexico, Adolfo de la Huerta, negotiated for the union an agreement that many hoped his prestige could persuade the strikers to accept. He achieved 20 cents per hour for a nine-hour day, transportation to the fields, abolition of the bonus system, and the supplying of picking equipment. Hill supported de la Huerta's efforts and urged the unionists to accept. Velarde, who had earlier supported and praised Hill's efforts with the CUCOM, urged opposition to the settlement, which did not include union recognition. Each side argued its position with the strikers as the growers called them all Communists and interlopers. Many of the workers were hungry. Velarde was banned from the meetings, and the strikers voted to accept the offer on July 24. There was no union recognition, some wage and working conditions benefits, and plenty of trouble.[89]

The growers and their vigilantes (with and without uniforms) essentially crushed the strike and saved their labor market with their counterattack. This violence provided an important reason for Mexicans to leave agricultural work for urban employment and for Anglos concerned about their labor and service needs to change their minds about Mexicans. People for whom George Clements spoke had seen the employment of Mexican workers as "a positive good" for all involved—for Anglo Southern Californians who needed work done and for Mexicans who were "undergoing active evolution" with the help of the Americans. These agricultural strikes of 1936 mark the change in Anglo perceptions of Mexicans, who were now considered "a necessary evil," since California was finally running out of other sources of such labor.

The strike of 1936 had been a community strike, a thoroughly Mexican affair that involved important Mexicans from both sides of the border, Mexican nationals and American residents, and a variety of ideological perspectives. It had been an effort against the market, a concerted effort on the part of Mexicans, acting essentially as a class to counter what agricultural employers as a whole did to them as a whole. Yet the strike contained other elements aside from this sense of solidarity of Mexicans as workers.

Mexicans were refusing to be "like the swallows at the old mission"—to come and go with the seasons and occasionally entertain gringo society. Many had decided to stay, usually with ambivalence, and they often wanted to partake of at least the material benefits of the society that they had helped build. This new consciousness took several forms.

Unions wrestled with employers for substantive equality. They fought for the right of Mexicans to wages and working conditions that would enable them to feed, clothe, and provide leisure time for their families at the same level as white workers. Certainly, conservatives maintained their allegiance to Mexico and what they asserted as the home country's cultural ways and norms.

This process challenged some of the dominant assumptions of the social and political landscape. The radicals of all ethnic and political persuasions, social democrats, and New Dealers all affirmed that the way things were regarding the distribution of wealth and power had to do with the actions and constructions of human beings. Americano suppositions about the blood of Mexicans, and Mexican and American mystical assumptions about national heritage and destiny, had explained, and continued to explain into the twentieth century, the hierarchies of owners and possessors, and races and countries. Now these historical conventions encountered assertions of human equality and the notion that since humans made society the way it was, they could change it in ways that affirmed equality and justice for all. Actually, this is still a big argument.

Certainly, though, Mexicans have re-presenced themselves on the landscape of Southern California, and become subjects in the history of the place. Mexicans forged social and institutional lives for themselves, but within the context of the demands of the labor market and a society that maintained its hostility toward their presence except as workers. Mexicans did not freely choose how their culture would evolve in Southern California, nor did the material conditions of their lives determine their cultural responses. The historical development of Spanish and Mexican Southern California framed and constrained what they would do and the nature of their culture. The attitudes and actions of elites, conflicts that they usually did not choose, the demands of the labor market, and, simply, the weight of 175 years of the history herewith briefly described and analyzed, all pressed upon the formation of the culture that they created out of a combination of adaptation, resistance, resignation, and the application of their familiar ways and beliefs. In addition to the theme that ideas about who should work remained constant through the Spanish, Mexican, and Anglo-American occupations of the landscape, these notions about the creation and evolution of culture have proved central to this narrative. This process, this hard journey, provides us an answer to the riddle of how the people in our story "were born, how they came to this certain place, how they continued."[90]

En Fin

*The Trajectories of
Mexican History
in Los Angeles*

This narrative could continue in at least two ways. One way would be to tell about how Mexicans in Los Angeles continued along the pathway toward Americanization. Just as accurately, we could proceed with how matters in México de afuera did not change much. In the 1930s what we might call "the American political system" simultaneously rejected Mexicans (deportation) and integrated them (the CIO). Such contradictory behavior could and did give rise to comments about the inscrutability of the americanos, but actually this is the way history works. Rather than creating a grand and encompassing narrative, we have analyzed how different strains led to often contradictory, or independent, historical flows. And this is how history would continue in the decades after those discussed here.

TRAJECTORY ONE

One scenario might emphasize how mexicanos de afuera began to protest and seek to reverse the discrimination they experienced in schools, the workplace, and other public places; how they began, in other words, to affirm their rights as Americans. We might focus on groups that fought for equality in the public schools, on the middle-class League of United Latin American Citizens, on the working-class Spanish-Speaking Peoples' Congress, or on the student-oriented Mexican American Movement. Perhaps above all else we would need to evaluate that greatest event in the creation of Mexican Americans, World War II. Each in its own way made the point to mexicanos de afuera that participation in the prevalent system in the new land, the American one, was the only way to meaningful advancement. If it was discrimination that kept Mexicans from participation, then that is what political efforts would have to address.

Discrimination in the schools pushed Mexican parents in the direction of American politics and law more than any other. Schools "which do not admit Mexican children," the typical distinction made in México de afuera in discussions about education, angered Mexican parents more than any other American institution. Segregation quite apparently derived from the americanos' dislike for Mexican kids rather than from any effort to help them learn or advance. The first major lawsuit took place in the community of Lemon Grove, near San Diego. There in 1930 parents filed suit and forced the school board to desegregate. The most famous case was *Mendez v. Westminster*, in which the California Supreme Court ruled in 1947 that segregation of Mexican children on the basis of race in Santa Ana was illegal.[1] The victories in these actions showed people that equal treatment of the children they cherished required participation in the American system, including becoming citizens, voting, and speaking English. In this way, what is sometimes called assimilation to American ways has been actually an expression of assertiveness and clearly has an oppositional quality.

Luisa Moreno, a Guatemalan-born labor activist, organized for UCAPAWA and is generally considered the organizer of El Congreso del Pueblo de Habla Española, or the Spanish-Speaking Peoples' Congress, which was founded in 1939 in Los Angeles with a wide variety of political views present. Fifteen hundred, including delegates representing 105 mostly Mexican-American and mexicano organizations, attended the convention. In strong contrast to middle-class organizations, the Congress stressed unity between workers from Mexico and Mexican Americans. It viewed Mexicans in the United States as an oppressed national minority but affirmed the necessity of allying with "all democratic forces among the Anglo-American and minority groups." Josefina Fierro de Bright assumed the position of executive secretary at age eighteen and was an energetic, pragmatic leftist. (Her mother, a restaurant owner in Los Angeles, was an exiled follower of Ricardo Flores Magón.) "The fight must be redoubled," she told the *People's World*. "The fight against discrimination and deportation, for economic liberty, for equal representation in government, for the building of a better world for our youth—this is our Congress's answer."[2]

The Congress's practical work, essentially confined to Los Angeles, consisted of agitating about police abuse, enabling Mexicans access to low-cost housing, helping with residence and citizenship forms and job applications, affirming equality for women in the organization, guaranteeing equal education for Mexican youth, and supporting access for Spanish-speaking people to defense jobs and unionization. Antidiscrimination activity, in other words. The membership included a genuine cross section of la gente, and the leadership stretched from liberal-moderate to radical-left. The Congress's history was destined to be brief. In 1942, like most Popular Front organizations, it folded itself up to promote unity for the war effort.[3]

More conservative in their outlooks were the League of United Latin American Citizens (LULAC) and the Mexican American Movement (MAM). For the 8 to 14 percent of Mexicans in Los Angeles who worked in white-collar, salaried positions or owned small businesses, the market system worked to their benefit, or at least it did not bind them or arrest their development the way it did working-class Mexicans. These Mexicans therefore sought not to counter or transform capitalism, but to reform it and to open up American society to talented people Anglo exclusiveness discouraged or discriminated against. LULAC, strongest in Texas and small in Los Angeles, represented this Mexican middle class and came to symbolize this political strategy. It mixed militancy and conservatism in its efforts to uplift Mexicans within the market system, integrate them into the dominant society's institutions, and make them into, as the name indicates, English-speaking citizens pledging allegiance to American political institutions. Such an organization had to defend the established system at the same time that it battled that same system to allow access to capable Americans of Mexican descent. LULAC more than any other group strove to provide formal equality, that is, equal opportunity to succeed, to Mexicans sinking down roots north of the border. The educational system was their primary arena of contestation.

MAM emerged from Southern California YMCAs in 1934. Mostly students, it sought "To promote good citizenship among Mexican-Americans and to inspire them to higher achievements in all phases of American life." "We believe," its articles of incorporation stated, "that the goal of our Movement, which is the upliftment of our people, can be achieved through a process of education." Once overlooked, now deemed "an important organization" by at least one historian, MAM published a newspaper, the *Mexican Voice,* and later the *Forward.* Actually, chapters tended to be very small, and the Supreme Council stated, "Bigness went to our heads, we became a board setting up policy. Now we find we have no one for whom to set policy." In Ontario the MAM chapter organizer "has endeavored to be the official interpreter of Mexican culture to the population at large. He has taken over the stereotypes of the Anglos that the Mexican excels in art, music, and dance." The Ontario chapter collapsed, and "the leadership of this man is not sought and not followed."[4]

Wars are transforming experiences in so many ways. Many mexicanos de afuera enlisted or were drafted, and they came back as Americans. "The very first result," said a Mexican-American navy man of entering the service, "is that without their civvies they [the sailors] have shed most of their 'differences.'" An article in MAM's *Voice* only five months into the war noted, "in our local draft board there was a high rate of volunteers of Americans of Mexican descent." "What this proves we cannot venture to guess . . . but at present he is thrown into constant contact with all backgrounds." We can reasonably suspect that the impulse to enlist arose from several factors: adventure, the desire to participate in a just war, peer pressure, and Mexican male youths' association of manliness and quality of character with physical prowess and fighting, a notion put forth in chapter 1.[5]

Nationally, between one-third and one-half million Mexicans entered the armed forces. They fought and died under the flag of the United States of America well out of proportion to their numbers. Soon notices of mexicanos de afuera wounded and killed in battle began to appear in *La Opinión*. "La lista de honor" grew and grew: on April 6, 1945, as the fighting pushed ferociously toward Okinawa and Berlin, 48 Mexicans from Los Angeles appeared on the list of those who had made the ultimate sacrifice. "Four More Mexicans Decorated," "7 More Mexicans in the List of the Fallen," "3 Mexicans Are Wounded Fighting against the Totalitarians" were typical headlines about Los Angeles's Mexican fighting men. A front page of February 1945 featured a picture of Doña R. de Alviso, of Maple Avenue in East Los Angeles, receiving a Bronze Star awarded posthumously to her son, Jesus, who had died fighting the Japanese, "este heroé de México de afuera."[6]

On the home front the number of blue stars (signifying a son or husband in the military) and gold stars (signifying a battle death) multiplied in the windows of the homes of the Mexican colonies. Support for the war extended beyond these ultimate sacrifices: after telling about Roosevelt High School graduate and "nuestro heroé" Corporal R. R. Martínez and his wounds at Saipan, *La Opinión* continued, "the members of this colony that buy War Bonds don't simply make the best investment of the epoch, but give moral and material support to the men, like Martínez, who chance their lives so that we civilians can enjoy the way of life that we have obtained."[7] It will be of interest, too, that although the Red Cross at first refused and then segregated blood donations from African Americans, the threat and dirtiness of Mexican blood had sufficiently declined that the Red Cross accepted it for transfusions into all wounded soldiers.

World War II was the good war, fought for democracy and against fascism. Like the southern blacks who returned from World War I to race riots and lynchings after having made "the world safe for democracy," returning Mexican GIs did not fail to notice the contradictions between the stated purposes for World War II and the treatment of Mexicans on the home front. It occurred to many that fighting for America, on the battle or home fronts, entitled them to partake of more of the American way of life, a notion that included not only no discrimination on the job, in public places, or in the schools, but equal opportunity to live in moderate comfort. Thus was born what is usually and accurately called "the G.I. Generation" of Mexican Americans. The efforts of returning Mexican-American military men, and CIO leaders who had suspended their fights with capitalists in the cause of the war, revolved in Los Angeles around the related issues of electing Mexican Americans to political office, most notably under the leadership of the Community Services Organization (CSO), which elected Edward Roybal first to the Los Angeles City Council and then to Congress; registering voters, for which an unprecedented number of Mexicans became citizens of the United States; advocating for a California State Fair Employment Practices Commission; and affirming equality in education. Most of this political agitation occurred in association with what CSO called "the liberal movement."[8]

Let us end this trajectory with a counterpoise to the floats at the Fiesta Days parade that introduced this narrative. The float that led the parade for the celebration of the Virgin of Guadalupe in December 1944 in Los Angeles flew the American flag and the Mexican flag: on its front appeared the words "E Pluribus Unum."[9]

TRAJECTORY TWO

In another scenario we would emphasize how Mexicans remained Mexicans on the landscape of Southern California. World War II, like its predecessor, created a manpower shortage. In response, an agreement of

April 1943 between the United States and Mexico authorized the U.S. government to arrange for and supervise the recruitment of railroad track labor. Of greater consequence, though, was Public Law 45, which in 1943 formalized the importation of *braceros* (literally but awkwardly translated as "offerers of strong arms"), or Mexican contract workers, to labor in the fields that previous immigrants had been abandoning for the cities or the military. Some drama accompanied the arrangement. Federal regulations concerning wages and housing led many growers initially to oppose the program, and Texas to reject braceros outright. Then in late 1943, when Texas acceded to the program, the Mexican government refused to allow braceros into the Lone Star state because of its nasty discriminatory practices. Braceros worked all over the West, Southwest, and California, under the most corrupt and harsh conditions. Employers saw them as ideal workers: if the braceros protested in any way, they would simply be sent back across the border; and their ready availability meant that employers could quash citizen or resident workers who attempted to unionize simply by replacing them with braceros. Growers liked this emergency policy so much that they made sure that it was continued for two decades after the war. (Indeed, only after the termination of the program in 1964 could the United Farm Workers have any hope of success.) The Bracero Program marked a new phase in the long history of the "dusky workmen."

The war years also saw a replay of legal and extra-legal violence against Mexicans on the streets of Los Angeles. In August 1942 the police and newspapers inflamed the general populace with allegations about the threat of hoodlumism after a young Mexican was killed at a party that had attracted zoot-suiters. The publicity around this Sleepy Lagoon case, in which only the barest rudiments of the legal process were followed, established Mexican youths as criminals in the minds of many americanos. While no more than 1,000 of the 36,000 Mexicans of school age in Los Angeles in 1943 were affiliated with anything resembling a gang, the image of the zoot-suited hoodlum came to be equated with male youths. The symbol of the zoot suit put Mexican youths outside of the Anglo-American normative order, in other words, made them aberrant people who could then be treated without regard for fair play or due process.[10]

The hysteria around the case set the stage for the Zoot Suit Riots that started in May of the following year. With the support of the press and many Anglo Angelenos, gangs of sailors from Long Beach and San

Pedro attacked the visibly distinctive zoot-suiters. Sailors, acting against orders, arrived on the East Side and downtown in trucks or taxi brigades and proceeded to first taunt zoot-suiters, then to strip them of their drapes, and often beat them up: Mexican blood splattered on the pavements of the East Side (figures 22 and 23).

Though race obviously played a role, this was not a race riot akin to the one in Detroit that same year, where thirty-four—mostly blacks— were killed. Indeed, historical retrospect allows us to suppose that this was more of a carnavalesque mutiny and that Mexicans became the objects of the sailors' rage over their own humiliations and frustrations with the military and war. Yet the riots certainly terrorized, and humiliated, the Mexican East Side. The police became involved only when they arrested those Mexicans who resisted the rioting sailors, who were usually portrayed as heroes. Finally, fearing more mutiny and international embarrassment, and pressured by the CIO Central Council, military authorities declared the areas of conflict off-limits to the hooligan sailors, who had beaten up scores of Mexican youths.[11]

The alarm on the East Side was as manifest as it was diffuse and futile. The barrio was unorganized and unable to oppose effectively either this attack on its youth or the tidal wave of popular hostility toward Mexicans. This lack of political organization resulted from a number of causes, among them the Mexico-oriented nature of the community's political interests and the involvement of many of the most articulate and capable Mexicans in the labor movement. The situation shocked many into an understanding of the need to develop organizations that spoke to the needs of the community in the United States. They realized the need to work through American institutions and legal processes, and with a consciousness of Mexicans as Americans, many of whom, let us remember, were fighting in (and, for a change, not against) the U.S. military.

Not only did the vulnerability of their community strike mexicanos de afuera so forcefully, but so too did the resurgence of wild notions about Mexican character traits being in the blood. At the grand jury investigation into the Sleepy Lagoon killing, Captain Edward Duran Ayres, chief of the Foreign Relations Bureau of the Los Angeles County Sheriff's Office, reported on the nature of Mexican criminality. He began with the Indian origin of the Mexican: "he shows many of the oriental characteristics, especially so in his utter disregard for human life." In contrast to "the Anglo-Saxon, [who] when engaged in fighting . . . resorts to fisticuffs . . . this Mexican element considers all that to be a sign

Figures 22 and 23. Blood on the pavements. The Zoot Suit Riots, 1943. (Both courtesy Security Pacific Collection, Los Angeles Public Library.)

of weakness, and all he knows and feels is a desire to use a knife or some lethal weapon." Captain Ayres continued that "his desire is to kill, or at least let blood." Now the Indianness that Dr. Clements and other defenders of Mexican immigration had credited for the passivity of Mexicans had been transformed into lethality: "When there is added to this inborn characteristic that has come down through the ages, the use of liquor, then we certainly have crimes of violence."[12]

In this second trajectory of Mexican history in Los Angeles, the continuities are much stronger than the transformations. Really, not much had changed: Mexicans were wanted as workers, and of a particular type; violence could be used to keep la gente in place; and fantastic but widespread beliefs about innate characteristics circulated to explain and justify the situation.

We have to wait until eight years after the end of the war to round out this picture of continuity. In 1953 Operation Wetback began, an effort of several years, which at its height in 1954 deported over a million Mexicans. In many ways readers should find the story familiar: transportation had improved in northern Mexico along a south to north trajectory, the Bracero Program had attracted people to the border, growers had eagerly hired vulnerable workers and encouraged their increase, and the end of the Korean War had brought a recession that needed scapegoats. This time the United States military swooped into colonias throughout the American West, arrested people, and sent them back to Mexico. Barrio and colonia dwellers lived in fear again.

The dream life of México de afuera improved not at all. The early 1930s witnessed the demise of any hope of having films that reflected the reality of México de afuera. Mexican stars of the silver screen still could not be themselves. Ramon Novarro starred opposite Greta Garbo in *Mata Hari* in 1931, but this was his only major talkie. He refused Louis B. Meyer's ultimatum that he enter a marriage of convenience in order to conceal his homosexuality. Gilbert Roland's accent also pushed him into the background. Dolores del Río shunned offers to make movies in Mexico, and her publicity now listed her as Spanish. But for both her and Lupe Velez, an accent was considered exotic and thus glamorous. In 1932 she starred in *The Girl of the Rio* (she's Brazilian even though the movie takes place along the U.S.-Mexican border), an immensely popular mainstream movie in which she introduced the two-piece bathing suit. The film so offended the Mexican government for its portrayal of Mexican justice that it was banned in Mexico, Panama,

Figure 24. "Good bye and good luck to you. Love, Lupe."

and Nicaragua. The film included Leo Carillo, famous as a participant in California Pastoral ceremonies. In his thirty movies of the 1930s, he usually portrayed foolish characters or ones that were a little "greasy." Dolores del Río and her americano husband divorced, and she returned to Mexico in 1943.[13]

Lupe Velez reemerged as the Mexican Spitfire, in a series of eight films beginning with *The Girl from Mexico* (1939). She was a comic wildcat, a goofball, and, in contrast to the estimation in which she and del Río were held in 1929, no credit to la raza. For only two days in *La Opinión*'s headlines from 1944 to the end of the combat did other news displace that of the war. The news of December 15 and 16, 1944, stunned mexicanos de afuera. Lupe Velez was pregnant with the child of a French actor who had jilted her: "soon to be a mother, and over-whelmed by a tremendous deception of the heart," she, in rather miserable fashion, killed herself in her Beverly Hills apartment. Her last words, which she wrote in English, shall end our second trajectory: "I see no other way out for me so good bye and good luck to you. Love, Lupe" (figure 24).[14]

THE MAKING OF MÉXICO DE AFUERA AND HISTORY

The trajectories presented above should not be taken as evidence of such notions as "the more things change the more they stay the same." Rather, what should be apparent here is that the people, but not all of them and none of them completely, changed while the conditions stayed the same. The above scenario of two trajectories presents a false dichotomy. We have less an either/or matter than we do one that illustrates how it is that history meanders; it picks up old material conditions and mixes them with new exigencies and fate. Some people, "born by the river," wound up along one shore in one situation, and those carried by other currents in time wound up on another in a different set of circumstances.

In other words, Mexicans in Los Angeles unloaded their cultural baggage into a chest of drawers at once familiar and unforeseen. In many ways these Mexican immigrants, presciently or not, made history when they picked and chose what they took from the drawers to deal with their new experiences in the north. This is how people make history and how, over time, history creates culture. The various generations of Mexican immigrants to the city neither passively received the messages of popular culture and schooling nor consciously assimilated the surrounding culture nor militantly protected their traditions. Rather, they drew on a storehouse, which included all of these means as each situation in the strange, threatening, attractive, and hostile environment appeared to require. This included cultural retrenchment, adaptation, and enigmatic new forms of relating to people and institutions. As they did so, knowingly or not and like it or not, they were sinking roots into the new land from which would grow new culture—first an immigrant one, later often a Mexican-American one—but one different from any the settlers of México de afuera had intended or imagined.

The movies, fashions, settlements and schools, and patterns of labor all worked to rumple what they unloaded and then even alter the pattern upon the fabric when passed on to their children. We miss much of the richness and diversity of the history of Mexicans in the United States either to lament the loss of the original culture (obviously a mixture of European and Indian ways anyway) or to celebrate the advent of modernity or progress. It should be obvious now that this complex cultural mestizaje that happened when Mexican immigrants encountered American popular culture in an industrial city had a variety of beguiling consequences, the sum total of which cannot easily be judged positive or negative. We can conclude only that some things were lost when the commodification of life replaced the affective bonds of non-industrial culture, and that some things were gained when notions of individual autonomy, particularly for women and children, challenged, often in a commercialized manner, the confinements of traditional culture. Surely, though, this course of history is one of poignant human endeavor and endurance. Some of the drawers in their cultural chest were closed forever, others altered beyond recognition, and in others Mexican immigrants found new ways of being that parents and children, and women and men, experienced with profoundly different sentiments. Their experience in Los Angeles entailed the full range of human emotions.

HISTORY AND MEXICAN AMERICA

Significantly, the conservatives in this Mexican political discourse affirmed ethnic nationalism. The language, in particular, but also the affirmation of other symbols of the Mexican nation—its religious rituals, particularly veneration of la Virgen; education about "los héroes de la nación"; and celebration of the great Mexican holidays, Cinco de Mayo and Diez y Seis de Septiémbre—provided the cultural underpinning for political activity.[15]

Thus we see here that, historically, those who have argued and organized for change, whether revolutionary or reform, of the productive system, have de-emphasized ethnic identification. The CIO did not want to make a point of distinguishing between national or ethnic groups. Mexicans, and other workers who suffered discrimination, received special emphasis from the Southern California CIO, but only toward the goal of achieving working-class solidarity. Obviously, organizations, whether anarchist, communist, or reformist CIO, that emphasized the Mexican as worker saw the Mexican worker as needing liberation from the status quo—the status quo of capitalism and the internalization of cultural notions that rendered people submissive.

In chapter 2 we saw how there were few stories and myths in the new place to tell people how to be and give them comfort. In their different ways the Liberales of the PLM and the liberals of the CIO rejected these stories and myths in favor of individual freedom, moving away from the past, and making art out of life (the PLM) or at least living in comfort (the CIO). Rejecting the old tales, which usually had proscriptive intent, these modern and articulate leaders could think about new ways that people could relate to each other and to machines and land, about new ways to love and to act in a humane way. They were of the Enlightenment. To many the aspirations of the Enlightenment have become passé—the masses have remained enthralled to baser pleasures: boxing, movie stars, la Virgen, machismo.

For better or for worse those who have appeared on this Mexican stage in America acted initially as residents of "México de afuera," combatively concerned with events in la madre patria and re-creating the familiar; or later as Mexican Americans, who have desired to maintain their ethnic identity, but primarily have aspired to acceptance within the American system; or minority workers who have wanted an end to discrimination on the job and a fairer share of the American pie; or as community members who have wanted respect for their people, access to good schools, protection from the police, and equitable political representation; or as nationalists who wanted thorough self-determination for mexicano people living in the United States. They all did so for the very good reasons outlined in this narrative. This genuineness, and the close connections each political view has had to reality as people experienced it, reveal why there always has been and always will be what can be called either diversity of political views or disunion. La raza will no more achieve political unity than any other group will.

Association with America will always diverge as well. In some ways Mexicans and Americans form two separate societies. Housing and job segregation, and distrust of each other's cultural ways, prevail. This can be said of México de afuera, of the border, and of the two nations as a whole. On the other hand Mexicans are integral to the functioning of many areas of the economy, Anglos are obsessed with the "Mexican threat," and Mexicans play a key role in the Anglo-American fantasy heritage of California. Mexico and America are intricately intertwined countries. Our two peoples must accustom themselves to one another.

There continues to be such peril and opportunity in our relationship. Let us end now with the words that began this account, ones that speak to the experiences of the mexicanos de afuera, ones that have offered me much while I constructed this narrative, words that speak to the tasks of the future:

> It has to do with stories, legends
> full of heroes and traveling.
> It has to do with rebirth and growing
> and being strong and seeing.

Notes

INTRODUCTION

1. Ricardo Romo, *East Los Angeles: History of a Barrio* (Austin, 1983); George J. Sánchez, *Becoming Mexican American: Ethnicity, Culture, and Identity in Chicano Los Angeles, 1900–1945* (New York, 1993).

2. Richard Griswold del Castillo, *The Los Angeles Barrio, 1850–1890: A Social History* (Berkeley, 1979); Antonio Ríos-Bustamante and Pedro Castillo, *An Illustrated History of Mexican Los Angeles, 1781–1985* (Los Angeles, 1986); Vicki L. Ruiz, *Cannery Women/Cannery Lives: Mexican Women, Unionization, and the California Food Processing Industry, 1930–1950* (Albuquerque, 1987); Juan Gómez-Quiñones, *Roots of Chicano Politics, 1600–1940* (Albuquerque, 1994), and *Mexican American Labor, 1790–1990* (Albuquerque, 1994); Rodolfo Acuña, *Occupied America: A History of Chicanos*, 3d ed. (New York, 1988); Abraham Hoffman, *Unwanted Mexican Americans in the Great Depression: Repatriation Pressures, 1929–1939* (Tucson, 1974); Francisco E. Balderrama, *In Defense of La Raza: The Los Angeles Mexican Consulate and the Mexican Community, 1929 to 1936* (Tucson, 1982); Carey McWilliams, *Southern California: An Island on the Land* (1946; reprint, Santa Barbara, 1979), and *North from Mexico: The Spanish-Speaking People of the United States* (1948; reprint, New York, 1969).

3. Lisbeth Haas, *Conquests and Historical Identities in California, 1769–1936* (Berkeley, 1995); Gilbert G. González, *Labor and Community: Mexican Citrus Worker Villages in a Southern California County, 1900–1950* (Urbana, Ill., 1994).

4. Octavio Paz, *The Labyrinth of Solitude: Life and Thought in Mexico* (1951; reprint, New York, 1962), 13; Robert M. Fogelson, *The Fragmented Metropolis: Los Angeles, 1850–1930* (1967; reprint, Berkeley, 1996).

CHAPTER 1. THE MAKING OF MÉXICO DE AFUERA

1. *Los Angeles Times,* May 7, 1903; *Los Angeles Express,* May 8, 1903. El Pueblo de la Reina de los Angles was the original name of the town.

2. *Los Angeles Times,* April 25 and 27, 1903; Charles Wollenberg, "Working on El Traque: The Pacific Electric Strike of 1903," *Pacific Historical Review* 42 (August 1973), 358–59, 365.

3. *Los Angeles Times,* April 26 and 27, 1903; Wollenberg, "Working on El Traque," 365–66.

4. Theodore Roosevelt, *The Strenuous Life* (New York, 1901), 21; *Los Angeles Express,* May 8, 1903.

5. *Los Angeles Times,* April 27 and March 15, 1903; *Los Angeles Socialist,* May 2, 1903.

6. *The Imperial Valley Press,* May 12, 1928, quoted in Charles Wollenberg, "Huelga, 1928 Style: The Imperial Valley Cantaloupe Workers' Strike," *Pacific Historical Review* 38, no. 1 (February 1969): 57. Haas, *Conquests and Historical Identities in California, 1769–1936,* 93–137; Martin Heidegger, "Building Dwelling Thinking," in *Poetry, Language, Thought,* trans. Albert Hofstadter (New York, 1975), 145–61; E. V. Walter, *Placeways: A Theory of the Human Environment* (Chapel Hill, N.C., 1988), 193.

7. *Los Angeles Times,* April 23, 1903; Catherine Coman, "Casa Castelar," *The Commons* 7 (January 1903): 13.

8. John Emmanuel Kienle, "Housing Conditions among the Mexican Population of Los Angeles" (master's thesis, University of Southern California, 1912), 23.

9. Coman, "Casa Castelar," 13.

10. *La Opinión,* December 15, 1944.

11. This discussion derives from Walter, *Placeways,* 23–43, 176–205.

12. Douglas Monroy, *Thrown among Strangers: The Making of Mexican Culture in Frontier California* (Berkeley, 1990), 144–54.

13. Nora Sterry, "The Sociological Basis for the Re-organization of the Macy Street School" (master's thesis, University of Southern California, 1924), 13.

14. Bessie D. Stoddard, "Courts of Sonoratown," *Charities and the Commons* 15 (December 2, 1905): 295–99; Coman, "Casa Castelar," 12; Pedro G. Castillo, "The Making of a Mexican Barrio: Los Angeles, 1890–1920" (Ph.D. diss., University of California, Santa Barbara, 1979), 19–20.

15. Coman, "Casa Castelar," 13. See also Stoddard, "Courts of Sonoratown," 298; Emory S. Bogardus, "The Mexican Immigrant," *Journal of Applied Sociology,* 11 (May–June 1927): 470; *La Opinión,* July 10, 1927; Workers of the Writers' Program, *Los Angeles: A Guide to the City and Its Environs* (New York, 1941), 155–56.

16. Clara Gertrude Smith, "The Development of the Mexican People in the Community of Watts, California" (master's thesis, University of Southern California, 1933), 20, 37–38; William Wilson McEuen, "A Survey of the Mexicans in Los Angeles" (master's thesis, University of Southern California, 1914), 40; Kienle, "Housing Conditions among the Mexican Population of Los Angeles," 8.

17. Smith, "The Development of the Mexican People in the Community of Watts," 37; Dana Webster Bartlett, *The Better City: A Sociological Study of a Modern City* (Los Angeles, 1907), 72–74.

18. Paul S. Taylor, *Mexican Labor in the United States: The Imperial Valley* (1930; reprint, New York, 1970), 1:29, 56–57; Bogardus, "The Mexican Immigrant," 473.

19. The following sources reveal the statistical imprecision and describe the house courts as "nuisances": Emory Bogardus, "The House-Court Problem," *American Journal of Sociology* 22 (November 1916): 393–97; Kienle, "Housing Conditions among the Mexican Population of Los Angeles," 7–9, 16–17; William H. Mathews, "The House Courts of Los Angeles," *The Survey* 30 (July 5, 1913): 461–65; Elizabeth Fuller, "The Mexican Housing Problem in Los Angeles," *Studies in Sociology* 5 (November 1920): 2, 6; California Commission of Immigration and Housing, *Second Annual Report (1916)* (San Francisco, 1916), 236; Los Angeles Housing Commission, *Report of the Los Angeles Housing Commission,* July 1, 1910, to March 31, 1913 (Los Angeles, n.d.), 19.

20. Bogardus, "The House-Court Problem," 395.

21. Mary Douglas, *Natural Symbols: Explorations in Cosmology* (New York, 1982), 26–36 (the quotation is from p. 28).

22. José E. Limón, "La Llorona, the Third Legend of Greater Mexico: Cultural Symbols, Women, and the Political Unconscious," in *Between Borders: Essays on Mexicana / Chicana History,* ed. Adelaida R. Del Castillo (Encino, California, 1990), 410–19.

23. Frank López, tape-recorded interview with author, June 10, 1976, Los Angeles, California; Jaime González Monroy, tape-recorded interview with author, May 30, 1976, Port Hueneme, California; McEuen, "A Survey of the Mexicans of Los Angeles," 42; Al William Grieve, "A Study of the Habitués of the Downtown Parks of Los Angeles, with a View to Ascertaining Their Constituency, Their Social Processes, and Their Relation to the Larger Community Life" (master's thesis, University of Southern California, 1926), 4, 60; *La Opinión,* February 12, 1928; Stoddard, "Courts of Sonoratown," 296.

24. California Commission on Immigration and Housing, *Report on Housing Shortage* (Sacramento, 1923), 13.

25. Letters from the Los Angeles Chamber of Commerce files quoted in Romo, *East Los Angeles,* 85.

26. Stoddard, "Courts of Sonoratown," 298; Kienle, "Housing Conditions among the Mexican Population of Los Angeles," 7–11; Bogardus, "The House-Court Problem," 397; California Commission on Immigration and Housing, *Second Annual Report,* 237; Gladys Emelia Patric, *A Study of Housing and Social Conditions in the Ann Street District of Los Angeles, California* (Los Angeles, 1917), 11, 13.

27. Los Angeles Housing Commission, *Report of the Los Angeles Housing Commission,* July 1, 1910, to March 31, 1913, 41; Helen W. Douglas, "The Conflict of Cultures in First Generation Mexicans in Santa Ana, California" (master's thesis, University of Southern California, 1928), 91; Paul S. Taylor, "Mexicans North of the Rio Grande," *The Survey* 66, no. 3 (May 1, 1931): 140–41.

28. Sterry, "The Sociological Basis for the Re-organization of the Macy Street School," 13.

29. California Commission on Immigration and Housing, *Second Annual Report,* 236; David Alexander Bridge, "A Study of the Agencies Which Promote

Americanization in the Los Angeles City Recreation Center District" (master's thesis, University of Southern California, 1920), 70; Patric, *A Study of Housing and Social Conditions in the Ann Street District,*" 16.

30. Bartlett, *The Better City,* 74.

31. Los Angeles Housing Commission, *Report of the Los Angeles Housing Commission,* July 1, 1910, to March 31, 1913, 41–42; Patric, *A Study of Housing and Social Conditions in the Ann Street District,*" 16–17.

32. Douglas, "The Conflict of Cultures in First Generation Mexicans," 60.

33. Patric, *A Study of Housing and Social Conditions in the Ann Street District,* 18. See also McEuen, "A Survey of the Mexicans in Los Angeles," 31; see also Sterry, "The Sociological Basis for the Re-organization of the Macy Street School," 47.

34. Smith, "The Development of the Mexican People in the Community of Watts," 39; Patric, *A Study of Housing and Social Conditions in the Ann Street District,* 20; U.S. Bureau of the Census, *Fifteenth Census of the United States, 1930, Population* (Washington, D.C., 1930), vol. 3, pt. 1, 266; U.S. Department of Labor, Bureau of Labor Statistics, "Labor and Social Conditions of Mexicans in California," *Monthly Labor Review* 32, no. 1 (January 1931): 88.

35. Patric, *A Study of Housing and Social Conditions in the Ann Street District,* 20; Christine Lofstedt, "The Mexican Population of Pasadena, California," *Journal of Applied Sociology* 7, no. 5 (May–June 1923): 22; Vernon McCombs, *From over the Border: A Study of Mexicans in the United States* (1925; reprint, New York, 1970), 34–35; City of Los Angeles, Department of Health, *Annual Report,* 1920 (Los Angeles, 1920), appendix.

36. Louis Reccow, "The Orange County Citrus Strikes of 1935–1936: The 'Forgotten People' in Revolt" (Ph.D. diss., University of Southern California, 1972), 17; Nelson S. Van Valen, "The Bolshiviki and the Orange Groves," *Pacific Historical Review* 22 (1953): 40; Mary Helen Ponce, *Hoyt Street: An Autobiography* (Albuquerque, 1993), 17.

37. John Berger, *Pig Earth* (New York, 1979), 203; Tomás Rivera, *Y no se lo tragó la tierra / And the Earth Did Not Part* (Berkeley, 1978), 115; see p. 64 in Rivera for the people "neither here nor there."

38. Taylor, *Mexican Labor in the United States: Imperial Valley,* 18–19, 39, 66–68, 79; Robert S. Elliott, "The Health and Relief Problems of a Group of Non-family Mexican Men in Imperial County" (master's thesis, University of Southern California, 1939), 16–17.

39. Francis Cahn and Bary Valeska, *Welfare Activity of Federal, State, and Local Governments in California* (Berkeley, 1936), 203; Taylor, "Mexicans North of the Rio Grande," 140; Norman D. Humphrey, "Employment Patterns of Mexicans in Detroit," *Monthly Labor Review* 61, no. 5 (November 1945): 913.

40. Ponce, *Hoyt Street,* 4–8.

41. Home Missions Council, *A Study of Social and Economic Factors Relating to Spanish-Speaking People in the United States* (n.p., [late 1920s?]), 23.

42. Mathews, "House Courts of Los Angeles," 466; Kienle, "Housing Conditions among the Mexican Population of Los Angeles," 7.

43. Douglas, "The Conflict of Cultures in First Generation Mexicans," 91; Cloyd V. Gustafson, "An Ecological Analysis of the Hollenbeck Area of Los An-

geles" (master's thesis, University of Southern California, 1940), 43; Los Angeles Housing Commission, *Report of the Los Angeles Housing Commission,* July 1, 1910, to March 31, 1913, 22–24.

44. *El Heraldo de México,* May 13, 1920; *La Opinión,* November 24, 1928.

45. Ernesto Galarza, *Barrio Boy* (Notre Dame, 1971), 200; Manuel Gamio, *Mexican Immigration to the United States: A Study of Human Migration and Adjustment* (Chicago, 1930), 236.

46. Blanche A. Sommerville, "Naturalization from the Mexican Viewpoint," *Community Exchange Bulletin* 6, no. 4 (May 1928): 11; Helen W. Walker, "Mexican Immigrants and American Citizenship," *Sociology and Social Research* 13 (1929): 468, 471; Emory Bogardus, "The Mexican Immigrant and Segregation," *American Journal of Sociology* 36, no. 1 (July 1930): 76–78; *La Opinión,* April 20, 1928.

47. U.S. Department of Labor, Bureau of Labor Statistics, "Labor and Social Conditions of Mexicans in California," 85; California Commission of Immigration and Housing, *Community Survey Made in Los Angeles* (San Francisco, 1919), 43–47; Walker, "Mexican Immigrants and American Citizenship," 465; Mason John Hart, *Revolutionary Mexico: The Coming and Process of the Mexican Revolution* (Berkeley, 1987), 180.

48. Nicolás Kanellos, *A History of Hispanic Theater in the United States: Origins to 1940* (Austin, 1990), 17–21.

49. Ibid., 19–39.

50. The examples here and in the next paragraph are taken randomly from ads in *El Heraldo de México,* January 7, November 15, 18, 22, and 30, 1919, January 7, 30, and 31, February 6, 20, and 24, and June 12, 1920; and from *La Opinión,* March 7 and 15, April 2, May 9 and 21, 1927; see also McEuen, "A Survey of the Mexicans in Los Angeles," 74; Kanellos, *A History of Hispanic Theater,* 26, 66.

51. The story of Ramona took place in the first decades of the American period of California history.

52. Kanellos, *A History of Hispanic Theater,* 44–59, 65–69.

53. In 1910, D. W. Griffiths directed Mary Pickford in the first cinematic presentation of the story of Ramona; in 1928 Dolores Del Río starred in another popular version and sang a jazzy hit song about Ramona; the 1936 version starring Loretta Young and Don Ameche remains the standard movie treatment, and in 1959 Raquel Welch won the right to portray Ramona in the undying Hemet pageant by winning its beauty contest. For a discussion of my attraction to the character and story of Ramona, see Monroy, *Thrown among Strangers,* 263–71.

54. See *La Opinión,* December 22, 1926, January 2 and March 14, 1927, June 3, 1928, and November 28, 1930, and *El Heraldo de México,* August 23, 1921, for examples of such advertisements; Sánchez, *Becoming Mexican American,* 182.

55. The text quotations are from *El Heraldo de México,* April 22 and 29, 1916; on the Couts family, see Monroy, *Thrown among Strangers,* 160, 192–93.

56. *La Opinión,* March 31, April 1, 21, and 22, May 6, 12 and 30, November 22, 1929, and December 21, 1930.

57. *La Opinión,* April 13, 14, 15, and 16 and May 13, 1929.

58. *La Opinión,* April 16, 20, and 21, 1929.

59. William E. North, "Catholic Education in Southern California" (Ph.D. diss., The Catholic University of America, 1936), 188–90; Sánchez, *Becoming Mexican American,* 157, 163; Manuel Gamio, *The Life Story of the Mexican Immigrant* (1931; reprint, New York, 1971), 28; Ponce, *Hoyt Street,* 162.

60. Karl Marx, "Contribution to the Critique of Hegel's *Philosophy of Right:* Introduction," in *Marx-Engels Reader,* ed. Robert C. Tucker (New York, 1972), 12.

61. The priest is quoted in Walter Goldschmidt, *As You Sow* (New York, 1947), 135.

62. *La Opinión,* June 10, 1928; Balderrama, *In Defense of La Raza,* 76–77; Sánchez, *Becoming Mexican American,* 167–68.

63. Mike Davis, *City of Quartz: Excavating the Future in Los Angeles* (New York, 1992), 330–31; Balderrama, *In Defense of La Raza,* 77; Sánchez, *Becoming Mexican American,* 168–69.

64. This discussion derives from Victor Turner and Edith Turner, *Image and Pilgrimage in Christian Culture: Anthropological Perspectives* (New York, 1978), 203–7. See also Rudolf Otto, *The Idea of the Holy: An Inquiry into the Non-rational Factor in the Idea of the Divine and Its Relation to the Rational,* trans. John W. Harvey (1923; reprint, New York, 1958), 63–65, 143–44.

65. *La Opinión,* December 12, 1929.

66. McCombs, "Stopping the Reds," *El Mexicano* 7, no. 3 (January–March 1919): 1; "Manifesto a la Nación del Plan del Partido Liberal Mexicano de 1906," reprinted in Juan Gómez-Quiñones, *Sembradores, Ricardo Flores Magón y el Partido Liberal Mexicano: A Eulogy and Critique* (Los Angeles, 1973), 96; *Regeneración,* November 6, 1910; Samuel M. Ortegon, "The Religious Status of the Mexican Population of Los Angeles" (master's thesis, University of Southern California, 1932), 22–23.

67. Sánchez, *Becoming Mexican American,* 168. See also Balderrama, *In Defense of La Raza,* 77–78.

68. *La Opinión,* December 12, 1929; Ena Campbell, "The Virgin of Guadalupe and the Female Self-Image: A Mexican Case History," in *Mother Worship: Theme and Variations,* ed. James J. Preston (Chapel Hill, N.C., 1982), 19–20. See the excellent and stimulating Ana Castillo, ed., *Goddess of the Americas / La Diosa de las Américas: Writings on the Virgin of Guadalupe* (New York, 1996).

69. *Los Angeles Times,* June 21, 1924; DeWitt Van Court, *The Making of Champions in California* (Los Angeles, 1926), 136; *La Opinión,* January 21, 1930; Joyce Carol Oates, "On Boxing," in *Reading the Fights* ed. Joyce Carol Oates and Daniel Halpern (New York, 1988), 298–99.

70. Jeffrey T. Sammons, *Beyond the Ring: The Role of Boxing in American Society* (Urbana, Ill., 1988), 27–29, 59–64, 257; *Los Angeles Times,* July 15 and 21, 1924; Van Court, *The Making of Champions in California,* 117. Van Court notes how Fidel LaBarba was senior-class president at Lincoln High School. After the Olympics he turned professional so that he could buy a house for his parents. In 1925 he quickly fought his way to the American flyweight championship and then became world champ in 1927, the same year he took a year off to go to Stanford.

71. Gerald Early, "'I Only Like it Better When the Pain Comes': More Notes toward a Cultural Definition of Prizefighting," in *Reading the Fights*, ed. Joyce Carol Oates and Daniel Halpern (New York, 1988), 44–45, 54; Oates, "On Boxing," 288.

72. Van Court, *The Making of Champions in California*, 136.

73. *La Opinión*, January 15 and March 21, 1928; April 1, 1927; January 21, 1930.

74. *La Opinión*, March 9, 1927; Gerald Early, "Three Notes toward a Cultural Definition of Prizefighting," in *Reading the Fights*, ed. Joyce Carol Oates and Daniel Halpern (New York, 1988), 28; Hugh McIlvanney, "Onward Virgin Soldier: Lupe Pintor v. Johnny Owen, Los Angeles, September 19, 1980," in ibid., 191.

75. Emory S. Bogardus, *The City Boy and His Problems: A Survey of Boy Life in Los Angeles* (Los Angeles, 1926), 86, quotes the playground director; Van Court, *The Making of Champions in California*, 2, 138–39, comments on Frankie García.

76. *La Opinión*, January 18, 1931; Ponce, *Hoyt Street*, 106–7.

77. *La Opinión*, May 26, 1927, and February 6, 7, and 9, 1928.

78. This discussion derives from Early, "Three Notes," Oates, "On Boxing," and especially my own observations of, and responses to, the fights.

79. Kay Lynn Briegel, "The Alianza Hispano-Americana, 1894–1965: A Mexican American Fraternal Insurance Society" (Ph.D. diss., University of Southern California, 1974), 60, 77, 79, 89, 92, 128–34; Romo, *East Los Angeles*, 152; *El Heraldo de México*, November 26, 1919.

80. *El Heraldo de México*, November 11 and January 16, 1919.

81. *La Opinión*, May 6, 1928, May 13, 1927, and August 17, 1929; Sánchez, *Becoming Mexican American*, 112–14.

82. *El Heraldo de México*, September 16, 1921, February 1 and 13 and March 6, 1919, and June 19 and July 2, 1920.

83. Sánchez, *Becoming Mexican American*, 108–9; Romo, *East Los Angeles*, 150–52; José Amaro Hernández, *Mutual Aid for Survival: The Case of the Mexican American* (Malibar, Fla., 1983), 79; *La Opinión*, November 29, 1926.

84. Balderrama, *In Defense of La Raza*, 37–38, 46–49, 52, n. 2; Romo, *East Los Angeles*, 153–54.

85. Balderrama, *In Defense of La Raza*, 40–46; Sánchez, *Becoming Mexican American*, 123; Robert N. McClean, "Goodbye Vicente!" *The Survey* 66, no. 3 (May 1, 1931): 196.

CHAPTER 2. BORN BY THE RIVER

1. *Los Angeles Express*, May 4 and 8, 1903; *Los Angeles Times*, May 7 and 9, 1903.

2. Roosevelt, *The Strenuous Life*, 229, 243, 241.

3. Marc Reisner, *Cadillac Desert: The American West and Its Disappearing Water* (New York, 1986), 115–21, Roosevelt is quoted on p. 115. See also Donald Worster, *Rivers of Empire: Water, Aridity, and the Growth of the American West* (New York, 1986), 156–69.

4. James D. Cockcroft, *Mexico: Class Formation, Capital Accumulation, and the State* (New York, 1983), 154, 167; Eric Wolf, *Sons of the Shaking Earth: The People of Mexico and Guatemala* (Chicago, 1959), 15–17; James W. Wilkie, *The Mexican Revolution: Federal Expenditure and Social Change since 1910* (Berkeley, 1970), 130–36.

5. Allen Kelley, *Historical Sketch of the Los Angeles Aqueduct* (Los Angeles, 1913), 13, 18–21. Other sources for this story include *Los Angeles Times*, June 13, 1907, and November 6, 1913; Reisner, *Cadillac Desert*, 61–92; Morrow Mayo, *Los Angeles* (New York, 1933), 220–46; Carey McWilliams, *Southern California: An Island on the Land* (1946; reprint, Santa Barbara, 1973), 183–94; Workers of the Writers' Program of the Works Projects Administration in Southern California, *Los Angeles: A Guide to the City and Its Environs*, 50–51.

6. City of Los Angeles, Department of Public Works, *First Annual Report of the Bureau of Los Angeles Aqueduct Power to the Board of Public Works* (Los Angeles, 1906–7).

7. Norris Hundley Jr., *Water and the West: The Colorado River Compact and the Politics of Water in the American West* (Berkeley, 1975), 17–52; Worster, *Rivers of Empire*, 194–99; Reisner, *Cadillac Desert*, 126–29.

8. Alexis de Tocqueville, *Democracy in America* (New York, 1945), 2:144. See also Taylor, *Mexican Labor in the United States: Imperial Valley*, 31; Worster, *Rivers of Empire*, 200.

9. Worster, *Rivers of Empire*, 201–5.

10. Reisner, *Cadillac Desert*, 101–3; McWilliams, *Southern California*, 195; *Los Angeles Times*, March 14, 1928; Barry Holstun Lopez, "Hanner's Story," in *River Notes: The Dance of Herons* (New York, 1980), 62.

11. Smith, "The Development of the Mexican People in the Community of Watts," 13–14.

12. Hart, *Revolutionary Mexico*, 33–51; Paul Friedrich, *Agrarian Revolt in a Mexican Village* (Englewood Cliffs, N.J., 1970), 2–3.

13. Hart, *Revolutionary Mexico*, 158–62.

14. Ibid., 161–62; Lawrence A. Cardoso, *Mexican Immigration to the United States, 1897–1931* (Tucson, 1980), 9–11.

15. Friedrich, *Agrarian Revolt in a Mexican Village*, 10–15, 43–46.

16. Hart, *Revolutionary Mexico*, 163–65, 183.

17. Ibid., 129–56.

18. Cockcroft, *Mexico*, 89.

19. Hart, *Revolutionary Mexico*, 63–64.

20. Ibid., passim, but esp. 11–15 and 258–86.

21. Paz, *The Labyrinth of Solitude*, 58. For the following information on the Revolution, see William B. Davis, *Experiences and Observations of an American Consular Officer during the Recent Mexican Revolutions* (Chula Vista, Calif., 1920), 147–50; Friedrich, *Agrarian Revolt in a Mexican City*, 98–130; Cardoso, *Mexican Immigration to the United States*, 71–73; Paul S. Taylor, *A Spanish-Mexican Peasant Community: Arendas in Jalisco, Mexico* (Berkeley, 1933), 33.

22. Taylor, *A Spanish-Mexican Peasant Community*, 40, 69; Paul S. Taylor, "Songs of the Mexican Migration," in *Puro Mexicano*, ed. J. Frank Dobie (Austin, 1935), 223, 239.

23. Berger, *Pig Earth*, 200–205; James Carl Gilbert, "A Field Study in Mex-

ico of the Mexican Repatriation Movement" (master's thesis, University of Southern California, 1934), 59–60, 83.

24. Gilbert, "A Field Study in Mexico of the Mexican Repatriation Movement," 79–80, 101; Richard Rodriguez, *Days of Obligation: An Argument with My Mexican Father*" (New York, 1992), 50.

25. Victor S. Clark, "Mexican Labor in the United States," *Bulletin of the Bureau of Labor*, no. 78 (September 1908), 468–74; Taylor, *A Spanish-Mexican Peasant Community*, 45; Cardoso, *Mexican Immigration to the United States*, 13–14.

26. Evelyn Hu-DeHart, *Yaqui Resistance and Survival: The Struggle for Land and Autonomy, 1821–1910* (Madison, 1984), passim; Dr. Balbás is quoted in Edward H. Spicer, *The Yaquis: A Cultural History* (Tucson, 1984), 141; the governor is quoted in Clark, "Mexican Labor in the United States," 500; and the émigré from Jalisco is quoted in Taylor, *A Spanish-Mexican Community*, 35.

27. Gilbert, "A Field Study in Mexico of the Mexican Repatriation Movement," 89; Cardoso, *Mexican Immigration to the United States*, 10–17, 55–70; Clark, "Mexican Labor in the United States," 470–71, 480, 490; Taylor, *A Spanish-Mexican Peasant Community*, 24–25; Romo, *East Los Angeles*, 50–55; Gamio, *Mexican Immigration to the United States*, 30.

28. McEuen, "A Survey of the Mexicans in Los Angeles," 12; the Jalisqueño is quoted in Taylor, *A Spanish-Mexican Peasant Community*, 45; Samuel Bryan, "Mexican Immigrants in the United States," *The Survey*, 28 (September 7, 1912), 728.

29. Gamio, *Mexican Immigration to the United States*, 1–12; Hoffman, *Unwanted Mexican Americans in the Great Depression*, 11–14; Cardoso, *Mexican Immigration to the United States*, 92–95; Romo, *East Los Angeles*, 58–59; U.S. Department of Labor, Bureau of Labor Statistics, "Labor and Social Conditions of Mexicans in California," 83–84; U.S. Bureau of Immigration, *Annual Report to the Commissioner General* (Washington, D.C., 1926), 9–10.

30. John Martinez, "Mexican Emigration to the U.S., 1910–1930" (master's thesis, University of California, Berkeley, 1957), 43–48, 69, 77–80; Cardoso, *Mexican Emigration*, 84, 114–116.

31. Paz, *Labyrinth of Solitude*, 73–88; Victor Turner, *The Ritual Process: Structure and Anti-Structure* (Ithaca, N. Y. 1977), 94–95; the grower is quoted in Carey McWilliams, *Factories in the Field: The Story of Migratory Farm Labor in California* (1939; reprint, Santa Barbara, 1971), 87.

32. Max S. Handman, "Economic Reasons for the Coming of the Mexican Immigrant," *American Journal of Sociology* 35 (January 1930): 604.

33. Otey Scruggs, "The First Farm Labor Program, 1917–1921," *Arizona and the West* 2 (winter 1960): 320–23; Harry Schwartz, "Agricultural Labor in the First World War," *Journal of Farm Economics* 24 (February 1942): 180; J. Blaine Gwin, "The New Mexican Immigration," The *Survey* 40, no. 18 (August 3, 1918): 491–92; "Regulations by United States Department of Labor for Admission of Mexican Laborers," *Monthly Labor Review* 7, no. 5 (November 1918): 416–18; Taylor, *Mexican Labor in the United States: Imperial Valley*, 16; Paul S. Taylor, "Some Aspects of Mexican Immigration," *Journal of Political Economy* 38, no. 5 (October 1930): 613.

34. The California railroad official is quoted in Linna E. Brestle, *Mexicans*

in the United States: A Report of a Brief Survey (Washington, D.C., 1929), re-
printed in *Church Views of the Mexican American,* ed. Carlos E. Cortez (New
York, 1974), 14. The statistics on the Mexican railroad workers are drawn from
U.S. Department of Labor, Bureau of Labor Statistics, "Increase of Mexican
Labor in Certain Industries in the United States," *Monthly Labor Review* 32
(January 1931): 82; and Taylor, "Some Aspects of Mexican Immigration," 611–
12. The AT&SF official is quoted in U.S. Congress, Senate, The Committee
on Immigration, *Restriction of Western Hemisphere Immigration,* 70th Cong.,
1928, 105. The Los Angeles Railway Company is quoted in Home Missions
Council, *A Study of Social and Economic Factors,* 16. Smith, "The Development of the Mexican People in the Community of Watts," 20.

  35. Castillo, "The Making of a Mexican Barrio," 149–51; Clark, "Mexican
Labor in the United States," 479.

  36. Clark, "Mexican Labor in the United States," 476–77; *Pacific Rural
Press,* September 6 and December 6, 1902, and February 24, 1912; Albert Ca-
marillo, *Chicanos in a Changing Society: From Mexican Pueblos to American
Barrios in Santa Barbara and Southern California, 1848–1930* (Cambridge,
Mass., 1979), 50–51.

  37. Statement of C. W. Thomas, *Pacific Rural Press,* September 6, 1902;
Senate, The Committee on Immigration, *Restriction of Western Hemisphere Immigration,* 26; Taylor, *Mexican Labor in the United States: Imperial Valley,* 40;
statement of S. P. Frisselle, U.S. Congress, House, Committee on Immigration
and Naturalization, *Seasonal Agricultural Labor from Mexico,* 69th Cong., 1926,
8; Senate, The Committee on Immigration, *Restriction of Western Hemisphere
Immigration,* 27, 70; George Clements to Governor C. C. Young, December 28,
1927, Clements Papers, box 64.

  38. U.S. Congress, Senate, Subcommittee of the Committee on Education
and Labor, *Violations of Free Speech and the Rights of Labor,* 76th Cong., 1940,
pt. 53, 1944 (hereafter cited as *Violations of Free Speech*); McWilliams, *Factories in the Field,* 134–51.

  39. McEuen, "A Survey of the Mexicans in Los Angeles," 29–30; Lloyd
Welker Fellows, "Economic Aspects of the Mexican Rural Population in California with Special Emphasis on the Need for Mexican Labor in Agriculture"
(master's thesis, University of Southern California, 1929), 24–26; Clark, "Mexican Labor in the United States," 500; Senate, The Committee on Immigration,
Restriction of Western Hemisphere Immigration, 27, 70.

  40. Jeremiah W. Jenks and W. Jett Lauch, *The Immigration Problem* (New
York, 1912), 212; Governor C. C. Young's Mexican Fact-Finding Committee,
Mexicans in California (San Francisco, 1930), 92.

  41. Statement of Fred J. Hart, in U.S. Congress, House of Representatives,
Committee on Immigration and Naturalization, "Western Hemisphere Immigration," *Hearings,* 71st Cong., 1930, 192.

  42. Ibid.

  43. George Clements to W. Frank Persons, October 16, 1935, in *Violations
of Free Speech,* pt. 53, 1969. The statistics come from House, Committee on
Immigration and Naturalization, *Hearings,* 203; Bogardus, "The Mexican Immigrant," 472–73; Taylor, "Mexicans North of the Rio Grande," 137–38; Tay-

lor, *Mexican Labor in the United States: The Imperial Valley*, 35; Fellows, "Economic Aspects of the Mexican Rural Population"; California Department of Employment, *Agricultural Activities, Crops, and Labor*, comp. Ellis S. Coman (Sacramento, 1939), n.p.

44. "Mexican Immigration—A Report by Roy L. Garis for the Information of Members of Congress," in House, Committee on Immigration and Naturalization, *Hearings,*, 427. See also Constantine Panunzio, "Intermarriage in Los Angeles, 1924–1933," *American Journal of Sociology* 47 (1942): 692.

45. Remsen Crawford, "The Menace of Mexican Immigration," *Current History* 31 (February 1930): 902–4.

46. Gompers is quoted in Philip S. Foner, *History of the Labor Movement in the United States*, vol. 3, *The Policies and Practices of the American Federation of Labor, 1900–1909* (New York, 1964), 262–63. Paul S. Taylor, *Mexican Labor in the United States: Chicago and the Calumet Region* (Berkeley, 1932), 34, 117; Francisco A. Rosales and Daniel T. Simon, "Chicano Steel Workers and Unionism in the Midwest, 1919–1945," *Aztlán*, 6, no. 2 (summer 1975): 267; David Brody, *Steelworkers in America: The Nonunion Era* (New York, 1969), 254.

47. The AFL statement of 1927 is quoted in Emory S. Bogardus, *The Mexican in the United States* (Los Angeles, 1934), 83–84. On the efforts for cooperation, see Santiago Iglesias, "The Child of the A.F. of L.," and "American Federation of Labor (Mexico—U.S. Immigration Conference)," both in *American Federationist* 32, no. 10 (October 1925): 928, 921–22, respectively; and Harvey A. Levinstein, "The AFL and Mexican Immigration in the 1920's: An Experiment in Labor Diplomacy," *Hispanic American Historical Review* 48 (May 1968): 207–19.

48. Crawford, "The Menace of Mexican Immigration," 905; Charles Clifford Carpenter, "A Study of Segregation versus Non-segregation of Mexican Children" (master's thesis, University of Southern California, 1935), 11; California Commission on Immigration and Housing, *Second Annual Report*, 236; Lofstedt, "The Mexican Population of Pasadena, California," 19.

49. *Los Angeles Times*, September 20, 1915; Congressman Box is quoted in Charles Wollenberg, "Huelga, 1928 Style," 57; Romo, *East Los Angeles*, 92–97.

50. Bogardus, *The Mexican in the United States*, 46; Reverend Vernon McCombs in the *New York Times* is quoted in "Mexican Invaders Relieving Our Farm Labor Shortage," *Literary Digest* 66, no. 3 (July 17, 1920): 54. See also *Angeles Times*, April 12 and 13, 1917; Romo, *East Los Angeles*, 97.

51. Bartlett, *The Better City*, 78; Crawford, "The Menace of Mexican Immigration," 905.

52. U.S. Congress, House of Representatives, Committee on Immigration from Countries of the Western Hemisphere, *Report*, 4, 7.

53. House, Committee on Immigration and Naturalization, "Western Hemisphere Immigration," *Hearings*, 59–61; Dr. George P. Clements to W. Frank Persons, October 16, 1935, in *Violations of Free Speech*, pt. 53, 19691; "Mexican Invaders Relieving Our Farm Labor Shortage," 53.

54. Clements to Governor C. C. Young, December 28, 1927, in Clements Papers, box 64; statement of S. P. Frisselle, House, Committee on Immigration

and Naturalization, *Seasonal Labor from Mexico,* 8; statement of A. C. Hardison, Senate, The Committee on Immigration, *Restriction of Western Hemisphere Immigration,* 50; statement of E. E. McInnis, ibid., 107; *Violations of Free Speech,* pt. 52, 19237.

55. Governor C. C. Young's Mexican Fact Finding Committee, *Mexicans in California,* 92.

CHAPTER 3. "LIKE SWALLOWS AT THE OLD MISSION"

1. Karl Marx, *The Eighteenth Brumaire of Louis Bonaparte* (1869, reprint: New York, 1963), 15.

2. Monroy, *Thrown among Strangers.*

3. Ibid., 51.

4. McWilliams, *Southern California,* 156–59; Fogelson, *The Fragmented Metropolis,* 13–20, 24–42, 72; Arthur G. Coons and Arjay R. Miller, *An Economic and Industrial Survey of the Los Angeles and San Diego Areas* (California State Planning Board, Sacramento, Calif., 1941, typewritten), 21–23; Notes by the Agents (Passenger Department Southern Pacific Company), *California South of the Tehachapi* (San Francisco, 1908), 15.

5. Grace Heilman Stimson, *Rise of the Labor Movement in Los Angeles* (Berkeley, 1955), 104–22; McWilliams, *Southern California,* 276–77.

6. Stimson, *Rise of the Labor Movement,* 366–89; Louis Adamic, *Dynamite: The Story of Class Violence in America* (1931, reprint: New York, 1958), 200–243; McWilliams, *Southern California,* 277–83; *Los Angeles Times,* October 1, 1910. Clarence Darrow defended the two machinists, the McNamara brothers, charged with the bombing that killed twenty people. Their innocence or guilt became the primary issue in the mayoral election, in which one of their defenders, the Socialist candidate Job Harriman, appeared to have the lead. In a deal that Lincoln Steffens and Otis concocted, Darrow apparently convinced the brothers to confess suddenly, on the eve of the election, in exchange for sparing them from the death penalty. This cost the Socialist Party the mayoralty of Los Angeles and paralyzed oppositional politics for a good while.

7. "Industrial Freedom" is the inscription on the Times Mirror Building in downtown Los Angeles. Otis is quoted in John A. Fitch, "Los Angeles, a Militant Anti-union Citadel," *The Survey* 33 (October 3, 1914): 4. McWilliams, *Southern California,* 274–78; *Violations of Free Speech,* pt. 52, 19017, 19025, and pt. 64, 23396; *Pacific Rural Press,* May 4, 1912, and August 26, 1922.

8. Clements to Young, December 28, 1927; Coons and Miller, *An Economic and Industrial Survey,* xviii; Los Angeles County, Board of Supervisors, *Southern California Crops, Annual Statistical Supplement, 1938* (Los Angeles, 1939), 2–3; California Department of Employment, *Agricultural Activities, Crops, and Labor.*

9. Coons and Miller, *An Economic and Industrial Survey,* 43; California Department of Employment, *Agricultural Activities, Crops, and Labor;* U. S. Department of Labor, United States Employment Service, *Annual Report, Wages Paid in Agricultural Occupations, All Counties, State of California, Year 1938* (Los Angeles, 1938); Cahn and Valeska, *Welfare Activity of Federal, State, and Local Governments in California,* 203.

10. Douglas, "The Conflict of Cultures in First Generation Mexicans in Santa Ana, California," 35; Taylor, "Mexicans North of the Rio Grande," 140; McWilliams, *North from Mexico*, 215–21.

11. Clark, "Mexican Labor in the United States," 494–95; the figure of one and a half months unemployment per year derives from California Unemployment Reserves Commission, *A Study of Seasonal Unemployment in California* (Sacramento, 1939), 37: Mexicans in the building and construction gangs suffered a 12.7 percent deviation from the norm of 100.

12. California Unemployment Reserves Commission, *A Study of Seasonal Employments in California*, 37, 86.

13. Ibid., 51–53.

14. Ibid., 67; Ruiz, *Cannery Women*, 21–32.

15. Clements to C. C. Young, December 28, 1927; California Unemployment Reserves Commission, *A Study of Seasonal Unemployment*, 67; Ruiz, *Cannery Women*, 18–20; Heller Committee for Research in Social Economics of the University of California and Constantine Panunzio, *How Mexicans Earn and Live: A Study of the Incomes and Expenditures of One Hundred Mexican Families in San Diego, California*, Cost of Living Studies, 5 (Berkeley, 1933).

16. U.S. Bureau of the Census, *Special Report on Foreign-Born White Families by Country of Birth of Head* (Washington, D.C., 1933), 217; Heller Committee and Panunzio, *How Mexicans Earn and Live*, 11.

17. Coons and Miller, *An Economic and Industrial Survey*, xviii, 113–15, 160; U.S. Bureau of the Census, *Fifteenth Census of U.S. Manufacturers, General Report* (Washington D.C., 1929), 1:243.

18. John Laslett and Mary Tyler, *The ILGWU in Los Angeles, 1907–1988* (Inglewood, Calif., 1989), 119; International Ladies' Garment Workers' Union, *Report and Proceedings of the Twenty-Fifth Convention of the International Ladies' Garment Workers' Union, 1945* (New York, 1945), 122.

19. Rose Pesotta, *Bread upon the Waters* (New York, 1945), 19–23; Unemployment Reserves Commission, *A Study of Seasonal Unemployment*, 69; *Western Worker*, February 28, 1935.

20. California Division of Industrial Welfare of the Department of Industrial Relations, *Biennial Report, 1938–1940* (San Francisco, 1940), 30, 33. Mexicans comprised 13.6 percent of laundry and dry-cleaning workers statewide, but the percentage was undoubtedly higher in Southern California; Governor C. C. Young's Fact Finding Committee, *Mexicans in California*, 83.

21. Los Angeles Bureau of Municipal Research Incorporated, *Unified Local Government and Tax Reform for Los Angeles County, California* (Los Angeles, 1934), 16–18.

22. Ibid., 111; Coons and Miller, *An Economic and Industrial Survey*, xxi, 26, 129, 141–43; *Violations of Free Speech*, pt. 52, 19006; *Los Angeles Times*, June 29, 1936.

23. Davis, *City of Quartz*, 386–88.

24. Unemployment Reserves Commission, *A Study of Seasonal Unemployment*, 86; Coons and Miller, *An Economic and Industrial Survey*, 137; The Citizens Industrial Fact Finding Committee, "Tentative Report on the Furniture Industry of Los Angeles" ([Los Angeles?], [1936 or 1937?]), 2–3; *Labor Herald*, October 31, 1941; *Los Angeles Citizen*, September 6, 1935; Scott Greer, "The

Participation of Ethnic Minorities in the Labor Unions of Los Angeles County"
(Ph.D. diss., University of California, Los Angeles, 1952), 117–20; Louis B. Perry
and Richard S. Perry, *A History of the Los Angeles Labor Movement, 1911–1941*
(Berkeley, 1963), 287, 463.

25. Greer, "The Participation of Ethnic Minorities," 62–63, 69–70, 73, 89,
100–104.

26. Bogardus, *The Mexican in the United States*, 46; Clements is quoted in
Home Missions Council, *A Study of Social and Economic Factors*, 10; McEuen,
"A Survey of the Mexicans in Los Angeles," 98; Merton E. Hill, *The Develop-
ment of an Americanization Program* (n.p., 1928), 5, 12.

27. Douglas Monroy, "Anarquismo y Comunismo: Mexican Radicalism and
the Communist Party in Southern California in the 1930s," *Labor History* 24,
no. 1 (winter 1983): 34–37; Jay S. Stowell, *The Near Side of the Mexican Question* (New York, 1921), 34; McCombs, "Stopping the Reds," 7; Romo, *East
Los Angeles*, 89–111; *Los Angeles Times*, March 10, 1916; Lofstedt, "The Mexican Population of Pasadena, California," 268.

28. Hill, *The Development of an Americanization Program*, is the fullest and
most characteristic of the reformer publications. See particularly p. 12 (on the
California Fruit Growers' Exchange) and p. 103 (on teaching procedures). See
also G. Bromley Oxnam, "The Mexican in Los Angeles from the Standpoint of
the Religious Forces of the City," *The Annals of the American Academy of Political and Social Science* 93 (January 1921): 130–33.

29. Commission of Religion, *Protestant Religious Work among Spanish-
Speaking Americans and Mexicans in the United States* (n.p., n.d., [1920s?]),
14; Bartlett, *The Better City*, 85.

30. Ortegon, "The Religious Status of the Mexican Population of Los Angeles," 31–32. On the Chicago settlements, see Christopher Lasch, *The New
Radicalism in America, 1889–1963: The Intellectual as a Social Type* (New
York, 1965), 3–37 (on Jane Addams) and 141–80 (on reform as social control);
and particularly Jane Addams, *Twenty Years at Hull House* (New York, 1960),
90–100, as well as 82, 121, 170 for her less-than-complimentary view of non-
Anglo immigrants.

31. Oxnam, "The Mexican in Los Angeles from the Standpoint of the Religious Forces of the City," 132; Edward Drewry Jervey, *The History of Methodism in Southern California and Arizona* (Los Angeles, 1960), 95–98; Ortegon,
"The Religious Status of the Mexican Population of Los Angeles," 37–41; Alberto Camarillo, "The Sociological Failure of the Catholic Church toward the
Chicano," *Journal of Mexican-American Studies* 1, no. 2 (winter 1971): 72–83.

32. Hill, *The Development of an Americanization Program*, 101, 106;
McEuen, "A Survey of the Mexicans of Los Angeles," 101–2.

33. Irving G. Hendrick, *The Education of Non-whites in California, 1848–
1970* (San Francisco, 1977), 60–69.

34. Leonard John Vandenbergh, "The Mexican Problem in the Schools," *Los
Angeles School Journal* 11 (May 14, 1928): 15; see also McEuen, "A Survey of
the Mexicans in Los Angeles," 100.

35. Vandenbergh, "The Mexican Problem in the Schools," 15–16.

36. Gilbert George González, "The System of Public Education and Its Function within the Chicano Communities, 1920–1930" (Ph.D. diss., University of

California, Los Angeles, 1974), 135–81: the *Los Angeles School Journal* 10 (February 14, 1923): 44, is quoted on p. 178.

37. Hendrick, *The Education of Non-Whites in California*, 81–82, 88, 91–92; Frank M. Wright, "A Survey of the El Monte School District, El Monte, California" (masters' thesis, University of Southern California, 1930), 25–28, 34.

38. Bogardus, "Second Generation Mexicans," *Sociology and Social Research* 13 (January–February 1929): 281–82; Ruth D. Tuck, *Not with the Fist: Mexican-Americans in a Southwest City* (New York, 1946), 188.

39. Steven Jay Gould, *The Mismeasure of Man* (New York, 1981), 146–92, and Terman is quoted on pp. 190–91. See also Gilbert G. González, *Chicano Education in the Era of Segregation* (Philadelphia, 1990) 62–66.

40. Kimball Young, *Mental Differences in Certain Immigrant Groups: Psychological Tests of South Europeans in Typical California Schools with Bearing on the Educational Policy and on the Problems of Racial Contacts in This Country* (Eugene, 1924), 60, 65–66.

41. González, "The System of Public Education," cites the Los Angeles City School study and effectively analyzes this one and several others on pp. 149–50.

42. Wright, "A Survey of the El Monte School District," 45–46, 60.

43. Hazel Peck Bishop, "A Case Study of the Improvement of Mexican Homes through Instruction in Homemaking" (master's thesis, University of Southern California, 1937), 87–88.

44. Ibid., 91, 94.

45. California Commission of Immigration and Housing, *First Annual Report* (Sacramento, 1915), 99–100; California Commission of Immigration and Housing, *Report on an Experiment Made in Los Angeles in the Summer of 1917 for the Americanization of Foreign-Born Women* (Sacramento, 1917), 12.

46. California Commission of Immigration and Housing, *Report on an Experiment Made in Los Angeles*, 5–6, 21–22; Bridge, "A Study of the Agencies Which Promote Americanization," 91–95, 106.

47. Hill, *Development of an Americanization Program*, 8, 103; *El Mexicano*, 7 (July–September 1918): 12.

48. *El Heraldo de México*, February 28, 1920.

49. *La Opinión*, March 26, 1927.

50. *La Opinión*, March 25, 1927.

51. Ruth Lucretia Martinez, "The Unusual Mexican: A Study in Acculturation" (master's thesis, Claremont College, 1942; reprint: San Francisco, 1973), 50.

52. Ibid., González, *Chicano Education in the Era of Segregation*, 77–93; Walter Karp, *Buried Alive: Essays on Our Endangered Republic* (New York, 1992), 65–68, and Wilson is quoted on page 66; *United Progressive News*, April 6, 1936.

53. *El Heraldo de México*, February 28, 1920.

54. Michel Foucault, "The Dangerous Individual," in *Michel Foucault: Politics, Philosophy, Culture*, ed. Lawrence D. Kritzman (New York, 1990), 137–51.

55. Samuel Maldonado Ortegon, "Religious Thought and Practice among Mexican Baptists of the U.S., 1900–1947" (Ph.D. diss., University of Southern California, 1950), 69–70; *El Heraldo de México*, July 18, 1920; Ortegon, "Religious Status," 21, 28, 53–54; Gamio, *Mexican Immigration to the United*

States, 114; Gamio, *The Mexican Immigrant,* 195; Bogardus, *The Mexican in the United States,* 63–64; Richard G. Thurston, "Urbanization and Sociocultural Change in a Mexican American Enclave" (Ph.D. diss., University of California, Los Angeles, 1957), 36.

56. Romo, *East Los Angeles,* 101–3; Juan Gómez-Quiñones, *Sembradores, Ricardo Flores Magón y el Partido Liberal Mexicano,* 48–49; Jesus González-Monroy, *Ricardo Flores Magón y su actitude en la Baja, California* (Mexico D.F., 1962) 110; Juan Gómez-Quiñones, "The First Steps: Chicano Labor Conflict and Organizing, 1900–1920," *Aztlán* 3, no. 1 (spring 1972): 29–30, 36; McWilliams, *Factories in the Field,* 158–64.

57. Hoffman, *Unwanted Mexican-Americans in the Great Depression,* provides an excellent analysis of repatriation in the United States and in Los Angeles, and he quotes Quinn on p. 47; Sánchez, *Becoming Mexican American,* 209–17.

58. Taylor, "Mexicans North of the Rio Grande," 205; U. S. Bureau of Immigration, *Annual Report of the Commissioner General* (Washington, 1927), 7; Balderrama, *In Defense of La Raza,* 40–42.

59. J. Blaine Gwin, "Back and Forth to Mexico," *The Survey* 39, no. 1 (October 6, 1917): 9; Acuña, *Occupied America,* 202–4; Robert McClean, "The Mexican Return," *The Nation* 135, no. 34 (August 24, 1932): 165; Sánchez, *Becoming Mexican American,* 211.

60. Ríos-Bustamante and Castillo, *An Illustrated History of Mexican Los Angeles,* reprints the front page of *La Opinión* for February 27, 1931, on p. 130. See also Hoffman, *Unwanted Mexican Americans,* 49–66; Balderrama, *In Defense of La Raza,* 15–19.

61. Balderrama, *In Defense of La Raza,* 20.

62. Sánchez, *Becoming Mexican American,* 216–26; Taylor, *A Spanish-Mexican Peasant Community,* 62–63; McWilliams, *Southern California,* 316–17.

63. Hoffman, *Unwanted Mexican Americans,* 83.

64. Hazel D. Santiago, "Mexican Influence in Southern California," *Sociology and Social Research* 16 (September–October 1931): 70–73.

65. C. Vann Woodward, *Origins of the New South, 1877–1913* (Baton Rouge, 1951), 150–58.

66. McWilliams, *North from Mexico,* 35–47, and *Southern California,* 70–83; comments by Clements, dated August 29, 1939, in Clements Papers, box 72.

67. Monroy, *Thrown among Strangers,* 258–63.

68. This analysis and the quotations come from Monroy, *Thrown among Strangers,* 261–67.

69. *Los Angeles Times,* March 5, 1919; Monroy, *Thrown among Strangers,* 3–96.

70. Clements to Young, December 28, 1927; note by Clements, August 25, 1939, Clements Papers, box 72.

71. Vandenbergh, "The Mexican Problem in the Schools," 15.

72. C. M. Goethe, "Danger of Unrestricted Mexican Immigration," *Current History* 28 (August 1928): 767.

73. *Los Angeles Express,* May 8, 1903; Booker T. Washington, *Up from Slavery* (New York, 1965), 147, 149; Roosevelt, *The Strenuous Life,* 19; Paul

T. Porter, "Handling Mexican Labor in California," *Electric Railway Journal* 72 (August 11, 1928): 222.

74. By contrast, the county's Japanese and black populations in 1930 totaled thirty-five thousand (2.8 percent) and forty-six thousand (3.7 percent), respectively. U.S. Bureau of the Census, *Fifteenth Census of the United States, 1930, Population*, vol. 3, pt. 1, 266; Roger Daniels and Harry H. L. Kitano, *American Racism: Explorations in the Nature of Prejudice* (Englewood Cliffs, N. J., 1970), 69; City Planning Commission, "Distribution of Racial Groups," chart, Los Angeles, 1940.

75. Griswold del Castillo, *The Los Angeles Barrio*, 51–61; Camarillo, *Chicanos in a Changing Society*, 166–74; Ricardo Romo, "Mexican Workers in the City: Los Angeles, 1915–1930" (Ph.D. diss., University of California, Los Angeles, 1975), 165–169; Romo, "Work and Restlessness: Occupational and Spatial Mobility among Mexicanos in Los Angeles, 1918–1928," *Pacific Historical Review* 46, no. 2 (May 1977), 169; Castillo, "The Making of a Mexican Barrio," 166–68; George Sánchez sampled naturalization forms and found "a few important differences." Twenty percent worked in "low blue-collar jobs," but I think we can be sure that those who were applying for citizenship would be the more successful Mexican immigrants (see Sánchez, *Becoming Mexican American*, 192–93).

76. Care was taken to select only those marriage partners with addresses in Los Angeles County. Every other Spanish surname in the records was selected. Other Latin Americans could be easily detected and excluded on the basis of their parents' place of birth. Listings in the city directories probably include non-Mexican Latinos. The marriage record sample included 644 couples, and the city directory sample, actually only a check of the marriage records, included only about 100. Like most quantitative sources, neither is perfect. The marriage records are biased not only toward younger workers, who were most apt to be new in the job market and therefore less skilled, but also toward those who were more settled and ready to marry and, therefore, those who had better jobs. Furthermore, the imbalance of Mexican men over women likely meant that women could be more selective in choosing a husband, and presumably they would select one with a good job. City directories, on the other hand, are notoriously sloppy about collecting names in poor neighborhoods. Undocumented people would have been afraid to register their names anywhere, and they therefore figure in neither sample.

77. Unskilled and semi-skilled workers are grouped together because at the time that I did this research (1976) I believed that unskilled and semi-skilled categories were a false dichotomization of one category. The semi-skilled worker actually is the creation of the statistician, and this upgrades masses of unskilled workers a new, higher level. Dr. Alba Edwards, an official of the Bureau of the Census in the 1930s, created the category to distinguish between laborers and those who operated machines. Connecting the use of machinery with a skill category guaranteed that as the mechanization of industry increased, the number of unskilled workers would decline and that of semi-skilled would rise. The U.S. Department of Labor's *Occupational Outlook Handbook* defines semi-skilled workers as ordinarily receiving "only brief on-the-job training. Usually they are

told exactly what to do and how to do it, and their work is supervised closely."
This definition is true, but the distinction between the two categories is actually
meaningful for the Mexican worker—it distinguishes between gang and factory
labor. See Harry Braverman, *Labor and Monopoly Capital: The Degradation of
Work in the Twentieth Century* (New York, 1974), 428–32, who cites and dis-
cusses the *Occupational Outlook Handbook*.

78. Mexican Occupational Structure in 1936:

WORKER	1936 MARRIAGE RECORDS (PERCENT)	1929 CITY DIRECTORY	1934 CITY DIRECTORY
Male			
Unskilled and semi-skilled	77.5	83.3	76.0
Skilled	9.5	8.9	14.0
White-collar or small business	13.76	7.8	10.0
Female			
Unskilled and semi-skilled	85.4		
Skilled	0.9		
White-collar or small business (including "saleslady" 3.3%)	13.6		

Source: Los Angeles County marriage records and Los Angeles city directories. See also
Douglas Monroy, "Mexicans and the Racial Politics of Growth in Los Angeles in the Interwar Period," *The Western Historical Quarterly* 14, no. 4 (October 1983), 438–40.

79. Kienle, "Housing Conditions among the Mexican Population of Los Angeles," 24; Faith M. Williams and Alice C. Hanson, *Money Disbursements of
Wage Earners and Clerical Workers in Five Cities in the Pacific Region, 1934–
1936: Mexican Families in Los Angeles* [United States Bureau of Labor Statistics Bulletin no. 639, part 2] (Washington D.C., 1939), 88; Romo, "Work and
Restlessness," 169.

80. Camarillo, *Chicanos in a Changing Society,* 168–69; Romo, *East Los
Angeles,* 120–21.

81. Home Missions Council, *A Study of Social and Economic Factors,* 23;
California Commission on Immigration and Housing, *Community Survey Made
in Los Angeles,* 70; U.S. Department of Labor, Bureau of Labor Statistics, "Sanitary Surveys in Los Angeles," *Monthly Labor Review* 20 (June 1925): 1371;
U.S. Bureau of the Census, *Fifteenth Census of the United States, 1930: Population, Special Report on Foreign-Born White Families by Country of Birth of
Head,* 212; Williams and Hanson, *Money Disbursements,* 88.

82. Greer, "The Participation of Ethnic Minorities in the Labor Unions of
Los Angeles," 77–78; Alice Bessie Culp, "A Case Study of the Living Conditions of Thirty-Five Mexican Families of Los Angeles with Special Reference to
Mexican Children" (master's thesis, University of Southern California, 1921),
45; Camarillo, *Chicanos in a Changing Society,* 166; Thurston, "Urbanization
and Sociocultural Change in a Mexican American Enclave," 33; Taylor, *Mexican Labor in the United States: Chicago and the Calumet Region,* 98; Humphrey,
"Employment Patterns of Mexicans in Detroit,"918.

83. *La Opinión,* December 20, 1928; Camarillo, *Chicanos in a Changing
Society,* 166; Thurston, "Urbanization and Sociocultural Change in a Mexican-
American Enclave," 138; Ponce, *Hoyt Street,* 169–70.

CHAPTER 4. "OUR CHILDREN GET SO DIFFERENT HERE"

1. Renato Rosaldo, *Culture and Truth: The Remaking of Social Analysis* (Boston, 1989), 96.

2. Merrill Leonard Harrod, "A Study of Deviate Personalities as Found in Main Street of Los Angeles" (master's thesis, University of Southern California, 1939), 14, 20–22, 65–74.

3. Smith, "The Development of the Mexican People in the Community of Watts," 52; Douglas, "The Conflict of Cultures in First Generation Mexicans in Santa Ana, California," 49; Mary Lanigan, "Second Generation Mexicans in Belvedere" (master's thesis, University of Southern California, 1932), 25–27.

4. *La Opinión*, March 18, 1928, May 23 and 26 and June 2, 1929.

5. George Hadley-Garcia, *Hispanic Hollywood: The Latins in Motion Pictures* (New York, 1990), 27–29.

6. *La Opinión*, November 27 and December 9, 1928, April 15, 1929, and September 16, 1927. See also Vicki L. Ruiz, "'Star Struck': Acculturation, Adolescence, and the Mexican American Woman, 1920–1950," in *Building with Our Hands: New Directions in Chicana Studies,* ed. Adela de la Torre and Beatríz Pesquera (Berkeley, 1993), 109–29.

7. *La Opinión* March 16, May 25, and July 13, 1928, May 26 and November 17, 1929, January 19, 1930, and March 3 and April 26, 1927.

8. *La Opinión*, June 2, 1928, May 26 and November 3, 1929, and March 21, 1930; Hadley-Garcia, *Hispanic Hollywood*, 52.

9. Rena Blanche Peek, "The Religious and Social Attitudes of the Mexican Girls of the Constituency of the All Nations Foundation in Los Angeles" (master's thesis, University of Southern California, 1929), 44–48, 80.

10. Stuart Ewen and Elizabeth Ewen, *Channels of Desire: Mass Images and the Shaping of American Consciousness* (New York, 1982), 98–99; Marjorie Rosen, *Popcorn Venus: Women, Movies and the American Dream* (New York, 1973), 39–41, 83–85, 159–60; *La Opinión*, January 8, 1930, and January 18 and 19, 1931; Arthur G. Pettit, *Images of the Mexican American in Fiction and Film,* ed. Dennis E. Showalter (College Station, Tex., 1980), 140–41; *Current Biography: Who's News and Why* (New York, 1945), 643; Williams and Hanson, *Money Disbursements of Wage Earners,* 108, 231.

11. Peek, "The Religious and Social Attitudes of the Mexican Girls," 44–48, 80.

12. Kenneth Munden, ed., *The American Film Institute Catalog of Motion Pictures Produced in the United States: Feature Films, 1921–1930* (New York, 1971), 283; Ewen and Ewen, *Channels of Desire,* 87.

13. Lanigan, "Second Generation Mexicans in Belvedere," 54–55.

14. *La Opinión*, October 27, 1929; José Gómez-Sicre, "Dolores del Río," *Americas* 19 (November 1967), 14.

15. *La Opinión*, February 1, 1931, and November 13, 1928.

16. Gamio, *The Mexican Immigrant, His Life Story* (Chicago, 1931), 103. See also McEuen, "A Survey of the Mexicans in Los Angeles," 74; and Peek, "The Religious and Social Attitudes of the Mexican Girls," 45–46.

17. Douglas, "The Conflict of Cultures in First Generation Mexicans," 59–60; Lanigan, "Second Generation Mexicans in Belvedere," 20; Gamio, *The Life Story of the Mexican Immigrant*, 68; Ewen and Ewen, *Channels of Desire*, 81.

18. Ewen and Ewen, *Channels of Desire*, 118–23, 173–78, 210; John Berger, "The Suit and the Photograph," in *About Looking* (New York, 1980), 33–35; Williams and Hanson, *Money Disbursements of Wage Earners*, 90, 107.

19. Lanigan, "Second Generation Mexicans in Belvedere," 18–19; Douglas, "The Conflict of Cultures in First Generation Mexicans," 4, 49.

20. Gamio, *The Mexican Immigrant*, 186, quotes the editor; Ewen and Ewen, *Channels of Desire*, 211–14; Lanigan, "Second Generation Mexicans in Belvedere," 18–19.

21. Paul J. Crawford, "Movie Habits and Attitudes of the Under-privileged Boys of the All Nations Area in Los Angeles" (master's thesis, University of Southern California, 1934), 19, 61, 67, 71, 73, 76, 79–80. Ramon Novarro, Lupe Velez, and Dolores del Río fared quite poorly in the survey of favorites.

22. Ibid., 95. See also Adam Garbicz and Jacek Klinowski, *Cinema, the Magic Vehicle: A Guide to Its Achievement* (New York, 1983), vol. 1; John Robert Nash and Stanley Ralph Ross, *The Motion Picture Guide* (Chicago, 1987), 7:2759–60.

23. Paz, *The Labyrinth of Solitude*, 12–18; Malcolm X, *The Autobiography of Malcolm X* (New York, 1966), 56–62.

24. Paz, *Labyrinth of Solitude*, is the most famous analysis of the pachuco; Luis Valdez's film *Zoot Suit* stunningly analyzes the pachuco and dramatizes the events of the Sleepy Lagoon case; Robin D. G. Kelley, "The Riddle of the Zoot: Malcolm Little and Black Cultural Politics during World War II," in *Malcolm X: In Our Own Image*, ed. Joe Wood (New York, 1992), 159–63.

25. Alice Miller, *For Your Own Good: Hidden Cruelty in Child-Rearing and the Roots of Violence* (New York, 1983), esp. 3–8, 63–98; Marcia Westkott, *The Feminist Legacy of Karen Horney* (New Haven, 1986), 136–39. In Latin *famulus* means "slave," and *familia* for the Romans denoted the patriarch on the one hand and his wife, children, and slaves on the other.

26. Lanigan, "Second Generation Mexicans in Belvedere," 26, 80; Douglas, "The Conflict of Cultures in First Generation Mexicans," 50; Smith, "The Development of the Mexican People in the Community of Watts," 47, quotes the following: "You see, my father and mother wouldn't let us get married. They always said, 'No!' Mother made me stay with her all the time. She always goes to church every morning at seven-thirty as she did in Mexico. I said I was sick. She went with my brothers and we just ran away and got married at the court . . . They were strict with my sister, too. That's why she took poison and died."

27. Smith, "The Development of the Mexican People in the Community of Watts," 63; Douglas, "The Conflict of Cultures in First Generation Mexicans," 50–51; Westkott, *The Feminist Legacy of Karen Horney*, 95–101; Michel Foucault, *The History of Sexuality*, Vol. 1: *An Introduction* (New York, 1980), 25–27.

28. Smith, "The Development of the Mexican Community of Watts," 48.

29. Bogardus, *The City Boy and His Problems*; Gamio, *The Life Story of the Mexican Immigrant*, 148.

30. Karl Marx, "Critique of Hegel's Philosophy of Right," in *The Marx-Engels Reader,* ed. Robert C. Tucker (New York, 1972), 12; Bogardus, "Second Generation Mexicans," quotes the statement about "freedom" by "Mrs. E." secured by Helen Douglas, 280; Douglas, "The Conflict of Cultures in First Generation Mexicans," 24; Lanigan, "Second Generation Mexicans in Belvedere," 20, 34.

31. Gamio, *The Life Story of the Mexican Immigrant,* 52–53.

32. Pettit, *Images of the Mexican American,* 131–35; Hadley-Garcia, *Hispanic Hollywood,* 36–39; Munden, ed., *The American Film Institute Catalog,* 218, 583.

33. *La Opinión,* February 7 and January 26, 1930; Hadley-Garcia, *Hispanic Hollywood,* 54.

34. *La Opinión,* January 30 and February 11, 1930.

35. *La Opinión,* March 2, 4, 5, and 23 and April 30, 1930.

36. *La Opinión,* November 30 and December 26, 1930, January 25 and February 15, 1931.

37. The *La Opinión* article is quoted in Kanellos, *A History of Hispanic Theater,* 42–43; see also pp. 51–52.

38. Douglas, "The Conflict of Cultures in First Generation Mexicans," 2; Smith, "The Development of the Mexican People in the Community of Watts," 120.

39. Gilbert, "A Field Study in Mexico of the Mexican Repatriation Movement," 54–56, 69–70.

40. Ibid., Ruth H. Landman, "Some Aspects of the Acculturation of Mexican Immigrants and the Descendants to American Culture" (Ph.D. diss., Yale University, 1953), 90; Martinez, "The Unusual Mexican," 37.

41. Gilbert, "A Field Study in Mexico of the Mexican Repatriation Movement," 141; Taylor, *A Spanish-Mexican Peasant Community,* 57; Landman, "Some Aspects of the Acculturation of Mexican Immigrants," 90.

42. Gilbert, "A Field Study in Mexico of the Mexican Repatriation Movement," 86, 160; Martinez, "The Unusual Mexican," 21–23, 33–34.

43. Clark, "Mexican Labor in the United States," 510; Evangeline Hymer, "A Study of the Social Attitudes of Adult Mexican Immigrants in Los Angeles and Vicinity" (master's thesis, University of Southern California, 1923), 36; Smith, "The Development of the Mexican Community of Watts," 49; Lanigan, "Second Generation Mexicans in Belvedere," 40.

44. McEuen, "A Survey of the Mexicans in Los Angeles," 87.

45. Lanigan, "Second Generation Mexicans in Belvedere," 40; Herman A. Buckner, "A Study of Pupil Elimination and Failure among Mexicans" (master's thesis, University of Southern California, 1935), 37, 65.

46. California Commission of Immigration and Housing, *Second Annual Report,* 237–38; Patric, *A Study of Housing,* 18; Sterry, "The Sociological Basis for the Re-organization of the Macy Street School," 94–95; Bridge, "A Study of the Agencies," 98–102, 107–10.

47. Carpenter, "A Study of Segregation versus Non-segregation of Mexican Children," 83; Summary of Survey of Economic Aspects of Mexican Agricultural Labor in Los Angeles County, 3.

48. California Commission of Immigration and Housing, *Second Annual Report*, 257; Sterry, "The Sociological Basis for the Re-organization of the Macy Street School," 80.

49. Gustafson, "An Ecological Analysis of the Hollenbeck Area of Los Angeles," 65–67.

50. Ibid., 67, 58, 122; Herbert Sidney Wood, "A Pupil Survey of James A. Garfield High School, Los Angeles" (master's thesis, University of Southern California, 1937), 13–14.

51. González, *Labor and Community*, 100–111; Haas, *Conquests and Historical Identities*, 189–96.

52. Laura Lucille Lyon, "Investigation of the Program for the Adjustment of Mexican Girls to the High Schools of the San Fernando Valley" (master's thesis, University of Southern California, 1933), 2, 36; Haas, *Conquests and Historical Identities*, 195.

53. Lyon, "Investigation of the Program for the Adjustment of Mexican Girls," 46; F. G. Mason, "A Case Study of Thirty Adolescent Mexican Girls and Their Social Conflicts and Adjustments within the School" (master's thesis, University of Southern California, 1929), 10, 20–22.

54. Landman, "Some Aspects of Acculturation," 112–17, 132–35.

55. *El Heraldo de México*, January 7, 1919; *La Opinión*, January 25, 1931, and January 28, 1930.

56. *La Opinión*, November 29, 1926, and September 1 and November 16, 1929; Sánchez, *Becoming Mexican American*, 116–17.

57. *La Opinión*, November 29, 1926, and May 5, 1928.

58. Sánchez, *Becoming Mexican American*, 118–19; *La Opinión*, November 16, 1929.

59. Charles Aranda, *Dichos: Proverbs and Sayings from the Spanish* (Santa Fe, 1977), passim.

60. *La Opinión*, February 7, 1930.

61. Douglas, *Natural Symbols*, 24–28; Barry Sanders, *A Is for Ox: Violence, Electronic Media, and the Silencing of the Written Word* (New York, 1994), 67–68.

62. Douglas, *Natural Symbols*, 26–27; Sanders, *A Is for Ox*, 68, 75.

CHAPTER 5. THE POLITICAL PASSIONS OF MÉXICO DE AFUERA

1. Ignacio Ramírez, *El Heraldo de México*, February 25, 1919.

2. *La Opinión*, May 23, 1927, and January 16, 1928.

3. On July 28, 29, and August 3, 1927, *La Opinión* reported the arrests of the "vagrants"; on January 16 and 23, 1928, it serialized the editorial; and on July 30, 1927, it described the episodes from the consul's point of view.

4. *La Opinión*, May 23 and 27, 1927; *El Heraldo de México*, February 25, 1919.

5. *La Opinión*, November 28, 1926.

6. *La Opinión*, January 16, February 5, and March 17, 1928.

7. *La Opinión*, October 29, 1929, and April 1, 1930.

8. The correspondence between Gompers and Lizarraras is quoted in Philip S. Foner, *History of the Labor Movement in the United States,* 3:276–77. See also McWilliams, *Southern California,* 93–94; Juan Gómez-Quiñones, *Mexican American Labor, 1790–1990* (Albuquerque, 1994), 76–77.

9. Gómez-Quiñones, *Mexican American Labor,* 78–79; McWilliams, *North from Mexico,* 190.

10. *Los Angeles Times,* February 1 and 9, March 2, 1919; *Los Angeles Record,* February 5, 1919; *El Heraldo de México,* February 6, 1919; Van Valen, "The Bolshiviki and the Orange Groves," 39–50.

11. *El Heraldo de México,* July 2, 1920; February 8 and 18, 1919; March 6, 1919; February 20, 1919; February 28, 1920.

12. *El Heraldo de México,* March 11, 1919. See also Perry and Perry, *A History of the Los Angeles Labor Movement, 1911–1941,* 85–92.

13. *El Heraldo de México,* February 28, 1920. On the worldwide peasant revolutions of the early twentieth century, see Hart, *Revolutionary Mexico,* 187–234.

14. W. Dirk Ratt, *Revoltosos: Mexico's Rebels in the United States, 1903–1923* (College Station, Tex., 1981), 25–31; Gómez-Quiñones, *Sembradores,* 13–1, which also reprints the 1906 founding manifesto of the PLM on pp. 95–98; James A. Sandos, *Rebellion in the Borderlands: Anarchism and the Plan of San Diego, 1904–1923* (Norman, Okla., 1992), 8–12; Friedrich, *Agrarian Revolt in a Mexican Village,* 64.

15. Gómez-Quiñones, *Sembradores,* 32–45, and the manifesto is reprinted on pp. 120–25. Calling himself a "chicken thief and a revolutionist," Jack London told a Los Angeles PLM meeting in February 1910: "we socialists, anarchists, hoboes, chicken thieves, outlaws, and undesirable citizens of the United States are with you heart and soul in your efforts to overthrow slavery and autocracy in Mexico." Emma Goldman spoke at Burbank Hall "in hearty sympathy" with the Mexican Revolution (proceeds from the event went to the PLM). Ethyl Duffy Turner edited the fourth page of *Regeneración* in English while her husband bought and shipped guns to Mexico in the winter of 1911 to fight the revolution. *Regeneración,* February 11 and October 1, 1910, May 6 and April 22, 1911, January 13, 1912; Ethel Duffy Turner, *Writers and Revolutionists, an Interview Conducted by Ruth Teiser* (Berkeley, 1967), 10, 22–23; Sandos, *Rebellion in the Borderlands,* 12–23.

16. *Regeneración,* September 23, 1911; Gomez-Quiñones, *Sembradores,* 41–45; Raat, *Revoltosos,* 33–35.

17. Lowell W. Blaisdell, *The Desert Revolution: Baja California* (Madison, Wisc., 1962); González-Monroy, *Ricardo Flores Magón;* Raat, *Revoltosos,* 56–59. Agnes Smedley, *Daughter of Earth* (New York, 1973), 186; and Elizabeth Gurley Flynn, *The Rebel Girl: An Autobiography, My First Life, 1906–1926* (New York, 1973), 181, both mention men going off to fight in Mexico.

18. For an example of Ricardo's railing at apathetic workers, see "Manifesto a Todos los Trabajadores del Mundo," *Regeneración,* April 3, 1911, reprinted in Gomez-Quiñones, *Sembradores,* 116–18.

19. "El Matrimonio," *Regeneración,* January 1, 1913; Sandos, *Rebellion in the Borderlands,* 128–29; Emma M. Pérez, "'A La Mujer': A Critique of the

Partido Liberal Mexican's Gender Policy on Women," in Del Castillo, ed., *Between Borders*, 468–69.

20. Ricardo Flores Magón, "A la mujer," *Regeneración*, September 24, 1910, reprinted in Gomez-Quiñones, *Sembradores*, 110–12; and an English translation is reprinted in Magdalena Mora and Adelaida R. Del Castillo, eds., *Mexican Women in the United States: Struggles Past and Present* (Los Angeles, 1980), 160–62. Praxedis Guerrero, "La Mujer," in *Regeneración*, November 6, 1910, is reprinted in Gomez-Quiñones, *Sembradores*, 105–108; *Regeneración*, January 1, 1913. See also Pérez, "'A La Mujer': A Critique," 464–67.

21. Ramírez's words are from her essay "!Surge!" *La Crónica*, April 10, 1910, reprinted in Mora and Del Castillo, eds., *Mexican Women in the United States*, 168; *Los Angeles Times*, September 19, 1907, quoted in Pérez, "A la mujer," 468–69. See also Emilio Zamora, "Sara Estela Ramírez: Una Rosa Roja en el movimiento," in Mora and Del Castillo, eds., *Mexican Women in the United States*, 163–67; Raat, *Revoltosos*, 32; Pérez, "'A La Mujer': A Critique," 470–71.

22. González-Monroy, *Ricardo Flores Magón*, 18, 64, plates following 64, 88, 110; Gómez-Quiñones, "The First Steps," 28–31; Gómez-Quiñones, *Sembradores*, 41; Melvin Dubofsky, *We Shall Be All: A History of the Industrial Workers of the World* (Chicago, 1969), 184–87; Friedrich, *Agrarian Revolt in a Mexican Village*, 67–70.

23. McCombs, "Stopping the Reds," 1, 7; Monroy, "Anarquismo y Comunismo," 36; McEuen, "A Survey of the Mexicans in Los Angeles," 69–70.

24. Ortegon, "The Religious Status of the Mexican Population of Los Angeles," 22–23; Gamio, *The Mexican Immigrant, His Life Story*, 127, 129.

25. Friedrich, *Agrarian Revolt in a Mexican Village*, 119–30.

26. Balderrama, *In Defense of La Raza*, 91–92, emphasizes the revolutionary rhetoric of the CUOM; González, *Labor and Community*, calls the CUOM "fundamentally conservative"; I once affirmed its revolutionary nature in Monroy, "Anarquismo y Comunismo," 39–41; Gómez-Quiñones, *Roots of Chicano Politics, 1600–1940*, 381, refers to the CUOM as "Progressive." Ricardo Romo, *East Los Angeles*, 154–55; Governor Young's Fact Finding Committee, *Mexicans in California*, 123.

27. The CUOM platform is reprinted in Governor Young's Fact Finding Committee, *Mexicans in California*, 123–24. On Pesqueira and CUOM, see *La Opinión*, May 12, 1928.

28. González, *Labor and Community*, 139; Governor Young's Fact Finding Committee, *Mexicans in California*, 125.

29. *La Opinión*, March 15, 1928.

30. *La Opinión*, February 5, 1929.

31. Devra Anne Weber, "The Organizing of Mexicano Agricultural Workers: Imperial Valley and Los Angeles, 1928–1934, an Oral History Approach," *Aztlán* 3, no. 2 (Fall 1972): 323, 328, 330; Ronald W. López, "The El Monte Berry Strike of 1933," *Aztlán* 1, no. 1 (Spring 1970); Cletus Daniel, *Bitter Harvest: A History of California Farmworkers, 1870–1941* (Berkeley, 1982), 146–47; Reccow, "The Orange County Citrus Strikes," 107–8; Charles B. Spaulding, "The Mexican Strike at El Monte, California," *Sociology and Social Research* 18, no. 6 (July–August 1934): 572–75.

32. Len De Caux, *Labor Radical: From the Wobblies to CIO, a Personal History, 1932–1940* (New York, 1971), 114–15; Nathaniel Honig, *The Trade Union Unity League Today: Its Structure, Policy, Program, and Growth*, rev. ed. (New York, 1934); Irving Howe and Lewis Coser, *The American Communist Party: A Critical History: 1919–1957* (Boston, 1957); James Weinstein, *Ambiguous Legacy: The Left in American Politics* (New York, 1975), 38–43; Al Richmond, *A Long View from the Left: Memoirs of An American Revolutionary* (New York, 1975), 145–48; Daniel, *Bitter Harvest*, 105–40.

33. Stuart M. Jamieson, "The Origins and Present Structure of Labor Unions in Agricultural and Allied Industries of California," in *Violations of Free Speech*, pt. 62, 22531–22540; Daniel, *Bitter Harvest*, 147–48; Lopez, "The El Monte Berry Strike," 104–5; Weber, "The Organizing of Mexicano Agricultural Workers," 328–29.

34. Lopez, "The El Monte Berry Strike," 105; Weber, "The Organizing of Mexicano Agricultural Workers," 328–30; Jamieson, "The Origins and Present Structure of Labor Unions," 22536.

35. On the contemporary comentator, see Spaulding, "The Mexican Strike at El Monte," 575. See also Daniel, *Bitter Harvest*, 148; Lopez, "The El Monte Berry Strike," 107–8; Weber, "The Organizing of Mexicano Agricultural Workers," 329; *Western Worker*, June 8 and June 12, 1933; *Los Angeles Times*, July 1, 1933; *La Opinión*, April 24, 1933.

36. On the American landowners, see Ross Gast to Dr. George Clements, June 28, 1933, Clements Papers, box 80. See also Bogardus, *The Mexican in the United States*, 41; Thurston, "Urbanization and Sociocultural Change," 10. The indomitable Dr. Clements "understood that undercover men would be put in with the Mexicans to try and encourage them to accept the Mexican Government's offer of free lands"; and he suggested that if that did not work, the Board of Supervisors should "make such moves as they legally can or reasonably can to turn some of this Mexican surplus into Mexico." More humanely, Clements suggested that the Mexicans be fed, since a "full-bellied Mexican rarely fights and is more tractable." Clements to Arnoll, July 12, 14, 20, 1933, Clements Papers, box 80; *Violations of Free Speech*, pt. 55, 20109, 20262.

37. Lopez, "The El Monte Berry Strike," 108–9.

38. R. A. Wellpott to Captain Hynes, memorandum, June 7, 1933, in *Violations of Free Speech*, pt. 64, 23629.

39. LaRue McCormick, interview by author, Los Angeles, January 1977; Weber, "The Organizing of Mexicano Agricultural Workers," 330–31.

40. Dorothy Healey and Maurice Isserman, *Dorothy Healey Remembers: A Life in the American Communist Party* (New York, 1990), 42–46; LaRue McCormick, interview; Ross Lawrence, "Lessons from the Southern California Strike," *Western Worker*, August 7, 1933; statement of Stanley Hancock, quoted in Healey and Isserman, *Dorothy Healey Remembers*, 46; Monroy, "Anarquismo y Comunismo," 41–42, 46–47.

41. *La Opinión*, November 29, 1926, and January 2, 1927.

42. Los Angeles Social Service Commission, *Annual Report, 1917–1919* (Los Angeles, 1918), 43.

43. Briegel, "Alianza Hispano-Americana," 152–53; David G. Gutiérrez,

Walls and Mirrors: Mexican Americans, Mexican Immigrants, and the Politics of Ethnicity (Berkeley, 1995), 98–99.

44. Gómez-Quiñones, *Roots of Chicano Politics*, 370–73, 495–96, n. 57; John Skirius, "Vasconcelos and *México de Afuera* (1928)," *Aztlán* 7, no. 3 (fall 1976): 479–94.

45. *La Opinión*, November 25 and December 9 and 14, 1928; January 5 and November 17 and 18, 1929.

46. *La Opinión*, August 17, 13, and 16 and May 4, 1929; Skirius, "Vasconcelos and *México de Afuera*," 486–87.

47. *La Opinión*, August 11 and 13, May 4, 1929, and November 29, 1928; Cockcroft, *Mexico*, 121.

48. Pesotta, *Bread upon the Waters*, 29–31.

49. Mark Starr, "Role of Union Organization," in *Industry and Society*, ed. William Foote Whyte (New York, 1946), 152; Lewis Lorwin, *The Women's Garment Workers: A History of the International Ladies' Garment Workers' Union* (New York, 1924); Julius Hochman, *Industry Planning through Collective Bargaining, a Program for Modernizing the New York Dress Industry as Presented in Conference with Employers on Behalf of the Joint Board of the Dressmakers' Union* (New York, 1941), 8, 19; *Los Angeles Illustrated News,* October 14, 1933.

50. Pesotta, *Bread upon the Waters*, 19–33; Perry and Perry, *A History of the Los Angeles Labor Movement, 1911–1941*, 251; International Ladies' Garment Workers' Union, *Report and Proceedings of the Twenty-Second Convention of the International Ladies' Garment Workers' Union, 1934* (New York, 1934), 107.

51. A bulletin from the Associated Apparel Manufacturers of Los Angeles, reprinted in Pesotta, *Bread upon the Waters*, 30–31; Congress of Industrial Organizations, Industrial Union Council, Los Angeles, *Unions Mean Higher Wages: The Story of the La Follette Committee Hearings in Los Angeles* (Los Angeles, 1940), 20.

52. *Los Angeles Illustrated Daily News,* October 9, 1933.

53. International Ladies' Garment Workers' Union, *Report and Proceedings of the Twenty-Second Convention*, 107–8; Pesotta, *Bread upon the Waters*, 34.

54. Pesotta, *Bread upon the Waters*, 24–25, 43; *Los Angeles Citizen*, October 25, 1935, and May 22, 1936.

55. International Ladies' Garment Workers' Union, *Report and Proceedings of the Twenty-Second Convention*, 108; Pesotta, *Bread upon the Waters*, 34–58; *Los Angeles Illustrated Daily News*, November 6, 1933.

56. *Western Worker,* October 30 and December 11, 1933; a Communist leaflet reprinted in Pesotta, *Bread upon the Waters*, 58–59.

57. International Ladies' Garment Workers' Union, *Report and Proceedings of the Twenty-Second Convention*, 108.

58. U.S. Department of Labor, Bureau of Labor Statistics, "Collective Agreements in the Ladies' Garment Industry," *Monthly Labor Review* 41, no. 5 (November 1935): 1301; *Los Angeles Citizen*, July 29, 1935; International Ladies' Garment Workers' Union, *Report and Proceedings of the Twenty-Third Convention of the International Ladies' Garment Workers' Union, 1937* (Atlantic City, 1937), 100.

59. *Los Angeles Citizen*, March 30 and August 14, 1936; Los Angeles Police Department, Office of Intelligence Bureau, September 30, 1937, memorandum, in *Violations of Free Speech*, pt. 64, 23614.

60. Pesotta, *Bread upon the Waters*, 23, 40; Frank López, interview.

61. *Los Angeles Illustrated News*, October 21 and 26, 1933; *Western Worker*, August 13, 1936.

62. Pesotta, *Bread upon the Waters*, 21–22, 32, 60–61, 91; Stanley Aronowitz, *False Promises: The Shaping of Working Class Consciousness* (New York, 1973), 173.

63. Gamio, *The Mexican Immigrant*, 127.

64. Perry and Perry, *A History of the Los Angeles Labor Movement*, 287; Frank López, interview.

65. There is some confusion about the Independent Furniture Workers Union. It may have been independently organized but affiliated with, if not weakly controlled by, the TUUL in 1933. Yet the Communists' newspaper, the *Western Worker*, refers to the "Furniture Workers' Industrial Union" as the TUUL union during 1934. Probably, as the Communists assumed more control, the IFWU lost its "independence" and the *I* in the acronym became "Industrial." I am assuming that these are one and the same union. Perry and Perry do not mention the FWIU; they refer to the IFWU simply as a TUUL union.

66. Frank López, interview; *Western Worker*, December 25, 1933, June 4 and September 4, 1934; Perry and Perry, *A History of the Los Angeles Labor Movement*, 287; Charles J. Evans and Sam Evans to Captain William F. Hynes, in *Violations of Free Speech and Rights of Labor*, pt. 64, 23578, 23579.

67. Frank López, interview; Perry and Perry, *A History of the Los Angeles Labor Movement*, 287.

68. Frank López, interview; *Los Angeles Citizen*, September 6, 1935; *Los Angeles Illustrated Daily News*, April 17, 1935; *Los Angeles Times*, April 30 and May 1, 1935; Merchants and Manufacturers to Bullock's Department Store, in *Violations of Free Speech and the Rights of Labor*, pt. 64, 23339, 23336.

69. *Los Angeles Citizen*, September 6, 1935, and January 22, 1936; *Los Angeles Times*, April 30 and May 1, 1935; Frank López, interview; Greer, "The Participation of Ethnic Minorities in the Labor Unions of Los Angeles County," 117–18.

70. Frank López, interview.

71. Irving Bernstein, *Turbulent Years, a History of the American Worker, 1933–1941* (Boston, 1971), 352–431; Taylor, *Mexican Labor in the U.S.: Chicago and the Calumet Region*, 34, 117; Rosales and Simon, "Chicano Steel Workers and Unionism in the Midwest, 1919–1945," 267; Brody, *Steelworkers in America*, 254.

72. Greer, "The Participation of Ethnic Minorities," 110; Tony Ríos, interview; and Jaime González Monroy, interview.

73. Tony Ríos, interview.

74. Ibid.

75. Perry and Perry, *A History of the Los Angeles Labor Movement*, 484; Bernstein, *Turbulent Years*, 727–34; Art Pries, *Labor's Giant Step: Twenty Years of the CIO* (New York, 1972), 392.

76. Tony Ríos, interview.

77. Ruiz, *Cannery Women*, 69–117.

78. Ibid., 21–39, 97.

79. The most famous telling of the Mine, Mill's story is in the magnificent film *Salt of the Earth;* the script is reprinted in "Salt of the Earth," *California Quarterly* 2, no. 4 (Summer 1953); Greer, "The Participation of Ethnic Minorities," 121–27; Pries, *Labor's Giant Step,* 410; Frank López, interview; and Jaime González Monroy, interview.

80. Frank López, interview; *Labor Herald,* November 7, 21, and 28, 1941, and February 13, 27, and July 31, 1942.

81. *Labor Herald,* October 9, November 6 and 20, December 11, 1942; Oscar Fuss, interview by author, March 7, 1977.

82. *Labor Herald,* January 16 and October 16, 1942; Frank López, interview.

83. *Labor Herald,* November 6, 1942, and see also July 24, 1942.

84. Balderrama, *In Defense of La Raza,* 97–101; he quotes Ricardo Hill on p. 98.

85. McWilliams, *Factories in the Field,* 243–50; Reccow, "The Orange County Citrus Strikes," 17, 67–68; *United Progressive News,* April 20 and May 1, 1936. The union is also referred to as the "Mexican Federation of Agricultural and Industrial Workers."

86. McWilliams, *Factories in the Field,* 244–49; *United Progressive News,* May 4, 1936. McWilliams notes that a golfer was wounded by a stray bullet intended for some picketers.

87. Sheriff Jackson is quoted in Reccow, "The Orange County Citrus Strikes," 177 (see also pp. 55, 83, 92, 122, 135, 211); and in Frank Stokes, "Let the Mexicans Organize!" *Nation* 143, no. 25 (December 19, 1936): 731. See also Balderrama, *In Defense of La Raza,* 102–3; McWilliams, *Factories in the Field,* 249–50.

88. Reccow, "The Orange County Citrus Strikes," 93, 137–43, 186; the *Times* is quoted in McWilliams, *Factories in the Field,* 250–51.

89. González, *Labor and Community,* 135–60; Balderrama, *In Defense of La Raza,* 104–5; McWilliams, *Factories in the Field,* 243–44.

90. Simon Ortiz, *Woven Stone* (Tucson, 1992), 153.

EN FIN

1. *La Opinión,* January, 25, 1931; González, *Chicano Education,* 28, 136–56.

2. Mario T. García, *Mexican Americans: Leadership, Ideology, and Identity, 1930–1960* (New Haven, 1989), 145–57; *Peoples' World,* December 4, 1939.

3. García, *Mexican Americans,* 159–73.

4. Articles of Incorporation of the Supreme Council of the Mexican-American Movement, December 19, 1945, MAM Papers 1-1; undated statement of the Supreme Council, MAM papers 1-7; Sánchez, *Becoming Mexican American,* 255–57; *La Opinión,* October 8, 1944; Landman, "Some Aspects of the Acculturation of Mexican Immigrants," 166–67.

5. *Mexican Voice* 1 (April 6, 1942), quoted in Martinez, "The Unusual Mexican," 63–64.

6. *La Opinión,* August 10, 25, and 30, 1944, and April 6 and February 2, 1945.

7. *La Opinión,* September 10, 1944.

8. The *CSO News,* November 15, 1950, in MAM papers 1-29; on the Sub-Comité Mexico-Americano Pro-FEPC, see *La Opinión,* June 2, 1945; Land-man, "Some Aspects of the Acculturation of Mexican Immigrants," 171.

9. *La Opinión,* December 19, 1944.

10. Ralph J. Turner and Samuel J. Surace, "Zoot-Suiters and Mexicans: Symbols in Crowd Behavior," *The American Journal of Sociology* 62, no. 1 (July 1956): 16–20; Mauricio Mazón, *The Zoot-Suit Riots: The Psychology of Symbolic Annihilation* (Austin, 1984), 18–30; Emory Bogardus, "Gangs of Mexican-American Youth," *Sociology and Social Research* 28 (September–October 1943): 57–58.

11. For a psychoanalytical approach to the nature of the riots, see Mazón, *Zoot-Suit Riots,* 78–97. McWilliams, *North from Mexico,* 235-24, puts the riots much more in terms of race conflict.

12. Ayers is quoted in Mazón, *Zoot-Suit Riots,* 22–23, and McWilliams, *North from Mexico,* 233-34.

13. Hadley-García, *Hispanic Hollywood,* 51–53, 61–62; Gómez-Sicre, "Dolores del Río," 14.

14. Ibid., 54; *La Opinión,* December 15 and 16, 1944.

15. *El Heraldo de México,* February 1 and March 6, 1919; September 16, 1921. *La Opinión,* November 29, 1926; May 6 and November 24, 1928; May 2 and 4, 1929; December 15, 1944.

Glossary

baile	Dance.
barrio	Neighborhood where *la gente* or *la raza* lived.
beneficiencia	Charity.
braceros	Literally "one who lends an arm," either to help a lady or to labor. *Braceros* officially came to the United States in an arrangement with Mexico to counter the agricultural labor shortage of World War II. Much like a guest-worker program, it continued for another two decades, keeping field wages low and unions out.
campesinaje, el	The peasantry.
campesinos	Poor people from the countryside either peasants or farm workers.
cesantes	Retired people.
Cinco de Mayo	The Mexican holiday that celebrates the victory of the village of Puebla against the French invaders on May 5, 1863.
colonia	Wherever a cluster of Mexicans lived in *México de afuera*. It could consist of house courts, shacks, well-kept working-class houses, an itinerant agricultural settlement, or a combination of the above. Sometimes the Spanish-language press used the word to refer to all the Mexicans residing in Los Angeles.
comisiones honoríficas	Usually formed for patriotic purposes, often with the active assistance of the consul to maintain the allegiance of Mexico's emigrated citizens, the *comisiones* sponsored Mexican national celebrations

and honored those who served the community in a manner that fostered the traditional ways.

compañeros   Buddies or compatriots.

corridos   Folk ballads or broadsides, usually celebrating an important person or event.

chicano   Used by Mexicans to refer to their lower-class, unsophisticated, or uncouth countrypeople. Much as middle- or upper-class Southern whites might refer to "crackers," *la chicanada* denoted the embarrassing riffraff. In the late 1960s, militant Mexican-American youth adopted the term "Chicano" as an affirmation of cultural pride and a rejection of assimilation. The origins of the word are unclear. It may derive from the Nahuatl pronunciation of *mexicano* (the "x" is pronounced "ch"), or from the state name Chihuahua.

cholos   Used in the nineteenth and early twentieth centuries to refer to lower-class, recently migrated workers. Now it describes rebellious youths who have created their own subculture, one that rejects both traditional Mexican and American ways.

deportiva   Sport.

desmexicanización   Demexicanization, or the loss of "traditional" Mexican ways to modernism or Americanization.

desocupados   Unemployed.

dichos   Sayings.

Diez y Seis de Septiémbre   Mexican holiday that celebrates Father Hidalgo's *Grito de Dolores* of September 16, 1810, the declaration of Mexico's independence from Spain.

ejido   The common lands surrounding traditional peasant villages. Based on a combination of Aztec communal corn farming ways and Spanish feudalism, these lands belonged "to everyone and no one" in the village and were used for grazing and foraging.

enganchistas   From the verb "to hook" or "to snare," these were labor contractors—American or Mexican—who recruited gangs of Mexican workers, from either side of the border, for American employers of unskilled labor.

estrellas   Stars, either in the sky, on the baseball diamond, or on the silver screen.

festejos   Celebrations, like those which the *comisiones honoríficas* organized.

gente, la	The people. *La gente trabajadora* were working people, and *la gente bién* were those who considered themselves the cultural elite, or "the better sort."
gringo	A mildly derisive term used by Mexicans for Americans. It originates probably not from hearing troopers sing "Green grow the rushes grow" in the Mexican-American War (as some have proposed), but from responding to English with "es griego a mi" (it's Greek to me).
hacendados	Large landholders in Mexico who control the labor of *peones*.
Liberales	Part of the radical opposition to the regime of Porfirio Díaz. After about 1908, the largest group, the Partido Liberal Mexicano under the leadership of Ricardo Flores Magón, espoused anarchism.
libre pensadores	Free thinkers.
limoneras	Where lemons are grown.
lloronas	Wailing women.
macizo, el	The native soil.
Magonista	A follower of the Partido Liberal Mexicano.
mestizaje	Mixing or miscegenation. A *mestizo* is the product of this.
mestizo	A person of mixed Indian and Spanish heritage. The word refers both to blood line and phenotype, and to culture.
México de afuera	A phrase originating in Mexico to refer to the communities of Mexicans who had moved *al norte*. It may be translated as "Mexico outside" or "Mexico away."
modos rancheros, los	The ways of the *campesinaje*, especially as *la gente bién* might refer to them.
mutualistas	Mutual-aid or insurance societies, which Mexicans founded north and south of the border. These were typical of many immigrant communities in the United States.
norte, el	Literally "the north," but when people went *al norte* they understood themselves to be going to places with jobs, discrimination, and Mexican colonies.
norteamericanismo	How some Latin American intellectuals and editorialist referred to the United States' unilateral, and sometimes reckless, military actions in Latin America.
pachuco/as	Mexican youth of the United States whose distinctive dress and conduct display their rejection of the ways of their parents and of the conformity of Anglo-

American Protestant culture. In the late 1930s and 1940s the males often wore zoot suits.

patrón	Boss, either an *hacendado* or a foreman.
pelado	*Pelar* means to cut or pull out someone's hair. Thus a *pelado* is a person not only destitute but without character or individuality.
películas hispanoparlantes	Spanish-speaking films.
peones	Peons, or peasants who work for an *hacendado*.
pobladores	Settlers.
pocho	The derisive name that people in Mexico use for Americanized Mexicans.
ranchero	A word used by *la gente bién* to refer to the allegedly rustic ways (*los modos*) of *la chicanada* or *el campesinaje*.
raza, la	In its typical usage the phrase simply refers to the Mexican people. It should not be confused with the English word "race"; it is more like "our people" when used in Mexican communities, newspapers, speeches, or chatter.
rebozo	The shawl that Mexican women have traditionally worn over the head. It may be seen as emblematic of her proper sheltering and protection, or of her subjugation and restraining.
repatriado	Someone who has gone back to Mexico either voluntarily or by forced deportation.
scientíficos	The technocrats associated with the regime of Porfirio Díaz. Influenced by French positivism, they sought to develop Mexico economically by attracting foreign capital.
sociedades	Mexican fraternal organizations. They may be for mutual aid (insurance and savings), politics, sports, service and charity, social pretense, professional association, simple fraternity, or even proto-union activity.
sólos	Men who are by themselves.
traque, el	The tracks. The word often refers to railroad track construction and maintenance labor.

Bibliography

ARCHIVAL SOURCES

George Clements Papers, University of California, Los Angeles, Special Collections
Dorothy Healey Papers, California State University, Long Beach, Library Collection
Carey McWilliams Papers, University of California, Los Angeles, Special Collections
Mexican American Movement, Papers of the Supreme Council, Urban Archives Center, California State University, Northridge

BOOKS, ARTICLES, AND PAMPHLETS

Acuña, Rodolfo. *Occupied America: A History of Chicanos.* Third ed. New York, 1988.
Adamic, Louis. *Dynamite: The Story of Class Violence in America.* New York, 1931; reprint, 1958.
Addams, Jane. *Twenty Years at Hull House.* New York, 1960.
"American Federation of Labor (Mexico-U.S. Immigration Conference)." *American Federationist* 32, no. 10 (October 1925).
Aranda, Charles. *Dichos: Proverbs and Sayings from the Spanish.* Santa Fe, 1977.
Aronowitz, Stanley. *False Promises: The Shaping of Working Class Consciousness.* New York, 1973.
Balderrama, Francisco E. *In Defense of La Raza: The Los Angeles Mexican Consulate and the Mexican Community, 1929 to 1936.* Tucson, 1982.
Bartlett, Dana W. *The Better City: A Sociological Study of a Modern City.* Los Angeles, 1907.
Berger, John. *Pig Earth.* New York, 1979.

————. "The Suit and the Photograph." In *About Looking*. New York, 1980.

Bernstein, Irving. *Turbulent Years: A History of the American Worker, 1933–1941*. Boston, 1971.

Blaisdell, Lowell W. *The Desert Revolution: Baja California*. Madison, 1962.

Bogardus, Emory. *The City Boy and His Problems: A Survey of Boy Life in Los Angeles*. Los Angeles, 1926.

————. "Gangs of Mexican-American Youth." *Sociology and Social Research* 28 (September–October 1943).

————. "The House-Court Problem." *American Journal of Sociology* 22 (November 1916).

————. "The Mexican Immigrant." *Journal of Applied Sociology* 11 (May–June 1927).

————. "The Mexican Immigrant and Segregation." *American Journal of Sociology* 36 (July 1930).

————. *The Mexican in the United States*. Los Angeles, 1934.

————. "Mexican Repatriates." *Sociology and Social Research* 18 (November–December 1933).

————. "Second Generation Mexicans." *Sociology and Social Research* 13 (January–February 1929).

Braverman, Harry. *Labor and Monopoly Capital: The Degradation of Work in the Twentieth Century*. New York, 1974.

Brestle, Linna E. *Mexicans in the United States: A Report of a Brief Survey*. 1929. Reprinted in *Church Views of the Mexican American*. Edited by Carlos E. Cortez. New York, 1974.

Brody, David. *Steelworkers in America: The Nonunion Era*. New York, 1969.

Bryan, Samuel. "Mexican Immigrants in the United States." *The Survey* 28 (September 7, 1912).

Cahn, Francis, and Bary Valeska. *Welfare Activity of Federal, State, and Local Governments in California*. Berkeley, 1936.

Camarillo, Alberto. *Chicanos in a Changing Society: From Mexican Pueblos to American Barrios in Santa Barbara and Southern California, 1848–1930*. Cambridge, Mass., 1979.

————. "The Sociological Failure of the Catholic Church toward the Chicano." *Journal of Mexican-American Studies* 1, no. 2 (winter 1971).

Campbell, Ena. "The Virgin of Guadalupe and the Female Self-Image: A Mexican Case History." In *Mother Worship: Theme and Variation*. Edited by James J. Preston. Chapel Hill, 1982.

Cardoso, Lawrence A. *Mexican Immigration to the United States, 1897–1931*. Tucson, 1980.

Castillo, Ana, ed. *Goddess of the Americas / La Diosa de las Américas: Writings on the Virgin of Guadalupe*. New York, 1996.

Citizens' Industrial Fact Finding Committee, The. "Tentative Report on the Furniture Industry of Los Angeles." N.p. [Los Angeles?], n.d. [1936?].

Clark, Victor S. "Mexican Labor in the United States." *Bulletin of the Bureau of Labor* 78 (September 1908).

Cockcroft, James D. *Mexico: Class Formation, Capital Accumulation, and the State*. New York, 1983.

Coman, Catherine. "Casa Castelar." *The Commons* 7 (January 1903).

Commission of Religion. *Protestant Religious Work among Spanish-Speaking Americans and Mexicans in the United States.* N.p., n.d. [late 1920s?].

Congress of Industrial Organizations, Industrial Union Council, Los Angeles. *Unions Mean Higher Wages: The Story of the La Follette Committee Hearings in Los Angeles.* Los Angeles, 1940.

Coons, Arthur G., and Arjay R. Miller. *An Economic and Industrial Survey of the Los Angeles and San Diego Areas.* California State Planning Board, Sacramento, Calif., 1941. Typewritten.

Crawford, Remsen. "The Menace of Mexican Immigration." *Current History* 31 (February 1930).

Current Biography: Who's News and Why. New York, 1945.

Daniel, Cletus. *Bitter Harvest: A History of California Farmworkers, 1870–1941.* Berkeley, 1982.

Daniels, Roger, and Harry H. L. Kitano. *American Racism: Explorations in the Nature of Prejudice.* Englewood Cliffs, N.J., 1970.

Davis, Mike. *City of Quartz: Excavating the Future in Los Angeles.* New York, 1992.

Davis, William B. *Experiences and Observations of an American Consular Officer during the Recent Mexican Revolutions.* Chula Vista, 1920.

De Caux, Len. *Labor Radical: From the Wobblies to CIO, a Personal History.* Boston, 1971.

de Tocqueville, Alexis. *Democracy in America.* New York, 1945.

Douglas, Mary. *Natural Symbols: Explorations in Cosmology.* New York, 1982.

Dubofsky, Melvin. *We Shall Be All: A History of Industrial Workers of the World.* Chicago, 1969.

Early, Gerald. "'I Only Like It Better When the Pain Comes': More Notes toward a Cultural Definition of Prizefighting." In *Reading the Fights.* Edited by Joyce Carol Oates and Daniel Halpern. New York, 1988.

———. "Three Notes toward a Cultural Definition of Prizefighting." In *Reading the Fights.* Edited by Joyce Carol Oates and Daniel Halpern. New York, 1988.

Ewen, Stuart, and Elizabeth Ewen. *Channels of Desire: Mass Images and the Shaping of American Consciousness.* New York, 1982.

Fitch, John A. "Los Angeles, A Militant Anti-union Citadel." *The Survey* 33 (October 3, 1914).

Flynn, Elizabeth Gurley. *The Rebel Girl: An Autobiography, My First Life, 1906–1926.* New York, 1973.

Fogelson, Robert M. *The Fragmented Metropolis: Los Angeles, 1850–1930.* 1967. Reprint, Berkeley, 1996.

Foner, Philip S. *History of the Labor Movement in the United States.* Vol. 3, *The Policies and Practices of the American Federation of Labor, 1900–1909.* New York, 1964.

Foucault, Michel. "The Dangerous Individual." In *Michel Foucault: Politics, Philosophy, Culture.* Edited by Lawrence D. Kritzman. New York, 1990.

———. *The History of Sexuality.* Vol. 1, *An Introduction.* New York, 1980.

Friedrich, Paul. *Agrarian Revolt in a Mexican Village.* Englewood Cliffs, N.J., 1970.

Fuller, Elizabeth. "The Mexican Housing Problem in Los Angeles." *Studies in Sociology* 5 (November 1920).

Galarza, Ernest. *Barrio Boy.* Notre Dame, 1971.

Gamio, Manuel. *The Mexican Immigrant, His Life Story.* Chicago, 1931. Reprinted as *The Life Story of the Mexican Immigrant.* New York, 1971.

———. *Mexican Immigration to the United States: A Study of Human Migration and Adjustment.* Chicago, 1930.

Garbicz, Adam, and Jacek Klinowski. *Cinema, the Magic Vehicle: A Guide to Its Achievement.* Vol. 1. New York, 1983.

García, Mario T. *Mexican Americans: Leadership, Ideology, and Identity, 1930–1960.* New Haven, 1989.

Goethe, C. M. "Danger of Unrestricted Mexican Immigration." *Current History* 28 (August 1928).

Goldschmidt, Walter. *As You Sow.* New York, 1947.

Gómez-Quiñones, Juan. "The First Steps: Chicano Labor Conflict and Organizing, 1900–1920." *Aztlan* 3, no. 1 (spring 1972).

———. *Mexican American Labor, 1790–1990.* Albuquerque, 1994.

———. *Roots of Chicano Politics, 1600–1940.* Albuquerque, 1994.

———. *Sembradores, Ricardo Flores Magón y el Partido Liberal Mexicano: A Eulogy and Critique.* Los Angeles, 1973.

Gómez-Sicre, José. "Dolores del Río." *Americas* 19 (November 1967): 8–17.

González, Gilbert G. *Chicano Education in the Era of Segregation.* Philadelphia, 1990.

———. *Labor and Community: Mexican Citrus Worker Villages in a Southern California County, 1900–1950.* Urbana, Ill., 1994.

González-Monroy, Jesus. *Ricardo Flores Magón y su actitude en la Baja California.* Mexico D.F., 1962.

Gould, Steven Jay. *The Mismeasure of Man* (New York, 1981).

Governor C. C. Young's Mexican Fact-Finding Committee. *Mexicans in California.* San Francisco, 1930.

Griswold Del Castillo, Richard. *The Los Angeles Barrio, 1850–1890: A Social History.* Berkeley, 1979.

Gutiérrez, David G. *Walls and Mirrors: Mexican Americans, Mexican Immigrants, and the Politics of Ethnicity.* Berkeley, 1995.

Gwin, J. Blaine. "Back and Forth to Mexico." *The Survey* 39, no. 1 (October 6, 1917).

———. "The New Mexican Immigration." *The Survey* 40, no. 18 (August 3, 1918).

Haas, Lisbeth. *Conquests and Historical Identities in California, 1769–1936.* Berkeley, 1995.

Hadley-García, George. *Hispanic Hollywood: The Latins in Motion Pictures.* New York, 1990.

Handman, Max S. "Economic Reasons for the Coming of the Mexican Immigrant." *American Journal of Sociology* 35 (January 1930).

Hart, Mason John. *Revolutionary Mexico: The Coming and Process of the Mexican Revolution.* Berkeley, 1987.

Healey, Dorothy, and Maurice Isserman. *Dorothy Healey Remembers: A Life in the American Communist Party.* New York, 1990.

Heidegger, Martin. "Building Dwelling Thinking." In *Poetry, Language, Thought.* Translated by Albert Hofstadter. New York, 1975.

Hendrick, Irving G. *The Education of Non-whites in California, 1848–1970.* San Francisco, 1977.

Hernández, José Amaro. *Mutual Aid for Survival: The Case of the Mexican American.* Malabar, Fla., 1983.

Hill, Merton E. *The Development of an Americanization Program.* N.p., 1928.

Hochman, Julius. *Industry Planning through Collective Bargaining, a Program for Modernizing the New York Dress Industry as Presented in Conference with Employers on Behalf of the Joint Board of the Dressmakers' Union.* New York, 1941.

Hoffman, Abraham. *Unwanted Mexican Americans in the Great Depression: Repatriation Pressures, 1929–1939.* Tucson, 1974.

Home Missions Council. *A Study of Social and Economic Factors Relating to Spanish-Speaking People in the United States.* N.p., n.d. [late 1920s?].

Honig, Nathaniel. *The Trade Union Unity League Today: Its Structure, Policy, Program, and Growth.* Rev. ed. New York, 1934.

Howe, Irving, and Lewis Coser. *The American Communist Party: A Critical History, 1919–1957.* Boston, 1957.

Hu-DeHart, Evelyn. *Yaqui Resistance and Survival: The Struggle for Land and Autonomy, 1821–1910.* Madison, 1984.

Humphrey, Norman D. "Employment Patterns of Mexicans in Detroit." *Monthly Labor Review* 61, no. 5 (November 1945).

Hundley, Norris, Jr. *Water and the West: The Colorado River Compact and the Politics of Water in the American West.* Berkeley, 1975.

Iglesias, Santiago. "The Child of the A.F. of L." *American Federationist* 32, no. 10 (October 1925).

International Ladies' Garment Workers' Union. *Report and Proceedings of the Twenty-Fifth Convention of the International Ladies' Garment Workers' Union, 1945.* New York, 1945.

———. *Report and Proceedings of the Twenty-Second Convention of the International Ladies' Garment Workers' Union, 1934.* New York, 1934.

———. *Report and Proceedings of the Twenty-Third Convention of the International Ladies' Garment Workers' Union, 1937.* Atlantic City, 1937.

Jamieson, Stuart M. "The Origins and Present Structure of Labor Unions in Agricultural and Allied Industries of California." In *Violations of Free Speech and the Rights of Labor.* Edited by U.S. Congress, Senate, Subcommittee of the Committee on Education and Labor, 76th Cong., 1940, 22531–40.

Jenks, Jeremiah W., and W. Jett Lauch. *The Immigration Problem.* New York, 1912.

Jervey, Edward Drewry. *The History of Methodism in Southern California and Arizona.* Los Angeles, 1960.

Kanellos, Nicolás. *A History of Hispanic Theater in the United States: Origins to 1940.* Austin, 1990.

Karp, Walter. *Buried Alive: Essays on Our Endangered Republic.* New York, 1992.

Kelley, Allen. *Historical Sketch of the Los Angeles Aqueduct.* Los Angeles, 1913.

Kelley, Robin D. G. "The Riddle of the Zoot: Malcolm Little and Black Cultural Politics during World War II." In *Malcolm X: In Our Own Image.* Edited by Joe Wood. New York, 1992.

Lasch, Christopher. *The New Radicalism in America, 1889–1963: The Intellectual as a Social Type.* New York, 1965.

Laslett, John, and Mary Tyler. *The ILGWU in Los Angeles, 1907–1988.* Inglewood, Calif., 1989.

Levinstein, Harvey A. "The AFL and Mexican Immigration in the 1920's: An Experiment in Labor Diplomacy." *Hispanic American Historical Review* 48 (May 1968).

Limón, José E. "La Llorona, the Third Legend of Greater Mexico: Cultural Symbols, Women, and the Political Unconscious." In *Between Borders: Essays on Mexicana/Chicana History.* Edited by Adelaida R. Del Castillo. Encino, Calif., 1990.

Lofstedt, Christine. "The Mexican Population of Pasadena, California." *Journal of Applied Sociology* 7, no. 5 (May–June 1923).

Lopez, Barry Holstun. "Hanner's Story." In *River Notes: The Dance of Herons.* New York, 1980.

Lopez, Ronald W. "The El Monte Berry Strike of 1933." *Aztlan* 1, no. 1 (spring 1970).

Lorwin, Lewis. *The Women's Garment Workers: A History of the International Ladies' Garment Workers' Union.* New York, 1924.

Marx, Karl. "Critique of Hegel's Philosophy of Right." In *The Marx-Engels Reader.* Edited by Robert C. Tucker. New York, 1972.

Mathews, William H. "The House Courts of Los Angeles." *The Survey* 30 (July 5, 1913).

Mayo. Morrow. *Los Angeles.* New York, 1933.

Mazón, Mauricio. *The Zoot-Suit Riots: The Psychology of Symbolic Annihilation.* Austin, 1984.

McClean, Robert. "Goodbye Vicente!" *The Survey* 66 (May 1, 1931).

———. "The Mexican Return." *The Nation* 135, no. 34 (August 24, 1932).

McCombs, Vernon. *From over the Border: A Study of Mexicans in the United States.* 1925. Reprint, New York, 1970.

———. "Stopping the Reds." *El Mexicano* 7, no. 3 (January–March 1919).

McIlvanney, Hugh. "Onward Virgin Soldier: Lupe Pintor v. Johnny Owen, Los Angeles, September 19, 1980." In *Reading the Fights.* Edited by Joyce Carol Oates and Daniel Halpern. New York, 1988.

McWilliams, Carey. *Factories in the Field: The Story of Migratory Farm Labor in California.* 1939. Reprint, Santa Barbara, 1971.

———. *North from Mexico: The Spanish-Speaking People of the United States.* 1948. Reprint, New York, 1969.

———. *Southern California: An Island on the Land.* 1946. Reprint, Santa Barbara, 1979.

"Mexican Invaders Relieving Our Farm Labor Shortage." *Literary Digest* 66, no. 3 (July 17, 1920).

Miller, Alice. *For Your Own Good: Hidden Cruelty in Child-Rearing and the Roots of Violence.* New York, 1983.

Monroy, Douglas. "Anarquismo y Comunismo: Mexican Radicalism and the Communist Party in Southern California in the 1930s." *Labor History* 24, no. 1 (winter 1983).

———. "Mexicans and the Racial Politics of Growth in Los Angeles in the Interwar Period." *Western Historical Quarterly* 14, no. 4 (October 1983).

———. *Thrown among Strangers: The Making of Mexican Culture in Frontier California.* Berkeley, 1990.

Mora, Magdalena, and Adelaida R. Del Castillo, eds. *Mexican Women in the United States: Struggles Past and Present.* Los Angeles, 1980.

Munden, Kenneth, ed. *The American Film Institute Catalog of Motion Pictures Produced in the United States: Feature Films, 1921–1930.* New York, 1971.

Nash, John Robert, and Stanley Ralph Ross. *The Motion Picture Guide.* Chicago, 1987.

Notes by the Agents (Passenger Department, Southern Pacific Company). *California South of the Tehachapi.* San Francisco, 1908.

Oates, Joyce Carol. "On Boxing." In *Reading the Fights.* Edited by Joyce Carol Oates and Daniel Halpern. New York, 1988.

Otto, Rudolf. *The Idea of the Holy: An Inquiry into the Non-rational Factor in the Idea of the Divine and Its Relation to the Rational.* Translated by John W. Harvey. 1923. Reprint, New York, 1958.

Oxnam, G. Bromley. "The Mexican in Los Angeles from the Standpoint of the Religious Forces of the City." *The Annals of the American Academy of Political and Social Science* 93 (January 1921).

Panunzio, Constantine. "Intermarriage in Los Angeles, 1924–1933." *American Journal of Sociology* 47 (1942).

Patric, Gladys Emelia. *A Study of Housing and Social Conditions in the Ann Street District of Los Angeles, California.* Los Angeles, 1917.

Paz, Octavio. *The Labyrinth of Solitude: Life and Thought in Mexico.* 1951. Reprint, New York, 1962.

Pérez, Emma M. "'A La Mujer': A Critique of the Partido Liberal Mexicano's Gender Policy on Women." In *Between Borders: Essays on Mexicana/Chicana History.* Edited by Adelaida Del Castillo. Encino, Calif., 1990.

Perry, Louis B., and Richard S. Perry. *A History of the Los Angeles Labor Movement, 1911–1941.* Berkeley, 1963.

Pesotta, Rose. *Bread upon the Waters.* New York, 1945.

Pettit, Arthur G. *Images of the Mexican American in Fiction and Film.* Edited by Dennis E. Showalter. College Station, Texas, 1980.

Ponce, Mary Helen. *Hoyt Street: An Autobiography.* Albuquerque, 1993.

Porter, Paul T. "Handling Mexican Labor in California." *Electric Railway Journal* 72 (August 11, 1978).

Preis, Art. *Labor's Giant Step: Twenty Years of the CIO.* New York, 1972.

Raat, W. Dirk. *Revoltosos: Mexico's Rebels in the United States, 1903–1923.* College Station, Texas, 1981.

"Regulations by the United States Department of Labor for Admission of Mexican Laborers." *Monthly Labor Review* 7, no. 5 (November 1918).

Reisner, Marc. *Cadillac Desert: The American West and Its Disappearing Water.* New York, 1986.

Richmond, Al. *A Long View from the Left: Memoirs of an American Revolutionary.* New York, 1975.

Ríos-Bustamante, Antonio, and Pedro Castillo. *An Illustrated History of Mexican Los Angeles, 1781–1985.* Los Angeles, 1986.

Rivera, Tomás. *Y no se lo tragó la tierra / And the Earth Did Not Part.* Berkeley, 1978.

Rodriguez, Richard. *Days of Obligation: An Argument with My Mexican Father.* New York, 1992.

Rosaldo, Renato. *Culture and Truth: The Remaking of Social Analysis.* Boston, 1989.

Romo, Ricardo. *East Los Angeles: History of a Barrio.* Austin, 1983.

———. "Work and Restlessness: Occupational and Spatial Mobility among Mexicanos in Los Angeles, 1918–1928." *Pacific Historical Review* 46, no. 2 (May 1977).

Roosevelt, Theodore. *The Strenuous Life.* New York, 1901.

Rosales, Francisco A., and Daniel T. Simon. "Chicano Steel Workers and Unionism in the Midwest, 1919–1945." *Aztlán* 6, no. 2 (summer 1975).

Rosen, Marjorie. *Popcorn Venus: Women, Movies, and the American Dream.* New York, 1973.

Ruiz, Vicki L. *Cannery Women / Cannery Lives: Mexican Women, Unionization, and the California Food Processing Industry, 1930–1950.* Albuquerque, 1987.

———. "'Star Struck': Acculturation, Adolescence, and the Mexican American Woman, 1920–1950." In *Building with Our Hands: New Directions in Chicana Studies,* ed. Adela de la Torre and Beatríz Pesquera. Berkeley, 1993, 109–29.

"Salt of the Earth." *The California Quarterly* 2, no. 4 (1953).

Sammons, Jeffrey T. *Beyond the Ring: The Role of Boxing in American Society.* Urbana, 1988.

Sánchez, George J. *Becoming Mexican American: Ethnicity, Culture, and Identity in Chicano Los Angeles, 1900–1945.* New York, 1993.

Sanders, Barry. *A Is for Ox: Violence, Electronic Media, and the Silencing of the Written Word.* New York, 1994.

Sandos, James A. *Rebellion in the Borderlands: Anarchism and the Plan of San Diego, 1904–1923.* Norman, Okla., 1992.

Santiago, Hazel D. "Mexican Influence in Southern California." *Sociology and Social Research* 16 (September–October 1931).

Schwartz, Harry. "Agricultural Labor in the First World War." *Journal of Farm Economics* 24 (February 1942).

Scruggs, Otey. "The First Farm Labor Program, 1917–1921." *Arizona and the West* 2 (winter 1960).

Skirius, John. "Vasconcelos and *México de Afuera* (1928)." *Aztlan* 7, no. 3 (fall 1976).

Smedley, Agnes. *Daughter of the Earth*. New York, 1973.

Sollier, J. F. "Communion of Saints." In *The Catholic Encyclopedia*. Edited by C. Herbermann et al. New York, 1911.

Sommerville, Blanche A. "Naturalization from the Mexican Viewpoint." *Community Exchange Bulletin* 6, no. 4 (May 1928).

Spaulding, Charles B. "The Mexican Strike at El Monte, California." *Sociology and Social Research* 18, no. 6 (July–August, 1934).

Spicer, Edward H. *The Yaquis: A Cultural History*. Tucson, 1984.

Starr, Mark. "Role of Union Organization." In *Industry and Society*. Edited by William Foote Whyte. New York, 1946.

Stimson, Grace Heilman. *Rise of the Labor Movement in Los Angeles*. Berkeley, 1955.

Stoddard, Bessie D. "Courts of Sonoratown." *Charities and the Commons* 15 (December 2, 1905).

Stokes, Frank. "Let the Mexicans Organize!" *The Nation* 143, no. 25 (December 19, 1936).

Stowell, Jay S. *The Near Side of the Mexican Question*. New York, 1921.

Taylor, Paul S. *Mexican Labor in the United States: Chicago and the Calumet Region*. Berkeley, 1932.

———. *Mexican Labor in the United States: Imperial Valley*. Vol. 1. 1930. Reprint, New York, 1970.

———. *Mexican Labor in the United States: Racial School Statistics, California, 1927*. Vol. 4. 1929. Reprint, New York, 1970.

———. "Mexicans North of the Rio Grande." *The Survey* 66, no. 3 (May 1, 1931).

———. "Some Aspects of Mexican Immigration." *Journal of Political Economy* 38, no. 5 (October 1930).

———. "Songs of the Mexican Migration." In *Puro Mexicano*. Edited by J. Frank Dobie. Austin, 1935.

———. *A Spanish-Mexican Peasant Community, Arendas in Jalisco, Mexico*. Berkeley, 1933.

Tuck, Ruth D. *Not with the Fist: Mexican-Americans in a Southwest City*. New York, 1946.

Turner, Ethel Duffy. *Writers and Revolutionists, an Interview Conducted by Ruth Teiser*. Berkeley, 1967.

Turner, Ralph J., and Samuel J. Surace. "Zoot-Suiters and Mexicans: Symbols in Crowd Behavior." *American Journal of Sociology* 62, no. 1 (July 1956).

Turner, Victor. *The Ritual Process: Structure and Anti-structure*. Ithaca, N.Y., 1977.

Turner, Victor, and Edith Turner. *Image and Pilgrimage in Christian Culture: Anthropological Perspectives*. New York, 1978.

U.S. Department of Labor. Bureau of Labor Statistics. "Collective Agreements in the Ladies' Garment Industry." *Monthly Labor Review* 41, no. 5 (November 1935).

———. "Increase of Mexican Labor in Certain Industries in the United States." *Monthly Labor Review* 32 (January 1931).

———. "Labor and Social Conditions of Mexicans in California." *Monthly Labor Review* 32, no. 1 (January 1931).

———. "Sanitary Surveys in Los Angeles." *Monthly Labor Review* 20 (June 1925).

Van Court, DeWitt. *The Making of Champions in California.* Los Angeles, 1926.

Van Valen, Nelson S. "The Bolshiviki and the Orange Groves." *Pacific Historical Review* 22 (1953).

Vandenbergh, Leonard John. "The Mexican Problem in the Schools." *Los Angeles School Journal* 11 (May 14, 1928).

Walker, Helen W. "Mexican Immigrants and American Citizenship." *Sociology and Social Research* 13 (1929).

Walter, E. V. *Placeways: A Theory of the Human Environment.* Chapel Hill, 1988.

Washington, Booker T. *Up from Slavery.* New York, 1965.

Weber, Devra Anne. "The Organizing of Mexicano Agricultural Workers: Imperial Valley and Los Angeles, 1928–1934, an Oral History Approach." *Aztlán* 3, no. 2 (fall 1972).

Weinstein, James. *Ambiguous Legacy: The Left in American Politics.* New York, 1975.

Westkott, Marcia. *The Feminist Legacy of Karen Horney.* New Haven, 1986.

Wilkie, James W. *The Mexican Revolution: Federal Expenditure and Social Change since 1910.* Berkeley, 1970.

Williams, Faith M., and Alice C. Hanson. *Money Disbursement of Wage Earners and Clerical Workers in the Five Cities in the Pacific Region, 1934–1936: Mexican Families in Los Angeles.* United States Bureau of Labor Statistics Bulletin, no. 639. Washington, D.C., 1939.

Wolf, Eric. *Sons of the Shaking Earth: The People of Mexico and Guatemala.* Chicago, 1959.

Wollenberg, Charles. "Huelga, 1928 Style: The Imperial Valley Cantaloupe Workers' Strike." *Pacific Historical Review* 38, no. 1 (February 1969).

———. "Working on El Traque: The Pacific Electric Strike of 1903." *Pacific Historical Review* 42 (August 1973).

Woodward, C. Vann. *Origins of the New South, 1877–1913.* Baton Rouge, 1951.

Workers of the Writers Program of the Works Project Administration in Southern California. *Los Angeles: A Guide to the City and Its Environs.* New York: 1941.

Worster, Donald. *Rivers of Empire: Water, Aridity, and the Growth of the American West.* New York, 1985.

X, Malcolm. *The Autobiography of Malcolm X.* New York, 1966.

Young, Kimball. *Mental Differences in Certain Immigrant Groups: Psychological Tests of South Europeans in Typical California Schools with Bearing on the Educational Policy and on the Problems of Racial Contacts in This Country.* Eugene, 1924.

Zamora, Emilio. "Sara Estela Ramírez: Una Rosa Roja en el Movimiento." In *Mexican Women in the United States: Struggles Past and Present.* Edited by Magdalena Mora and Adelaida R. Del Castillo. Los Angeles, 1980.

THESES AND DISSERTATIONS

Bishop, Hazel Peck. "A Case Study of the Improvement of Mexican Homes through Instruction in Homemaking." Master's thesis, University of Southern California, 1937.

Bridge, David Alexander. "A Study of the Agencies Which Promote Americanization in the Los Angeles City Recreation Center District." Master's thesis, University of Southern California, 1920.

Briegel, Kay Lynn. "The Alianza Hispano-Americana, 1894–1965: A Mexican American Fraternal Insurance Society." Ph.D. diss., University of Southern California, 1974.

Buckner, Herman A. "A Study of Pupil Elimination and Failure among Mexicans." Master's thesis, University of Southern California, 1935.

Carpenter, Charles Clifford. "A Study of Segregation verses Non-segregation of Mexican Children." Master's thesis, University of Southern California, 1935.

Castillo, Pedro G. "The Making of a Mexican Barrio: Los Angeles, 1890–1920." Ph.D. diss., University of California, Santa Barbara, 1979.

Crawford, Paul J. "Movie Habits and Attitudes of the Under-privileged Boys of the All Nations Area in Los Angeles." Master's thesis, University of Southern California, 1934.

Culp, Alice Bessie. "A Case Study of the Living Conditions of Thirty-Five Mexican Families of Los Angeles with Special Reference to Mexican Children." Master's thesis, University of Southern California, 1921.

Douglas, Helen W. "The Conflict of Cultures in First Generation Mexicans in Santa Ana, California." Master's thesis, University of Southern California, 1928.

Elliott, Robert S. "The Health and Relief Problems of a Group of Non-family Mexican Men in Imperial County." Master's thesis, University of Southern California, 1939.

Fellows, Lloyd Welker. "Economic Aspects of the Mexican Rural Population in California with Special Emphasis on the Need for Mexican Labor in Agriculture." Master's thesis, University of Southern California, 1929.

Gilbert, James Carl. "A Field Study in Mexico of the Mexican Repatriation Movement." Master's thesis, University of Southern California, 1934.

González, Gilbert George. "The System of Public Education and Its Function within the Chicano Communities, 1920–1930." Ph.D. diss., University of California, Los Angeles, 1974.

Greer, Scott. "The Participation of Ethnic Minorities in the Labor Unions of Los Angeles County." Ph.D. diss., University of California, Los Angeles, 1952.

Grieve, Al William. "A Study of the Habitués of the Downtown Parks of Los Angeles, with a View to Ascertaining Their Constituency, Their Social Processes, and Their Relation to the Larger Community Life." Master's thesis, University of Southern California, 1926.

Gustafson, Cloyd V. "An Ecological Analysis of the Hollenbeck Area of Los Angeles." Master's thesis, University of Southern California, 1940.

Harrod, Merrill Leonard. "A Study of Deviate Personalities as Found in Main

Street of Los Angeles." Master's thesis, University of Southern California, 1939.

Hymer, Evangeline. "A Study of the Social Attitudes of Adult Mexican Immigrants in Los Angeles and Vicinity." Master's thesis, University of Southern California, 1923.

Kienle, John Emmanuel. "Housing Conditions among the Mexican Population of Los Angeles." Master's thesis, University of Southern California, 1912.

Landman, Ruth H. "Some Aspects of the Acculturation of Mexican Immigrants and Their Descendants to American Culture." Ph.D. diss., Yale University, 1953.

Lanigan, Mary. "Second Generation Mexicans in Belvedere." Master's thesis, University of Southern California, 1932.

Lyon, Laura Lucile. "Investigation of the Program for the Adjustment of Mexican Girls to the High Schools of San Fernando Valley." Master's thesis, University of Southern California, 1933.

Martinez, John. "Mexican Emigration to the U.S., 1910–1930." Master's thesis, University of California, Berkeley, 1957.

Martinez, Ruth Lucretia. "The Unusual Mexican: A Study in Acculturation." Master's thesis, Claremont College, 1942. Reprinted by R and E Research Associates, San Francisco, 1973.

Mason, F. G. "A Case Study of Thirty Adolescent Mexican Girls and Their Social Conflicts and Adjustments within the School." Master's thesis, University of Southern California, 1929.

McEuen, William Wilson. "A Survey of the Mexicans in Los Angeles." Master's thesis, University of Southern California, 1914.

North, William E. "Catholic Education in Southern California." Ph.D. diss., The Catholic University of America, 1936.

Ortegon, Samuel M. "The Religious Status of the Mexican Population of Los Angeles." Master's thesis, University of Southern California, 1932.

———. "Religious Thought and Practice among Mexican Baptists of the U.S., 1900–1947." Ph.D. diss., University of Southern California, 1950.

Peek, Rena Blanche. "The Religious and Social Attitudes of the Mexican Girls of the Constituency of the All Nations Foundation in Los Angeles." Master's thesis. University of Southern California, 1929.

Reccow, Louis. "The Orange County Citrus Strikes of 1935–1936: The 'Forgotten People' in Revolt." Ph.D. diss., University of Southern California, 1972.

Romo, Ricardo. "Mexican Workers in the City: Los Angeles, 1915–1930." Ph.D. diss., University of California, Los Angeles, 1975.

Smith, Clara Gertrude. "The Development of the Mexican People in the Community of Watts, California." Master's thesis, University of Southern California, 1933.

Sterry, Nora. "The Sociological Basis for the Re-organization of the Macy Street School." Master's thesis, University of Southern California, 1924.

Thurston, Richard G. "Urbanization and Sociocultural Change in a Mexican American Enclave." Ph.D. diss., University of California, Los Angeles, 1957.

Wood, Herbert Sidney. "A Pupil Survey of James A. Garfield High School, Los Angeles." Master's thesis, University of Southern California, 1937.

Wright, Frank M. "A Survey of the El Monte School District, El Monte, California." Master's thesis, University of Southern California, 1930.

GOVERNMENT DOCUMENTS

California Commission of Immigration and Housing. *Community Survey Made in Los Angeles.* San Francisco, 1919.
——. *First Annual Report.* Sacramento, 1915.
——. *Report on an Experiment Made in Los Angeles in the Summer of 1917 for the Americanization of Foreign-born Women.* Sacramento, 1917.
——. *Report on Housing Shortage.* Sacramento, n.d. [1923?].
——. *Second Annual Report (1916).* San Francisco, January 2, 1916.
California Department of Employment. *Agricultural Activities, Crops, and Labor.* Compiled by Ellis S. Coman. Sacramento, 1939.
California Division of Industrial Welfare of the Department of Industrial Relations. *Biennial Report, 1938–1940.* San Francisco, 1940.
California Unemployment Reserves Commission. James L. Mathews, Chair. *A Study of Seasonal Unemployment.* Sacramento, 1939.
Los Angeles Bureau of Municipal Research Incorporated. *Unified Local Government and Tax Reform for Los Angeles County, California.* Los Angeles, 1934.
Los Angeles City Planning Commission. "Distribution of Racial Groups." Chart. Los Angeles, 1940.
Los Angeles County. Board of Supervisors. *Southern California Crops, Annual Statistical Supplement, 1938.* Los Angeles, 1939.
Los Angeles Health Department. *Annual Report, 1920.* Los Angeles, 1920.
Los Angeles Housing Commission. *Report of the Los Angeles Housing Commission.* Los Angeles, July 1, 1910, to March 31, 1913.
Los Angeles Social Service Commission, *Annual Report, 1917–1919.* Los Angeles, 1918.
U.S. Bureau of the Census. *Fifteenth Census of the United States, 1930, Population.* Vol. 3, pt. 1. Washington D.C., 1930.
——. *Fifteenth Census of U.S. Manufacturers, General Report.* Vol. 1. Washington D.C., 1929.
——. *Fifteenth Census of the United States, 1930: Population, Special Report on Foreign-Born White Families by Country of Birth of Head.* Washington D.C., 1933.
U. S. Bureau of Immigration. *Annual Report of the Commissioner General.* Washington, 1927.
U.S. Congress. House of Representatives. Committee on Immigration and Naturalization. *Seasonal Agricultural Labor from Mexico,* 69th Cong., 1926, 8.
U.S. Congress. House of Representatives. Committee on Immigration and Naturalization. "Western Hemisphere Immigration." *Hearings,* 71st Cong., 1930, 192.
U.S. Congress. Senate. The Committee on Immigration. *Restriction of Western Hemisphere Immigration.* 70th Cong., 1928.
U.S. Congress. Senate. Subcommittee of the Committee on Education and

Labor. *Violations of Free Speech and the Rights of Labor.* Pts. 52–55, 64–65.76th Cong., 1940, (The La Follette Hearings.)

U.S. Department of Labor. United States, Employment Service. *Annual Report, Wages Paid in Agricultural Occupations, All Counties, State of California, Year 1938.* Los Angeles, 1938.

PERIODICALS

El Heraldo de México
El Mexicano
La Opinión
Labor Herald
Los Angeles Citizen
Los Angeles Examiner
Los Angeles Express
Los Angeles Illustrated News
Los Angeles School Journal
Los Angeles Socialist
Los Angeles Times
Pacific Rural Press
People's World
Regeneración
United Progressive News
Western Worker

INTERVIEWS

Fuss, Oscar. Interview by the author. Los Angeles, March 7, 1977.

López, Frank. Interview by the author. Los Angeles, June 10 and 15, 1976.

McCormick, La Rue. Interview by the author. Los Angeles, January 26, 1977.

Monroy, Jaime González. Interview by the author. Port Hueneme, May 30, 1976.

Ríos, Tony. Interview by the author. Los Angeles, December 12, 1976.

Index

Text: 10/13 Sabon
Display: Sabon
Compositor: Prestige Typography
Printer and binder: BookCrafters, Inc.